EMPIRE AND COLD WAR

Also by Scott L. Bills

KENT STATE/MAY 4: Echoes Through a Decade (*editor*)

Empire and Cold War

The Roots of US-Third World Antagonism, 1945–47

Scott L. Bills

Associate Professor of History
Stephen F. Austin State University

St. Martin's Press   New York

First published in the United States of America in 1990

Printed in Hong Kong

ISBN 0–312–03641–8

Library of Congress Cataloging-in-Publication Data
Bills, Scott L.
Empire and cold war: the roots of US-Third World antagonism,
1945–47/   Scott L. Bills.
p.   cm.
Includes bibliographical references.
ISBN 0–312–03641–8
1. Developing countries—Foreign relations—United States.
2. United States—Foreign relations—Developing countries.
3. Cold War.   I. Title.
D888.U6B55   1990
327.730172'4—dc20

89–37559
CIP

For
Robert and Dolores Bills
and also
KD-B and SHB

Contents

List of Illustrations

Preface

This is not a book about Great Events. There are no keening ideological desiderata. Rather, it is a story, in part, about people whose lives and goals were seldom found at the core of cold war disputes or crises: a story about the aspirations of the colonized amidst big-power intrigues and jostling. The status of colonial regimes in Afro-Asia was greatly influenced by the global mobilization which characterized the Second World War, then further affected by the onset of Soviet-American hostility and its widening ripple effect. If there ever has been anything like an operative 'domino theory' in this century, it was sparked by world war, especially the second one, when every possible domino was flattened, battered, pushed, shoved, twirled, spun, kicked, rocked or brushed by the wind. It was an awesome and horrible war in so many ways: methodically brutal and genocidal, leavened with powerful racist imagery, marked by the great advance of death-dealing technology, ending, as so many contemporary observers noted, with a fireball fist of power which forever transformed grand strategy. Yet, it was also a war which many were somewhat sad to see end: (1) because (for a few) it offered adventure nowhere else available, to be followed perhaps by a return to drab opportunities at home; (2) because (for more) its continuation postponed the scary, uncertain task of taking stock and trying to rebuild lives, families and thriving nations from the rubble; and (3) because (for more yet) the war's wreckage provided the best moment in generations to petition for or fight for freedom. Had the war in Asia lasted much longer, the Chinese communists would have improved their military position, perhaps in step with advancing Soviet armies. As well, native nationalists would have been much stronger in Vietnam, likely well established in both the north and south through an effective campaign of anti-Japanese resistance, perhaps working closely with an expanding American intelligence/guerrilla effort. In the Netherlands East Indies, a longer war might well have produced a widespread uprising by the same nationalists whose collaboration enabled them to build a formidable paramilitary force under Japanese overlordship. Even so, the end of war, coming when it did – expectedly in Europe in May, then quite suddenly in Asia in mid-August 1945 – set in motion the kind of systemic turmoil which, for a short time, provided leaders of big, small and nascent powers the chance to re-evaluate traditional policies, to rethink national goals, and to ponder the meaning and vitality of freedom.

This book examines the wide-ranging impact of the Second World War throughout the colonial territories which sprawled along the southern rim of Eurasia. To be sure, colonial areas were not central to the winning strategy of the Grand Alliance. Yet, heartening Allied victories had come first in North Africa; and the steady accumulation of men and *matériel* in India, Southeast Asia and the Pacific island chains played an important role in stemming – then turning – the Japanese advance. As the air war expanded, colonial territories provided vital advance bases for direct attacks on Axis homelands. Also, overseas dependencies continued to be valued for their raw materials and agricultural output. For the Western imperial powers, holding onto their colonies appeared to be one of the few sure ways to re-establish any kind of claim to big-power status. But would the effort be worth the candle?

The word 'rimlands' is an apt geopolitical designation for the belt of colonial territories to the south: along the Mediterranean littoral, through the Northern Tier, across the Indian subcontinent and into the mountainous jungles of Southeast Asia. For American policymakers, such lands had long been merely the dimly lit, exotic exterior of European imperialism: closed spheres, little known, little cared about. The United States tended its own few colonies with intermittent passion. But the Second World War changed all that, as many historians have noted. The United States emerged from the war as the most powerful economic and military dynamo on the planet. Its armies were scattered over several continents. Its trucks, jeeps and tanks sat along the dusty roadsides from Casablanca to Kunming.

The shape of the new world order was not long in coming and we are quite familiar with its overall characteristics: a litany of Soviet-American incidents, crises and polemic. While the early cold war era often appears now to have become a burnt-over district within the historiography of American diplomacy, it remains the centerpiece of post-1945 history. And Europe was the central theater of the cold war until the mid-1950s. For American officials, accomplishments in Europe – relief, economic recovery, political stabilization – would percolate outward (or downward) to the poorer, less stable dependencies. Colonial peoples would be asked to be patient, to trust the United States to deliver belatedly on such wartime promises as the Atlantic Charter, and to co-operate in the consolidation of the Western bloc in Europe before taking up the reins of an eager nationalism. Unfortunately, the themes of tutelage, moderation and evolutionary change had little appeal for the peoples of what would later be called the Third World. Later, the southern rimlands would seem less remote: instead, the acceleration of cold war contention would spread United States–Soviet rivalry far beyond Europe, to contend and clash in the colonies. The term 'Third World' is both wonderfully inclusive and frustratingly imprecise; it is simply the best we have.

Hence, this book examines also the early cold war years, which were the seedbed for the crystallization, spread and institutionalization of anti-Americanism as a lasting if not permanent feature of Third World culture – a ritualistic denunciation of the pervasive and alien influence of

US power. Those actions taken and not taken by American policymakers in the immediate post-war period – when nationalist leaders throughout the colonial rimlands hoped and expected the United States to lead the way in the dismantling of empires – had great impact. It led to great disappointment, followed by great disillusionment. Certainly the ability of the United States to underwrite dramatic global revolution was much overrated; but just as surely, there was no interest in using American power in this way. 'Anticolonialism' is a slippery word. Nevertheless, it is reasonable to suggest that any national policy which does not seek directly to empower native nationalists cannot be referred to as anticolonial. Heartfelt sentiments that imperial rule was corrupt, oppressive, decadent, unjust, unfair and needlessly exclusive were shared by some American policymakers, even by President Franklin Roosevelt. But such sentiments, for reasons outlined in this book, did not translate into a consistent, viable US policy which can be called 'anticolonialism'.

My interest is primarily in American policymaking, though obviously European (especially British) diplomacy had something to do with it. The role of the United States in the Third World is an interest I have held through a number of years of on-again, off-again research because (1) US foreign policy toward colonial areas in the early cold war years appeared so haphazard or *ad hoc* and yet was not; (2) American officials often acted as if they had little information upon which to base sound policy judgments about such nebulous wartime goals as self-determination and yet they did have adequate information; and (3) American involvement with the Third World has been such a tragic story of mistakes and misunderstanding. Indeed, there was a consistent purpose and pattern to American colonial policy during the critical period of 1945–47, when the Second World War ended, reconstruction was undertaken and the cold war became the dominant motif of international relations. It was not a purpose supported by every policymaker at every level in American government; but the State Department elite, the top presidential advisers and President Harry Truman all shared a metropolitan outlook which conditioned the US response to pleas for assistance from nationalists in colonial dependencies. This was not a product of ignorance. The pluses and minuses were listed and compared. The policy ledgers simply did not balance in favor of active support for colonial independence, not for the short term. For the long term, possibly so – but colonial peoples were not that patient and for good reason.

Acknowledgments

Without institutional assistance, I could never have contemplated the kind of research necessary for this book. For my being able to travel to London and repeatedly to Washington, I must thank the Stephen F. Austin State University Research Council for several grants. Other university support provided me with a Macintosh SE computer, which greatly facilitated completion of the manuscript. James V. Reese, Vice-President for Academic Affairs and William J. Brophy, Dean of Liberal Arts, have offered steady administrative support for faculty research. As well, my department chair, Robert N. Mathis, has been always helpful and encouraging.

A number of archivists have been very helpful in locating important materials. I must especially thank Terri Hammett and John Taylor of the Military Reference Branch, National Archives, for their efforts in directing me to recently opened OSS materials. Also, Sally Marks and Kathy Nicastro of the Diplomatic Branch always offered useful recommendations for work in State Department record collections. Erwin Mueller and Dennis Bilger of the Harry S. Truman Library were both impressive in their ability quickly and effectively to direct me toward materials scattered through several different collections. There never is, it seems, any single individual to thank at the Public Record Office in London; so I will simply express my appreciation for the very professional organization and knowledgeable staff.

I would like to thank those people who read and commented upon the manuscript at various stages: Lawrence Kaplan, Steven Thulin, Lynne Dunn, Calvin Hines and Alvin Cage. Their comments and ideas more than once spawned efforts to rethink and rewrite sections of the manuscript. Larry Kaplan deserves special thanks for his years of gently prodding me toward completion of this book. It was Al Cage who suggested that I reduce the intended scope of the book and thus gave an increasingly unmanageable project new focus and energy. At the SFASU library, the assistance of Ann Chandler, Lee Sullenger and Jimmi Fischer in securing research materials was ever important and much appreciated. Also, the enthusiasm and support from Simon Winder of St Martin's Press was a lively antidote to manuscript fatigue.

More than anyone else, however, I wish to say a heartfelt thanks to my family: to my wife, Kris Dixon-Bills, and to my son, Seth – for the long discussions about book-related topics, for the many evenings and weekends I worked at the computer, for the wrestling, bike-riding and beachcombing delayed, for the vacations planned around research trips, for all the times that love somehow overcame the cramp and press of academic life.

1 Introduction: Living in the Atomic World

Third grader Chizue Sakai stood outside a temple in the small town of Yae-machi on the morning of 6 August 1945. It was early still, quiet and the sun was bright. 'All of a sudden, we saw a flash of light like lightning in . . . the southeastern sky. Then there was a boom and the clouds turned red.' In Hiroshima, young Shigeru Tasaka walked to his bedroom window 'when suddenly there was a flare of bluish-white light'. It was 8.15 a.m. Other children awakened to the same awesome flash – blue pulse, white heat. Then, within a few moments, all was darkness and a great fist of wind pressed everyone and everything to the ground. Shortly, fires sprouted throughout the collapsed tinderbox houses in the center of the city. As the people poured from their homes – stunned, bleeding, frightened, burnt, bent and dying – they stepped onto an alien landscape. 'Men covered in blood and women with skin flapping around them like kimonos were plunging into the river, screaming.' High above, a 34-year-old American physicist surveyed the scene from inside the *Great Artiste*: 'I looked in vain for the city that had been our target. The [mushroom] cloud seemed to be rising out of a wooded area devoid of population'. It looked peaceful, he recalled, 'from seven miles up'. The buglike, swollen and blackened bodies; the flapping, flayed, shredded skin; the unquenchable thirst and unrelieved moaning of the badly burned; the lingering deaths of family members from the heavy dose of radiation – these were the images painfully recalled by the children of Hiroshima. Three days later there was a further 'rain of ruin from the air'.[1] It was terrible and it was wondrous.

A long and bitter war thus entered its final days. While the full spectacle of the unearthly, searing heat and crushing power launched at Hiroshima and Nagasaki would not be widely understood for some years, Americans knew that death and destruction were widespread in the afflicted cities. 'This transcendent display of determination and power', wrote one historian, 'seemed to announce to a battered and war-scarred world that the young giant, America the invincible, had taken the fate of the world and indeed the very atomic stuff of the universe, into its hands'.[2] Indeed, much more arresting than the flattening of Japanese cities was the flamboyant imagery of cosmos grasped, thresholds crossed and new eras begun.

The Atomic Age became the reigning metaphor of the day – inaugurated through a fascinating display of collective technological ingenuity organized in response to a massive government-sponsored mobilization of muscle and expertise. The twin August flashes above Japanese cities proclaimed to all the pervasive prowess of distant, smokestack America. In

1

September 1945, for instance, a team of US intelligence personnel in Saigon jokingly declared that a Signal Corps device they carried – 'a flashlight with a stock and sights' – was an 'atomic gun'. It made a strong impression upon the local population. 'After that,' recalled Lt. Emile R. Counasse, 'we had no need of any other weapons. On the few occasions when we carried the 'atomic gun', people cleared off the streets in a hurry.'[3]

The Atomic Age was 'a new room', read *Time* magazine, 'rich with hope, terrible with strange dangers. The door that slammed behind man at Hiroshima had locked'. The new age was here to stay. 'The bomb rendered all decisions made so far, at Yalta and at Potsdam, mere trivial dams across tributary rivulets.' According to an article in the *New York Times Magazine*, a 'mighty revolution' had occurred in human society. What was the shape of this new morning? Had humankind really been 'tossed into the vestibule of another millennium'?[4]

The British Labour prime minister, Clement Attlee, wrote to President Harry Truman in September 1945 to warn that the advent of atomic weaponry signalled for the world community 'entirely new conditions' regarding both strategic and diplomatic matters. 'We can set no bounds', he feared, 'to the possibilities of airplanes flying through the stratosphere dropping atomic bombs on great cities'. Later, there would be rockets as delivery vehicles. Even the new United Nations Organization had not been founded upon a framework of international security compatible with the new dimensions of warfare. Attlee asked, 'Am I to plan for a peaceful or a warlike world? If the latter I ought to direct all our people to live like troglodytes underground as being the only hope of survival, and that by no means certain'.[5] It was an excessively grim portrait, born from the view of a prostrate continent; but Attlee spoke eloquently of the necessary revision of established patterns of thinking and acting in global affairs.

Yet, for American strategists, it was important to emphasize the limited short-term impact of atomic bombs in order to avoid zealous calls for instant military demobilization. Everyone could admit (indeed, could hardly deny) that a long-range adjustment of military planning and global relationships was on the event horizon. However, scientist Vannevar Bush agreed with the secretary of war that the growing popularity of 'push-button' war scenarios was harmful. Bush complained, 'The tendency of the American people to seize upon slogans and to rationalize their way out of predicaments by facile expressions gives such a term far more force than it would have in a country that did not have these characteristics'. It was unfortunate that so many people seemed to feel that the next war would be fought with 'dials and tubes'. Bush observed: 'I think the general public has now gotten a Buck Rogers slant on a possible warfare of the future that is going to be very hard to overcome'. Within the Office of Strategic Services, analyst Gregory Bateson was more concerned with the impact of atomic technology upon 'indirect methods of warfare'. His concerns meshed with ongoing discussions within the agency regarding the shape of American intelligence-gathering in the aftermath of the war – such that the United States must not be 'lulled into inattention'. Bateson predicted that all major powers would have atomic weapons within ten years, possibly sooner; and while this would change the overall character of future warfare, it would not affect certain kinds of politico-military activity. 'Guerrilla tactics, white and black propaganda, subversion, social and economic manipulation, diplomatic pressure, etc. – all of these are immune to atomic attack.'[6]

For the short term the coming of the Atomic Age meant far less than many people imagined. Undeniably, the atomic bomb was a fierce and merciless destroyer; but the notion that this was now 'a world whose peoples have suddenly perceived that they live under the shadow of death'[7] was much overblown. Or rather, the most fearsome shadows were cast by such hauntingly familiar specters as disease, famine, economic collapse, debilitative civil war, political uncertainty and human despair. In fact, the legacy of the wartime summits was a durable one. In the afterglow of Axis defeat, the dazzle of new weaponry had little immediate impact upon either the shape of international relations or the collective psyche of the world's population.[8] The American atomic monopoly was merely one element of the massive global imprint left by the passing of the Second World War.

Adam B. Ulam has suggested that atomic weaponry exercised a 'baleful fascination' for American policymakers, limiting their ability to discern the urgency of re-establishing a world balance of power. Certainly the appeal of such technology was seductive, opening a new channel for enhancing America's post-war influence. It seemed logical to Gregory Bateson, for instance, that the United States would seek to use its atomic arsenal as 'a disciplinary threat' against potentially aggressive nations. Nevertheless, as Theodore Draper has observed, the 'evanescent fantasy of absolute power induced by the bomb' was gripping but not decisive. Likewise, Barton J. Bernstein affirmed the subtle influence of the atomic monopoly; however, his careful study revealed that while US leaders were 'inured to the mass killing of [enemy] civilians', use of the bomb was not primarily a cynical attempt to intimidate the Soviets.[9] All too clearly, US hopes for an easily emplaced Pax Americana were rapidly dispelled – by the frustrating complexity of global politics as well as by the Soviets' studied indifference to atomic affairs. Equally important, looking beyond the European theater toward the colonial rimlands, the blue-white dawn of the Atomic Age had little relevance except to further solidify the image of the United States as a great technological power. The dreams of the colonized in Algiers, Tripoli, Benghazi, Damascus, New Delhi, Hanoi, Saigon or Batavia were stubbornly rooted in an affirmation of indigenous culture and a desire for self-governance.

Without a doubt, the war had been profoundly and universally disruptive, festooning governments with new bureaus, new tasks and new means
to power, generating fundamental societal change. Admiral William D.
Leahy, chief of staff to both Franklin Roosevelt and Truman, pondered the
meaning of Allied victory in late summer 1945: 'It was my conviction on
this night of August 14 that we would be paying for this war in many ways
long after we, and our children too, had passed away'.[10] The physical
devastation was immense, leading to prolonged anxiety and suffering
throughout Europe and much of East Asia. The war's turmoil had set in
motion forces which would dramatically alter the international balance of
power and reshape the means and ends of competition and rivalry in the
world arena. Yet, for many Americans, this outcome of the war was poorly
perceived. From the perspective of the home front, the Allied victory was a
product of American military and industrial might; further, the war had
lifted up the United States from economic despair and had restored the
dynamism of its capitalist system. Such a viewpoint, observed Bradley F.
Smith, distanced Americans 'not only from the condition, but also from the
outlook and general longing, of most of the rest of the world's population'.
Both Truman and his new secretary of state shared this parochial
outlook.[11]

For American policymakers at war's end, there were many questions to
be asked and, once proffered, few certain answers. By late summer 1945,
there were severe shortages of food and coal throughout Europe – what
were the prospects for convincing economic recovery, both short-term and
long-term? What was the likelihood that new demagogues would arise
from the rubble-strewn landscape? What was the Soviet agenda for
Europe, the Middle East and East Asia – was it as ambitious as some
feared? What was going on in all the untidy nooks and crannies of the
world? There were so many of them. What were the ultimate goals of
nationalist movements in colonial areas? Which nation or doctrine would
most effectively mobilize this mass of black, brown and Asian peoples?

American officials generally considered the peoples of the colonial
rimlands to be simple folk, largely indifferent to and unaware of the
complex swirl of global politics. Enthusiasm for self-government could be
understood, of course. Nearly all US policymakers routinely expressed an
aversion to imperialism of any stripe and believed themselves to be
exemplars of a deep-rooted belief in self-determination. 'Anticolonialism
was one of America's dearest and most respected traditions', wrote Robert
M. Hathaway. 'This had not prevented the United States from assuming
the role of colonial master itself, but it did mean that Americans virtually
without exception believed that their rule over foreign peoples was so
benevolent as to constitute a totally different type of relationship from
traditional metropolitan-colonial ties.'[12]

Yet, as the post-war system remained stubbornly unsteady, untested and

inexperienced regimes in dependent territories hardly appeared an acceptable alternative to colonial administrations that at least offered interim
stability. Surely, a careful, scrupulous period of tutelage would be the best
sort of transitional program for dependent peoples. However, success
would then depend upon the strength and integrity of French, British or
Dutch commitments to meaningful autonomy for their dependencies. Was
there still sufficient trust between the rulers and the ruled for protectorates, mandates and colonies to be made over into benign trusteeships?
Freedom, after all, was tricky: it rested, *inter alia*, on the complicated
interplay of an educated citizenry, formal constitutional safeguards and
continuity, a respect for civilian governance and relatively untrammeled
enterprise. At least that was how it worked in the United States; and
Roosevelt, Truman, and all other advocates of self-determination through
tutelage were certain that the American national experience transferred
most adequately and appropriately to colonial areas.

It was difficult to anticipate the pattern of impending events. Alone
amongst the Western powers, the United States was unburdened by
physical devastation, economic and social disorganization, and mounting
political frustration and discontent. American officials sought an effective
way to export their policy principles in order to uplift and educate (or
re-educate) friends, foes and unknowns alike, and to do so without being
unduly abrasive or patronizing. As many historians have pointed out, the
uncertainty following FDR's death in April 1945 was in part the result of
his own vague policy planning, his off-hand optimism, his buoyant faith in
a bright new order.[13] The natural inclination of US leadership was toward
gradualist programs; but increasingly, time appeared short – events and
incidents blurred in a rushing cascade. The questions and answers became
more urgent as US–Soviet relations steadily worsened. The world was a
singularly large stew; the pots were boiling; the masses were stirring;
metaphors clashed and mixed; solutions were elusive and inevitably
expensive.

AMERICAN ANTICOLONIALISM

The French historian, Philippe Devillers, has described the vain hopes of
France for post-war colonial restoration in Southeast Asia, noting that
unrealistic national ambitions could only be avoided by attacking popular
myths.[14] The significance of myths, whether it lay in their continued sway
or in their destruction, was undeniable. Their influence was pervasive
throughout the immediate post-war period: myths of imperial grandeur
and racial superiority, myths of innocence and benevolence, myths of
mission and markets, myths of conspiracy and apocalypse. For US
policymakers, the well-heeled shibboleth of anticolonialism was treated as

a root tenet of the American worldview. It was so described repeatedly, earnestly, and most typically with reference to the nation's founding. As John D. Hickerson, head of the Office of European Affairs during the latter 1940s, remarked: 'We won our independence against a colonial power and we have always tended to sympathize with people trying to achieve independence'.[15] Indeed, such sentiment became a common referent for sardonic comments by European diplomats, especially the British, who perhaps heard it most often.

American anticolonialism, however, was more a leap of faith, a self-conscious testament to virtue, than a coherent doctrine or policy. The argument was simple enough: the United States had never been a serious imperial power, certainly not one which methodically extended its sway over numerous distant territories and alien populations. While the record was not entirely devoid of adventurism, to be sure, aberrations whether great or small could be explained and excused as accident, zeitgeist or some similar yet inconsequential lapse of vigilance. 'When we practiced colonialism ourselves, as we did during the first third of the present century', wrote Julius W. Pratt in the late 1950s, 'it was with an uneasy conscience and a more or less steady purpose to return to the paths of virtue.'[16] Was there, after all, something unique about the American character and system? Compared to other big powers, was US foreign policy more freedom-loving and better attuned to the aspirations of the world's oppressed? It was certainly true that the United States had long advocated the opening of restrictive imperial trading spheres. It had extended its dominance of foreign lands more through a reliance upon economic power than military conquest and formal colonial administration. During the 1930s, the impact of the Great Depression had much restrained American overseas activity. Thus, on the eve of the Second World War the United States found itself tending a few minimally garrisoned Pacific territories, with promises already made for Philippine independence. If the promises were kept, then surely the American claim to special virtue would have wide impact among colonial peoples.

The American self-image had been well served after 1900 by the logic of the open door, a policy which functioned well as an adjunct to the rhetoric of anticolonialism. Informal empire as a product of economic penetration and geographic propinquity was not without complications, as demonstrated by the pattern of US military intervention in Central America and the strategic problems posed by Pacific outposts. Still, for most Americans, such activity seemed different enough from the methodology of European imperialism: at least it was less of a bad thing.

When the time came for American entry into the Second World War, US policymakers believed that they had learned important lessons from the collapse of the world economy in the early 1930s and the Anglo-French policy of appeasement represented by the Münich Agreement. For Franklin

Roosevelt and his State Department – two somewhat asynchronous entities – the open door was one of several keys to a successful re-ordering of the post-war world: to smooth commercial rivalry and facilitate economic recovery, thus to encourage international co-operation on vital issues; to provide the United States with necessary new markets and assured supplies of raw materials; and to spur an evolutionary dissolution of empires. The open door thus served a pre-eminent self-interest, promised a healthier and more co-operative global community, and could readily be presented in terms which suggested a latent empathy with the needs of dependent peoples.[17]

However, the 'clarion-clear anticolonialism'[18] of the pre-war period was progressively less clear, less clarion. American anticolonialism had always been a vague notion – strongly held it seemed, an inviolable tradition perhaps; yet, the essential ambiguity of the term permitted the rapid accumulation of contradictions once the United States became a major player in a global war. The principles of the open door had worked to reconcile the reality of expanding American power in international affairs with the fragments of an antediluvian anti-imperialism; but after 1941 the anticolonial ideal encompassed too many opposing tendencies to remain unchallenged by events. For instance, were spheres of influence in fact not created equal, such that some were more acceptable than others? At a moment in history when US military forces were active in many colonial theaters, why did the Roosevelt administration offer repeated commitments to restore European sovereignty at war's end? Each major ally was intransigent on specific issues: how hard and how profitably could Britain or the USSR be pushed on the matter of strategic spheres and self-determination of peoples? How could the post-war defense needs of the United States, especially in the Pacific, be credibly reconciled with broad-ranging theories of international trusteeship? These were not questions that were impossible to answer, but they were questions which posed unavoidably the dilemma of a nation with metropolitan priorities trying to ride the new tide of militant nationalism cresting in the colonial rimlands. Interim understandings, *modi vivendi*, military occupations: this was the language of the Grand Alliance. And yet, Roosevelt, his secretary of state, Cordell Hull, and others in the State Department pursued through the wartime labyrinth an effort to win recognition from within and without that the post-war era would bring new regimes to colonial areas: a system of humane and forward-looking trusteeships amidst a world community rededicated to co-operation and economic development.

By the spring and summer of 1945, US policy toward dependent territories was frequently *ad hoc* and seldom envisaged quick independence. There were some exceptions: India, for one, a topic of sustained interest for the American public. Or further east, the State Department was firm in its commitment to a fully independent Thailand after the war.

Overall, however, the colonial question did not represent a focal point of big-power politics during the final phase of the war. The agendas for the Yalta and Potsdam summits indicated the pecking order for thorny issues, and the matter of sovereignty over areas like French Indochina, the Netherlands East Indies or Algeria was hardly a priority topic. Historians have thus looked for but not found a meaningful, systematic American advocacy of an end to empires at the close of the war.[19]

THE ATLANTIC CHARTER

For colonial peoples perhaps the most influential document of the Second World War was the Atlantic Charter, issued by Franklin Roosevelt and Winston Churchill in mid-August 1941. The declaration was conceived as a means to reinforce the image of twin democracies, hand in hand, dedicated to the future application of certain just propositions amidst clear and present dangers to world civilization. In the Charter's imprecision lay its wide appeal, looking beyond the anti-Hitler struggle to a world of freer trade, more widely shared economic advance, and global peace vaguely assured by 'a wider and permanent system of general security'. America and Britain pledged their respect for 'the right of all peoples to choose the form of government under which they will live; and they [FDR and Churchill] wish to see sovereign rights and self-government restored to those who have been forcibly deprived of them'.[20]

The role of Churchill, as well as the politico-military context in which the declaration appeared, suggested a Eurocentric appeal. Such was the theme of the prime minister's remarks on 9 September 1941, emphasizing that the Charter concerned 'general principles' only. Respect for self-determination, he said, referred to peoples suffering 'under the Nazi yoke' and did not alter the imperial commitments of Britain.[21] A similar sentiment was suggested by the context of Roosevelt's explanation of the Atlantic Charter in his remarks to Congress on 21 August:

> It is so clear cut that it is difficult to oppose in any major particular without automatically admitting a willingness to accept compromise with Nazism; or to agree to a world peace which would give to Nazism domination over large numbers of conquered Nations. Inevitably such a peace would be a gift to Nazism to take breath – armed breath – for a second war to extend the control over Europe and Asia to the American Hemisphere itself.

And yet, the phrasing of the principles bespoke a broader ethic at work – not simply 'an interchange of views relating to the present and the future', but something more profound.[22]

The expression of a more universal application of the Charter came with Roosevelt's comments in a fireside chat of 23 February 1942, when he asked his listeners to 'spread before you a map of the whole earth, and to follow with me the references which I shall make to the world-encircling battle lines of this war'. All could see, he noted, that the oceans had become 'endless battlefields', that America must wage war over 'vast distances' and reject the 'turtle policy' of awaiting a confrontation with Axis forces in the Western Hemisphere. Roosevelt pointed to the strategic importance of Japanese bases on Pacific islands and the Southeast Asian peninsula. But his point, of course, was to inspire. America would gain back its lost ground; its vision would be sustained by a new spirit of national unity and self-sacrifice. The Grand Alliance was committed to a common cause: 'The Atlantic Charter applies not only to the parts of the world that border the Atlantic but to the whole world ...'.[23] A global struggle demanded a global doctrine: this was the thrust thereafter of official statements about war goals.

Sumner Welles, under-secretary of state and close associate of the president, described the war as a major watershed in world development. In a speech of 30 May 1942, he termed the conflict a 'people's war': 'Our victory must bring in its train the liberation of all people. Discrimination between peoples because of their race, creed or color must be abolished. The age of imperialism is ended. ... The principles of the Atlantic Charter must be guaranteed to the world as a whole – in all oceans and in all continents'.[24] And Roosevelt was no less emphatic on many occasions during the war, as when he spoke with his son Elliott in Casablanca in January 1943. 'The thing is, the colonial system means war. Exploit the resources of an India, a Burma, a Java; take all the wealth out of those countries, but never put anything back into them, things like education, decent standards of living, minimum health requirements – all you're doing is storing up the kind of trouble that leads to war.' The United States, said FDR, would not be a partner to the restoration and maintenance of the British or French imperial systems.[25] Roosevelt's anticolonial views were only strengthened by the geographic twists and turns of wartime summitry, taking him through French and British colonies in North Africa: a drive through poverty-ridden Bathurst, Gambia; a dinner with the Sultan of Morocco; a view from a Marrakesh parapet of the sun setting behind the Atlas Mountains; a shipboard interview with King Ibn Saud at Great Bitter Lake, Egypt. As the war progressed, Roosevelt typically directed his strongest criticism against the French colonial record in Indochina, insisting that France should not return to the region with its sovereignty intact.

While Robert Dallek has asserted that the Atlantic Charter was 'too vague to capture the [American] public attention',[26] its universalist phrasing and widespread use as Allied propaganda ensured rising expectations among colonial peoples that the United States had committed

itself to their postwar liberation. From the countryside of Southeast
Asia, the Muslim communities of the Maghreb, the native assemblies of
the Levant and elsewhere, nationalist leaders petitioned for American
support. They co-operated with US military forces; they wrote letters to
the president or the secretary of state; they deposited speeches, com-
muniqués and manifestoes with US consular staffs – believing that they
addressed themselves to the only major power which would listen
sympathetically to their entreaties and possibly intervene on their
behalf.

This surge of pro-American sentiment in the colonial rimlands
reflected two related judgments: first, that the United States intended an
abolition of empires, and second, that it had the requisite power to do
so. The wartime prowess of America and the wide-ranging nature of its
military commitments had become familiar points to colonial peoples.
There were troubled times ahead, but for the moment the phenomenal
popularity of America was a heady realization: as when Wendell Willkie
returned from a 49-day world tour and reported 'a gigantic reservoir of
good will toward us, the American people'. He continued:

> The existence of this reservoir is the biggest political fact of our time. No
> other Western nation has such a reservoir. ... The preservation of this
> reservoir of good will is a sacred responsibility, not alone toward the
> aspiring peoples of the earth, but toward our own sons who are fighting
> this battle on every continent. For the water in this reservoir is the clean,
> invigorating water of freedom.[27]

However, American advocacy of a universalistic application of the
Atlantic Charter's principles was not matched by similar sentiments among
British officials. In this way, promulgation of the Charter marked the
opening of a low-level but persistent dispute between the two governments, a disagreement about the character and utility of empire which
continued throughout Roosevelt's presidency. While FDR did not advance
many specific ideas concerning trusteeship and self-government, his general intent, as Walter LaFeber has shown, was to 'eliminate most colonial
holdings [in the post-war period] including those of Great Britain'. Roosevelt seemed especially fond of poking and prodding British officials, who
were the only avowed imperialists to whom he had regular access and with
whom he could good-naturedly and off-handedly discuss a variety of
anticolonial scenarios, fully expecting the ripostes he invariably received.
British diplomats were determined to avoid acquiescence to FDR's proposals for Indochina, as when Ambassador Halifax commented in January
1944 that trusteeship over a French colony would tempt Roosevelt to seek
similar arrangements over British or Dutch possessions. FDR then reiterated his assurances that Britain and the Netherlands had done a much
better job of administering their empires than had the French. Afterward,

Halifax reported to the Foreign Office that it was 'all very good tempered, but I am left feeling that he has got this idea in his mind a bit more than is likely to be quite wholesome'. Still, as William Roger Louis has emphasized, the US and British policymaking establishments were both dominated by men of similar gradualist views regarding the status of colonies after the Axis surrender.[28] While Roosevelt entertained various schemes for decolonization, few State Department officials hoped for or expected abrupt change in the control of dependent areas.

Privately, British policymakers complained about the 'ancient grudge' evidenced in the periodic rise and fall of anti-British sentiment in the United States. Too often and too unfairly, the British empire was chastised as the epitome of a self-centered, oppressive colonialism. Further, the Foreign Office worried about American trusteeship proposals which might stimulate nationalist agitation in British possessions. J. C. Donnelly, of the North American Department, grumbled about the difficulty of anticipating what kinds of proposals might emerge from the 'vapour' of American politics. Americans had continually to be educated, it seemed, to the reality of a benevolent British imperial system. Frederick Puckle, an adviser with the British embassy in Washington, observed that Americans 'have little patience with any situation which looks to them like a senseless mess and traditionally cling firmly ... to the belief that there is always a short cut to a solution of any practical problem'. The 'simple minds' of most Americans, he averred, could not understand the concept of a 'self-liquidating Empire'.[29]

Overall, the Americans would require considerable instruction. 'According to the Foreign Office', wrote Terry H. Anderson, 'the United States was a lumbering giant, a powerful nation but a novice in foreign affairs, lacking leadership, aimlessly wandering down international paths'.[30] Still, it was not clear whether Roosevelt himself was fully committed to any sustained effort to disestablish empires. Nevile Butler, assistant under secretary in the Foreign Office, suggested in early 1945 that Roosevelt 'will be prepared to condone imperialism if tempered by publicity and economic co-operation'. But the response from Permanent Under-Secretary Alexander Cadogan was pessimistic: 'Pres. Roosevelt is determined that the U.S. shall not become an "Imperial" Power, so that he can reserve all his criticisms for us and the French and the Dutch and others'.[31]

Delivering the 32nd Anniversary Lecture to the Royal Central Asian Society in 1943, Lord Hailey, a noted authority on colonial matters, addressed two interrelated issues: (1) the American tendency toward wide application of the Atlantic Charter, and (2) the character of an American idealism based both on ignorance of and simplistic views toward international relations. Great Britain, asserted Hailey, already had a tradition of self-government in its dependencies; and while the government must now plan to move further toward granting self-rule, it must do so carefully.

Merely to add to the number of sovereign nations with small populations
and economic resources, without an effective affiliation to more compe-
tent political and economic units, would be of very limited benefit to
the peoples themselves, and would certainly be no contribution to the
maintenance of future world order.

Hailey identified a frequently cited (in London) contradiction in US
policymaking: 'The questions of "internationalism" and "isolation" ... do
not have the same meaning for Americans where European commitments
are concerned as they might have when Pacific security is at stake'. He
predicted that as British military forces achieved greater success on the
battlefield, there 'will perhaps be less tendency to discuss the ethical
aspects of our policy'.[32]
    As the war progressed, British officials spoke less about the limited
applicability of the Atlantic Charter and more about the natural compat-
ibility of its principles with their traditional imperial aspirations. This trend
was noted in an analysis produced by the Office of Strategic Services, in
August 1944: 'In a word, the official British position is that there is actually
no need for the specific application of the Atlantic Charter ... to British
dependencies in Africa or elsewhere, since present British policy is in
keeping with the aims and objectives of that declaration'.[33]

THE YALTA FORMULA

A freeze-frame which symbolized both the new global presence of the
United States and also the special prestige and charisma of Franklin
Roosevelt was the moment of his arrival in Valletta harbor, Malta, on 2
February 1945. It was to be a short stopover en route to the Crimea for the
second tripartite summit meeting. Anthony Eden, then British foreign
secretary, described the scene in his memoirs:

> At half past nine President Roosevelt's cruiser hove into sight. As the
> great warship sailed into the battered harbor every vessel was manned,
> every roof and vantage point crammed with spectators. While the bands
> played and amid so much that reeked of war, on the bridge, just
> discernible to the naked eye, sat one civilian figure. In his sensitive hands
> lay much of the world's fate. All heads were turned his way and sudden
> quietness fell. It was one of those moments when all seems to stand still
> and one is conscious of a mark in history.

Charles Bohlen, adviser to the president, recalled the occasion in much the
same way, as a 'memorable spectacle' with the sun 'glistening on the waves'
and flags snapping in the breeze as the cruiser *Quincy* sailed into the
harbor. 'Roosevelt sat on deck, his black cape around his shoulders,

acknowledging salutes from the British men-of-war and the rolling cheers of spectators crowding the quays. He was very much a historical figure.'[34] It was the rare moment when image and aspiration resembled reality, when the mid-twentieth-century components of national power – production, technology, military strength and charismatic personality – were assembled on distant, gleaming shores. It was not, however, what Roosevelt himself would have called a 'headliney' event.[35]

Plate 1.1 *The Big Three at the Yalta Conference, February 1945.*
Source: National Archives photo no. #169A-1, Box 169, RG 208-PU, Still Pictures Branch.

Perhaps the best recognized depictions of the wartime alliance are the group photographs from the summit conferences, particularly the meeting at Yalta: Churchill, Roosevelt and Stalin posed somewhat awkwardly on the patio of the Livadia Palace on 10 February 1945. The post-war world took shape uneasily in the background. The photographs do something to illuminate the people and their conflicting concerns: Stalin wrapped tightly in a drab uniform, indifferent, calling to mind Bohlen's account of their first meeting – 'He had a round, tubby figure and walked clumsily, like a small bear'. But the dictator was an admired, personable, pragmatic negotiator. Churchill, on the other hand, brilliant in his rallying of the British polity against Hitler, could be an inconsistent spokesman at the summits. Portly, alternately animated and somber, shrewd and defensive, Churchill called to mind Charles de Gaulle's reference to 'the heavy

servitude of an alliance with giants'.[36] The prime minister was steadily
more disturbed about and preoccupied with Britain's precipitous slide into
the basket of second-class powers. Roosevelt sat clear-eyed but gaunt, his
deep fatigue and declining health scarcely hidden by a dark cape. Unfortunately, the New World emissary to battle-scarred Eurasia had little in the
way of new solutions for old problems and persistent exigencies. The
post-war era, it appeared, was being stretched tightly over the bones of the
recent past.

Alexander Cadogan considered all three leaders to be a bit overrated:
'The Great Men don't know what they're talking about and have to be
educated and made a bit more tidy in their methods'.[37] But tidiness was
not the real problem. True, the discussions of the Great Men were often
slow-moving and imprecise, but not because they needed to study more
carefully their briefing papers – rather because the course of the war
already had redrawn the political map of Europe. Robert L. Messer has
pointed to 'the unspoken but very real Western sense of indebtedness,
even guilt, concerning the current military situation and the Allies' relative
responsibility for the defeat of Germany'.[38] Adjustments would have to be
made and acknowledged; and there was still the Pacific war to conclude
and burnish. Less apparent than the impending difficulties in Europe was
the extent to which the war had also reconfigured the relationship between
metropoles and colonies.

At Yalta, Roosevelt remarked that fifty years of peace were possible if
the three powers could grasp the opportunity to stimulate security and
stability for all peoples.[39] Stalin later alluded to the fact that preservation
of the alliance would become more problematic with the close of the war.
Churchill responded with shining imagery:

> He said that in the modern world the function of leadership was to lead
> the people out from the forests into the broad sunlit plains of peace and
> happiness. He felt this prize was nearer our grasp than anytime before in
> history and it would be a tragedy for which history would never forgive
> us if we let this prize slip from our grasp through inertia or carelessness.

This exchange about hardships and prizes occurred during elaborately
friendly toasts at a dinner meeting on 8 February. Roosevelt's trusteeship
plans were scuttled the next day, when mention of the issue elicited from
Churchill a protest that Britain would not yield 'one scrap' of its empire to
any international supervisory agency. Secretary of State Edward R.
Stettinius hastened to assure him that any trusteeship system established by
the projected United Nations Organization would not apply to the British
Empire. Nor, it soon became clear, would it apply to the French, Dutch or
any other empire.[40] The final protocol of the conference stated that
trusteeships would only be considered for (1) former mandates of the
League of Nations, (2) territories 'detached' from the Axis powers, and (3)

territories voluntarily placed under UN supervision. The protocol was made public in late March and Stettinius indicated in early April that the Yalta formula for trusteeship would be the basis for US proposals at the founding conference for the United Nations in San Francisco. This formula, acknowledged the acting secretary of state, 'would preclude the establishment of a trusteeship in Indochina except with the consent of the French government. The latter seems unlikely'.[41]

INTERNATIONAL TRUSTEESHIP

In January 1945, British official J. C. Donnelly observed, 'The question of the Japanese mandated islands is going to provide one of the most interesting and significant issues in the American attitude towards post-war settlement. The needs of strategy and the traditional (if ill informed and hypocritical) view held tenaciously by majority opinion in the U.S. on colonies come into outright collision'. In fact, exclusive US control of former Japanese mandates in three island chains in the Pacific was a virtual *sine qua non* of the projected peace settlement. The Marshall, Mariana and Caroline Islands (also referred to as Micronesia) would be retained by the United States as strategic bases; the only question to be answered was under what rubric American control would be legitimized. The American military establishment was adamantly opposed to any system of genuine international control over the islands. As Secretary of War Henry Stimson told Roosevelt on 3 March 1945, 'I pointed out again to him the difference between the mandates which occupied the attention of statesmen after the last war and the present Pacific island problem where there is no population to be imperialized and where the reason for national defense was paramount'.[42]

As Donnelly might have predicted, American officials found it important to explain why retention of military bases throughout the Pacific did not constitute an expression of imperial will. Secretary of the Navy James V. Forrestal, appearing before the House Committee on Appropriations, asserted that the Pacific Ocean has become 'a great American lake' and that any formula devised to protect US security interests through the region would not represent 'the march of imperial power'. He continued: 'Mostly they are sandpits in the Pacific, islands of small area, that represent no great economic asset, and, to that extent, they are quite different ... from the acquisition of territory in the old imperial sense. We are talking only of security. We have no concern with adding to our territory or our wealth or our economic assets'.[43]

The fate of the Pacific mandates was not a difficult issue to resolve. The territories had been seized from the Japanese at (in Stimson's words) 'much cost of life and treasure' by US military forces, and there were typically put forward emotional as well as strategic claims. The islands were conquered territory from a just war; their retention represented an outward-reaching defense perimeter which would preserve stability through the region. If there were going to be an umbrella trusteeship system to which the United States would adhere, argued Stimson, then the former island mandates must be placed in a special, separate category which protected American hegemony.[44] This was the solution pursued in San Francisco.

The American delegation to the founding conference of the United Nations, which opened on 25 April, thus had clear guidelines for dealing with colonial issues: the Yalta formula on trusteeship and an intragovernmental resolve to protect American control over strategic bases in the Pacific. It was not surprising then that those articles of the UN Charter pertaining to dependent territories, largely a product of State Department committees, expressed no new or radical principles.[45] In addition to detailing trusteeship arrangements and designating a Trusteeship Council to oversee the limited field, a provision of Chapter XII (International Trusteeship System) established a special category of trust territory – a 'strategic area' – to be assigned to a particular power and supervised directly by the Security Council rather than the General Assembly. Control of the former Japanese Pacific mandates was then duly conferred upon the United States as a strategic trust.

More promising to colonial peoples than the limited scope of international trusteeship arrangements was Chapter XI of the UN Charter, the Declaration Regarding Non-Self-Governing Territories. This section committed all signatory nations to accept as a 'sacred trust' the following: respect for indigenous cultures, the development of institutions for self-government, and metropolitan assistance for economic and social development. Also included was a pledge 'to transmit regularly to the [UN] Secretary-General for information purposes . . . statistical and other information of a technical nature relating to economic, social, and educational conditions'. This provision plus the authority of the Trusteeship Council to accept petitions from and arrange for periodic visits to the trust territories convinced Benjamin Gerig, who had played an important role in drafting the Charter's sections on dependent peoples, that the new system would quickly begin to benefit the colonized. He believed that a new accountability to the UNO would spur imperial powers toward greater concern with indigenous welfare. In addition, despite the small number of trusteeships initially given over to the United Nations, 'these territories are scattered throughout the colonial areas of the world in such a way that they will undoubtedly influence and affect the administration of neighboring colonial territories'. Hence, the UN trusteeship system 'may be regarded somewhat as a world laboratory of colonial administration'. Or, as State Department official Ralph J. Bunche argued, the new 'guiding principles' *vis-à-vis* colonies and trusteeships, 'while admittedly not revolutionary, nevertheless very definitely open an encouraging new vista for dependent peoples'.[46]

However, Bunche also acknowledged, 'The policies of governments alone can breathe life into the dependent-territory arrangements devised at San Francisco'. This was the point emphasized by Norman Thomas, spokesman for American left-liberal sentiment, in his remarks about the UN Charter: 'While it contains provisions which may make a little easier the abandonment of imperialism, there is no sign whatever that the three Great Powers will use it'.[47] In July 1945, he was certainly right. The breath of life was yet to come: the unforeseen by-product of heightened big-power squabbling and competition.

In hearings before the Senate Foreign Relations Committee, Secretary Stettinius and Sen. Tom Connally both made it clear that America's strategic needs in the Pacific had not been compromised. Said Connally, 'We signed the Charter on the theory that our interests in the Pacific and elsewhere were amply protected. . . . In short, it was our attitude that if we are in possession of an island which we have conquered from Japan at the cost of blood and treasure we can remain in possession of it, if it is within a strategic area, until we consent to have it go under the trusteeship'.[48]

An ambitious inspection tour of Pacific islands by members of the House Naval Affairs Committee, a trip covering 21 500 miles, produced a report extolling the virtues of a US-controlled 'chain of security' through the region. American management of the former Japanese mandates, assured the committee's report, 'will be predicated solely upon the desire and responsibility to maintain peace in the Pacific, rather than upon imperialism'. The map which accompanied the report well illustrated the desired swath of influence to be cut through the strategic seas.[49] For the immediate future, it seemed clear that the number of trusteeships would remain small and that any UN role in reducing the scope of colonial controls would be measured largely in terms of its offering a new forum for the discussion of disputes between colonizer and colonized.

During the second half of 1945, then, nationalist leaders in colonial areas could appeal to the principles of two charters in their search for legitimacy and assistance from the big powers. British and Dutch imperial administrations had been discredited by military defeat, the French by collaboration with Japan. Western imperialism appeared to be in the midst of an irreparable systemic crisis: a weak, tottering superstructure, on the brink of collapse. 'Colonial peoples everywhere now recognized', wrote Stewart C. Easton, 'that European powers were no longer invincible. Never again would they feel they were struggling against insuperable odds.'[50] But would the big powers honor their new commitments? Did they agree on what those commitments signified? Would US policymakers seek vigorously and directly to protect the interests of dependent peoples? Third-World

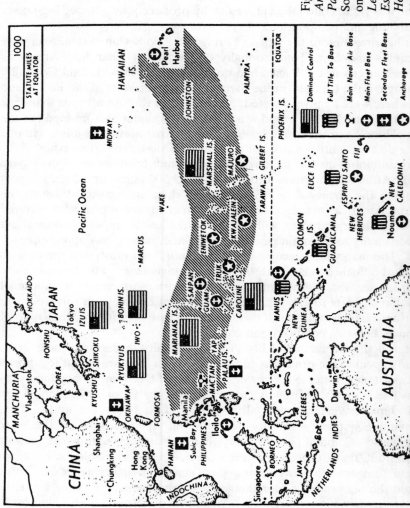

Figure 1.1 *Projected American influence in the Pacific.*
Source: House Committee on Naval Affairs, *Sundry Legislation Affecting the Naval Establishment, 1945, Hearings,* 79th Cong., 1st sess., 1946, p. 1021.

nationalists measured their chances for success; they surveyed the immediate post-war horizon to divine American intent, to identify test cases, to determine if their struggle would be short or long.

COLD WAR VISTAS

In May 1945, Gen. William J. Donovan, director of the Office of Strategic Services, forwarded to the White House a policy commentary titled 'Problems and Objectives of United States Policy'. The paper's author or authors (not named) offered tentative conclusions, phrased as suggestions, about the general shape of the post-war world and likely US priorities. While the analysis was not a blueprint and did not reflect high-level discussions in the spring of 1945, it proved to be an interesting augur of things to come over the next year and a half.

To begin with, the OSS analysis pointed to the dangers posed by the Soviet geostrategic position at the end of the war: 'Russia will emerge from the present conflict as by far the strongest nation in Europe and Asia – strong enough, if the United States should stand aside, to dominate Europe and at the same time to establish her hegemony over Asia'. While Soviet aims were unpredictable, there seemed good reason to expect the merging of the 'predatory tradition' of Tsarist Russia with the 'dynamism' of communist ideology to fuel a formidable expansionism. Avoiding an 'unreasoning antagonism' of the Soviet Union, US policymakers must determine how best to serve their 'prime interest', national security. The task was made urgent because 'the present war has shown conclusively that with airpower and ships, a great power can move huge masses of men and supplies over vast ocean distances' despite strong opposition.

'Unfortunately', continued the paper, 'recent events indicate that the Soviet Government puts but little store by proposals of compromise or by international agreements'. Given the imposition of Soviet control over Eastern Europe, it was apparent that 'Russian expansion has already gone to such lengths' that US 'counter-moves' were required. Soviet dominance of Eastern Europe must be met by the creation of a 'Western-European-Mediterranean-American bloc'. France and Britain must be quickly resuscitated.

In this connection the United States should realize also its interest in the maintenance of the British, French and Dutch colonial empires. We should encourage liberalization of the colonial regimes in order the better to maintain them, and to check Soviet influence in the stimulation of colonial revolt. We have at present no interest in weakening or liquidating these empires or in championing schemes of international trusteeship which may provoke unrest and result in colonial disintegration, and may at the same time alienate from us the European states whose help we need to balance the Soviet power.

A European balance of power might thus be preserved, and the ties of empire would enhance rather than undermine stability and security.

Asia presented similar opportunities for possible Soviet aggrandizement, but in that region the United States had an advantage. 'Since military operations in the Pacific area have been carried out almost exclusively by United States forces, we find ourselves in that ocean and its islands roughly in a position comparable to that of Russia in Eastern Europe. . . . What we hold, we can retain, if we are so minded.' The goals in Asia should be consolidation of a democratic regime in China and the limitation of Soviet influence in post-war Japan. In Southeast Asia, American interests would be served neither by espousing anticolonial doctrines nor by seeking trusteeship arrangements. In addition, American policymakers should ensure adequate military facilities in the Philippines and keep control of military bases in Micronesia.[51]

This was not Roosevelt's policy, nor was it in 1945 yet the policy of the Truman administration. Roosevelt's belief that the maintenance of imperial spheres would only abet further conflict was soon proved accurate. He was correct in pointing to French rule in Indochina as a dispirited and discredited administration, tarred by collaboration with the Japanese at a time when indigenous nationalists had proved themselves to be useful allies of the United States. But despite his genuine sympathy for the aspirations of dependent peoples, FDR's anticolonialism always acknowledged broader American foreign policy objectives, such as strategic bases in the Pacific. Further, as Lloyd C. Gardner has stressed, Roosevelt's 'free-floating style' somewhat disguised a firm determination to expand the American role in the post-war world. 'After all, he could hardly predict what the situation would be at war's end, what could be done immediately and what would simply have to be anticipated without a precise plan.[52]

At the conclusion of the Yalta Conference, Roosevelt accepted a definition of international trusteeship which eliminated the prospect of imminent movement toward self-government in rimland dependencies.[53] What colonial power was willing to place any of its overseas territories under UN supervision? In 1945, the answer was obvious: none. Roosevelt's acquiescence may simply have reflected his awareness that the wartime cauldron within which his anticolonial stance found expression was soon to empty. Warren F. Kimball has suggested that FDR's efforts to forge a wide-ranging agreement at the Crimea meeting 'betray his suspicions that Yalta would be his last chance. Spurred on, perhaps, by his failing health, Roosevelt seemed intent upon creating great-power harmony then and there, a difficult task even without the suspicion that characterized Anglo-Soviet-American relations. Desperate to satisfy so many constituencies, Roosevelt ended up pleasing none'.[54] As such, a trusteeship formula which outlined the rationale for and benefits of international supervision, even with serious limits, was better than nothing at all. Within several years after Roosevelt's death, it looked better still.

Hence, President Truman inherited a policy toward colonial areas which was replete with contradictions and imbalances, as it always had been, within a political environment which forced him to make the kinds of decisions that Franklin Roosevelt had consciously postponed. The course of Truman's decision-making then contributed to the opening of a new level of hostility toward and rivalry with the USSR. In the process, the attitudes and priorities discussed in the OSS paper summarized above became, by 1947, the basis for American foreign policy: a Eurocentric focus, a global struggle to contain Soviet influence, a retreat from advocacy of anticolonial views which might interfere with consolidation of a Euro-American security system.

The colonial situation at war's end, the ripple of rimland crises which both marked and contributed to the onset of the cold war, and the rationale and impact of US policymaking toward dependent areas – such are the subjects of the chapters which follow. The Big Three were divided by big issues, and it was obvious where those divisions lay. But as Timothy Garton Ash has pointed out, 'The real intentions and interests of the Big Three are often more clearly revealed in what they said and did to "lesser" parties than in what they said and did to each other'.[55] Of course, there was an abundance of lesser parties in latter 1945 and early 1946, and, geopolitically, some were lesser than others. Often, those policy debates and decisions which were the most troublesome, the most revealing, and the most far-reaching were those concerning the colonial world. For that reason, the years 1945–47 mark more than the collapse of the Grand Alliance and the beginning of the cold war. In fact, the breakup of the anti-Hitler coalition and the struggle for Europe were only the curtain rising on the more profound global drama rooted in the emergence of millions of people from the shadow realm of colonial and neocolonial control.[56] The phenomenon of deep-seated anti-Americanism in the Third World, so evident by the late 1960s, was largely a product of the immediate post-war years. Tracing the origin of such widespread disappointment, anger, and envy among the colonized provides a fuller portrait of the main events as well as the political undertow. The dilemma faced by American policymakers was summarized by one observer in an article which appeared in 1958:

Our European allies, primarily England and France, are vitally dependent on the economic advantages colonialism gives them in Asia and Africa for their political and military strength in the world. Only thus can they maintain themselves as strong allies in our mutual struggle against

Communism. Yet, if we support European colonialism in order to keep
our European allies strong, we alienate the people of Asia and Africa,
making it easier for Communism to win them over and thereby deprive
the Europeans of these economic areas.[57]

State Department officials expressed similar sentiments during the latter
1940s, but the options posed were not of equivalent weight. The collapse of
Western Europe, projected as imminent during the winter of 1946–47,
boded immediate and disastrous ills for US foreign and domestic policy: on
this, everyone could agree. The growth of communist influence in the
colonial rimlands, real or imagined, was a more gradual cancer and further
away, out in the desert dunes and dense jungles. Presumably it could be
arrested later. After the reconstruction of Western Europe, there would be
new opportunities to reverse damaging trends and restore American
prestige among native nationalists in the colonies. 'Hopes and illusions are
two different things', wrote Stettinius in defense of Roosevelt's diplomacy
at Yalta, 'and the President was well aware of the difference'. Each
president has brought his own set of hopes and illusions with him, and
Harry Truman was no different. During the war, geographer Nicholas J.
Spykman observed that 'times were never so propitious for the dreamers
of dreams and the architects of vast political mansions'.[58] In fact, to
American leaders, the opportunities for adjustment and change, for the
realization of global dreams, seemed much greater in 1945 than ever
before.

2 Rivalry in the Mediterranean, 1945: French North Africa and the Levant

On 8 November 1945, the Reverend W. S. Boyd of Morgantown, West Virginia, appeared before the House Foreign Affairs Committee to speak in favor of the creation of a Department of Peace. While the hearings were merely scheduled as a courtesy to a long-time colleague, the setting gave Boyd an opportunity to describe his hopes for the post-war order. The United States, he said, remained a young and vital nation: 'In the brief period of our national existence it has already become tradition with us to be imaginative and daring and resourceful in the achievement of the goals we set for ourselves. We have become specialists in the impossible'. Indeed, such resourcefulness would be required to handle the difficult challenges of the coming years. The end of the war, Boyd commented, must be followed by greater gains for the 'little people' of the world. 'Sooner or later, we will have to make good on our promises of freedom and justice and equal opportunity and perpetual peace'.[1] As the Reverend Boyd looked outward, beyond his own hemisphere, toward the little people – the poor, the dispossessed, the colonized – perhaps he realized how intently they were staring back.

As the aftershocks of war rippled through virtually every region of the world, numerous controversies and conflicts soon emerged. For the superpowers, the key grappling ground was Europe, the vortex of the geostrategic game. But there were volatile flashpoints in the developing world as well: native uprisings in North Africa, Anglo-French conflict in the Levant, explosive big-power rivalry in Iran, upheaval in India, inter-necine warfare in China, armed resistance to colonial restoration in French Indochina and the Netherlands East Indies. Disposition of the former Italian colonies in Africa – Libya, Eritrea and Somaliland – was an issue which dogged the major powers, continuing to elude resolution in the immediate post-war years. Strategic questions loomed large on the foreign policy agenda of the Big Three: the Soviets and Eastern Europe, the Americans and the Pacific, the British and the Middle East.

American government officials, policy analysts both in and out of government, and newspaper columnists were all aware that the post-war years promised some fundamental changes. The rhetoric of war's end was soaring and hyperbolic. Proclaiming victory over Japan on 16 August 1945,

President Truman announced, 'This is the end of the grandiose schemes of the dictators to enslave the peoples of the world, destroy their civilization, and institute a new era of darkness and degradation. This day is a new beginning in the history of freedom on this earth'. Two weeks later, in Tokyo Bay, from the deck of the battlecruiser *Missouri*, General Douglas MacArthur declared that Japan's defeat opened 'the vista of a new emancipated world' for the peoples of East Asia. 'Today, in Asia as well as in Europe, unshackled peoples are tasting the full sweetness of liberty, the relief from fear.'[2] In truth, however, few people beyond the shores of America were tasting this sweetness; and it was soon pointed out that many Americans still needed relief from fear and want. As European society continued reeling from the devastation of war, it became obvious to American policymakers that the 'little people' would have to wait. 'Ain't it awful what a difference it makes where you sit!' wrote Harry Truman for obvious reasons.[3]

From where a good many Americans sat, the character of post-war regimes in the colonial world posed interesting but complex and dilemmatic questions. Sumner Welles, having left the State Department in 1943, continued to write about the fate of empires. In *The Time for Decision* (1944), he identified the need soon for 'a radical readjustment of international relationships throughout Asia and the regions of the Pacific ... if there is to be any hope at all of political stability, economic security, and peaceful progress'. Although he did not feel that colonial peoples were sufficiently advanced to handle self-government, Welles advised that restoration of the status quo in Asian dependencies was no longer feasible. In early 1945 Welles described 'the whirlwind which is looming': an outburst of anticolonial sentiment and activity in the Far East. 'To the Oriental mind, the Atlantic Charter unequivocally promises an end to imperialism.' He believed that the British Commonwealth could become a bulwark against widespread conflict and chaos if former dependencies joined with the metropole in a co-operative, voluntary association.[4] Another author, H. W. Wieschhoff, pointed to the impact of the Atlantic Charter in African colonies, likewise praised the British model of administration, and predicted that Anglo-American military activity in French North Africa would leave a mark on Arab attitudes through the region. In a lecture delivered in October 1946, Rupert Emerson observed: 'The United States has a very real choice to make. As the wealthiest and most powerful country in the world the way in which it swings, or fails to swing, cannot but help have a vast influence in every corner of the world'.[5]

Because their nation was so wealthy and now so powerful, US leaders were exuberant but cautious in surveying the range of possible or desirable modifications in the world system. American policymakers desired economic restoration and free trade; they favored a world economy centered upon and flowing from the dynamism of the US productive system.

Vis-à-vis the colonial question, it was a time for ingenuity rather than innovation. Nonetheless, given the continued attractive power of the image of an innate and wholly anticolonial spirit in the United States, there was no shortage of appropriate public remarks expressing official sympathy for the problems of dependent peoples. For instance, John Carter Vincent, director of the Office of Far Eastern Affairs, speaking a year after the Japanese surrender, warned against US support for the status quo in the Pacific, favoring instead the adoption of 'progressive policies' and the avoidance of 'short-term expedients'. Philip Jessup, wartime economic consultant to the State Department and later member of the US delegation to the United Nations, affirmed the need for an 'imaginative sympathy' with Asian peoples, 'looking at their problems from their point of view rather than ours'. He concluded: 'Clearly a policy which approaches the problem of the Far East from any other direction would have little chance of succeeding'.[6] The same sentiments could have been offered, and were, about movements and events in Africa or the Middle East.

The lessons of history were clearly drawn: an effort willy-nilly to impress dependent peoples into the service of Western interests, without recognizing deeply held aspirations for self-government, would be foolish. Worse, it would be counterproductive – it would fail and it would tarnish the name and image of America. There was little doubt that, to the world's poor and oppressed, America was the shining city. Everyone talked about it. From every colonial theater came the good word: America was loved and admired; Americans were different from Europeans. Nevertheless, US diplomatic and military observers in or near dependent territories typically advised that indigenous peoples were not ready to assume the responsibilities of national independence. As Harold D. Finley, US consul general in Algiers, wrote in May 1946: 'Administrative chaos and progressive retrogression would, it seems likely, follow the setting up of any Moslem state in this country. In fact such a development is presently unthinkable'.[7]

Progressive retrogression, in fact, might become an epidemic if chronic instability became rooted throughout the long belt of colonies and mandates curving along the power periphery. Festering colonial sores would become what Cordell Hull called 'kernels of conflict'. The old-style imperialism was outmoded. As Sen. Karl E. Mundt observed after a brief sojourn through the Mediterranean area in latter 1945, 'I think the mandate system is about dead. It is about to join the dodo bird in somebody's museum'. Further, the rigid maintenance of spheres of influence would imperil global economic recovery. There must be a franker and freer discussion of access to raw materials and markets. 'The preservation of peace ... requires, in a world as complicated and as closely interknit as this modern world of ours, a great design', remarked Stettinius. Part of that design, he advised, should be development strategies for the colonial rimlands: 'The more wealth they produce and the higher their national income, the more they will wish to buy from us and be able to pay for'.[8] But what policies might promote economic development yet discourage premature political agitation?

The Philippines was the logical model for American leaders to exult as proof of their liberal principles and good intentions. Minus a few ugly episodes, which Americans preferred to forget, here was a colony which had undergone patient tutelage since the turn of the century, one whose native population had been acclaimed for courageous resistance against the Japanese, and one which was scheduled to and did become independent on 4 July 1946. Among American officials, the word 'Philippines' was always prominent amid lectures upon or suggestions for better management of European colonies. To Third-World peoples, the Philippines was offered as proof of American benevolence and goodwill. An informational booklet prepared by the US embassy in Manila began this way:

> The Philippine Republic stands as a symbol of democracy in the Far East and as concrete evidence of the fairness and unselfishness of the United States. . . . The countries of Asia . . . watch carefully the growth of this country as the testing ground for judging whether the democratic way of life can provide adequately in the Far East for the welfare of the people and as a testing ground of United States policy.[9]

In truth, the Philippines was perhaps a more useful example than many officials realized. There was, no doubt, a ritualistic character to the frequent trotting out of the US–Philippines relationship, but Franklin Roosevelt had used it creatively to explain the boundaries of American anticolonialism. There were, he said, two important factors in the pattern of recent Philippines history: (1) the need for a 'period of preparation', through expansion of the educational system and socio-economic development, and (2) the need for a 'period of training for ultimate independent sovereignty' via the steady growth of self-governing institutions. Even the United States, he pointed out, had passed through 'preliminary stages', a 'whole process of political training and development' beginning in the local assemblies and town meetings of the colonial era, before achieving its independence.[10] The latter statement expressed a kinder view of the British Empire's historical imperative than FDR typically acknowledged.

Thus, the Philippines was proffered as a successful testing ground for the efficacy of American tutelage. But the immediate post-war years were littered, it seemed, with a bewildering array of test cases involving fundamental principles and doctrines. What was the appropriate test, for instance, of Allied sincerity in making far-ranging wartime promises? Was it American policy in North Africa, British policy in the Levant or Palestine, Soviet policy in Iran or French policy in Indochina? The war years contained sufficient *ad hoc* actions and declarations to supply nearly any policy precedent desired.

An early indicator of US wartime policy toward colonial spheres was the outcome of Operation TORCH in November 1942: the Anglo-American invasion of French North Africa. Here was the Maghreb: the Muslim peoples of Morocco, Algeria and Tunisia. The territories represented an important adjunct to the French economy. The region's strategic import- ance was much upgraded by the expanding role of air power in the war. French dominance of the Maghreb had been well established in the pre-war years, through docile Muslim rulers in Morocco and Tunisia, through direct rule in Algeria. In the latter colony, the northern coastal area was divided into three departments (Oran, Algiers and Constantine), presided over by a governor-general; and the arid southern region (Territoires du Sud) was administered by the French military. In the autumn of 1942, despite uncertainty and unease among the Arab com- munities, life was reasonably quiet in the French territories. After the humiliation of French military defeat and the imposition of the armistice in June 1940, North African colonial officialdom had quickly accommodated itself to the intrigues and policies of the Vichy regime. As William A. Hoisington, Jr., has pointed out, the code of Vichy was quite compatible with the ethos of the colonial situation: 'Discipline, obedience, order; duty, hierarchy, unity – these words that saturated [Marshal] Pétain's speeches had always been part of the language of the empire builders'. On the other hand, the strong sense of a greater and glorious France, which previously animated the *mission civilisatrice*, was largely absent, replaced by the need to protect and preserve French domains in the face of multiple enemies. Thus, Vichy rule in the Maghreb was also a 'regime of resignation',[11] one which appeared only loosely and unenthusiastically committed to active collaboration with Nazi Germany.

FRENCH NORTH AFRICA

'Foreign policy, in time of a great war, is directly conditioned by the ebb and flow of military events', wrote William L. Langer in his 1947 study of US policy toward Vichy France. Julian G. Hurstfield, in a more recent analysis, has pointed to the lack of easy distinctions between military and political goals for wartime policymakers.[12] In North Africa and elsewhere, the calendar of events produced a constant interweaving of short-term and long-term objectives and expectations. While military expediency might rule in a particular instance, the war's progression created each moment new situations in which the presence or absence of firm political goals inevitably shaped the character of the expanding struggle. For Churchill and Stalin, the two considerations were inexorably intertwined; however, Roosevelt believed that military affairs could be handled separately and preferred to postpone the unravelling of difficult political tangles until after the Axis surrender. The pursuit of military objectives in colonial areas while seeking to ignore such broader political questions as sovereignty and native nationalism was a pattern first established in the aftermath of the TORCH landings, in French North Africa, with early indications that it was an inadequate policy.

While the United States maintained regular consular relations with each of the colonial regimes in French North Africa, additional American personnel began arriving in the territories in the spring of 1941. The establishment of a small but widely dispersed network of US observers in Algeria, Morocco and Tunisia resulted from a February 1941 agreement between presidential emissary Robert Murphy and General Maxime Weygand, the French delegate general in North Africa. This accord was a by-product of Roosevelt's policy of maintaining ties with the Vichy government in hopes of limiting German influence and preventing an Axis occupation of French overseas territories. The Murphy-Weygand agreement established the terms for the shipment of such US goods as coal, cotton and foodstuffs to the French colonies; ostensibly to help avert economic and social collapse, the purpose of this arrangement was primarily political. Roosevelt and Murphy sought to bolster, with the promise of American assistance, those Vichy officials whom they regarded as only half-heartedly pro-Axis. The Murphy-Weygand agreement also stipulated that American products could neither be stockpiled by the colonial regimes nor reshipped to Axis territories; to verify local compliance with this provision, a limited number of US observers, soon designated 'vice consuls', were permitted to oversee the distribution of goods.[13]

Robert Murphy remained in North Africa as the equivalent of an American High Commissioner and co-ordinated the activity of the vice consuls, whose work in intelligence gathering quickly eclipsed their other responsibilities. As Murphy later recalled, he frequently told French officials 'that the only interest of the American Government in Africa was strategic, and that we considered relations between France and the African peoples in French Africa to be purely an affair between them'.[14] This attitude was also typical of the vice consuls. Kenneth Pendar, who served as a vice-consul in both Casablanca and Algiers, was one of the few Americans who acquired a genuine (if paternalistic) interest in Arab culture; nevertheless, he likewise desired to maintain smooth relations with the French administration. 'We were not there to preach democracy or independence', he wrote. 'We were there to find out what the Arabs really thought about the Axis and about the democratic nations, what sort of propaganda swayed them, how much the Axis infiltrated and corrupted the Arab world, and how receptive that world would be if American action were ever necessary in Africa.' Thus, the Murphy-Weygand agreement, noted Hurstfield, 'enhanced, rather than impaired, Vichy's control over her empire'.[15]

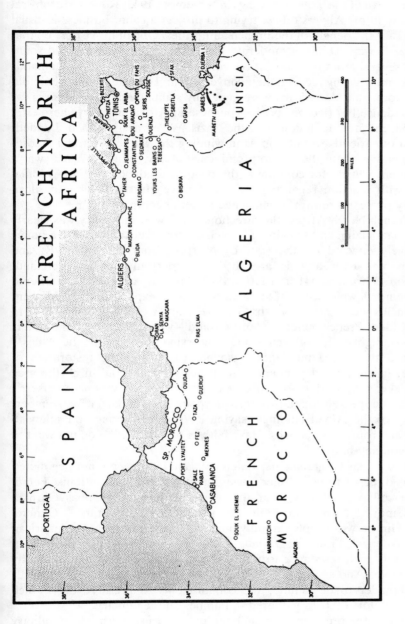

Figure 2.1 *French North Africa.*

Source: Map dated 3 August 1943, Office of Strategic Services, R & A, OSS-2529-C, RG 226, Cartographic and Architectural Branch, National Archives and Records Administration.

On the eve of the TORCH landings in November 1942, Robert Murphy sat anxiously in his Algiers office, trying to project a calm, business-as-usual manner for the benefit of the French authorities. One of his visitors on that day was Ferhat Abbas, a moderate Muslim nationalist who would soon, within several months, confront the colonial administration with demands for reform. Murphy recalled their conversation: 'I repeated what I had told him before, that Americans were generally sympathetic to all desires for independence but that our present purpose in Africa, as everywhere else, was concentrated upon defeating the Nazis. We earnestly hoped, I added, that all our friends would join us in winning the war'.[16] Franklin Roosevelt's parable about the rise to prominence of 'Dr. Win-the-War'[17] was a convenient vehicle for combining the continued advocacy of anticolonial views with inaction regarding any substantive efforts to use American military power to reform or challenge imperial controls.

In French North Africa, the direction of US wartime policy was clearly toward stabilizing and sustaining French control over the region – a policy effectively enacted on the spot by Murphy, approved by FDR, and implemented over a wide area by the American military command. Between February 1941 and latter 1942, Murphy authored or brokered arrangements which constituted a steadily more explicit acknowledgment of French sovereignty in North Africa. His letter of 2 November 1942 to the dissident French general, Henri Giraud – whom Roosevelt and others believed might rally colleagues and countrymen to fight for the Allies – promised that the United States sought to ensure 'the restoration of France, in all her independence, in all her grandeur and in all the area which she possessed before the war, in Europe as well as overseas'. Roosevelt appeared to reaffirm this viewpoint in remarks on 7 November, the day of the Allied landings, saying, 'We come among you solely to defeat and rout your enemies. Have faith in our words. We do not want to cause you any harm'.[18]

Of course, such agreements, statements and letters were not negotiated with or directed to established governments. The collaborationist Pétain regime collapsed shortly after the North African invasion as German troops moved to new positions throughout southern France. General Henri Giraud was simply an individual who appeared to serve American aims. Admiral François Darlan, whose co-operation was secured in aborting French resistance to the landings, was a stopgap figure, clearly expendable. And so on. Still, as the war progressed, despite Roosevelt's cold shoulder to de Gaulle, US commitments to preserve the French empire in North Africa gathered in number and legitimacy.

Here was the problem: only an open policy of using American military forces to supersede Vichy colonial authorities and methodically to replace them with either a US protectorate or a network of indigenous appointees would have brought self-determination to North Africa. Such was never proposed by any American official, military or civilian. The native Muslim population, alternately pictured as a sleeping dog being let lie or an unfocused effervescence in danger of reaching critical mass, was not to be stirred too deeply. The Allies wanted Arab support, certainly, but largely in the form of non-interference (so as to avoid behind-the-lines sabotage), labor services (albeit with a higher pay scale than offered by the French), and useful intelligence concerning Axis activity. Fuelling popular discontent was only on the agenda for occupied Europe, where unrest disrupted Nazi rather than Allied planning.

At the Roosevelt-Churchill Casablanca summit in January 1943, FDR's handling of the colonial question assumed its usual perplexing character for his subordinates. In a conversation with General Giraud, Roosevelt insisted that a discussion of political questions must wait until North Africa had been cleared of German armies – presumably, this referred to final decisions on sovereignty and administrative responsibility.[19] It was instead a different political question which concerned the conferees: the matter of establishing a unified directory for Fighting France. Hence, the real test for whether or not an issue was suitable for detailed discussion was not its political character but rather its immediate and direct impact upon US military planning.

Roosevelt hosted a pleasant dinner for Morocco's Sultan, Mohammed V, on 22 January, and then met with Charles de Gaulle, a reluctant visitor to the Anglo-American compound. In his remarks to the resistance leader, FDR asserted that there was no government, provisional or otherwise, currently able to exercise French sovereignty over North Africa, a situation which justified both the American negotiations with Vichy officials and also Roosevelt's desire to delay judgment on long-term administrative responsibility for the Maghreb. According to Captain John L. McCrea, who listened to the conversation from outside the room, 'The President pointed out that it was, therefore, necessary to resort to the legal analogy of "trusteeship" and that it was his view that the Allied Nations fighting in French territory at the moment were fighting for the liberation of France and that they should hold the political situation in "trusteeship" for the French people'. Then, at war's end, France could reassert its sovereignty over both homeland and empire.[20]

What did this mean? No one was sure. Roosevelt's remarks reflected his belief in several things: (1) that the French had a particularly bad record in administering their colonies, or at least some of them, (2) that France was no longer a great power and would not recover that status, and (3) that de Gaulle did not deserve American trust and recognition. Yet, none of these thoughts necessarily governed the ultimate disposition of French colonial areas. Murphy was understandably confused as he catalogued the president's various comments at Casablanca.[21] Were empires indivisible, or could some territories be detached while others remained under the authority of the metropole? How were trusteeships to be planted over the dying bodies of recalcitrant imperialists? Before leaving Casablanca, Roosevelt approved the substance of Murphy's work in North Africa.

Native Nationalism

American resources for gathering information were impressive, but processing it – consolidating the reports of military personnel, State Department officials, and intelligence agencies – was more difficult. In French North Africa, as elsewhere, FDR preferred to spread authority among different and even competing bureaucracies. It was a tactic which sometimes served his purposes well, other times not so well, but nearly always prevented the aggregation of ideas and data necessary to forge a realistic appraisal of foreign policy options. This characteristic of Roosevelt's presidency was not so critical for developing military strategy, where the primacy of war-related considerations and the hierarchical system of command enabled a few individuals to speak authoritatively to the president. But for the lesser important and more complex political issues raised by the path of war, this division of authority and responsibility hindered the assimilation of accurate information and precluded the formation of a bloc of officials who might have spoken more persuasively and powerfully in support of indigenous nationalist movements. In North Africa as well as other colonial territories, State Department representatives were typically uninterested in native politics, except as a sideshow of sorts, and the department's bureaucracy in Washington was dominated by the views and concerns of its Europeanists, both during and after the war.

Field operatives of the Office of Strategic Services (OSS) often had the best vantage point for accurately evaluating the attitudes and expectations of Third-World nationalists. Consequently, reports prepared by OSS personnel, including the papers produced in the Research and Analysis Branch, generally revealed a better understanding of and greater sympathy for nationalist movements than was found in other agencies. However, OSS activities in colonial areas were skeletal compared to the scale of intelligence operations in the European theater; and the observations of agents out on the war's periphery were muted in the brief summary materials that reached the White House. The State Department itself, so often bypassed in wartime decision-making, was unlikely to be attentive to external advice in those areas of foreign relations where its expertise still flourished and its influence might still determine the line of march.

As the first liberated zone in the war, French North Africa became a laboratory for an ambitious American-sponsored aid program: a civilian lend-lease venture designed to restore economic stability and thus reduce the likelihood of popular discontent. While the pre-invasion aid program, initiated by Murphy, had failed to reach significant levels,[22] American officials now hoped that a large-scale assistance effort might enable North African farmers to produce surplus commodities for export to Europe, with a concomitant increase in US prestige among Arab peoples. Yet, problems regularly arose over procuring adequate supplies of goods, shipping arrangements and administration of the program. 'At best', wrote James J. Dougherty, 'the civilian assistance to North Africa represented a qualified success. It provided basic subsistence, which pacified the population and thereby prevented any political upheavals.' But civilian lend-lease failed to rehabilitate the region's economy, and by the end of the war food shortages in Muslim communities had become common throughout North Africa.[23] Hence, the American wartime presence in the Maghreb created tension without resolution, and the overall impact of the US occupation was difficult to determine. While US troop activity and economic aid provided further proof of the decline of French power, American policy relied heavily upon and thus strengthened the French colonial administration. While US officials carefully avoided advocacy of Moroccan, Algerian or Tunisian independence, the American intervention quickened the indigenous impulse toward self-determination. And perhaps, as Arthur L. Funk has suggested, the American military occupation of French North Africa 'established a precedent for unilateral control of a liberated area'.[24]

During 1943–44, OSS analysts produced several detailed evaluations of the colonial situation in French North Africa. The reports were prepared in the Research and Analysis Branch and offered the following observations:

1.   There had been a rapid decline of French prestige in the Maghreb in the wake of the 1940 armistice;
2.   Hatred of the French colonial system was widespread among the Muslim population of the region;
3.   There was a dynamic nationalist movement, with expanding influence, in each territory, although the movement was not unified across the Maghreb;
4.   While Arab nationalists initially had reacted favorably toward appeals from the Axis powers, few leaders had actively collaborated with the Nazis;
5.   Arab nationalists sought to take advantage of the interim American occupation to force concessions from the French administration; and
6.   Maghreb Arabs were increasingly disappointed by apparent US indifference to their political aspirations.[25]

The decline of metropolitan prestige and the rising strength of nationalist groups were themes soon sounded by American observers in other colonial areas. Expressing what became a common generic refrain, an OSS analyst noted: 'French North Africa may well prove a testing-ground of United Nations democratic pronouncements and, from the point of view of colonial populations, any pattern established there can hardly fail greatly to influence their destiny for years to come'.[26]

Intelligence operatives, however, were not responsible for the day-to-day task of representing US foreign policy objectives in North Africa. That labor fell naturally to American consular representatives, who showed some interest in but little enthusiasm for Arab nationalist movements. In late 1943, Under-Secretary Edward Stettinius requested more detailed reports on political and social conditions in the Maghreb, noting 'the close relation of the native question in North Africa to Arab problems elsewhere'. But, he warned, US officials must neither publicly criticize the French administration nor interfere in local affairs.[27]

The problem with this policy of non-interference, as indicated by Robert Murphy, was that Arab leaders *expected* the United States to support the demands put forward in nationalist manifestos. 'The American military authorities, of course', wrote Murphy, 'are interested in attaining their objective, namely the wholehearted cooperation of the Arab population during the coming critical months, for purely military reasons.'[28] From US consulates in Algiers, Casablanca, Rabat and Tangier, the viewpoint was identical: the American government was not prepared to extend any official approval to nationalist groups seeking wartime adjustments to the colonial status quo. Thus, it was a mistake to interpret too literally Senator Arthur H. Vandenberg's remark concerning the principles of the Atlantic Charter: 'They march with our armies. They sail with our fleets. They fly with our eagles. They sleep with our martyred dead'.[29] On the other hand, the presence of large numbers of 'uninhibited, forthright, rollicking' American soldiers was not unnoticed by North African Arabs. Various war-related activities, wrote Mohammed Khenouf and Michael Brett, 'brought personal contact between the Muslim population and the new-comers, from which Muslims undoubtedly drew their own conclusions about themselves, the French, the Americans and the British'.[30]

As it happened, there were few occasions during the war when violent protest erupted against the French administration in North Africa. OSS informants reported a policy of harsh repression in Tunisia following its reoccupation in spring 1943. There was a spiralling confrontation between Algerian nationalists and French officials, but no serious outbreak until VE Day. In Morocco, however, there were rumors of impending street demonstrations in early January 1944. American diplomats in the territory worked closely with the new French resident general, Gabriel Puaux, and were reluctant to make any contacts with Arab leaders not closely associated with the Sultan. But having met with two such leaders in early January, Ernest Mayer, the US consul at Rabat, wrote:

> In reply to their request for my views and advice, I stated that I did not think that the American people and Government would look with favor

upon any political movement which would tend to distract us from our present all-encompassing absorption in the prosecution of the war. ... I also advanced the opinion that broad changes might be anticipated after the war in the concepts of colonial administration and the administration of mandates and protected countries. My interlocutors replied that they could not wait until after the war to take action because then France, having presumably regained her power, could not be driven from her privileged position in Morocco.[31]

J. Rives Childs, chargé at Tangier, believed that Arab nationalists 'are bent upon using the American and British authorities to play them off against the French, and I would respectfully suggest that while avoiding giving offense to legitimate Moorish Nationalist aspirations, we refrain from being made cat's-paws for the circumlocutory intrigues to which the Moors are so addicted'. Further, argued Childs, discussion in Morocco of the Atlantic Charter and other idealistic principles had been premature and dangerous amongst a people so politically immature.[32] The consuls were agreed: Arab nationalists who pressed for immediate reforms were opportunists; and, overall, North African peoples were inadequately prepared for self-determination.

Following disorders in Rabat and other Moroccan cities in latter January 1944, Secretary Hull re-emphasized the priority which must be given to the military situation: 'It is obvious that any agitation likely to hamper the war effort cannot be regarded with favor by this Government and that a political movement designed to alter the character of the French protect-orate at this critical juncture of the war would be inopportune to say the least'.[33] Despite such official caution, however, an OSS study of 27 January suggested a rise in anti-American sentiment among the French settlers, or *colons*, of the region, noting their dissatisfaction with continued US reliance upon Vichyite administrators, with the level of American lend-lease assistance, and with the behavior of US soldiers. Also a cause of discontent were the inevitable reservations about American contacts with Muslims, 'The French know that they are cordially disliked by the Arabs; they suspect, and perhaps rightly, that the Arabs would welcome any change of masters'. The report found that local Arabs remained reasonably friendly and continued to hope that the American government would ultimately act to improve their situation.[34]

Another OSS report, written several months later, warned that the causes of the Moroccan outbreaks must be 'carefully understood': 'The recent disturbances ... are significant not because they indicate the impatience of a few hot-blooded leaders, but because they focus the spotlight on the explosive potential of the Maghreb problem'.[35] But it was only several weeks to D-Day, and American policymakers resisted the idea that North African nationalism was a genuinely potent political force or

that Muslims were becoming seriously disillusioned with a praxis that
buttressed the colonial regime and accomplished little in the way of
improving daily life.

VE Day in Algeria

By the time of the Yalta meeting in February 1945, there were two
well-established nationalist groups in Algeria, both with roots in the
inter-war period. Ferhat Abbas had initially represented the interests of
the Francophile Muslim elite, the *evolués*, and in 1943 he was among those
moderate nationalists who presented to French officials a manifesto calling
for a greater native voice in the colony's affairs. His subsequent arrest and
stiff French resistance to reform prompted Abbas to espouse a more
fundamental change in the Franco-Algerian relationship by war's end. His
group of followers was generally referred to as the Amis du Manifeste until
the founding in 1946 of the political party Union Démocratique du
Manifeste Algérien (UDMA). Messali Hadj was the other, and more
radical, leading nationalist figure, head of the Parti Populaire Algérien
(PPA), an underground organization during the war and one which
demanded complete and unconditional independence from France. This
group was reorganized as the Mouvement pour le Triomphe des Libertés
Démocratiques (MTLD) in 1946.

On the evening of 23 March 1945, the US consul general in Algiers,
Edward P. Lawton, talked with Paul Alduy of the Governor General's
staff. As was usual among French officials in both North Africa and Paris,
Alduy lamented the fact that external influences, including the Atlantic
Charter, were making it harder for the colonial administration to control
the native population. He mentioned rumors that the nationalists were
receiving encouragement from Lawton, who responded: 'I stated that this
was absurd since I had not met a single nationalist leader since arriving in
Algiers over a year ago and that I had not, in fact, even laid eyes on any of
them. I said that ... I had scrupulously refrained from becoming ac-
quainted with them because I did not wish to give the slightest pretext for
any rumors to develop'. Alduy noted the unsettled nature of French
politics and observed that efforts to entrench American interests in North
Africa would result in France's moving closer to the Soviet Union. 'To this
I replied that I did not see how there could be any doubts regarding our
good intentions in French North Africa', wrote Lawton. 'I said that I knew
of no postwar interests that we had in this region other than maintenance in
Morocco of our treaty rights and of the open-door regime in commerce.'[36]

A month later, Ferhat Abbas did in fact visit the US consulate to deliver
some materials he thought appropriate for the founding meeting of the
United Nations Organization. Lawton remained aloof, reporting: 'I attach
no importance to Abbas' visit, except as indicative of increasing self-con-

fidence in Moslem circles and their rising hope that out of the San Francisco conference may come some measures beneficial to their status and future welfare'. Lawton mentioned again the 'disturbed state of the French mind' regarding Anglo-American intentions toward North Africa. He echoed the opinion of Paris embassy staffer Harry A. Woodruff, who had discussed the North African situation with Jacques Vimont, a Foreign Ministry official associated with Maghreb affairs. Vimont recognized that there was a high degree of Arab discontent, which he blamed on a depressed economy (marked by serious shortages in foodstuffs and clothing) and the chaotic nature of the international situation. Regarding the issue of trusteeships, 'Vimont thinks that if any such plans were pushed by us to[o] far we would have to count on a close understanding developing between Great Britain, France, Holland, and Belgium to oppose its effective application'.[37]

On 1 May 1945, there were small-scale clashes in Algiers between Muslim demonstrators and French police as Arab marchers carried banners calling for independence. According to French officials, the demonstration was organized by pro-Nazi activists. But then on VE Day, 8 May, suppression of a similar demonstration in the town of Sétif, located in the northeast Constantine Department, had led to a general uprising throughout the region. Consul General Lawton reported the deaths of perhaps 60 to 70 Europeans with heavy though undetermined Arab casualties. He noted: 'While it is generally agreed that the situation is serious, no one doubts that the French can and will enforce order by whatever measures are necessary'. An OSS report termed the Sétif affair a 'full-fledged rebellion', lasting for several days, with perhaps 6000 Arabs killed and another 10 000 to 14 000 wounded. 'Using troops, armor, police, planes to bomb and strafe villages, and warships to shell coastal settlements, the French quickly broke the backbone of the revolt. Troops were flown to Algeria from France, Morocco, and Tunisia, partly in borrowed British transport planes.'[38]

Yves Chataigneau, Algerian governor-general, characterized the outbreak as a product of food shortages and the lingering influence of Nazi propaganda. Certain native elements, claimed the French, had been inspired by 'Hitlerism', particularly the nationalist PPA and perhaps even the Amis du Manifeste.[39] Messali Hadj was already under house arrest, and French authorities quickly exiled him to the southern desert; Ferhat Abbas was arrested shortly after the disturbances began. A PPA circular issued after the Mayday violence in Algiers read, in part: 'While the Government General accuses a "party known for its attachment to Hitlerism", it forgets that Hitler partisans are still in their [French officialdom's] midst'. The OSS summary, noted above, asserted that allegations of Nazi sympathies or other insidious influences obscured the real issue: the character of French colonial policy. Muslim dissatisfaction was widespread and the colonial administration had no plans for significant reform. Further: 'The severity of the current suppression will undoubtedly deepen anti-French sentiments in Algeria, and it is likely to have powerful repercussions throughout Moslem North Africa'.[40]

A letter to President Truman, sent from the Parti Populaire Algérien several months after the Sétif uprisings, condemned the 'shameful' record of French colonialism and argued that Arab support for the Allies during the war had earned 'certain rights' that deserved to be respected.

> The Algerian people are unanimous in their determination to fight fiercely to free themselves from their slavery and their more than secular misery. They are, however, sure that their contribution to victory will not have been in vain and that the kindly help of the United Nations will not fail them in these critical moments when, after the events of the Department of Constantine, the Algerian problem presents itself with a new clarity. . . . The deep and underlying causes of these latter events are multiple, but they are all corollary to one fact: the colonial regime of the French, imposed and maintained by force and subject to maneuvers of military divisions. . . . The fundamental evil of which the Algerian people suffer is colonialism.

The Allies, contended the PPA, bore a 'noble responsibility . . . to defend the liberty of the individual and of peoples, of justice and of peace'.[41] A similar viewpoint was expressed by Azzam Bey, secretary-general of the newly formed Arab League, in June 1945. In a discussion with S. Pinckney Tuck at the American legation in Cairo, Azzam Bey insisted that Arabs had been 'killed by the thousands' in Algeria and charged the United States with 'the full moral responsibility' for events in North Africa. In a prepared note, he wrote, 'This responsibility which all the Arabs know emanates from the fact that it was the United States Forces that saved France's possession of North Africa and re-established complete French domination over these Arab lands'. Rather than compelling the French to make concessions to native nationalists, the United States had given 'the Colonial Imperialism of the French an opportunity to revive'.[42]

In fact, the State Department informed its Paris embassy that the French government must be told about Azzam Bey's note and informed 'that the present situation in Algeria to which it refers is a source of anxiety not only to this government but to American public opinion which is deeply conscious of the sacrifices in American lives and material expended in the liberation of North Africa and of the subsequent economic aid given to and planned for that area'. While this would be done with the 'friendliest motives', nonetheless the French should be aware of US concerns regarding events in North Africa 'which could have the most serious consequences not only to the French but to the relations of all Western Powers with the Arab world'.[43] This was the cutting edge of the issue: the possible domino-like effect of anticolonial discontent and the suppression of that discontent upon the attitudes of dependent peoples writ large. However, such voicing of US concerns did not, according to Acting Secretary Dean Acheson, suggest that American officials acknowledged responsibility for events in North Africa.[44] The Normandy landings of June 1944 had well marked the shift of American military and diplomatic attention away from the colonial areas of North Africa and the Middle East. In addition, so little information about the Sétif uprisings was released by the French government that upheavals in Algeria were quickly overshadowed by the very public Anglo-French imbroglio in the Levant in the spring of 1945.[45]

THE LEVANT CRISIS

'This is a political memorandum', began a lengthy commentary by Sir Edward Grigg, British Minister Resident in the Middle East in 1945. He believed that meaningful post-war defense arrangements in the Middle East would have to be based on a realistic appraisal of Arab aspirations, 'because we are now entering an era in which political considerations will infallibly predominate'. The British Empire, wrote Grigg, was a 'co-operative commonwealth of widely separated peoples' and, as such, its survival 'depended upon the freedom of its communications'. While powerful allies were always an asset, Britain's first priority in the immediate post-war period must be preservation of the 'coherence' of the Empire: the fundamental source of the nation's influence and prestige. The Middle East was 'an essential link in the Imperial system, a centre in which are gathered essential arteries of communication and an essential source of power'. The economic and strategic importance of Egypt and the Suez Canal, the Levant countries of Syria and Lebanon, and the Mideast oilfields was undeniable.

Grigg believed that British military exploits during the war years had generated an 'atmosphere of friendliness' toward Great Britain throughout the Near East. 'This friendliness is a very important element; it spreads an absolutely invaluable aura about the immense prestige which the record of the Empire in the war has restored to us. But it cannot be taken for granted.' Britain must therefore be alert to the strength of the nationalist spirit in Arab states. 'We must ride them with the loosest possible rein asking rather for co-operation than insisting upon rights, unless compelled to do so, humouring their national sensitiveness in every possible way, caring for their essential interests, and remembering that Imperial security in the future will depend in no small degree upon the skill and tact with which we now discharge a very exacting and complex task'. While the greatest threat to Britain's security in the region would be political and social discontent, wrote Grigg, British imperialism had the requisite flexibility to accommodate rising nationalist fervor in the dependencies.

Thus, the essential elements of British post-war policy 'will be close attention to the trappings of national independence (the outer form will always
matter more than the inner method in this part of the East), and the use of
all the influence we can exert to secure progressive policies in questions of
land tenure, employment, justice, education, poverty, and health'.

Military strength would naturally be quite important but would not by
itself protect and secure Britain's position in the Middle East. In working
out a 'general scheme of defence' for the region, thought Grigg, the British
should focus upon negotiating base rights rather than seeking automatically
to keep large numbers of troops stationed in the area. The key territories
would be Egypt, Palestine, Transjordan, and Iraq – countries which
formed a 'strategic spine in which all four are essential vertebræ'. Partition
of Palestine, however, would destroy the integrity of this configuration,
raising the specter of 'alienation of the whole Arab world'. As the core
territories for British military planning, Palestine and Transjordan were
necessary as 'reliable buttresses in all weathers'. Syria and Lebanon, both
in transition from mandate status to independence, constituted something
of a 'military vacuum'. Instability in the Levant could only harm overall
British security interests; therefore, it was important that those states
'should not remain a debatable land exposed to strife between competing
neighbours and systems of Government, but should come into the
co-operative system of Middle Eastern security set up by us as reasonably
stable partners'.

Other powers might certainly affect the outcome of British plans in the
Middle East, especially France, the United States and the USSR. Like
most British diplomatic appointees serving in the region, Grigg had little
praise for French policy. Despite 'a powerful cultural influence' in the area,
France had discredited itself among Arab peoples. But rather than
embarrassing England, thought Grigg, the decline of French power would
likely benefit British interests. From the Muslim perspective, any Western
power too closely linked with French intrigues suffered identification 'with
a colonising aim and method which are anathema to all the Arab States.
... France seems unable to produce men capable of understanding the
mind and winning the heart of the virile, inconstant and warm-blooded
Arab peoples'. It was, observed Grigg, a 'psychological impossibility' for
the French genuinely to co-operate with Britain in the region. 'There is no
room in the Middle East for a French and a British sphere of influence. ...
The Arab League is solid in two things only – opposition to French preten-
sions in the Levant and to the creation of a Jewish State in Palestine.'

Friends were hard to find. Grigg did not believe that the Soviet Union
was necessarily or inevitably hostile toward Britain, but he felt that the
USSR would naturally try to enhance its influence in the Middle East in
ways which could only test British skill and determination. On the other
side was the United States. 'America', wrote Grigg, 'is the only true

partner which we shall find in building up a solid structure of social and military security in the Middle East.' The United States was a 'natural ally, because her leaders at home and her representatives on the spot for the greater part think and feel as we do upon the welfare of the Middle Eastern States, and because her major interests coincide with ours in that she needs security for the exploitation of mineral oil, aviation bases, and social contentment rather than unrest'. The only noticeable discord in US-British relations lay with disputes over Palestine 'and in the ignorant ideas of British Imperialism which hold the American mind with unrelenting force'. Hence, without sacrificing its own vital interests, Britain should 'make room for American partnership' in the Middle East. In return, the US government should acknowledge that Britain carried the primary responsibility for Mideast security.[46]

Edward Grigg's paternalistic vision of a wise and careful British pre-eminence in the Middle East soon foundered upon the weakness of Britain's economy, the network of bitter intra-regional rivalries, the destablizing partition of Palestine, and irreparable strains in the Anglo-Egyptian relationship. As well, Anglo-American partnership appeared to wane in the first half-year of peace. Such developments forced a rethinking of British strategic policy, with the result that previously marginal territories, such as Cyrenaica, temporarily assumed greater importance. Further, it soon became apparent that within the Commonwealth there was more disarray than consensus and co-operation. Also, there were challenges to the basic strategic assumptions which informed and undergirded Grigg's theses. Prime Minister Clement Attlee, for instance, averred that the British Empire could only be defended effectively through its membership in a strong United Nations, that to believe otherwise was to rely on 'outworn conceptions'. He wrote:

> Quite apart from the advent of the atomic bomb which should affect all considerations of strategic area, the British Commonwealth and Empire is not a unit that can be defended by itself. It was the creation of sea power. With the advent of air warfare the conditions which made it possible to defend a string of possessions scattered over five continents by means of a Fleet based on island fortresses have gone.[47]

However, the prime minister's iconoclasm regarding imperial defense was not widely shared within the military establishment and foreign policy bureaucracy. Instead, as Lord Hood minuted in response to Attlee's commentary,

> I would submit ... that the advent of air power has in no way altered the fact that the first vital interest of this country is not merely the defence of the shores of these islands, but also the security of communications between this island and the outer world, from which our food supplies

and other vital war materials are derived. ... The maintenance and strengthening of our position in the Middle East must thus remain a cardinal feature of Imperial policy.[48]

By the time Edward Grigg's memorandum was considered by the Cabinet, in July 1945, Britain had launched a controversial intervention in Levant affairs which undercut the authority of the French administration in order to prevent widespread upheaval. While Britain's future in Middle East affairs could not be readily fathomed in the summer of 1945, it did seem that resolute military action in Syria and Lebanon, after months of rising tension and frustrating mediation efforts, had cooled a hotspot and increased British prestige as a respecter and possibly a guarantor of Arab independence.

The Free French effort to preserve the Levant as a sphere of influence, despite a wartime promise of independence, led to a crisis in 1945 which presented problems and opportunities for American as well as British policymakers. Unlike the precise goals of Britain's Foreign Office, however, US policy toward the Middle East was rather amorphous, characterized largely by a new sense of the region's strategic importance and oft-repeated concerns that expanding American economic interests not be curtailed by a born-again European hegemony. Franklin Roosevelt's Near East policy was also, and purposefully, little directed toward divining the post-war shape of regional political ferment.

Economic concerns were paramount for American policymakers. During the war, Roosevelt had assured Winston Churchill that the United States was 'not making sheep's eyes' at British oilfields in the Middle East, and Churchill had confirmed the legitimacy of US investments in Saudi Arabia.[49] British officials were wary of American entry into the politics of oil, yet they generally accepted (like Grigg) the inevitability of such involvement and believed that Britain's strategic position would improve through acquiring a junior partner. Roosevelt noted in March 1944 that the United States had a 'vital interest' in the Middle East, especially 'in seeing that itself and other nations should not be discriminated against in dealing openly and fairly with these territories in the exchange of goods and resources'. In a February 1945 meeting with King Ibn Saud aboard the USS *Quincy* at Great Bitter Lake, Egypt, FDR casually referred to the imperialistic temper of Great Britain, which, as he was fond of pointing out, was a national pastime which the United States did not share. He promised that the American government would support Syrian and Lebanese independence in the event of French intransigence, and he spoke warmly about the benefits that would accrue from an open door regime in the Middle East.[50]

The open door was central to FDR's perspective on the post-war reorganization of dependent territories, just as was his belief that decolonization would be the logical, inexorable outcome of the war. For American leaders, broadly speaking, the open door was cast as epitomic of enlightened self-interest: the United States would prosper, and all nations would surely benefit from a restored, expanded, interlocking network of trade. The fading of spheres of influence would allow for an orderly devolution of empires – a gradual transformation which, it was hoped, would maintain political stability, preserve critical economic ties, and avoid the growth of anti-Western movements in colonial areas.

France and the Levant

'There is in the French philosophy of the Empire no inclusion of a commonwealth of free but federated nations', concluded an OSS report of March 1944. 'The overseas territories, vaguely classified as colonies, protectorates, and mandates, have become regarded as separate units, and are administered as such, but they continue to exist on a political level below that of the *métropole*.' While French colonial regimes were reasonably successful 'in handling local peoples of relatively undeveloped regions', as in North Africa, their frequent resort to military force became problematic in more complex societies requiring skillful political manipulation, as in the Levant.[51]

The territories of Syria and Lebanon had been formally assigned to France as League of Nations mandates in the wake of the First World War; at the same time, Britain had been designated the mandatory power for Iraq, Palestine and Transjordan. The two Middle East spheres of influence co-existed uncomfortably, side by side but not in tandem. By the mid-1930s, the British were pursuing what A. B. Gaunson has termed a policy of 'modest devolution', negotiating new treaties which granted limited autonomy to Iraq and Egypt. The French government, resisting liberalization of its own colonial policy, viewed British reforms as an effort to undermine France's prestige in the region. Thus was created an atmosphere of 'resentful competition' which continued through the eve of the Second World War.[52] Following the Franco-German armistice of June 1940, Levant colonial officials adhered to the Pétain regime, and the authoritarian ethos of Vichy found expression in Damascus and Beirut as well as in Algiers. By the spring of 1941, as recorded in the OSS study mentioned above, 'The Near and Middle East had become a vitally strategic area. Through this gateway the Axis planned to encircle the Mediterranean and, after the entrance of Japan into the war, to join the East and West in a vast pincer movement that would crush the British Empire in Africa and Asia and at the same time isolate Russia'.[53]

Especially threatening to Britain's precarious position in the region was the potential for German use of Syrian military facilities as a staging ground for offensive operations. In May 1941, the German government was granted access to air bases in Syria, which were then used for refueling planes carrying military aid to rebels in British-controlled Iraq. As a result, on 8 June 1941, a small Anglo-Free French force, commanded by General Henry Maitland-Wilson and General Georges Catroux, invaded the Levant; after a month's hard fighting, the joint expedition wrested control from the pro-Vichy directorate. At the beginning of this campaign, General Catroux had proclaimed an end to the mandatatory regime and the independence of both Syria and Lebanon.[54] A cease-fire agreement was signed on 14 July at Acre, Syria. A subsequent exchange of letters between British Minister of State Oliver Lyttelton and Free French leader Charles de Gaulle defined an interim, hybrid administration for the Levant. Lyttelton assured de Gaulle 'that on the British side we recognise the historic interests of France in the Levant. Great Britain has no interest in Syria or the Lebanon except to win the war. We have no desire to encroach in any way upon the position of France'.[55]

The Free French were to handle internal affairs and maintain order in the two territories while British forces co-ordinated external defense. Soon, however, this distinction became muddied by renewed Anglo-French rivalry, shaped by the conflicting desires of Catroux, as delegate general in the Levant, for a full reassertion of French sovereignty and the British demand for genuine reform leading to Syrian and Lebanese independence. Gaunson's study of the Levant situation points to several key themes of British activity in the Near East during 1942–44: (1) that policy was often determined more by local officials than the London Foreign Office, (2) that Britain's chief concerns were regional military exigencies and encouraging favorable Arab sentiment, and (3) that British policymakers were committed to a contradictory policy of supporting Syrian and Lebanese independence while encouraging at least nominal recognition of French special interests in both countries.[56] Once it became clear in latter 1943 that nationalists would refuse to grant the French special privileges and that the French would resort to military force to maintain their authority, London officials were compelled, reluctantly, to think more seriously about choosing sides.

In March 1943, Catroux proclaimed the restoration of native assemblies in the Levant and promised that free elections would soon be scheduled. But all was not well. Following an August referendum in which nationalists won strong support, Lebanese leaders demanded that French officials – responsible to the French Committee for National Liberation (FCNL) as of June 1943 – agree to a series of concessions which would initiate the dismantling of the colonial regime.[57] When the FCNL balked at surrendering its mandatory authority, the Lebanese government attempted to enact the desired reforms without French approval. This action prompted the colonial administration on 11 November 1943 to suspend the Lebanese constitution, dissolve the newly elected assembly, and arrest and imprison

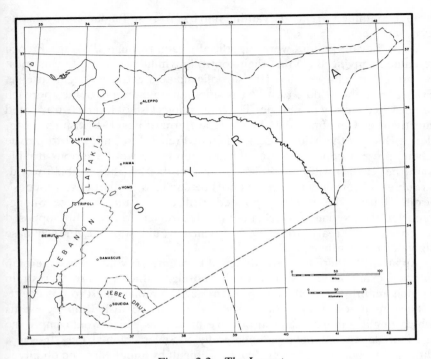

Figure 2.2 *The Levant*

Source: Map dated 18 April 1942, Geographic Division, COI, OSS-467-C, RG 226, Cartographic and Architectural Branch, National Archives and Records Administration.

nationalist leaders. Here was another potential test case of Allied intentions. However, under intense pressure from London, the FCNL defused the crisis by announcing the release of all detainees and the reinstatement of constitutional government. On 24 November, Catroux declared to the peoples of the Levant, 'Now France has restored what has been undone. She remains faithful to her promises, engagements, and obligations. Have confidence in her therefore to respect your rights and liberties as she has confidence in you to respect all that constitutes in your land her patrimony and situation'.[58]

The confrontation of November 1943 was eased but not resolved by Catroux's cautious retreat. An OSS study asserted: 'From a strictly realistic standpoint it is not so much Fighting France which is on trial before the bar of Arab opinion, as Britain and the US'. While the Arabs had never believed in the sincerity of French promises of Levant independence, the United States and Britain had established considerable goodwill throughout the region.[59] Thus, the latter two nations would certainly profit from a peaceful settlement in Syria and Lebanon, but they also stood to lose much from a continued Franco-Levantine impasse over so fundamental an issue as sovereignty.

While Levant politics were superficially calm through 1944, the French remained convinced (1) that their controlling influence in the Levant must be protected, and (2) that British policymakers actively sought to eject France from the Middle East.[60] The situation simmered until the approach of an Allied victory in Europe. The impending clash of interests was noted shortly after Christmas 1944 by General Bernard Paget, British commander-in-chief in the Middle East: 'If [the] French [are] allowed to pursue [their] present policy in Syria and Lebanon there will be serious trouble and [the] British will be held largely responsible by [the] Arabian world. Trouble will certainly not (repeat not) be confined to [the] Levant States'. From Beirut, the newly appointed British minister, Terence Shone, reported that Syrian and Lebanese officials remained adamantly opposed to concluding treaty arrangements which would stipulate French base rights or other privileges.[61]

Apparently, there was little that could be done to avoid renewed tension in the Levant states. Adding to the Foreign Office's desire to restrain French ambitions was the ever-present need to remain alert to precedents which might jeopardize relationships within the British Empire: events which might diminish English prestige or actions which would imply the right of dependent peoples unilaterally to sever colonial ties. It was a difficult balancing act, one made more difficult by impatience and obduracy on the part of others. Count Stanislas Ostrorog, second in authority to the French delegate general in the Levant, informed British representatives that it was a psychological necessity for France to maintain its sphere of influence in the region. France retained only such a small foothold, he said – surely the British with their many dependencies and national honor unstained by German conquest could acquiesce to French claims. Within the Foreign Office, Nevile Butler summarized the issue: 'A great deal depends upon the French themselves, and their "psychological needs" deriving from the unhappy past are not a sound foundation for the treatment of rising Arab aspirations to freedom sponsored by the Americans and the Russians'.[62] From Damascus, Shone wrote that the only hope for improved conditions lay with 'a real change of heart and methods on the part of the French'. The native governments, he argued, were 'far from perfect', but overall they had been 'commendably patient'. The British ambassador in liberated Paris, Alfred Duff Cooper, a consistent Francophile, was told to make certain that French authorities understood Britain's policy: the French must replace their recalcitrant officials in the Levant, stop thinking of Syria and Lebanon as part of the French Empire and get on with the task of setting 'France-Levant relations on a new basis of confidence and co-operation'.[63]

The Crisis of 1945

'We are about to embark on a serious attempt to bring the French & Levant States together on a settlement of some sort', observed Eastern Department official Robert M. A. Hankey on 19 January 1945. But what sort of accord would either side accept? French leaders were wrong in believing that the British Foreign Office was pursuing a policy explicitly tailored toward evicting France from the eastern Mediterranean; and French officials in the Levant refused to reconcile themselves to a new relationship wherein they were first among equals. Those nationalist leaders in Syria and Lebanon who believed that Great Britain would give them unconditional backing were also wrong. Terence Shone was instructed to tell the Syrians and Lebanese that Britain had a two-part policy: independence for the Levant states and new treaties with France. 'The [Levant] States must not think that they have *carte blanche* under some guarantee from His Majesty's Government to accept part of our policy and reject the other.' Or as Major General Edward L. Spears recalled Churchill's saying, 'He spoke to me of the dangers in the Levant ... What people might learn to do against the French in the Levant might be turned against us later. We should discourage the throwing of stones since we had greenhouses of our own – acres and acres of them, he said'.[64]

The source of this policy dilemma was well articulated by Foreign Secretary Anthony Eden, who noted that Anglo-French co-operation was a cornerstone of Britain's post-war planning. The Levant governments must behave themselves and 'regularise' their relationship with France; the French must recognize British strategic interests. 'The French', wrote Eden, 'must be made to see that there are limits to the extent to which we are prepared to incur odium and hostility or still more endanger our position in the Middle East on their behalf.' As Edward Grigg phrased it, the Middle East was 'a region of life-and-death consequence for Britain and the British Empire'; and a Levant which became a 'running sore' could only damage efforts to build friendly relations with Arab states.[65]

From the British perspective, the most sensible solution was a new treaty arrangement between France and the Levant states, one which would be in force by the time war's end brought the departure of the bulk of Allied troops from the Middle East. Since both the French and the Levant governments found it difficult to negotiate directly without mutual recrimination, a third party would have to apply pressure at both ends in order to produce a realistic settlement. Britain had, after all, associated itself in June 1941 with the Free French promise of independence. If such action did not signify a British guarantee, it was at least an 'undertaking' on behalf of Syria and Lebanon and one which put English prestige at risk. Lord Killearn, having issued the 1941 declaration from Cairo, believed that his government owed the Syrians and Lebanese a fair deal. Churchill commented to his Foreign Secretary, 'There is no question of our turning the French out of Syria and Lebanon. They are out already, except in-so-far as they may be able to negotiate a treaty with the Syrians and Lebanese'. But Levant independence, Churchill believed, should not be contingent upon France's gaining a preferential position through new treaties: 'If she gains it we do not oppose it; if she does not, we cannot work for it'.[66]

British goals were neatly summarized by Nevile Butler in late February 1945:

> We wish to keep the present tense situation in the Levant under control by getting the French to state moderate demands, and the Levant Governments to consider them in a conciliatory spirit and to make counter proposals as necessary, and anyhow not to indulge in offhand rejection. Time may thus be secured for the new League of Nations to take shape, and for other Powers to share with us some of the present thankless and dangerous duties of broker.[67]

Yet, the situation remained confused and polarized. A visit to the Levant by Robert Hankey failed to generate any sense of lurking or impending peace. He reported that native political leaders hated the French 'like poison' and that they denounced the colonial administration 'lock stock and barrell, often quite unreasonably – but the French have a very bad record'. About a month after returning to London, Hankey wrote, 'The dislike of the French and British officials for each other in Syria and the Lebanon has got to such a pitch that neither are sane about the other'. In fact, at the time of his trip, 'hardly anybody in the whole place' was sane, he said, except for Terence Shone and a few members of his legation staff.[68]

The American government was also interested in a sensible resolution of the Franco-Levant dispute. Looking toward the post-war era, the State Department identified a set of shared Anglo-American goals in the Middle East and offered its version of an open door regime as the best means to guarantee Western access and local stability. As summarized in a departmental policy paper, 'The end in view would be the creation of conditions favorable to the orderly development of the area's resources, free from the exploitative, discriminatory and restrictive practices that have caused friction in undeveloped areas in the past'. This need not be an aggressive approach: the United States should co-ordinate its policy with other powers and not seek 'to disturb long established commercial and economic relations between any country and the Middle East, so long as these relations result in efficient and adequate service and rest on valid economic bases rather than on hampering controls'. However, to most State Department analysts, it seemed clear that, upon examining the record, only the British had 'long established commercial and economic relations' which could be adjudged as resting on appropriate treaty relationships.

For American policymakers, the sharp discord between French authorities and Levant nationalists represented the predictably bitter fruits of a badly managed colonial administration wedded to an anachronistic and self-defeating insistence upon a preferential position. 'The Middle East is and will remain', concluded the State Department policy paper, 'one of the principal testing grounds of the ideals for which the war is being fought and of the world security system now being constituted.'[69] By the spring of 1945, when this paper was completed, it was clear that one nation especially threatened the stability of the Near East and demonstrated a callous disregard for the overall Western position in the region. That nation was France, and the flashpoint was the Levant, where American and British diplomats actively co-operated to convince both sides of the controversy that moderation in the pursuit of a new era was definitely a virtue.

A British aide-mémoire presented to the State Department on 1 February 1945 noted the lack of improvement in Franco-Levant affairs and asked for US support in spurring Syrian and Lebanese officials to begin serious negotiations with the French. A further aide-mémoire of 9 February repeated the request. At the Yalta Conference, the British delegation produced a memorandum asking again for US assistance.

> The Syrians have, we believe, in the past harboured a feeling that the United States Government would approve of their resisting any understanding at all with the French. We hope that in the interests of a peaceful and fair settlement of the position in the Levant States the President [Roosevelt] will, if he sees the President of Syria while in Egypt, urge him to adopt a circumspect and forthcoming attitude.[70]

Franklin Roosevelt did not, as it happened, meet with the Syrian president, Shukri al-Quwatli, on the way home from Yalta. However, an impressive group of British policymakers gathered together with Quwatli in Cairo on 17 February. Present were Prime Minister Churchill, Foreign Secretary Eden, Permanent Under Secretary Cadogan, Minister Resident Grigg, Minister Shone and Robert Hankey of the Eastern Department. There must be a free and open exchange between the French and the Levant states – this was the point of the meeting. As the record of the conversation noted, 'The Prime Minister said that the French should say what they wanted, the Syrians should say what they were prepared to give. Then the situation could be examined and an agreement reached'. Churchill wanted a resolution of the matter:

> The Prime Minister in the course of the conversation emphasised repeatedly that the Syrians should handle the question tactfully and settle it without serious quarrels. They should give the French a reasonable settlement and not trample on French *amour propre* which had been greatly shaken by the war. They should retain their rights but

they should be confident in their friends and in the world organisation which would be set up. Constant rows with the French were very annoying to His Majesty's Government. [The Syrian government] ... should go as far as possible. If they remained intransigent and gave no consolation to the French there would certainly be trouble. De Gaulle was a dangerous man and he [Churchill] himself could not foresee the outcome. It might be very unpleasant for all parties. He pointed out that British troops would not stay indefinitely in the country.[71]

On 16 February, the State Department cabled George Wadsworth, the US diplomatic representative to the Levant States since latter 1942, instructing him to advise the local governments that they must 'adopt a more moderate and realistic attitude' and work with the French to adopt new treaties consistent with Syrian and Lebanese independence 'and non-discriminatory as regards third powers'. Wadsworth was to assure both governments that his statements did not reflect any change in US recognition of Levant independence. Meanwhile, in Paris, Ambassador Jefferson Caffery similarly urged the French government to show moderation in its negotiations with the Levant states and to refrain from the use of military force in the area. Caffery was instructed: 'You should also make it clear, if the need arises, that we regard our policy toward the independent Levant States as entirely distinct and separate from our policy toward France and the French Empire'.[72] This case was different, then, from the situation in French North Africa or in other dependent territories where the United States was unlikely to interfere with imperial affairs.

Charles de Gaulle and other French leaders did not, however, acknowledge that either British or American officials, at any level, had useful suggestions to offer regarding Levant politics. French antipathy toward the British position in the Middle East was well established. In Washington, Francis Lacoste, counsellor at the French embassy, argued with officials of the Division of Near Eastern Affairs (NE). He pointed to cultural benefits derived from French rule over the Levant states and contended that France deserved a return on its investment through maintenance of a special position in the territories. The French would not accept an open door regime for the Levant. As recorded by Foy D. Kohler, assistant chief of NE, Lacoste 'said that at the turn of the century, when this policy was defined, the United States was only one of a number of powers in the world of relatively equal size and strength. However, we had now become so colossal that if the open-door policy were followed, the others would be unable to compete with us.' Paul H. Alling, chief of NE, vigorously disputed Lacoste's viewpoint, 'emphasizing the decreasing size and the increasing interdependence of the whole world. He pointed out that equality of opportunity was high on our list of war aims and that we had no intention of fighting this war and then abandoning our objectives'.[73] From

Paris, the British ambassador, Duff Cooper, reported that French officials were virtually unanimous in opposing concessions to Levant nationalists. Foreign Minister Georges Bidault, for instance, publicly attributed Levant difficulties to outside intervention and stated that France could not surrender its privileged position.[74] Though typically exaggerated, the presence of a sizeable contingent of British troops in the Near East was often assailed by French officials as proof of English malevolence.[75]

By March the pattern which would govern Levant affairs over the next two months had emerged. British and American entreaties to Syrian and Lebanese officials met with limited success; Anglo-American pressure upon de Gaulle's government was most often ignored; and France pursued a policy of claiming pre-eminence in the Levant and purposefully delaying meaningful negotiations on revised treaties. Outwardly, French officials in Paris, Beirut and Damascus remained calm, even complacent, about the potential for violent upheaval in the Near East. In mid-March, stopping briefly in Algiers on his way to Paris for new instructions, Delegate General Paul E. Beynet told the press that the Levant situation was generally satisfactory, despite the effects of 'propagandes étrangères', and that mutual good will could resolve whatever problems had arisen. In early April de Gaulle complained to Duff Cooper again about the presence of British troops in Syria but then downplayed French demands: 'General de Gaulle said the French had no wish to govern Syria or the Lebanon. They were quite prepared to leave it to the inhabitants. The[y] would be badly governed no doubt, but that did not concern France. All they wanted was a military and air base, and proper treatment for their schools and universities'.[76]

By late April, US and British policymakers sensed a greater urgency to their efforts to midwife a settlement in the Levant. After receiving reports that the French were sending additional troops to the area, Acting Secretary Joseph Grew feared that all possibility of mutual accommodation would be destroyed by the use of military force. Potentially troublesome also, in this context, was the 25 April opening of the UNO conference in San Francisco, placing the issue of relations between large and small powers at center stage. 'Even a minor act on the part of a major power at this time which could be regarded as provocative, would have an effect out of proportion to its intrinsic importance.' Joseph C. Satterthwaite, US consul in Damascus, reported that French policy 'at the moment revolves around a . . . belief in the necessity for delay'. General Beynet had not yet returned from Paris with new proposals. British Minister Terence Shone remarked, 'The Syrian Government have constantly complained of the long delay and maintain that the French are trying to spin things out'. Shone also informed London that Syrian and Lebanese officials would feel misled by the British if the French now failed to offer reasonable terms for the reopening of negotiations. He added: 'While the two Governments still have confidence in us and the populations still consider us as sympathetic to their cause and powerful enough to aid them, the sands are running out'.[77]

A letter from Churchill to de Gaulle, dated 4 May, announced that the British were willing to withdraw all their troops from Syria and Lebanon once new Franco-Levant treaties had gone into effect. An increase in French troop strength before the conclusion of an accord, however, could well 'cause unrest or a rise of temper. . . . As you imagine it is a matter of great importance to us not to have [the] Arab world roused up with [the] probability of sympathetic reactions in Iraq'.[78] On 6 May the French cruiser *Montcalm* debarked about nine hundred soldiers at Beirut; three days later, after boarding five hundred Senegalese troops, it departed. On VE Day, Shone and Grigg witnessed 'wild enthusiasm' in Beirut, though they were surprised 'to find the French enclosures decorated with large pictures of Marshal Stalin as well as General de Gaulle but no other Allied leader'. Shone commented parenthetically, 'The French are playing this Russian line here while at the same time trying as you know, to make our flesh creep about possible dangers from that quarter'. He reported 'an undercurrent of deep anxiety' among Lebanese nationalist leaders concerning the likely arrival of further French forces.[79]

The issue of French reinforcements quickly became the lightning rod for nationalist discontent at the arrogance of French officials and the glacial pace of negotiations. The American and British ministers continued to urge caution, to recommend patience and restraint. As Acting Secretary Grew wrote to Wadsworth, 'It is essential that the Levant Govts. should not misconstrue our sympathetic understanding of their difficulties as encouraging violence or disturbances of any sort'. Or in Shone's words, Syrian and Lebanese officials must avoid 'putting a foot wrongly'. In San Francisco, the Lebanese delegate told Secretary Stettinius that he feared spreading disorder, even to neighboring states, if the French attempted to land additional troops.[80] On 17 May the *Jeanne d'Arc* debarked six hundred additional troops at Beirut. Franco-Levant negotiations then resumed on the eighteenth, in Damascus, as the Lebanese and Syrian foreign ministers met with Delegate General Beynet and received identical aides-mémoire. The French government demanded protection of its cultural, economic, and strategic interests (including bases). Once those requirements were embodied in a new treaty, native troops under French control (the *troupes spéciales*) would be transferred to the local governments 'under reservation of maintaining the troops under the High French Command as long as circumstances do not permit the full exercise of a national command'. The terms of the aides-mémoire were clearly unacceptable to Syrian and Lebanese leaders. Wadsworth and Shone immediately reported a new deadlock and the increased likelihood of violence.[81]

Wadsworth met with General Beynet on the nineteenth and found him surprisingly unconcerned with the situation. Shone spoke with an equally optimistic Beynet, who was convinced that 'if disorders occurred, a few shots in the air were generally enough to send [the] crowd packing'. On 20 May, Shone called upon Beynet again, accompanied by both General Paget, British commander-in-chief in the Middle East, and Major General Gerald A. Pilleau, commander of the British 9th Army. According to Shone, 'General Beynet was obviously more concerned than the day before. ... While he was at times cynical he struck us all as tired and worried'. As an explanation for his two-month absence and the arrival of French reinforcements at the same time as the aides-mémoire, Beynet said that it made no difference – the Syrians and Lebanese would have rejected whatever proposals he had brought with him.[82]

Loy W. Henderson, director of the Office of Near Eastern and African Affairs (NEA), produced a memorandum sharply critical of French policy in the Levant. 'While we in San Francisco are talking about world security and are devising methods for combating aggression', he wrote, 'France is openly pursuing tactics which are similar to those used by the Japanese in Manchukuo and by the Italians in Ethiopia.' Allowing France to intimidate the Levant states would undercut the credibility of the United Nations Organization at the very moment of its founding. Referring to the imposition of Soviet control in Eastern Europe, Henderson argued: 'It is possible for the small countries of the world to differentiate between the great democratic powers of the West and the Soviet Union. They are almost certain, however, to judge all the Western powers in the light of policies pursued by any of them'. Thus, it apeared that French actions constituted a test of American sincerity in championing the rights of small nations.[83]

Incidents mounted in Syrian towns. The British consul in Damascus predicted an imminent showdown, writing, 'I feel we have shot our bolt here'. On the morning of 26 May, President Truman approved a note to the French government expressing 'deep concern' about the Levant situation, pointing to the importance of avoiding such strife while the UN conference was in session and urging that the French review their Near East policy. On the evening of the 26th, London time, the Foreign Office released a statement to the press which expressed regret that the dispatch of French reinforcements 'should have been the occasion for breaking off negotiations ... between the Levant States and the French Government'. It was hoped that this development would not preclude an amicable settlement. From Syria, however, General Paget reported continuing acts of French provocation. 'Tanks remain in Damascus. Aircraft fly low over mosques during [the] hour of prayer. Machine guns are prominently sited on roofs of buildings. ... In my opinion [the] French are deliberately courting [a] clash with the [Levant] states.' From the US legation in Jidda, Saudi Arabia, William A. Eddy cautioned:

I do not wish to labor the point of reviving Arab doubts about Allied faith, a point which has been made so clearly by Minister Wadsworth in his reports. It is worth noting, however, that Saudi Arabians as well as other Arabs are saying that history is repeating itself dangerously, that Arab expectations are again being dashed, that the French are establishing themselves in Syria and the Lebanon, as if they were colonial possessions, just as they did after the last war.

Azzam Bey, of the Arab League, warned, 'The situation is becoming worse day by day and warns us that a devastating storm is about to break'.[84]

The French remained obdurate. An official communiqué of 29 May expressed surprise that the Syrian and Lebanese governments 'can have any real fears as to the intentions of France regarding their independence. . . .'. From Beirut, Shone reported: 'The position in Syria is nothing short of critical and Lebanon if quiet on the surface is according to our information simmering'. From Cairo, Lord Killearn advised taking a 'stronger line with de Gaulle . . . [and] doing it quickly[,] i.e. before the main explosion up north occurs'. In San Francisco, chairmen of the Arab delegations to the United Nations conference called upon the secretary of state to register their concern over Levant affairs.[85]

On the evening of 29 May, following several days of growing disorder and armed conflict in the Syrian towns of Homs, Hama and Aleppo, French forces began using their artillery against Damascus. George Wadsworth, speaking over the phone with his vice-consul in the capital, could hear machine guns firing. The British representative in Homs reported much destruction from French bombing: 'Many buried in debris. Have given assistance to police in digging out the dead and carrying wounded. For God's sake do something to [? grp. omitted] this beastly mess without delay'. Terence Shone watched the French shelling of Damascus from the roof of the British legation, saying, '. . . I urge that the time has come when our considerations should be the effect on Allied [grp. undec.] in the Middle East of this treatment of an ancient and holy city of Islam, and the effect on our own prestige if we should stand aside while it is pulverised'. From Cairo, Edward Grigg declared angrily 'that the French have now put their hands to a German process of butchery and blind destruction in Syrian towns. . . . What remained of French influence in the Levant is now completely lost. Nothing we can do will help the French to recover it'. The US consul, Satterthwaite, was likewise appalled at the level of violence; he was driven in a British armored car to visit President Quwatli, who asked plaintively, 'Where now is the Atlantic Charter and the Four Freedoms?'[86]

Winston Churchill, amid the reports of destruction in Syria and mounting tension in Lebanon, sought support from President Truman before ordering the British 9th Army to intervene and halt French military action.

However, by the time his request was received and approved in Washington, Churchill already had felt compelled to authorize General Paget to take control of Levant affairs. According to the official record of the 11.30 a.m. Cabinet meeting of 31 May: 'The situation at Damascus had grown rapidly worse, and the conduct of the French troops had become reckless and irresponsible. In addition to indiscriminate shelling, French troops were spraying the streets with machine-gun fire from vehicles and buildings; and even vehicles flying the British flag were not immune from attack'.[87]

De Gaulle instructed French units to observe a cease-fire, thus avoiding direct conflict between two European armies in Syria. Wadsworth arrived in Damascus on 1 June, the day after the British intervention. After viewing Syrian governmental offices, he reported, 'They were unguarded, empty, gaping with bullet holes, littered with shattered glass, Parliament benches overturned, papers scattered'. When British tanks and armored cars appeared and were positioned throughout the city, he wrote, 'People emerged from houses and cheered'. That enthusiasm was matched by the Syrian foreign minister, who remarked, 'This gesture of Great Britain is a new victory for the principles of democracy and justice of which she has always been a champion'. The British delegation to the UN conference received kind words from Arab spokesmen. In Washington, Joseph Grew remarked to the cabinet on 1 June: 'I said that the Near East is a powder keg, that the French action might well have resulted in blowing off the lid and that a general conflagration might have resulted throughout the Arab world'.[88]

The crisis was over, but its impact could be measured in part through the bitterness expressed by Charles de Gaulle in his press conference of 2 June, wherein the villains were Syrian guerrillas and British diplomats. De Gaulle sought to embarrass the British government by proposing that there be scheduled an international conference on Middle East issues – one which would necessarily examine affairs in British territories and include delegations from the United States and the Soviet Union. But playing the Soviet card was never very effective for de Gaulle, as in this case when American and British leaders successfully opposed any plan which would allow the USSR 'to have her foot firmly in the Near Eastern door'.[89]

However, though it was a noisy affair, the Levant crisis did not reveal a dramatic change in British or American foreign policy toward either the Middle East or the colonial world in general. During May 1945, British and American ministers in the Levant had spoken as one voice to both the native nationalists and to the French Délégation Générale. Such Anglo-American co-operation, when backed up by military force, could thus effectively discourage a third power from pursuing colonial aims which were incompatible with US and British global interests.

The Middle East, in the spring of 1945, had emerged as the strategic heartland for the defense and maintenance of the British Empire; yet,

Britain's tenure in the region would depend ultimately upon Arab sufferance. There was firm American support for British policy, inspired by the recognition that a hemorrhage of Western prestige would greatly complicate the politics of oil, especially with regard to Saudi Arabia, 'one of the three great puddles left in the world'.[90] In effect, US leaders grasped perhaps their last opportunity to piggyback American interests, at little risk, on a British readiness for direct military intervention.

Yet, the character of Anglo-American co-operation in the Levant was an aberration in several important ways. Overall, the British Foreign Office anticipated a post-war system in which France and England would be closely allied in both European and imperial goals. Only in the Levant did the British feel compelled to challenge the legitimacy of French overseas administration. Only in the Levant did US and British interests so well coincide in resisting the re-imposition of a colonial regime. After the Levant crisis had passed, Great Britain did not again oppose the French government on any substantive issue involving the operation of their respective colonial empires.

For American policymakers, the Levant crisis of spring 1945 provided an opportunity to observe the possible costs of a Europe-first strategy, including the likely damage to US overseas prestige caused by an intransigent ally. The actions of one member of the Western community could certainly if not irrevocably affect the attitudes of emergent peoples toward the whole Western bloc. However, while the Levant was a logical focal point for a crisis of imperial devolution, the pertinent policy guidelines were much clearer than in other geopolitical areas. The nations of Syria and Lebanon already had been granted their independence, albeit ambivalently, and that independence had been formally recognized by the United States in 1944. Hence, the matter of sovereignty was easily resolved. Broad policy declarations applicable to other independent countries occupied by Allied troops could be appropriately applied to the Levant. Further, and equally important, the native governments in both Syria and Lebanon were moderate and pro-Western. It was easy to characterize the Levant nations as, in the words of one congressman, 'the two youngest republics with American ideals and American principles. They are the youngest republics in the world, just fresh out of the shell'.[91] Thus, in policy terms, Syria and Lebanon were not at all in the same generic grouping of overseas dependencies as Algeria or Indochina. Also, the Levant crisis could be speedily resolved by France's meeting specific and justifiable demands from the native governments, such as surrendering control of the troupes spéciales, replacing the colonial administration with a regular diplomatic mission, and withdrawing foreign troops.

While the French were behaving badly, even stupidly, in the Levant, there was no intent to punish them beyond taking the steps necessary to restore calm and protect Anglo-American interests in the region. In fact, as de Gaulle later noted, the British were eager to make amends for the Levant affair by co-operating with France in other colonial areas.[92] While some degree of French emnity toward both Britain and the United States persisted beyond the Levant crisis, it did not interfere with the major policy goals of those powers. No lasting rifts were produced. Still, the Levant upheaval posed for the US government a series of vital questions concerning official attitudes toward:

1. the matter of lofty principles versus political expediency;
2. the requirements and outcome of a Europe-first priority in the immediate post-war years;
3. the problems likely generated by cynical or duplicitous behavior on the part of Western imperial powers;
4. the importance of accountability in the councils of the new United Nations Organization; and
5. the possibilities for expanded Soviet influence through the exploitation of economic hardship and political discontent in the colonies or ex-colonies of European allies.

The diplomatic solution to Syrian and Lebanese demands as well as Anglo-French wrangling began slowly to emerge in mid-summer 1945 when the Quai d'Orsay stated its intent to transfer the troupes spéciales from French to local jurisdiction. In August negotiations began between French and British officials for arranging joint troop withdrawals from the Levant. Progress was slow on all fronts. Asked by a British diplomat, in December, to comment informally on draft Anglo-French agreements, NEA Director Loy Henderson objected to the use of the phrase 'leading role'. It was, he said, too anachronistic; it spoke to a lingering European desire for predominance in the affairs of independent nations. Henderson also objected to a provision allowing the French to maintain troops in Lebanon until the UNO might develop a security shield for the area.[93] His was a perspective widely shared within the State Department, as was demonstrated during a half-hour meeting between Harry Truman, Henderson, and the Middle East chiefs of mission on 10 November 1945.

The Foreign Service officers at the meeting were S. Pinkney Tuck, minister to Egypt; William Eddy, minister to Saudi Arabia; George Wadsworth, minister to the Levant states; and Lowell C. Pinkerton, consul-general in Jerusalem. 'Kippy' Tuck had previously served as chargé in Vichy and consul in Algiers. William Eddy, born in Syria, had been a Marine lieutenant colonel and was active in OSS intelligence gathering throughout North Africa during the war; he was fluent in Arabic and had served as translator during the Roosevelt-Ibn Saud conversations at Great Bitter Lake. Both George Wadsworth, well liked by Lebanese leaders, and Lowell Pinkerton, serving in Jerusalem since early 1941, were also seasoned observers of Middle East politics. 'These Ministers are very anxious', wrote Henderson, 'before returning to their posts, to get the President's ideas with regard to what our overall policy in the Near East is to be in the postwar era'. In particular, Henderson hoped to have the president affirm that the United States would seek to expand its influence in the Near East and continue to advocate a regional open door trade policy.

Acting as spokesman for the group of Foreign Service officers, Wadsworth offered as their collective judgment the view that Arab states deserved a prominent position in American post-war policy – not simply because of the Palestine dispute or economic-strategic considerations, but also because the Middle East was in ferment, its peoples determined to manage their own affairs without external interference. Arab officials desired American assistance for economic development and hoped that a US presence in the Middle East would counteract expected efforts by Britain and France to rekindle pre-war influence in the region.

Truman agreed with his diplomats' assessment of the overall importance of the Arab world. He was enthusiastic in support of the open door, saying: 'We want this to be the basis of our relations with China and with every country of the world'. The president agreed that the United States must play an active role in Mideastern affairs, but he was uncertain how to provide guidance on the matter of 'political Zionism' – 'That *is* the sixty-four-dollar question', he commented.[94] Truman realized that there would not be quick solutions to any of the troublesome issues stemming from the European administration of Arab territories in the Near East and North Africa. The post-war controversies in the Middle East were a product of both the arbitrary nature of pre-war boundaries and the wartime surge of indigenous nationalism – conditions replicated throughout much of the colonial world. Whereas the Levant crisis had revealed the potential for damaging Anglo-French discord over imperial spheres, a throwback to the halcyon days of empire, such rivalry did not become endemic to the restructured international system after the Axis defeat. That it did not was a product of the weakened state of both France and Britain, though the latter was better able to reassert traditional prerogatives, and the fact that their decline from the top rank of world powers created a natural rapprochement in the interest of preserving and restoring sovereignty over dependencies. A 'European' versus an 'American' agenda, where avowed principles and/or economic-strategic interests appeared to be in conflict, had surfaced over various issues during the war: the second front, the soft underbelly, the Vichy regime, the Italian armistice, trusteeships, and the character of the Allied offensive in the Far East. It was with considerable acrimony that a clash of Anglo-American agendas flared in Southeast Asia during 1944–45 as British policymakers tried to garner US approval and support for the recapture of colonial territories.

3 War's End in Southeast Asia

As Canadian diplomat Escott Reid walked through the streets of San Francisco on VE Day, 8 May 1945, he detected only minimal public enthusiasm or display over Germany's defeat. It had been a long, bloody, frightening war and there was little evidence that Californians much appreciated the significance of the Nazi collapse. Reid surmised that for people on the west coast, the Pacific War was the encounter of real import; and, apparently, Japan's final defeat was yet a good many months in the future.[1] Celebration in May would be premature. The enemy lurker, while banished from the threshold, still maintained large armies in the field in Asia and was preparing by most accounts a desperate defense of the home islands. More grisly battlefields awaited in a war which had encouraged a 'visceral hatred' of the Japanese, stoked by 'racist codewords and imagery': treacherous, simian-like, a monolithic swarm.[2] The anxiety and humiliation of December 1941 was not forgotten as San Francisco hosted the founding conference of the United Nations Organization, dedicated to reconciliation and international co-operation as the capstones of a new world order.

Privately, Reid was not optimistic about the UNO's future as he sat through tedious meetings which muted both spirit and imagination. He feared that the post-war world was being shaped much more profoundly by the day-to-day press of events in battle-scarred Europe than by the work of effete committees in San Francisco. He complained about the performance of the American secretary of state, Edward Stettinius, whom he viewed as an effervescent mediocrity poorly suited to the great tasks required. He complained about the plodding character of the assemblage, where already the Western delegations judged Soviet diplomats to be robotic and obstructive. But for Reid, with the war over in Europe, the future looked surely less terrible than the immediate, ravaged past.[3]

Hope did not spring eternal, and the ultimate shape of peace remained elusive. The precise configuration of post-war Europe was yet painfully to be pieced together through the desultory work of the Council of Foreign Ministers. French North Africa shuddered through the tension-filled transition from Vichy to Gaullist administration as native nationalists tested the bounds of colonial authority. Among the Senussi tribesmen of Cyrenaica and the Muslim townsmen of Tripolitania there arose ever stronger demands for self-government. The Near East was a scene of turmoil at war's end, with Arab uncertainty exacerbated by unrest in the Levant and the rapid rise of Zionist influence in Palestine. The balance of power in the Pacific basin and the Far East had shifted, with the United States intent now on playing a commanding role. What of the other interested powers? Japan was a wasteland, targeted for indefinite American occupation. The country was to be demilitarized, its imperial armies returned home and demobilized, its society reformed and rehabilitated. The Soviets, successfully excluded from a meaningful role in Japan's occupation regime, seemed unlikely to be assertive elsewhere in Asia while consolidating control in Central and Eastern Europe. The situation in China was too chaotic to sustain any stable regime; instead, the country was poised on the edge of a debilitative civil war. Following devastating defeats, especially the fall of Singapore, British forces had fought with limited success to recapture colonial territories in Southeast Asia. Dutch rule in the East Indies had quickly collapsed in the face of a Japanese invasion in early 1942; and by August 1945, the Netherlands had insufficient military forces to reoccupy the islands. The French administration in Indochina had aligned itself with Vichy and collaborated with the Axis, thus preserving the colonial superstructure and allowing its territory to serve as a base for Japanese assaults against neighboring countries. Yet, scattered French resistance against a Japanese coup which overturned Vichy rule in March 1945, while predictably futile, bespoke a glint of new vitality for the tarnished French record in Southeast Asia. French military action, however brief, provided a slim but usable reed upon which to build, for those so minded, a rationale for continuing to recognize French sovereignty over Indochina.

Hence, the spring and summer of 1945 was not a period of endearing, magnanimous gestures and moving rapprochement among the complex array of opposing forces in the Far East: the powerful and the weak, the colonizer and the colonized, the left and the right – the victors, the vanquished and the wary *attentistes*. Somewhat prematurely, Leonard Woolf had observed in 1928 that colonialism was a dying enterprise, the only unresolved matter being 'whether it will be buried peacefully or in blood and ruins'. In the aftermath of French military action in Algeria and Syria in 1945, combined with the legacy of race war in Asia, it certainly appeared, in the words of V. G. Kiernan, that 'bleeding was still the imperial cure for all political distempers...'.[4] Along the horizon there strode many shadows.

The Japanese conquest of Southeast Asia had irrevocably strained and shattered the bonds of Western empire in the region. Native societies were left 'in shambles'[5] – so many people killed, wounded and displaced, the countryside devastated, economies distorted and crippled, disease and famine rampant. 'War telescopes social time', wrote Gabriel Kolko, 'bringing together new forces and new interactions with traditional institutions, producing predictable as well as original mutations in human experiences and social systems'.[6] Nowhere was this more true than in Southeast Asia. War was a crucible, out of which were forged durable new struggles – new blood and new ruins.

For many American observers, in Washington and on the spot in East Asia, there was little doubt that the age of European overseas empires was over; and for equally as many, the crumbling of such empires initially appeared to be a good thing. During the war, a hortatory book by George E. Taylor, *America in the Pacific*, pictured the state of Asian politics after Japan's defeat. With special attention to the colonial areas of Southeast Asia, Taylor sought to explain the roots of American foreign policy interests in the region and to differentiate the United States and its traditions from those of its European allies, especially the British. Yet the book was also designed to affirm a basic similarity of purpose in Anglo-American objectives. Thus, while the Allies were all portrayed as nations of virtue, each pursuing worthwhile and essentially laudatory goals in the Far East, the United States, Taylor noted, acted according to unique and superior principles.

The most ticklish question for Taylor concerned the spread of US power through the Pacific basin in the late 1800s. How was American imperialism different from and more altruistic than British, French or Dutch overseas expansion? Americans were eager to believe that such a distinction could be made. Taylor first wanted to disabuse the reading public of any notion that the United States had been pulled into a faraway conflict over colonies, asserting, 'America is not fighting to defend the relics of nineteenth century empires and domination'. He argued that the United States 'has never taken her own empire so seriously as have the other powers; she has done more to encourage rather than prevent the political independence of Asiatic peoples'. Rather than seeking to control and exploit, America traditionally favored 'westernization . . . under native leadership'. To put it another way, while US expansion was admittedly 'far from a drawing-room story', American influence had been on balance progressive. 'Few powers', wrote Taylor, 'have been so embarrassed by the possession of empire, none has been so ready to be rid of colonies. . . . The possession of colonies has not made her general policy imperialistic.' This war, he observed, was creating new opportunities for US influence to win colonial reforms favorable to the subject peoples of Asia.

Despite this important distinction between the New and Old Worlds, wrote Taylor, all of the Western powers could stand together, and proudly, as exemplars of a gentle imperialism, especially when compared to the 'Japanese leopard'. Here was the rub, however: despite their innate and calculated ruthlessness, the Japanese had succeeded in destroying the myth of white racial superiority in Asia. The destruction was complete. The myth could not be convincingly resurrected. But what should take its place – independence for subject peoples? Taylor quickly answered his own question. 'Freedom for what? Freedom to set up tiny states under native sultans – more reactionary than the worst imperialism? Freedom to Balkanize the Pacific and set up tariff walls every few miles?' No, this would not do. Yes, empires would be transformed, and the United States could take the lead in shaping this transformation; but such change would necessarily take different turns in different areas. There might be a quick route to self-rule, for instance, for the peoples of India, Egypt and the Philippines; on the other hand, the 'politically backward and economically exploited native peoples' of Southeast Asia could hardly aspire toward the same goal, certainly not during the immediate post-war years.

Taylor believed that the United States, with its 'cleaner record', was thus well suited to enlist the support of colonial peoples and to do so without sacrificing a realistic policy advocating independence only for peoples ready for it.[7] Taylor's diagnosis was reminiscent of a statement by John Carter Vincent, veteran Asian specialist in the State Department, in October 1945, when he noted: 'We can be sentimental as well as practical – as long as we *are* practical'.[8] Such was clearly the direction of wartime thinking among American policymakers, despite appearances.

Nonetheless, even the practical, paternalistic anticolonialism of the State Department raised the hackles of European allies, as when Cordell Hull spoke with Anthony Eden in Quebec in late summer 1943. The secretary had in March of that year handed Eden a draft policy statement titled 'Declaration by the United Nations on National Independence', to which the British were reluctant officially to respond. Though vague and hardly radical in tone, the declaration proposed that the Atlantic Charter be read as a promise, among other things, 'that [the] opportunity to achieve independence for those peoples who aspire to independence shall be preserved, respected, and made more effective'. It should be the duty of those Allies responsible for colonial and mandate territories 'to cooperate fully with the peoples of such areas toward their becoming qualified for independent national status'. For those peoples clearly unprepared for self-rule, a period of tutelage would be necessary – but a timetable for the 'earliest practicable' independence should be established for all colonies.[9]

Only after several tries was Hull able to persuade Eden to take up this issue at the subsequent 1943 Quebec meeting of Roosevelt and Churchill. Hull assured the British foreign secretary that the proposal was not intended to countenance impromptu self-government. As recorded in the meeting minutes: 'The Secretary said that the thought behind his dealing with this problem had been to give encouragement to the peoples in dependent areas, not with any view to their being given, tomorrow or next week, complete independence as a separate entity, but to offer them, at some time when they might have proved that they were capable of independence, the possibility of so conducting their political development that they might hope for this achievement at some future time'. Predictably, Hull pointed to the US promise of Philippine independence as the kind of progressive policy he had in mind. However, Eden countered with the practised British argument: the empire was a conglomerate of territories whose peoples represented quite different stages of political awareness and maturity – some having already achieved the status of self-governing dominions – and the concept of 'independence' represented a dangerous and destabilizing ambiguity as a policy goal. As J. C. Sterndale Bennett, head of the Foreign Office Far Eastern Department, later remarked, 'We have been pursuing a long process of education in the direction of self-government'. Interrupted by the war, he wrote, the British were duty-bound to renew their task. 'I suppose it is too much to hope that the Americans will come to realise that our attitude towards our Colonies is one of responsibility and not of privilege.'[10]

Roosevelt did little better with Churchill in challenging British imperial policy. In fact, both leaders well realized the potential gaps between their arguments for or against empire and the often uncomfortable realities of history and Allied warfare. As Christopher Thorne has shown, Roosevelt and Churchill chose to avoid an extended, acrimonious dispute over colonies, believing that the outcome of the war, more than anything else, would determine the future of dependent peoples. Further, while Churchill remained firm in his imperial desiderata, he paid little attention to Asian affairs. Franklin Roosevelt – for different reasons – likewise offered little leadership on Far Eastern questions.[11]

As FDR frequently commented, he had chosen French Indochina as the site for a post-war trusteeship arrangement, one which would place the territories of Vietnam, Laos and Cambodia under international administration. He did this, he explained from time to time, because the French had performed so poorly as colonial masters, and the Indochinese had suffered long enough their heavy imperial yoke. However, the political significance of French Indochina as a playground for US trusteeship schemes was not matched by its strategic rank. As the American cross-Pacific offensive against Japan began to absorb greater resources during 1943–44, securing the forward base sites necessary for air attacks against the home islands, American military planners increasingly viewed Southeast Asia as a minor theater: a chain of dependencies and convoluted terrain best left to British forces, given London's clear self-interest. Despite the frequent assertion in wartime Washington that Britain was fighting in Southeast Asia primarily to recover imperial territories – in the process demonstrating its Old World enervation – the US Joint Chiefs were quite eager to avoid costly entanglements in French Indochina and the Netherlands East Indies. And while British policymakers sought strategic control over Allied military planning for Southeast Asia, they did so with the hope that American *matériel* and troops would continue to flow into the theater as part of a broad regional offensive. British officials realized that their military operations and political future in the Far East were increasingly dependent upon American support. A Foreign Office brief of 28 March 1945 noted: 'In thinking of Anglo-American co-operation, we are not thinking merely of the war period, but of the wider field which opens out beyond'.[12]

THE SOUTHEAST ASIA COMMAND

As the institutional expression of divergent Anglo-American strategic priorities, the Southeast Asia Command (SEAC) was a product of the Quebec summit of August 1943. The Joint Chiefs of Staff (JCS) anticipated an expanded American offensive through the central Pacific combined with large-scale air attacks against Japan mounted from yet-to-be-established bases in China. Therefore, a major American objective was to increase military assistance to Chinese forces via completion of a supply route through northern Burma. As to British goals, a memorandum by the Joint War Plans Committee observed: 'Fundamentally, it is believed that the British are guided by the aim to re-establish the prestige of the British Empire in the Far East (with which we have no quarrel)'. However, US planners predicted difficult logistical problems for the British military in Asia following the defeat of Germany – and it was already an established axiom of Anglo-American wartime partnership that a German surrender must precede final, full-scale offensive action against Japan.[13]

At the Quebec conference, General George C. Marshall explained the American desire to bring maximum force directly against Japan by the 'speediest method', avoiding a long, difficult campaign through the East Indies. United States support for greater assistance to China, he explained, was a political principle rather than simply a military requirement. Roosevelt subsequently underlined the limited American commitment to operations in Southeast Asia: the shortest overland route to Japan was through Burma into China. Fighting through the East Indies might take many years. Gently turning aside Churchill's suggestion that after liberating Burma the Allies launch an attack southward against Sumatra, FDR simply pointed out that such action was in the wrong direction – away from Tokyo.[14]

Earlier in the conference, a memorandum by the British Chiefs of Staff had proposed a reorganization of the command structure in the China-Burma-India (CBI) Theater. As formally approved by Roosevelt and Churchill, the Southeast Asia Command (SEAC) was created – adjoining but separate from CBI – as a joint Anglo-American affair with responsibility for military operations in Burma, Ceylon, Thailand, the Malay Peninsula and the island of Sumatra.[15] Lord Louis Mountbatten was appointed Supreme Allied Commander, SEAC, with General Joseph Stilwell designated as the second-in-command, controlling US forces in Burma while retaining his position as chief of staff to Chiang Kai-shek.[16] Mountbatten's appointment reflected the open recognition by American policymakers that Southeast Asia was logically and primarily an imperial theater and was of secondary importance to the final invasion and defeat of Japan. The Joint Chiefs of Staff appeared little concerned with the political outcome of SEAC's operations; however, American civilian and military personnel in Southeast Asia soon chafed at restrictions imposed by the British command.

John Paton Davies, Jr., a Foreign Service officer in China throughout the 1930s, served as Stilwell's political adviser following the creation of SEAC. Davies brought to his position a well-travelled skepticism about the virtue of Western imperialism, and he worried about European efforts to undercut US prestige in the Far East. His memorandum of November 1943, for instance, sought to define the difference between American and British goals in East Asia. In particular, he addressed the need to identify a separate American agenda within the command and operations tangle of SEAC. While Anglo-American co-operation in the battle against Japan was of course legitimate and necessary, Davies cautioned that US military efforts must not be seen as snatching 'British, French and Dutch colonial chestnuts out of the Japanese fire'. Yet, this advice was easier given than carried out: 'The repossession of the British Empire in Asia is merged with the war against Japan. Military and political strategy are so intermingled that the distinction between the two is easily blurred'.

The United States, observed Davies, risked a serious loss of prestige by not distinguishing its goals from those of the British. '[The] obvious American disinclination to engage in colonial expansion, the American record of championing Asiatic states threatened by aggression and repeated American pronouncements extolling the virtues and benefits of liberty and self-determination have in the past given the United States a good reputation in Asia'. While American anticolonialism, even haphazardly expressed, embarrassed and worried the British, wrote Davies, their military forces were dependent upon US lend-lease assistance to sustain any offensive aimed at recapturing Southeast Asian colonies. Thus, he asserted, SEAC represented, at heart, a British ploy to guarantee the continued inflow of US *matériel* while minimizing (or compromising) the possible political ramifications of the American presence in a colonial theater. Davies warned, 'Our collateral involvement in the British imperial enterprise will affect our relations not only with colonial Asiatics, but also with the free peoples of Asia'. Among the latter, he counted especially the Chinese and Thais, who might conclude that the United States had aligned itself with a 'whiteocracy'.

Still, as long as the war continued, the British and the Americans needed each other in Southeast Asia. Hence, the United States must preserve 'a purely American identity' within SEAC, primarily through independent psychological warfare programs amongst the native population. And to whatever extent possible, Davies urged, American personnel should remain aloof from civil administration in colonial territories.[17] In this way, Davies' memorandum highlighted issues which would soon be routinely discussed and debated by policymakers in London and Washington as well as their representatives in the Southeast Asia Command: especially (1) the matter of American short-term and long-term goals for the region, (2) US fears regarding the emergence of a broadly anti-Western pan-Asian movement, and (3) the problematic issue of jurisdiction over intelligence/psychological warfare operations in Southeast Asia.

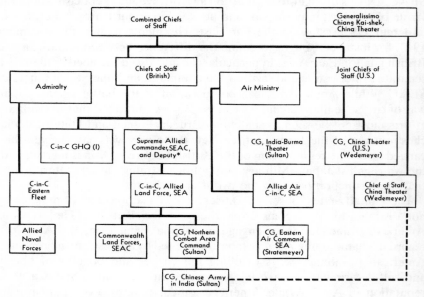

*Lt. Gen. Raymond A. Wheeler, U.S. Army, was Deputy SAC, SEA.

Figure 3.1 *Allied Chain of Command in Asia, November 1944.* Following the splitting of CBI into two separate commands in October 1944, three distinct military organizations competed for resources in East Asia: the China Theater, the India-Burma Theater, and the Southeast Asia Command.
Source: Charles F. Romanus and Riley Sunderland, *Times Runs Out in CBI* (Washington: Department of the Army, 1959), p. 30.

WARS'S END

From the beginning, SEAC was riddled with discord between its American and British wings. As John Davies later commented, 'SEAC was neither a tight nor a happy ship'. The organizational structure, according to one American attached to command headquarters, was a 'monstrosity', its operations fraught with 'bureaucratic duels' between US and British intelligence agencies throughout the theater.[18] The chief problem was not, as it sometimes appeared, a battle between strong personalities or intrusive bureaucratic staffs, but rather the result of divergent expectations for SEAC activities. The Joint Chiefs looked upon the theater as an adjunct of US planning to improve Chinese military performance while British policymakers posited a legitimate intra-theater agenda of recapturing strategic territory (particularly Singapore), interdicting enemy communications, waging an attritive struggle against Japanese forces, and restoring British prestige. 'It was a command suffering from an inner conflict', wrote Davies. 'It was designed for an amphibious offensive aimed at Singapore, but instead was dragged northward into land warfare in the mountains and jungles of the India-Burma border.'[19] Rivalry in the realm of clandestine warfare between the Office of Strategic Services (OSS) and the British Special Operations Executive (SOE) was only a symptom of this larger divergence. In effect, there were five problems, all interrelated.

1. The supreme commander, Mountbatten, was faced with the need to co-ordinate military operations over a wide area, through difficult terrain, with inadequate resources – in the midst of Anglo-American wrangling over grand strategy;
2. Washington provided little specific political guidance to US military and intelligence personnel in Southeast Asia, so that officials on the spot were left to formulate their own *ad hoc* arrangements;
3. There was a growing and increasingly bitter competition between US and British clandestine/psychological warfare agencies for controlling contacts with the native peoples of the region – a rivalry which signified a jockeying for post-war influence among resistance leaders who might head new governments or, unchecked, threaten existing colonial administrations;
4. There was discord and feuding within the respective American and British camps as well; and
5. OSS operatives, US political advisers attached to SEAC, and State Department appointees in Southeast Asia tended to become progressively more unforgiving toward the colonial system within which SEAC operated, convinced that their actions reflected official US policy as embodied in the Atlantic Charter and the principles of the open door.

Lieutenant Colonel Richard A. Heppner, chief of OSS operations in Southeast Asia, was able to report in July 1944: 'During the last month, it has become clear that we are a major operator in this part of the world. . . . This mission has progressed from a small operation to a large one with dramatic suddenness'. On the downside, however, this success had spawned increased opposition from SOE, which now actively sought to interfere with OSS efforts to recruit agents in Malaya and the East Indies. 'In all of our dealings with this agency', wrote Heppner, 'we note a lack of good faith on their part, and a willingness to indulge in tactics which can be characterized only by the word, underhanded.' Heppner's September 1944 mission report noted generally favorable relations with SEAC headquarters but continuing problems with SOE.

> While everything is very friendly on the surface, we are the targets for constant subrosa attacks by this organization. ... They continue to follow the line which they followed in the Near East and Balkans, that is to claim the right to make first contacts with any group inside the country, following which they will permit us to enter on their terms. Thus far we have succeeded in holding our own.[20]

Outside the Southeast Asian theater, political questions continued to cloud American policy. In August 1944, British ambassador Lord Halifax had left with the State Department an aide-mémoire proposing to accept a French military mission within SEAC and to establish in India a special Corps Léger d'Intervention for later service in Indochina. Secretary Hull referred the matter directly to Roosevelt, noting: 'Although these suggestions are ostensibly military in character, they have wide political implications'. Clearly, they did, and the implications suggested an early restoration of French authority in Indochina, which FDR had consistently opposed. Roosevelt chose to delay a response to the proposal until his September meeting with Churchill in (again) Quebec.[21] On that occasion, however, the issue of Indochina was not discussed.

In spite of this official silence on the topic, the State Department had produced for the conference a comprehensive memorandum, dated 8 September, dealing with the Southeast Asian situation. The memo represented an apparent synthesis of the opposing viewpoints on colonialism held by the department's European and Asian experts. Responding to the British aide-mémoire, the memorandum's authors questioned the value of French military intervention in Indochina, observing that French forces in the colony were generally considered ineffective and that the Japanese would likely soon move to disarm them because of rising 'mutual distrust'. The British had made their request, it appeared, in order to strengthen the ability of France to retain its hold on Indochina and perhaps also to enhance British colonial claims. For this reason, the British government could be expected to seek an expansion of SEAC's boundaries to include Indochina, the East Indies and Hong Kong. Significantly, the memo acknowledged the potential impact of indigenous nationalism: 'It would seem of substantial military importance to secure for the United Nations [alliance] the good will of the native peoples of southeast Asia among whom, for some years, there has been increasing nationalistic sentiment, and who, for the past three years, have been subjected to intense Japanese propaganda exploiting the old slogan of "Asia for the Asiatics"'.

In line with previous State Department thinking, the memorandum proposed a joint Allied declaration setting forth a program for native self-determination and a regional open door trade regime. Nodding in the direction of Roosevelt's well-known interest in colonial peoples, the authors advised that a joint endeavor would have greater impact if it were accompanied by support for trusteeships under the auspices of an international organization; however, 'it might be unwise for the United States to attempt to insist upon such a declaration of trusteeship by one country if similar declarations could not be secured from the others'.

> In addition to their great value as psychological warfare, such announcements would appear to be directly in line with American post-war interests. These areas [of Southeast Asia] are sources of products essential to both our wartime and peacetime economy. They are potentially important markets for American exports. They lie athwart the southwestern approaches to the Pacific Ocean and have important bearing on our security and the security of the Philippines. Their economic and political stability will be an important factor in the maintenance of peace in Asia. Emergence of these regions as self-governing countries would appear desirable as soon as they are capable of self-rule, either as independent nations or in close voluntary association with western powers, for example as dominions. Such association might indeed lend them political and economic strength (the weakness of Asiatic powers has long been a cause of war) and help prevent future cleavage along regional or racial lines.
>
> Failure of the western powers to recognize the new conditions and forces in southeast Asia and an attempt to reestablish pre-war conditions will almost surely lead to serious social and political conflict, and may lead to ultimate unifying of oriental opposition to the west.[22]

In a separate memorandum, the secretary of state advised the president:

> All reports indicate that the military operations of SEAC are aimed primarily at the resurgence of British political and economic ascendancy in Southeast Asia and the restoration of British prestige. To minimize American association in the public eye with restoration of British imperialism which is admittedly highly unpopular in Asia, no American civil affairs officer is to serve in any area in the SEAC theater unless under independent American command, and no American officer may collaborate in SEAC political warfare.[23]

While reasonably clear to Washington officials, such guidelines were rife with ambiguity in the field – especially given the fact that some political warfare, and probably a good deal of it, was directed chiefly against the Japanese. It was no simple matter for field officers to disentangle political and military ramifications for operations that inevitably included both by the very nature of the theater.[24]

The State Department's anxieties regarding trade, American prestige,

Figure 3.2 *India-Burma Theater 1944–45.* By the end of October 1944, the China-Burma-India Theater had been split into two separate commands.
Source: Charles F. Romanus and Riley Sunderland, *Times Runs Out in CBI* (Washington: Department of the Army, 1959), p. 7.

and any 'future cleavage' between Western and Asian peoples were echoed by Max W. Bishop, who was added to the consular staff in Colombo, Ceylon, during early summer 1944. Formerly an assistant to Ambassador Joseph Grew in Tokyo, Bishop won quick praise from Colonel Heppner for his 'wide knowledge of the Far East, and . . . thorough appreciation of the value of [the] OSS'.[25] In November, after nearly six months in the theater, Bishop produced a report on SEAC operations and morale which affirmed the command's importance to American strategic planning but commented at length on the deterioration of Anglo-American relations at the headquarters in Kandy. Differences between Moutbatten and Stilwell had prevented proper co-ordination of military planning between CBI and the Southeast Asia Command. SEAC was sarcastically referred to as 'Supreme Example of Allied Confusion'. The 'country club' atmosphere of SEAC headquarters and the 'failure... to accomplish large military operations' frustrated American officers. Fairly or unfairly, wrote Bishop, American personnel had developed 'an uneasy or resentful attitude' toward the British. 'SEAC badly needs a major victory', he observed, in order to reduce tension and restore morale.

In the political sphere, however, SEAC had been quite active – perhaps too active, at least from the American perspective. Bishop was critical of SOE, for instance, for transporting a Gaullist agent into Indochina in July, and of the British command in general for its unilateral decision to accept a French liaison group headed by General Roger Blaizot. 'Upon arrival', noted Bishop, 'General Blaizot was installed in a large SOE bungalow. British preparations were complete, even to the detail of a new flag pole in front of SEAC Headquarters, presumably for the French flag.' Whether Bishop realized it or not, such had become the pattern of OSS-SOE competition, one of dueling *faits accomplis*.

Observing the same events, Heppner remarked, 'There can be little doubt that the British and Dutch have arrived at an agreement with regard to the future of Southeast Asia, and now it would appear that the French are being brought into the picture'. Bishop reached the same conclusion, commenting further: 'If unity in policies and programs for Malaya, Thailand, Indochina, the Netherlands East Indies, and Burma is established under British aegis, the predominance of British influence in this area will be assured so long as the native populations are kept in line'. However, he was not sanguine about the future of empires.

Pressure of native peoples in this area against outside control will continue to grow. It is believed that in the face of that pressure empires will be forced sooner or later to change their character or disappear. It hardly seems possible that the political and economic evolution of Asiatic and colonial peoples can be stopped. ... Asia and its peoples seem destined to present future generations with most difficult problems. This part of the world may easily become a malignant source of irritation and a threat to peace and stability.

There is much bitterness, whether justified or not, among leading and important Asiatics and colonial peoples toward 'white' imperial or colonial powers. Propaganda associating the United States with such powers did not begin with this war and has not always fallen on barren soil.

Thus Bishop raised the specter of Soviet policies and ideology having 'gained a real hold over many progressive leaders in Asia and nearby areas'. This growing influence would have to be recognized and dealt with. In order to avoid alienating Asian peoples, Bishop urged a collaborative

Allied effort to devise a 'progressive and forward-looking program for non-self-governing peoples'. In lieu of such an effort, the obvious problem of differentiating US goals from the colonial policies of its allies argued for reconsideration of the American role in SEAC.[26]

It was a dismal picture of the Southeast Asia Command: confusion, infighting, low morale, an unenviable military record, and a possible European cabal to reassert imperial rule by subverting American ideals. As a filip, Bishop had tossed in a hint of anxiety about post-war Soviet influence in the region. It was a persuasive and cautionary composite. Bishop's report, as with other similar commentaries, captured for US policymakers the chronic duality of Southeast Asian affairs: a region of secondary importance militarily but potentially very damaging (in the future) to American hopes for stable pro-Western regimes in resource-rich developing areas.

The British view, of course, was somewhat different – the Americans relentlessly complained and criticized, they constantly raised niggling questions about military operations in an underappreciated theater while denying the British Chiefs any operational role in the final assault against Japan. American leaders waxed eloquent about self-determination and independence while prying up the lid covering the imperial pie. British officials also identified in US policy a simplistic vagueness in overall strategic thinking, a sense that power itself was its own reward. The United States represented an undirected might, an 'unwieldy barge',[27] too much akin to an adolescent's witless euphoria. Such characteristics, if they did not bespeak hubris, nonetheless typically ignored enduring political questions. What about the Soviet colossus astride Europe? Equally important, what about the integrity of imperial communications and the continuity of colonial governance? Were empires to become casualties of American whimsy? Maberly Esler Dening, political adviser to Mountbatten, reported to the Foreign Office that US officials were not giving adequate thought to the post-war order in the Far East.

> American thinking so far as United States public and press is concerned seems to have been concentrated on a brave new world in which all men of all colours are equal. That is admirable, but Asia can no more divorce itself from its past than Europe, and little practical consideration appears to have been given to the situations which this war has created and continues to create and which will force themselves upon American as well as British attention at the close of hostilities.[28]

For the governments of Britain and France in particular, empires represented access to the physical and strategic resources necessary for metropolitan reconstruction, and they symbolized renewable national prestige and big-power status. It would be recognized, surely, that European countries controlling global networks could not sensibly be discounted in future international councils. American naïveté and lack of planning could do great damage. A largely visceral anticolonialism, poorly attuned to political realities, threatened to reduce Western Europe to the status of an American dependency – the mere tail of the dog, and one which could never wag the dog quite effectively enough to preserve real power and influence. Further, the dog would likely be too self-absorbed to know its own best interests. Yet, the long-range imperial vision of London officials began to collide with the intuitive pragmatism of British military commanders in Southeast Asia, those who faced directly the rise of strong nationalist movements. It happened first and not unexpectedly in Burma, where Mountbatten chose to accord nationalist forces a significant role in Allied military operations. It happened later, following the Japanese surrender, in Vietnam and Indonesia, where there emerged surprisingly stiff local resistance to Allied reoccupation.

Philip Ziegler, Mountbatten's official biographer, has written that the 'Supremo', as he was frequently called, was influenced by two major considerations regarding native peoples: (1) the 'practical and military' necessity for establishing stable interim regimes and encouraging anti-Japanese activity, and (2) his 'personal and idealistic' strain, favoring recognition of the desires of indigenous peoples for some degree of autonomy. 'He believed that people should be allowed as far as possible to control their own destiny. The territories of South-East Asia might not yet be ready for full independence, but the aspirations of their peoples could not be ignored. It must be made clear to them that the former imperial powers accepted that they were on the road to self-government.'[29] However, the prospect of nationalists working in tandem with SEAC forces (under British direction) was somewhat different from the scenarios which unfolded in Vietnam and Java, where nationalists declared their independence in the face of a high-level British desire to restore French and Dutch colonial control.

There was no active 'conspiracy' among the imperial powers, something which would have involved complicated negotiations and required the kind of precise military commitments which the British Chiefs of Staff could not make. The simpler truth was that London policymakers accepted as axiomatic the proposition that British imperial interests mandated an effort to re-establish stability in overseas dependencies; and in Southeast Asia such considerations appeared to require protection of French and Dutch pre-war colonial claims to whatever extent feasible. As one British official minuted, 'Our main reason for favouring the restoration of Indo-China to France is that we see danger to our own Far Eastern Colonies in President Roosevelt's idea that restoration depends upon the United Nations (or rather the United States) satisfying themselves that the French record in Indo-China justifies the restoration of French authority'.[30]

There was, nevertheless, agreement within the Combined Chiefs of Staff in early 1945 that neither the French nor the Dutch should yet participate in political warfare in the SEAC theater. For the United States, this attitude reflected an effort to prevent collusion among European powers. For the British, it was a matter of avoiding additional impediments to the conclusion of war-related tasks: they had had enough of a disruptive and recalcitrant ally in the Levant. On the other hand, it would be only a matter of months before Britain's military and diplomatic activity in Southeast Asia was aligned close alongside its European colleagues.

Decisions reached at the Potsdam Conference of July 1945 provided a new framework for the unfolding of the last days of war in Southeast Asia. Main items for discussion between the Anglo-American military staffs included French military activity in the SEAC theater, adjusted boundaries of command responsibility in Southeast Asia, and decision-making responsibility for the final assault on Japan. The American Joint Chiefs approved the use of French troops in Indochina 'in due course', but they rejected a British bid for greater involvement in Pacific strategic planning. For the JCS, Southeast Asia was now obviously a secondary front, constituting 'an area of British Empire responsibility associated with the Portuguese, the Dutch, and perhaps eventually the French. The initial operational interest of the United States in this area has now greatly decreased'. Thus, the US military role in Southeast Asia would be restricted to (1) reviewing planned operations with regard to their impact upon overall US strategy, and (2) assessing the necessary level of lend-lease assistance required by Mountbatten's command.[31] The combined chiefs of staff also agreed to an arbitrary revision of theater boundaries, splitting French Indochina at the 16th parallel, with the northern zone remaining in the China Theater and areas to the south of the line passing to SEAC.[32] Thus, after Japan's capitulation, Chinese forces would arrive in Hanoi, and British forces would occupy Saigon.

Although British policymakers had favored the extension of SEAC boundaries to include additional colonial territories, they did not foresee the sudden collapse of Japanese resistance. Rather, it had been expected that a steady but gradual increase in SEAC forces throughout 1945 and early 1946, including the arrival of French troops, would provide the basis for convincing military liberation of occupied terrorities and the concomitant restoration of European prestige among native peoples of the region. The announcement of impending Japanese surrender following the atomic bombings of 6 and 9 August found the Southeast Asia Command without adequate resources to carry out such immediate tasks as repatriating Japanese soldiers and securing the release of prisoners of war and civilian internees, many of whom had spent several years in cruel confinement. Further, and worse for SEAC, Mountbatten was prevented from dispatching reoccupation forces to the wide-ranging territories of his theater until after the formal surrender ceremonies of 2 September.

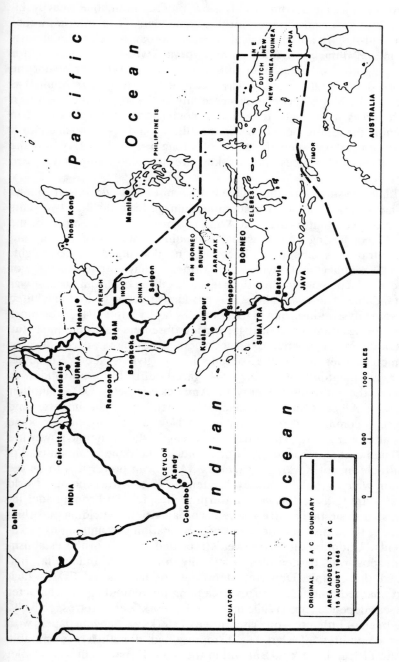

Figure 3.3 *Revised Boundaries of the Southeast Asia Command, August 1945.*
Source: Peter Dennis, *Troubled Days of Peace: Mountbatten and South East Asia Command, 1945–46* (New York:
St Martin's Press, 1987), p. 18.

The result was an uncomfortably slow reoccupation, one heavily influenced by the disposition of local commanders. The interim weeks
between mid-August and the arrival of British forces to such colonial ports
as Saigon and Batavia provided an opportunity, wrote one observer, for
the 'sleeping fires' of Asian nationalism to blaze up. Whether or not the
fires were sleeping, the interval was a crucial one. As Peter Dennis has
remarked: 'The hiatus between the ceremony in Tokyo Bay and the return
of allied forces in strength to former colonial territories was critical in
determining the atmosphere in which the allies would re-establish control.
And the contrast between the show of strength in Tokyo Bay and the
dribble of SEAC's forces into its key areas could hardly have been
greater'.[33]

The Japanese surrender aboard the battlecruiser *Missouri* was of course,
largely an American show. A predominant image from the final two years
of war, alongside that of the Red Army juggernaut, had been one of the
United States flexing new muscles, extending tentacles of power into
disparate frays east and west. There was no denying American might.
When US military and civilian authorities behaved patronizingly or
adopted a didactic pose toward their lesser brethren of the alliance, it was
understandable if not laudable. The productive capacity of the United
States was truly awe-inspiring in its global display by latter 1944, even more
so by the spring and summer of 1945; and few observers were immune to the
charms of the raw, exuberant dynamo, whether the sinews were military or
economic. Charles de Gaulle, despite his misgivings about Roosevelt
during a Washington visit of July 1944, gazed out of his hotel window in
wonder at the pulse and energy of American society. Or as another
Frenchman, Albert Camus – a celebrated member of the underground
resistance – commented upon arriving in New York City harbor some
months after war's end, 'The order, the strength, the economic power are
there. The heart trembles in front of so much admirable inhumanity'.[34]

Admirable or not, feckless or reckless, American power was to be the
rock upon which Franklin Roosevelt intended to construct the new world
order. His strengths and flaws as a wartime president and commander-in-
chief existed in subtle balance – here his broad vision overriding parochial
viewpoints, there his vagueness and procrastination succumbing to rapid-
fire events. Undoubtedly, Roosevelt's repeated interest in the establishment of post-war trusteeships, especially for French Indochina, had
energized those State Department officials of like views. FDR's tacit
support sparked ambitious wartime planning for remolding the character
of overseas dependencies. While much of this work seems, retrospectively,
to have been of little use – one committee of clerks exchanging papers with
another committee of clerks – it represented nonetheless a sizeable
aggregate of true believers. But within the State Department as a whole,
there was no broad consensus in favor of challenging the imperial sway of

Western European allies. This lack of solid institutional support undercut Roosevelt's planning, as did his own actions in postponing the discussion of vital political issues and accepting an emasculated trusteeship formula at Yalta.

In addition, the progress of the war militated against any firm US hand in the final disposition of colonial territories, for several reasons: US military planners were not directly involved, the issue became a subject for multilateral negotiations, or American policymakers chose not to press for decolonization at the expense of regional stability. As noted by an *ad hoc* group of the State-War-Navy Coordinating Committee (SWNCC), inaction by the US government regarding Indochina in particular had the 'practical effect' of giving England and France free rein in determining the post-war status of that colony.[35] Also, US recognition of the Gaullist French Committee for National Liberation (FCNL) in latter 1944 made it much more difficult for the American government to renege on its wartime promises to respect the territorial integrity of the French Empire. Thus it was that policy confusion became the mainstay in what Evelyn Colbert has called 'the cat's cradle of conflicting objectives, command rivalries, free-wheeling clandestine operations, personal and national jealousies and antagonisms, aborted plans, and frustrated hopes within which the Allies conducted the war on the Asian mainland'.[36] Nowhere were the feelings of confusion and frustration greater than in Southeast Asia, notably with regard to affairs in Vietnam and on the island of Java.

FRENCH INDOCHINA

In his September 1944 mission report, Lieutenant Colonel Richard Heppner had indicated that OSS intelligence work was well under way in Sumatra, Malaya and Thailand, with operations planned for Burma and Indochina. To mount greater efforts, however, Heppner needed additional forces: 'conducting officers', language specialists, and all types of operational personnel. He wrote, 'The ideal conducting officer who is required for every intelligence operation should be young, vigorous, have a sympathy with the native races with whom he must work and wherever possible should have a knowledge of the language and the areas where he or his group will operate'. Meanwhile, Heppner did not anticipate much improved relations with either British or Dutch intelligence personnel attached to SEAC.[37] The French liaison mission, under General Blaizot, had arrived, but there was no reason to believe that Gaullist appointees would approve US intelligence-gathering operations in Indochina. An OSS Research and Analysis Branch paper argued that FCNL colonial policy was identical with that of the pre-war period, directed essentially toward establishing 'an Empire unity giving France the political and economic power necessary to regain its position as a world power'. The report concluded: 'There is little likelihood that French colonial policy anywhere will take on a self-government tinge'. A diplomatic note from the FCNL in January 1945 reaffirmed the intent of the provisional regime to see full French sovereignty restored in Indochina.[38]

Through late 1944 and early 1945, conditions within Indochina continued to worsen as the Allies made steady gains elsewhere against Japanese forces. Major Austin O. Glass, OSS, reported in December 1944: 'The French [forces in Indochina] are always in a state of expectancy believing that sometime – somehow – their troops will be disarmed by the Japanese'. The larger French garrisons had been surrounded, and the Japanese command had conducted extensive war games in the colony as well as sending troops across the northern border into China. The Japanese had improved older airfields and begun construction of new ones in both Vietnam and Cambodia. The economy deteriorated, with strict rationing of food and medicine. The success of Allied air and naval forces in destroying Japanese shipping had resulted in shortages of coal and gasoline, with tons of rice rotting on the docks in Saigon. 'As the Allies make further gains to the detriment of the Japanese, the latter become more arrogant and exacting in their attitude towards the French.' The native population, despite enemy propaganda, had remained strongly anti-Japanese; and greater efforts were urged to enlist help from Vietnamese guerrillas in recovering downed pilots.[39]

As the Japanese prepared to defend their occupied zones, the Vichy French army, largely idle since 1942, could not be relied upon for resilient fighting to contest control of Indochina – this was the conclusion of most observers. Nevertheless, the British Special Operations Executive had begun work in late 1944, in concert with the Blaizot mission, to seed a French-led resistance movement in Indochina, one which might offer useful assistance to an Allied offensive. To supplement its efforts, SOE pressed for the early arrival of additional French troops from North Africa. However, such planning was pre-empted on 9 March 1945 when Japanese forces overthrew the collaborationist regime of Governor-General Jean Decoux and disarmed and interned nearly all French military forces. While such action had been anticipated for several months, only a very limited number of French units, those not in their barracks, were able to resist the Japanese coup and escape into China. Isolated units fought a desperate struggle for survival, assisted by limited Allied airdrops, and had little opportunity for sabotage or other guerrilla activity. Charles Cruickshank, in his official history of SOE activity in the Far East, described British hopes for a successful special-operations French underground in Indochina as a 'broken reed'.[40]

On the surface, little or nothing had changed regarding US policy toward Southeast Asia. Roosevelt had reiterated at the beginning of 1945 that

resolution of the Indochina tangle remained an item for post-war deliberations; and as before, this general statement did not resolve specific military
questions arising within the SEAC theater. But in the absence of clear
guidelines from the White House, US military planners, by default, took
responsibility for American policy toward SEAC-related affairs. That is,
while the notion of colonial trusteeships lingered and languished, it was the
joint chiefs of staff, primarily for military reasons, who routinely vetoed a
high-priority effort to transport French troops to Southeast Asia. Indochina remained part of an 'Outer Perimeter', beyond the sphere of
projected US military operations. In the words of Brigadier General
George A. Lincoln, Indochina 'is not considered to be in [the] area
required for [the] direct defense of [the] US, leased areas, and possessions
(including the Philippines) following [the] defeat of Japan . . . and [its]
future disposition is of minor military signficance'.[41] At the same time,
such military considerations did not dictate any rationale for opposing the
return of French administration to Southeast Asia. With Roosevelt's death
in April, the last glimmer – and it was only that – of an American-initiated
effort to reorder Indochinese affairs was gone.

The Japanese coup of 9 March and the abortive resistance which
followed was the signal for French officials to dun every echelon of US
wartime authority in order to win (1) a commitment to deliver French
troops to Asia, and (2) a clear recognition of French sovereignty over
Indochina. Particularly active were Henri Bonnet, the French ambassador,
and Vice-Admiral Raymond Fenard, chief of the French Naval Mission in
the United States.[42] The effort bore fruit. The combined chiefs of staff
authorized the immediate transport of the Corps Léger d'Intervention to
Ceylon.[43] At a SWNCC meeting of 13 April, Assistant Secretary of War
Robert A. Lovett called for a high-level reconsideration of US policy
toward Indochina. According to the meeting minutes:

> He added that the question of our Indo-China policy is a matter of lively
> military interest and that the lack of a policy is a source of serious
> embarrassment to the military. He pointed out that Admiral Fenard has
> been using a technique of submitting a series of questions to various
> agencies of the United States Government and by obtaining even
> negative or non-committal responses thereto has been in effect writing
> American policy on Indo-China.

H. Freeman Matthews, director of the Office of European Affairs, noted
that there was discord within the State Department about such colonial
issues, but he agreed that the US position should be clarified. And indeed,
it soon was. As Gary R. Hess has shown, there was only an 'artificial
consensus' between the Europeanists and Asianists in the State Department before Roosevelt's death – represented by the September 1944
memorandum which favored a firmer Allied commitment to self-

determination.[44] With Roosevelt's prodding no longer a factor and with a new president uninterested in the fate of Indochina, the SWNCC meeting produced the desired policy reassessment.

The staff of the Office of European Affairs (EUR) prepared the first draft of the new policy statement on Indochina, one intended to be markedly different in emphasis from previous assessments. It was noted that French officials had no intention of placing the colony under international trusteeship, that the US government acknowledged French sovereignty over Indochina, and that the continued advocacy of anti-colonial views was having a 'harmful effect' upon Franco-American relations. EUR officials recommended that the United States 'neither oppose the restoration of Indo-China to France, with or without a program of international accountability, nor take any action toward French overseas possessions which it is not prepared to take or suggest with regard to the colonial possessions of our other Allies'. While the American government might choose to press for a 'liberalization' of French colonial policy, this was not to be a condition for military or other assistance.[45]

The response from the Office of Far Eastern Affairs (FE) was prompt. Essentially, the Asian experts sought to redirect the draft memorandum back toward (1) identifying the French record in Indochina as a poor one, especially in view of collaboration with the Japanese, (2) recognizing that 'independence sentiment' was widespread in the colony, and (3) asserting a strong US interest in the region's future. As Abbot Low Moffat, head of the newly created Division of Southeast Asian Affairs (SEA), later commented: 'We could and we should, we felt, be very specific and actually use the power we had to try to secure self-government in Indochina. . . . If we informed the French . . . that we would not oppose the return of Indochina[,] we would negate our influence in securing French policies consonant with our interests'. Still, FE officials agreed that France must regain its strength in Europe, that no special trusteeship for Indochina would be necessary, and that the return of French rule to Indochina was acceptable provided that 'adequate assurances' were given of concessions to native nationalists.[46]

Many staffers in the Office of Far Eastern Affairs would have agreed with the views Moffat expressed in March 1945 to a French diplomat. The SEA director averred that, 'personally', he hoped 'the ultimate development in Southeastern Asia would be autonomous countries in close voluntary association or federation with various European powers; that in the long run completely independent countries not so associated might lead to wars among themselves or possibly a Pan-Asian movement hostile to the West'. Hence, an FE lecture on the virtues of self-determination did not constitute a demand for full self-government. Post-war uncertainties encouraged caution. Under the tutelage of Assistant Secretary James Dunn, a hearty Europeanist, a compromise memorandum did incorporate some of FE's proposals. The exchange had reflected substantial agreement regarding the post-war relationship between the United States and Western Europe. The final memorandum advised: 'It seems particularly important that at this time the United States should draw close to France and Great Britain, the strongest Western Powers, and attempt to remove the sources of friction between the United States and France, which include French apprehensions that we are going to propose that French territory be taken away'.[47] This compromise paper of April 1945 was never officially approved by Truman, but it accurately reflected the new balance of power within the State Department regarding colonial issues. On 8 May, from San Francisco, Secretary Stettinius reported his assurance to French Foreign Minister Georges Bidault 'that the record is entirely innocent of any official statement of this government questioning, even by implication, French sovereignty over Indo-China'.[48]

A separate State Department policy study, completed in June 1945, examined the expected state of affairs in East Asia at war's end. To begin with, future peace and security in the region must rest upon certain principles: more broadly representative governments among the independent Asian powers, an end to imperial preference, and the extension of some measure of self-rule to dependent peoples. Western colonialism had facilitated enemy conquests through the region, and Japanese propaganda had lent encouragement to indigenous nationalism. The problem for US policymakers was to 'harmonize' the goal of greater political autonomy for colonial peoples with the desire for continued close co-operation with European allies. The ideal solution 'would be a Far East progressively developing into a group of self-governing states – independent or with Dominion status – which would cooperate with each other and with the Western powers on a basis of mutual self-respect and friendship'.

Such dreams aside, the June policy paper looked toward a chaotic political and economic environment following Japan's surrender: conflict in China, upheaval in Korea, and potential US-Soviet rivalry. The post-war situation in Indochina would probably be 'particularly unstable'; pre-war nationalist uprisings had demonstrated 'that the supporters of independence are neither apathetic nor supine and are willing to fight'. American recognition of French sovereignty over Indochina was stated simply and directly, as if there had never been any dispute over the matter. In the Netherlands East Indies, State Department planners expected 'a generally quiescent period' at the end of the war, with good relations between the Dutch and the native population.[49] Therefore, the American policy toward Asian colonial dependencies was essentially to be one of non-intervention – explained as a hopeful aloofness, designed to offer other Western powers the opportunity to realize for themselves the need to make meaningful (even if minimal) concessions to native nationalists.

VIETNAM, THE VIET MINH, AND THE OSS

The political unrest and economic dislocation in Southeast Asia in 1945 were not simply a result of wartime conditions. Food shortages and inadequate medical care as well as native nationalist sentiment were inextricably linked to the character of the pre-war colonial regimes. Indigenous peoples had responded unevenly to Japanese pan-Asian propaganda, though nowhere as genuinely as American and European policy-makers initially had feared. A Japan-centered empire was no more appealing, in the long run, than one managed by Western powers. Nonetheless, significant advantage had accrued to colonial peoples in Southeast Asia: the politics of war made it impossible for Western armies to return in force to their colonies during August–September 1945. The exception was Burma, the only Southeast Asian colony won back from Japanese control by the action of SEAC forces. Hence, within SEAC, the good news from Tokyo in mid-August was a mixed blessing. As OSS officer Archimedes Patti later recalled, 'Early in August the end of the war ... had been nowhere in sight. There were, we thought, many battles to be fought before V-J Day; we therefore felt locked in a conventional time sequence. But as the aftershock of the atomic explosions spent itself, everyone in Asia came to the realization that this was a new ball game.'[50] For Charles de Gaulle, there was new hope for the entry of French forces into Indochina. For Admiral Mountbatten, there was the need to marshall SEAC resources and convert the timetable for impending offensive operations into the so-called RAPWI effort – Repatriation of Allied Prisoners of War and [civilian] Internees – and to do so through a much expanded theater as a result of agreements at Potsdam. For OSS operatives, the new ball game called for a quickly emplaced information network to report on local conditions and look after US interests in the region. For Southeast Asian nationalists, there appeared a window of opportunity: Japan acknowledged defeat, and its occupation forces withdrew to their barracks or were ordered by Mountbatten to perform police tasks until the arrival of SEAC forces. In either case, local nationalists were free, with or without Japanese assistance, to set up independent governments in Vietnam and Java. In doing so, they could rely upon widespread popular support. In Java, a sizeable Indonesian military force trained and equipped by the Japanese stood ready to defend the new regime.

Despite its unremarkable record and resources, Mountbatten's Southeast Asia Command, in its final, groping actions of the war, provided the only available vehicle for reasserting European power in the region. Ironically, it also served as the chief entrepôt for those few Americans, largely OSS operatives, who were able accurately to observe if not influence the unstable political environment in southern Vietnam and the East Indies. American personnel, including OSS teams, appeared in northern Vietnam courtesy of the US command in China. Such people brought with them the image of the United States as a virtuous, virile, freedom-loving republic and found frequent reaffirmation of that portrait among Asians. This had been the point of Wendell Willkie's *One World* in 1943: the existence of a wondrous reservoir of goodwill toward Americans. Certainly it was a resilient faith that dependent peoples had placed in US material largesse and political support. But the faith was not boundless. American leaders understood the risks: if the United States did not act decisively to uphold a universalist application of self-determination, the disappointment of colonial peoples might surface rapidly and palpably – or possibly it might not. In the immediate post-war period, much depended on the depth of nationalist sentiment in Southeast Asia, on the attitude of charismatic nationalist leaders, on the policies of the imperial powers, and on the intent of the Allies quickly to terminate war-related tasks and move toward reform and renovation. This set of variables consisted, however, of unknowns or things unknowable at the time of the Japanese surrender.

An OSS report of July 1945 referred to the Vietnamese (or 'Annamites' as they were often called) as 'the most politically-conscious people of Indochina'.[51] And it was toward the Vietnamese nationalist stronghold in Tonkin province that the newly designated OSS Southern [China] Command, headquartered in Kunming, turned its attention that same month. As an experiment, American personnel were to be sent into Tonkin, to link up with the Viet Minh resistance movement. On 9 July, Colonel Harry L. Berno, attached to OSS/India-Burma Theater (formerly OSS/SEAC), pointed out that plans for French guerrilla activity in Indochina were effectively quashed by the Japanese coup in March; since that time British efforts to keep afloat a clandestine French organization had met with only limited success. 'It has not been a serious or large-scale operation', wrote Berno, 'and at the present time there is nothing to indicate that it will develop into anything of important significance to the French, USA, or [the] Chinese.' Hence, contact with native nationalists offered an alternative route to fomenting guerrilla-style attacks against Japanese forces.[52]

An advance group from an OSS Special Operations (SO) team, codenamed 'Deer', was dropped into northern Vietnam on 16 July, landing near the village of Kimlung. Deer team was assigned the task of interdicting enemy lines of communication out from Hanoi and training/equipping guerrilla forces. Major Allison K. Thomas, commander of the group, untangled his parachute from a tree, delivered a few extemporaneous remarks (in fluent French) to the 200-member 'guard' sent to greet him, and was escorted with the rest of his party to meet Ho Chi Minh (frequently 'Mr Hoe' or 'Mr Hoo' to American ears). 'We were ... led through the forest paths, then under a bamboo archway with the sign in English above "Welcome to our American Friends" and then conducted to our quarters which had been recently built for us. ... We were then introduced to Mr Hoo, Party Leader, who welcomed us and presented us with a fatted calf and some Hanoi beer for our supper.'[53] The next day, Ho insisted that a French officer accompanying the team must leave. The Viet Minh would welcome ten million Americans, said Ho, but no Frenchmen. Thomas was impressed with Ho and sympathetic to his nationalist credo. On 17 July he wrote: 'Forget the Communist bogy. VML [Viet Minh League] is *not* Communist. Stands for freedom and reforms from French harshness'. Three days later, Thomas had concluded that OSS operations in Vietnam would be ineffective without Viet Minh assistance, that the VML had legitimate grievances against the French colonial administration, and that French forces would probably have to be excluded from future American-initiated military activities in the territory.[54]

The remainder of Deer team arrived on 30 July, as well as the personnel for 'Cat' team commanded by Captain Charles M. Holland, who soon led his group to a separate base site. Major Thomas and Ho Chi Minh began planning an attack against the Japanese garrison in the provincial capital of Thai Nguyen; and weapons instruction to a hundred-man Vietnamese contingent started in early August. At mid-month, Thomas recorded: 'Training continuing at high speed in carbines, M-1's, Tommyguns, Bazookas, LMG's, Brens, Mortars and Grenades. Received news that Jap surrender imminent'. In spite of the news, Thomas' team and a group of Vietnamese guerrillas prepared to advance toward Thai Nguyen. The major wired his OSS command in China and offered to accept the surrender of Japanese forces in the area. 'The answer . . . was that as far as we were concerned the war was over and under no circumstances were we to accept any Jap surrenders. This was indeed extremely disheartening to me as we all felt we had risked our lives in coming here and now when the going was to be easy we were not allowed to get in on the gravy.' Leaving Kimlung, Thomas had a final meeting with Ho, 'who indicated to me he would like me to stay in FIC [French Indochina] as long as possible. I . . . doubted if it would be possible inasmuch as his party was not recognized nor was his country independent as yet'.

Subsequently, Thomas was ordered to remain on the outskirts of Thai Nguyen rather than proceeding to Hanoi. He later recalled: 'This . . . was stunning news. We could not understand this. If Hanoi was safe to enter and we being Americans we couldn't see the point but guessed that Hq thought we would not be strictly neutral inasmuch as we worked for a few weeks with the VIETMINH'. Yet, it seemed that the United States had hardly been neutral when issuing arms to the French for use in Indochina. 'Of course, the counter argument and quite plausible one was that the French were our Allies and the VIETMINH party was a secret party working against the French whose existence was not recognized by any power'. Deer team was later permitted to visit Hanoi, from 9–16 September, and Thomas noted that it 'was an extremely festive city for everyone except the

French'.[55] It was a city strewn with political banners proclaiming Vietnamese independence, castigating the French, and welcoming representatives of the victorious Allies.

Indeed, much had happened during the month of August. While Deer team had been carrying out its small-scale, experimental mission in the interior of Tonkin, larger forces had closed down the entire Asian theater. Allied planning quickly shifted gears in order to arrange for appropriate surrender ceremonies and to implement the RAPWI program. But Colonel John O. Coughlin, Strategic Services Officer for Southeast Asia, reported on 18 August that 'this surrender business is going much slower than it was initially thought it would'.[56] It was one thing for the Japanese to stop fighting; it was quite another for the Allies to transport the requisite troops to enemy headquarters and prison camp sites. From the India-Burma command, OSS personnel were organized into special rescue teams for Saigon, Batavia and Singapore; as well, additional operatives were scheduled for Bangkok, where the US intelligence network had already surfaced. Americans reached the Hanoi area as part of a similar effort co-ordinated from China. Such teams, in addition to their RAPWI work, recalled Patti, 'would also provide opportunities to cover intelligence objectives and postsurrender political warfare activities'.

The matter of post-war intelligence was addressed in an 18 August memo by Colonel Coughlin: 'By the time all these teams or missions are established, sufficient information should be available to determine the shape of the future organization out here'. He urged a rapid increase in the number of civilians involved in intelligence activity. 'It will undoubtedly become increasingly difficult for us to maintain a military or even a quasi-military organization out here after a very few months, and every effort should be made for the continuation of our organization after the military is withdrawn'.[57] Americans in Indochina, their tenure uncertain, sought information on two major and related points: (1) the likelihood of long-term guerrilla resistance to restoration of the colonial status quo, and (2) the ideological orientation of Ho Chi Minh and the Viet Minh leadership generally.

HO CHI MINH

In the swirl of military-political events and aspirations and clashing interests which marked Southeast Asia in latter 1945, the dominant personality was not British, French, Chinese or American. Instead it was Ho Chi Minh. He was the man to come to terms with. This was all the more remarkable because of his slight build and his gentle, soft-spoken manner – and the fact that he was Vietnamese in a corner of the world where Europeans had long been dominant. Ho Chi Minh's charisma was etched in his intellect and piercing eyes, evinced in his quiet resolution, expressed via his repeated ability to win respect and admiration from nearly all who talked with him. A realist, a pragmatist, a veteran communist, an unyielding nationalist, Ho Chi Minh seldom failed to inspire adjectives which suggested a feisty, indomitable spirit within a frail, even sickly, frame. Amongst Vietnamese, he liked to be known as 'Uncle Ho', the kindly, tireless champion of the nationalist cause.

In latter 1946, correspondent George Weller wrote, 'Pin Uncle Ho down and you find him a master of the soft answer'.[58] Though Ho Chi Minh had been well schooled in France in doctrinaire Marxism-Leninism, he rarely impressed his interviewers as a hard-bitten revolutionary. On the contrary, from his first contacts with American journalists, OSS personnel or diplomatic representatives, Ho consistently emphasized his desire for Vietnamese autonomy or independence – without ideological strings attached – and his willingness to negotiate with the French government in order to arrange an acceptable compromise solution. Initially, Ho rarely acknowledged his communist affiliation and frequently denied it when dealing with Americans. If questions were later raised, as they inevitably were, he declared that his leftist politics would not translate into a harsh Marxist-Leninist regime with close ties to the Soviet Union.[59] Ho Chi Minh always insisted that his first priority was Vietnamese freedom. And he promised with equal spirit and frequency that there would be a long, bloody armed struggle if the French were not willing to give way. In an AP wire story from Hanoi, Ho Chi Minh appeared as 'the slight, bearded rebel', the 'mystery man of the Annamite revolutionary movement',[60] even as Franco-Vietnamese contention accelerated.

In the spring of 1945, Archimedes Patti was the OSS officer in charge of developing plans for special operations in northern Indochina, above the 16th parallel. Believing that the Viet Minh might be a useful ally, Patti arranged a meeting with Ho Chi Minh in late April, at a teahouse in a small Chinese village. He recalled: 'Ho's sincerity, pragmatism, and eloquence made an indelible impression on me. He did not strike me as a starry-eyed revolutionary or a flaming radical, given to cliches, mouthing a party line, or bent on destroying without plans for rebuilding'. Ho Chi Minh was eager for US support. Major Patti believed that Ho could be trusted as an ally against the Japanese and that co-operating with the Viet Minh did not conflict with American goals in the region.[61] Several months later, from inside Vietnam, Major Allison Thomas reported effective Viet Minh harassment and interdiction actions; and he was equally enthusiastic about US-Viet Minh co-operation. Thomas was moved by the image of Americans living in bamboo huts alongside Vietnamese freedom-fighters, plotting guerrilla strategy, listening sympathetically to grievances against the colonial system. Ho was 'our friend of the forest'. He was 'extremely sincere and able and believe[s] 100% in the independence of F.I.C.' But

Ho and other Viet Minh leaders were 'vehement', wrote Thomas, in denying that the nationalist movement concealed a communist agenda, telling Americans that political questions would come to the fore only after independence had been achieved. 'The leaders made an analogy to the USA at the time it was seeking independence. There were no parties but only patriots. Politics came later.' While the Viet Minh were openly anti-French and distrusted the Chinese government, its leaders had 'nothing but praise and kindness for the Americans'.[62]

United States soldiers, arriving in Southeast Asia in small numbers, were warmly received as the forerunners of heightened American interest in the region. For US personnel, contact with native peoples could be an edifying experience, even a heady one. As Edmund Taylor, an OSS officer with SEAC, remarked: 'The longer we stayed in the theatre the more OSS became permeated with the suspicion and disapproval of Western imperialism'. The experience also fed the American self-image of exemplar and liberator. Such was the response, for instance, of Arthur Hale of the United States Information Service, who visited Indochina within a month after the Japanese surrender. He reported that the Vietnamese were no strangers to American culture, politics, and political personalities, estimating that 70 per cent of the motion pictures shown in Hanoi before the war had been US films. He observed that the Vietnamese were 'true movie fans' and had an immense curiosity about all things American. Hale was surprised to hear pre-war US slang spoken in the streets of Hanoi. He found deep-seated anti-French feeling, and he soon identified Ho Chi Minh as the 'outstanding personality' of the Viet Minh leadership. Hale also reported: 'Nowhere did the coming of Americans, in this case a mere handful of them, mean so much to a people as it did to the population of northern Indo China. To Annamites, our coming was the symbol of liberation not from Japanese occupation but from decades of French colonial rule'.[63] Captain Herbert J. Bluechel, arriving in Saigon, commented that Vietnamese did not treat Americans the same as Europeans.

> Americans are considered to be a separate people and the Viet Minh leaders expressed the hope that Americans would view favorably their bid for independence, since we ourselves fought for and gained our independence under a situation considered to be similar to that as exists in Indo China to-day.[64]

Ho Chi Minh expressed familiar themes, then, in his one-sided correspondence with high-level US officials which began in October 1945 and continued through early 1946. On a number of occasions, Ho tried to contact directly the secretary of state and the president. A telegram of 17 October to the White House, via Chungking, established Ho's basic argument: that the Vichy capitulation to Japan had betrayed the Allies and severed Franco-Vietnamese links, and that the provisions of the Atlantic

Charter had promised the people of Vietnam their independence.[65] A letter of 22 October, for the secretary of state, claimed that the principles of the Atlantic Charter 'strongly appealed to the Vietnamese and contributed in [the] making of the Vietminh resistance in the war zone a nation-wide anti-Japanese movement which found a powerful echo in the democratic aspirations of the people. The Atlantic Charter was looked upon as the foundation of future Vietnam'. Ho asserted: 'As a matter of fact, the carrying out of the Atlantic and San Francisco Charters implies the eradication of imperialism and all forms of colonial oppression'. The situation in Vietnam required 'immediate interference' on the part of the United States.[66]

In fact, five days later, on 27 October, President Truman delivered what appeared to be pertinent remarks at the Navy Day ceremonies in New York City. Truman declared that the United States represented 'righteousness and justice', that it would not approve 'any compromise with evil', and that it would seek 'steady progress toward international cooperation'. He then proclaimed a list of 12 fundamental principles which governed American foreign policy. The fourth point essentially restated a provision of the Atlantic Charter, though with less ambiguity:

> We believe that all peoples who are prepared for self-government should be permitted to choose their own form of government by their own freely expressed choice, without interference from any foreign source. That is true in Europe, in Asia, in Africa, as well as in the Western Hemisphere.[67]

It meant less than it seemed. By late October, as US wartime intelligence units had been or were being ordered home from Southeast Asia, American policymakers had already come to terms – if somewhat uncomfortably – with the restoration of imperial sovereignty. Ho Chi Minh's letters were not answered. It may be that his only appeal which actually reached the White House was a short paragraph in a routine summary memorandum prepared by the acting director of the OSS in late September 1945.[68] With this one exception, Ho's correspondence was filed and forgotten in the State Department – with the approval of the head of the Division of Southeast Asian Affairs. As Abbot Moffat later recalled, a response from the president would have entailed recognition of the Viet Minh government. Had Truman written back to Ho Chi Minh, said Moffat, 'that would have been taken by the French . . . as a really serious affront and possibly a breach of international etiquette'. France, noted Moffat, was ultimately a 'more valuable ally' than the Vietnamese.[69]

The role of the OSS personnel in Southeast Asia during the final days of the war and for several months thereafter has been misunderstood in two ways in the interim years. At one point, before the availability of a large collection of OSS documents, it seemed logical to some historians to assume that American intelligence operatives were the first to sound the alarm about communist influence in the Viet Minh.[70] More recently, it has been asserted that OSS officers in Vietnam were generally naïve, sometimes actively anti-French, and thus easily seduced by the wily, soft-answer Ho Chi Minh – that he told them what they wanted to hear and they believed him.[71]

Neither allegation was accurate. The easy political intimacy of Americans and Vietnamese nationalists was a product of pragmatism and parallel idealism. By the summer of 1945, OSS analysts believed that the Viet Minh could provide valuable assistance against the Japanese and that co-operative endeavors might serve as an opening for enhanced US influence in Indochina. Ho Chi Minh knew that the nationalists needed US support in order effectively to challenge the French for control of the country, at least for the short-term. The Viet Minh pictured themselves as freedom-fighters; the Americans pictured themselves as freedom-fighters.[72] In fact, the seduction was reciprocal. Some OSS officers were obviously overenthusiastic about the Viet Minh program, as a result of conversations with Ho; and just as clearly, Ho Chi Minh and perhaps other nationalists developed unrealistic expectations of American assistance on the basis of their association with the same OSS personnel.

Further, those Americans who made contact with the Viet Minh were rarely unequivocal in their praise of the nationalist movement. OSS operatives understood that their viewpoint might be distorted and that broader policy considerations might well and justifiably govern US foreign policy for the region and the world. Also, while nearly everyone praised Ho Chi Minh, such was not true for other Viet Minh leaders, who appeared less contemplative, less flexible, less deferential to the Americans – and who also seemed more stereotypically communist in their bearing. There was the suggestion, for instance, that Vietnamese mouthed slogans without understanding what democracy and independence were all about. The Viet Minh organizational structure and even its yellow-star-on-red flag suggested a Leninist imprint. And when Viet Minh leaders had the opportunity to test their administrative skills before the arrival of reoccupation troops, it was common to attribute mistakes to political immaturity or to identify acts of anti-white violence as part of an undercurrent of ideological or racial terror that boded ill for a native regime.

In truth, OSS personnel had no more affinity for an overtly communist regime, anywhere, than did policymakers in Washington. However, one important difference between the two groups – those who were in Southeast Asia and those who were not – was that Americans who worked and travelled among the Vietnamese, who talked with Ho Chi Minh or other Viet Minh officials, could *feel* the strength of nationalist fervor in the countryside. Americans 'in country' during 1945 thus understood and even admired the nationalists' determination in a way that US policymakers in

Washington did not and could not. 'Communism' as a 'demon theory'[73] had not yet fully reared its head, and OSS operatives in the summer and fall of 1945 were able to glimpse the possibility of an independent leftist regime in Southeast Asia and were free to consider it a reasonable variation on old themes. The outlines of approaching conflict were easy to see. As Edmund Taylor advised, 'The importance of this theater, in my opinion, arises mainly from the fact that after the war it is going to be a power vacuum, or partial vacuum, and therefore a storm center'.[74]

Post-surrender policies and politics in Southeast Asia were greatly complicated by the onset during 1945–46 of heightened US-Soviet rivalry which spilled over from Europe into a host of thorny rimland encounters. While unilateralism was one response to rising Soviet-American hostility, many issues were entangled in difficult but necessary multilateral negotiations which were an outgrowth of wartime optimism and summitry. Especially complex were questions which went to the heart of the European balance of power: occupation regimes, provisional governments, frontier adjustments, peace treaties and the disposition of Italian colonies in Africa. As noted by Benjamin Rivlin, the need for big-power agreement on the fate of strategically located Italian dependencies – Libya, Eritrea and Italian Somaliland – provided a 'made-to-order issue' for Soviet-American wrangling.[75]

Particularly problematic were the discussions regarding Libya: administered as a unified colony beginning in 1934, liberated from Axis control largely by British forces, and split into three separate occupation zones by VE Day. British military authorities administered the lion's share of the territory, controlling the areas of Cyrenaica and Tripolitania along the Mediterranean shore, while a French military regime supervised affairs in the interior region of the Fezzan. The apparent solution at war's end, possibly for all the Italian colonies, was trusteeship; but negotiations were complicated not only by rival claims and conflicting proposals (including a desire to restore the Italian administration) within the newly created Council of Foreign Ministers, but also by uncertainty about the wisdom and necessity of recreating a unified Libya. In the end, wisdom was in short supply.

4 Loose Change: Cyrenaica, Tripolitania, and the Council of Foreign Ministers

In September 1944, Major A. W. Schmidt of the Office of Strategic Services tendered his assessment of the future importance of Africa to American policymakers. As an OSS mission chief in British West Africa, his wartime travels had included Egypt, Morocco, Senegal, Portuguese Guinea, Liberia and the Belgian Congo. Because Africa ceased to be an active theater of war in 1943, Schmidt felt that he and his fellow officers of the OSS African Division were forced to consider, sooner than others, the direction of post-war intelligence-gathering and the character of US policy through the region. Believing that the State Department had not yet formulated its policy agenda for Africa, Schmidt presented his own analysis in the shape of two poles: isolationism versus internationalism. He noted that US–African trade had been very limited before the war, largely because most African raw materials could be gotten more cheaply elsewhere, usually from the Netherlands East Indies. However, wartime needs had prompted increased US imports of bauxite, manganese, copper, uranium and industrial diamonds. Schmidt then argued forcefully for the internationalist viewpoint: 'simply that the United States, having finally emerged as a major world power ... must of necessity be interested and continue to be interested in important developments in every nook and cranny of the world'.

American leaders must learn more about global conditions in order to compete successfully with other nations for influence and prestige. This was one very important lesson from the war: 'Who would have thought in the year 1935 that the guage [sic] of the track of the Benguela [Angola] railroad or the condition of its rolling stock would be important to United States interests in case Rommel had been successful at El Al[a]mein in November 1942? In the same year who would have thought that the defenses at Dakar were of particular importance to the people of the United States?' Schmidt noted that the course of warfare had transformed northern Africa's strategic significance. 'Since the Mediterranean Sea will always remain a vital supply route to operations in Europe or in Asia, a continuing knowledge of and interest in the developments in North Africa and the southern shores of the Mediterranean will be of vital importance.'[1]

Although 'nook and cranny' was a phrase later used to illustrate Soviet acquisitiveness,[2] the war had amply demonstrated in theater after theater the importance of accurate intelligence – not simply espionage (though that counted too), but primarily the collecting of pertinent data: topography, harbor depths, tide schedules, crop figures, average temperatures and rainfall, industrial production, mineral resources, population growth. Also of interest were surveys of peoples' attitudes: were they friendly or unfriendly, changeable or hidebound, Christian, Muslim or Jew? Did they want independence or not? Were they willing to fight for it? Would they favor communism? Presumably, as many OSS officers observed, the collection of such information would continue to be a requirement of US foreign policy in the post-war era. The war had opened virtually every corner of the world to Americans of one sort or another; and, as noted earlier, the tremendous expansion of US productive power and the international array of its military forces naturally encouraged feelings of pride and ebullience among American leaders. Anything could be done and very likely Americans were the ones to do it.

The dominant sentiment in Western Europe was, however, much different, where the loss of life had been so catastrophic, where the landscape bore open testament to the new destructive fury of combat, and where the Holocaust stood now as a milestone of human barbarism and forever as a metaphor for technocratic horror. In January 1945, an English academic named J. R. R. Tolkien sat down to write a letter to his son in the Royal Air Force. Throughout the war, Tolkien had continued to labor over a long manuscript detailing a lively, intricate history of alliances of hobbits, elves and wizards fighting recurrent evil. Having just heard that Soviet troops were 60 miles from Berlin and that the roadways of the continent were glutted with refugees, Tolkien wrote, 'There seem no bowels of mercy or compassion, no imagination, left in this dark diabolic hour. . . . Well the first War of Machines seems to be drawing to its final inconclusive chapter – leaving, alas, everyone the poorer, many bereaved or maimed and millions dead, and only one thing triumphant: the Machines'. On 1 February, Secretary Stettinius sat with a dreary, despondent Churchill: 'He said there were probably more units of suffering among humanity . . . as of this hour when we sat down to dinner, than at any time during the history of the world . . . and as he looked out on the world, it was one of sorrow and bloodshed'. The prime minister enjoyed eloquent overstatement; but even so, the European scene undeniably evoked an eerie uncertainty and exhibited a pervasive mood of irreplaceable loss – as in Camus' image of 'destroyed buildings at the very edge of a wounded earth' at the port of Le Havre. So it was that Europeans accepted the end of the Second World War with, as Christopher Thorne has written, a 'mixture of widely differing thoughts and emotions'.[3]

Chief among the immediate problems was the inadequate supply of food and fuel. Several weeks after VE Day, John Colville, a private secretary to Churchill, was pessimistic about the near future: shortages, massive displacement and meager hope. 'The situation is no easier, nor are the prospects apparently brighter', he thought, 'than before the first shot was fired.' President Harry Truman, arriving in Washington following the war's final summit, told the American people: 'I have just returned from Berlin, the city from which the Germans intended to rule the world. It is a ghost city. . . . How glad I am to be home again! And how grateful to Almighty God that this land of ours has been spared!' A pinched and penniless Western Europe badly needed US assistance if its peoples were to avoid a cruel winter of discontent. 'Desperate men', said Truman, 'are liable to destroy the structure of their society to find in the wreckage some substitute for hope. If we let Europe go cold and hungry, we may lose some of the foundations of order on which the hope for worldwide peace must rest.'[4]

Americans, as it turned out, were to hear this theme again and again over the next several years, articulated with increasing urgency and in ever more apocalyptic tones. In the summer of 1945, the danger lay in widespread deprivation. By late 1946 and early 1947, the danger was a malevolent ideology seeking to use that deprivation as a vehicle to despoil and enslave the human spirit. Caught in the fray were a host of issues, few of them clearcut, which became hostages to the browbeating rhythm of US-Soviet diplomacy. Peering into 'the early post-military period'[5] was difficult for everyone, and the status of colonies and mandates was typically determined in conjunction with other, larger matters. The progressive strangulation of East-West diplomacy in the months after Potsdam guaranteed a rapid gridlock over trusteeships as well as other points of dispute. It was a situation which encouraged partition and other interim expedients, introducing long-lived anomalies into a post-war international system dominated by two superpowers.

POST-SURRENDER TASKS: ITALIAN LIBYA

Foreign policy analyst Vernon McKay wrote in 1946 that 'Mediterranean Africa' was of 'paramount significance' for the United States, that the American stake 'goes far beyond our natural concern for native welfare'. Like others, McKay discerned a better awareness of African affairs amongst Americans as a result of wartime action and news reporting. Amidst the implicit globalism of the post-war era, he wrote, the disposition of the Italian colonies very much affected a variety of US military and economic interests.[6] North Africa was strategic terrain because it comprised the southern flank of a Mediterranean security zone, one broadened by the new range and capabilities of air power. North Africa was a vital link in Western-dominated networks of trade and communication, as proven by the history of British involvement in Egypt, and the region represented a land bridge of sorts between Eurasia and the New World.

The British were in a very strong position in northeastern Africa at war's end, with a clear military preponderance in the Near East and occupation armies controlling the Italian colonies. For this reason, English aims for the region leaned toward the familiar requirements of imperial security. After Germany's surrender, noted William Roger Louis, the British Chiefs of Staff 'surveyed the Middle East as a landowner might gaze over his estates with an eye towards more or less desirable places of accommodation (Egypt and Palestine) and those more suitable merely for outdoor relief (Cyrenaica). It was important that the natives be kept friendly'. The Levant crisis, noted R. D. J. Scott Fox of the Foreign Office, had been 'a warning as to the complications likely to ensue from a European Power trying to establish itself in an Arab country where it is not wanted'.[7] The subsequent course of Middle East affairs effectively demonstrated the paradox posed by the Labour government's foreign policy: a reduced scope for empire, resulting from a pragmatic reassessment of economic and strategic capabilities, combined with a determination to remain a significant player in new great games, whatever their ultimate shape.

In northeastern Libya, the territory of Cyrenaica had been an active theater of war through early 1943, by which time all of Italian Africa was under British control. Unlike Tripolitania to the west, the countryside of Cyrenaica was much battered, crossed and recrossed by German and English armies. Lord Rennell's official history of British military administration in occupied Africa identified several key themes for Libya: (1) the Civil Affairs Branch of the military consolidated its control by replicating the pattern of a colonial regime, although officials remained uncertain about the future status of the territory and thus focused upon interim measures; (2) the shift of Anglo-American military activity away from North Africa in the summer of 1944 stimulated Arab expectations of rapid progress toward self-rule; and (3) despite inevitable problems, Arab-British relations remained generally cordial in both Cyrenaica and Tripolitania.[8] But such friendliness – however extensive it might be – could not survive the frustration of Arab hopes for self-determination.

Unlike the population in other areas of Libya, Cyrenaican Arabs had begun long before 1945 to develop a national identity through the unifying force of the Islamic Sanusiya Order. Also referred to as the Sanusi or Senussi Order, this group represented a sizeable fundamentalist fraternity within the Sunni Muslim faith. Sayed Mohamed Idris al-Mahdi al-Senussi, grandson of the founder, had become head of the Order in 1916, after which he sought to preserve Cyrenaican autonomy in the face of Italian expansionism. Following Italian occupation of the territory in 1923, Sayed Idris went into exile in Egypt and thereafter encouraged his followers in an active guerrilla resistance through 1931. In the view of E. E. Evans-Pritchard, the years of the Second World War marked the final transition of the

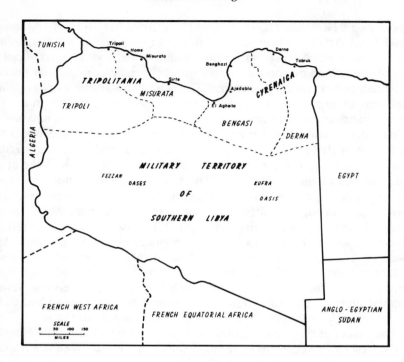

Figure 4.1 *Libya, 1945–46.*
Source: Map drawn by John Yarbrough, based on a map drawn in the Office of the Geographer, Department of State, 19 October 1943, OSS-A-3567-A, RG 226, Cartographic and Architectural Branch, National Archives.

fraternity from a religious to a political movement: 'Amid the roar of planes and guns the Bedouin learnt to see themselves more clearly as a single people, the Sanusi of Cyrenaica, in a wider world, and came to be regarded as such by those engaged in the struggle'.[9]

With the onset of the Second World War, Sayed Idris quickly lent his support to the British military effort in North Africa. It was this assistance which prompted Anthony Eden, as foreign minister, to pledge in the House of Commons in January 1942 'that at the end of the war the Sanusis in Cyrenaica will in no circumstances again fall under Italian domination'. The value of Senussi allies was seconded from the field by Lt. Col. J. N. D. Anderson in December 1944: 'The inhabitants of Cyrenaica helped us greatly, at considerable risk to themselves, by feeding, hiding and leading back to our lines hundreds of British personnel. The motive for this assistance was largely our "alliance" with Sayed Idris'. During a July 1944 visit to the territory, reported Anderson, Sayed Idris had been 'cheered to the echo'.[10]

The overall situation in the coastal regions of Libya was summarized in a report of 13 November 1944, prepared by Brigadier R. D. H. Arundell, Chief Civil Affairs Officer in the Middle East. Anticipating that Allied victory and a peace treaty with Italy would not for several years stipulate formal disposition of occupied territories, the brigadier urged clarification of British policy toward Cyrenaica. The sentiments of the local populace appeared to augur well for sustained British influence in the area: 'The Cyrenaicans' aspirations can be summed up as a progressive measure of independence under the banner of Sayed Idris el Senussi and under the protection of Britain, for which they harbour the friendliest feelings'. Still, with extensive physical destruction and social dislocation in the wake of the war, life remained chaotic. Most of the Italian population had been evacuated during the seesaw Anglo-German campaigns, and the resource-poor character of the territory hampered stabilization. 'The [Arab] townsmen are politically precocious, but otherwise backward and ill-educated, while the majority of the population are semi-settled tent dwellers. The country is seriously lacking in the professional classes and craftsmen and technicians. The Cyrenaicans could not possibly stand alone.' Given this situation, British officials had discarded the Italian colonial superstructure and 'have been compelled to improvise and to lay the tentative foundations for a European-protected Arab State'.

'The object of this paper', noted Arundell, 'is to emphasise the fact that His Majesty's Government is, through conquest, responsible for a country whose future is unknown, but on which money must be spent and a progressive policy initiated without delay if that future is not to be seriously prejudiced. Unless we can make an early beginning in the task of both economic and political reconstruction, the people of Cyrenaica will soon begin to look askance at those whom they have hitherto welcomed and we shall be accused of failing to discharge responsibilities which have been forced upon us by the accidents of war.' Hence, a policy of 'bare care and maintenance' must be upgraded. For Arundell, British strategic interests and the aspirations of native Arabs happily coalesced. Cyrenaica, he wrote, 'must be regarded as the western bastion of the Middle East. The Power which controls this territory sits astride the sea lanes of the Eastern Mediterranean, and can threaten the Nile Valley by land and air'. Cyrenaica could provide important base and training sites for all three military services and offered advantages as a 'concentration area' for the army and air force. 'We can station there considerable forces without arousing resentment which is liable to be excited in other territories of the Middle East, and such troops will be sufficiently accessible to be employed at short notice anywhere in the Middle East.' While complex questions about land tenure and economic reconstruction were still to be resolved, Arundell contended that a careful and thoughtful tutelage could lay the groundwork 'for an easy transition from a B.M.A. [British Military Administration] to an Arab State with an Emir and a British Resident'.[11]

Brigadier Arundell produced an updated study of the Libyan situation in July 1945, only a few days before the opening of the Potsdam Conference in Germany. As before, he reaffirmed traditional British concerns in the region, stressing: 'Cyrenaica has no intrinsic value for a foreign power except through its strategically important geographical position'. Sayed Idris, Arundell observed, was 'intelligent, reasonable, loyal and dignified, and should prove at least a reasonably satisfactory figure-head'. Through their attachment to the Sanusiya Order, local Arabs comprised a cohesive society; and they 'prefer British tutelage to any other . . . [and] they would welcome the presence of British troops for economic reasons'.[12]

Neighboring Tripolitania, reported Arundell, represented a more diverse society than Cyrenaica, one in which Sayed Idris could claim only limited influence. A large number of Italians remained in the territory, concentrated near the port of Tripoli; and Arundell believed that Tripolitanian Arabs had been generally more tolerant of the colonial administration than had Cyrenaicans. Nonetheless, Arab nationalist sentiment was steadily increasing: 'No backward race . . . likes to be subject to a defeated and discredited power. . . . The demand that the territory should not be handed back to Italy has become widespread and insistent'. Arundell warned that any effort to return Tripolitania to Italian control would be greatly resented and likely lead to armed resistance; and he reported that abundant weapons were available for protracted guerrilla struggle.

Arundell argued that British strategic interests in Tripolitania were 'entirely negative': the area need not be administered by Britain, but it must be denied to a hostile power – otherwise, the British position in Cyrenaica would be compromised. Such negative interests were also pertinent to the political situation: 'It is important to avoid the opprobrium throughout the Arab world which HMG would certainly incur by disposing of the territory in a way regarded as contrary to the principles of the Atlantic Charter and democratic self-determination'. Therefore, Britain must either assume responsibility for Tripolitania or devise an acceptable alternative. 'Most intelligent Tripolitanians realise that they cannot hope to stand alone for many years to come and their political aspirations may be summed up in the desire for some form of liberal protection with a guarantee of eventual independence after a period of progressive tutelage. And for such a role they favour Britain.' Ultimately, however, the population would 'look to the east – to Egypt, the Levant and the Arab League – rather than to the west and the shackles of French colonising methods'. Arundell believed that Muslims were particularly hostile toward the French because of the latter's consistent effort to Europeanize Arab society. Tripolitanians were no exception, especially with French forces holding and claiming the Fezzan region in southern Libya.[13]

Such reports from the field were clear: British responsibility for Cyrenaica was a strategic necessity; a friendly power must be trustee over neighboring territories; and while Arabs of the region were reasonably pro-British, they would strongly oppose a restoration of Italian control or an extension of French influence. In Cyrenaica, Sayed Idris was a dignified anachronism who personified a nascent nationalist sentiment amenable to British tutelage. All in all, the situation looked promising. On the other hand, the skein of Middle East politics appeared more convoluted the closer one looked.

Foreign Office minutes in late June 1945 revealed substantial agreement with the military's assessment of Cyrenaica's strategic importance; however, the matter of a trustee for Tripolitania offered several reasonable scenarios. Viscount Samuel Hood of the Reconstruction Department doubted that a 'British solution' for both Libyan territories was possible. There appeared few alternatives, he wrote, to a restoration of Italian administration in Tripolitania. 'The extent to which satisfaction is to be given to the French [claims in the Fezzan] will turn I should imagine on much wider issues: whether in return for their abdication in the Levant we shall recognise French predominance in North Africa.' Charles W. Baxter, head of the Eastern Department, found merit in the suggestion that French losses in the Levant could be assuaged by new responsibilities in Libya, including the administration of Tripolitania as well as the Fezzan.[14]

As might be expected, Arthur V. Coverly-Price of the Egyptian Department preferred a British-controlled Cyrenaica chiefly for its contribution to the defense of the Suez Canal. Frederick R. Hoyer Millar, head of the Western Department, felt that while Britain must retain control of Cyrenaica, Italy could administer Tripolitania under some form of international trusteeship. In what would become an oft-heard argument over the next several years, Hoyer Millar observed:

> For political reasons we do not want our [Peace] Treaty to be unduly harsh on the Italians, since we want not only to retain Italian friendship, but to build Italy up into a useful member of society, to encourage her to look to the West rather than to the East and to make use of her for our own purpose as a 'bastion of democracy in the Mediterranean'. ... I think ... we ought to let Italy retain direct interest in one of her colonies, and the obvious colony to cho[o]se for this seems to be Tripolitania where she can do us least harm and where she would seem not to have done too badly for the local population in the past.

He believed that the American government would favor a lenient policy toward Italy and cautioned, 'We shall have to be very careful to avoid giving the Americans the impression that we want any of the Italian colonies for ourselves'. Philip M. Broadmead, head of the North American Department, agreed with this assessment of the likely US attitude. He affirmed that actions taken in the name of international trusteeship would be palatable to American policymakers: 'It will be the way in which it is handled that will matter'.[15]

In mid-July, Lord Hood complained that despite frequent discussion of the fate of the Italian colonies, the Foreign Office had 'been unable to formulate definite recommendations for Ministerial approval. . . . It is time that we arrived at some firm conclusions'. Hood noted that only 'at the last moment' was a brief prepared for the British delegation to the Potsdam summit – one which began:

We have a strategic interest in ensuring that these Italian overseas possessions do not come under the control of potential enemy states as they flank our sea and air communications through the Mediterranean and the Red Sea, and provide bases from which Egypt, the Sudan and Kenya could be attacked. At the same time we have no wish to annex these possessions and indeed could not do so compatibly with the Atlantic Charter. They are economic liabilities and we do not want to incur the additional expense and responsibilities. Moreover we do not want to lay ourselves open to accusations of British Imperialism. The best way of providing for the future of these territories would appear to be to bring them within the scope of international trusteeship.

That having been said, the Foreign Office posited an Italian peace treaty which ceded the colonies collectively to Britain, France, the Soviet Union and the United States. The four powers would then develop some formula for apportioning trusteeship duties. Seeing little reason for a unified Libya ('a purely artificial creation'), the position paper recommended British administration of Cyrenaica and Italian control of Tripolitania.[16]

The State Department's preliminary views regarding the Italian colonies were summarized by Cordell Hull in an August 1944 memo. For Libya, the department preferred a single trusteeship under the auspices of the United Nations Organization. 'This would not preclude the establishment of an autonomous Amirate of the Senussi. . . . However, if it should prove difficult to obtain British agreement to this over-all solution, a feasible, though less desirable, arrangement would be to establish Cyrenaica as an autonomous Senussi Amirate under Egyptian (or possibly British) trusteeship . . . and to place Tripolitania under an International Trusteeship to be exercised by Italy.'[17]

In effect, Hull acknowledged that Libya was not of great concern to American policymakers, and he was aware that the Joint Chiefs of Staff thought likewise. For this reason, State Department briefing books prepared for the Potsdam Conference contained no specific proposal for the future of Libya. Instead, it was suggested that the American delegation support, in order of preference, (1) Italian administration of a unified Libya, subject to whatever international controls were later devised; (2) autonomy for Cyrenaica under Sayed Idris, with ties to Egypt or Britain, and Italian trusteeship over Tripolitania; or (3) autonomy for Cyrenaica and international trusteeship for Tripolitania.[18]

THE POTSDAM CONFERENCE

When British official Alexander Cadogan described to his wife the conference preparations on 15 July, he recognized the unease which attended the meeting. 'I wrote to you from Yalta that that was the oddest spot I'd struck yet. In some ways I think this is odder. Here we are, in the midst of this devastated and denuded country, living in a little town of our own, consisting of villas set amidst trees ... with more or less every comfort of a somewhat rough and ready kind.' The next day he rode into Berlin: 'It's a staggering sight. The roads cleared, but no traffic on them. Hardly a house undamaged and 90% mere shells. I don't think it could ever be rebuilt. The whole thing would have to be pulled down and several millions tons of rubbish carted away'. A week earlier, Assistant Secretary of State Dean Acheson had met with members of the House Foreign Affairs Committee, in executive session, and briefed them on the grave situation in Europe. In particular, he stressed the desperate plight of Italy and its immediate need for US assistance. Without such outside help, he predicted, 'You will have a complete collapse, economically, politically, spiritually, and every other way'. Senator Frances P. Bolton of Ohio asked, 'Will that not be true of every country [in Europe]?' 'Yes', replied Acheson, 'it will'.[19]

It was appropriate that the Big Three gather near Berlin to celebrate their victory over Nazi Germany. It was appropriate, too, that the physical destruction, economic chaos, and political uncertainty unleashed by the war should be viewed directly by the conference participants. For the Soviet and British delegations, such ruins and rubble were, if not common-place, hardly unexpected. For American leaders, including President Truman, the setting was a poignant reminder of the magnitude of Europe's necessary reconstruction after the defeat of Japan. For Truman, whose previous overseas visit had been in 1918 as commander of an artillery battery in France, this was an abrupt introduction to international diplomacy. And as Robert Messer has shown, both the president and his secretary of state, James F. Byrnes, viewed the war experience from a profoundly different perspective than had Roosevelt. 'Like most other Americans who saw the war from the homefront, Truman assumed that Hitler had been defeated primarily as a result of America's superior productive capacity.'[20] Thus, it appeared to be a moment for manly handshakes and brisk, businesslike diplomacy; Truman shared little of the war weariness, cynicism, and foreboding which alternately animated Churchill and Stalin.

As the Potsdam Conference opened on Tuesday, 17 July, the first plenary meeting featured discussion of what were to be two closely interwoven policy threads: the US proposal for a five-member Council of Foreign Ministers and Stalin's interest in a Soviet trusteeship in the eastern Mediterranean. The Council was approved the following day, to take responsibility for the preparation of peace treaties with Axis allies in Europe. Such quick approval for the CFM 'was regarded as a cheering sign that the wish to cooperate would rule', wrote Herbert Feis. 'But actually, while this agreement ... was being conceived, a cold and separating argument was going on about the attitude to be assumed toward Italy and the smaller Axis satellites.'[21] And while the grander issues held center stage, there were also 'cold and separating' exchanges over colonies and trusteeships which reflected differing intradelegation as well as inter-governmental perspectives.

At the sixth plenary meeting, on 22 July, the Soviet foreign minister, V. M. Molotov, asked specifically about the disposition of Italian colonies in Africa. What was to be done with them? Churchill explained that the territories were being administered by the British military and that his government believed, and had said publicly, that Italy forfeited its colonial claims by its alliance with Germany. Churchill asked, Who wants these colonies? Who has a claim to make? After Truman voiced disinterest, the prime minister quickly addressed the key issue: 'Churchill said he had not considered the possibility of the Soviet Union desiring to acquire a large tract of the African shore. If that were the case it would have to be considered in relation to many other problems'.[22]

Churchill's concern was based on a vaguely worded Soviet proposal of 20 July, one which invoked the new UN trusteeship system and sought its application to the Italian colonies. Either individual or tripartite trustee-ships would be acceptable; implicit perhaps was the thought that Italy's three colonies could easily translate into three or four separate administra-tions – something for everyone. In addition, the Soviet proposal raised, also ambiguously, the matter of pre-war mandates, as if to suggest that new administrative machinery might be fashioned for them as well.[23]

At Molotov's request, the trusteeship matter was discussed on 23 July and, as it turned out, effectively shunted aside for the short-term. Anthony Eden and Secretary of State James Byrnes argued that conclusion of the Italian peace treaty should precede further negotiation over the colonies. That is, agreement on draft treaty provisions formally stripping Italy of its dependencies should logically precede discussions concerning the future status of overseas territories. Byrnes argued convincingly that disposition of the colonies should be deferred to the first session of the Council of Foreign Ministers, to which Eden and Molotov assented. On the last day of the conference, it was further agreed, again at Byrnes' suggestion, that CFM trusteeship discussions would be limited to the Italian colonies and that the Council would not consider a broader range of adjustments to colonial or mandatory territories.[24]

As with subsequent big-power discussions about the shape of the post-war international system, the Potsdam meetings reflected the priority of European questions – the fate of Germany and its Axis allies, the status of interim governments in Poland and the Balkans – as well as concerns about the war against Japan. For American policymakers, the formula for disposition of Italy's African colonies would be dependent on several factors: (1) plans for the economic and political reconstruction of Italy and the restoration of its close relationship with the West; (2) the overall shape of US–Soviet relations and the continued ability of Allied diplomats to hammer out compromises for a satisfactory European settlement; and (3) the course of Soviet policy in Eastern Europe, which would serve as a measure of Stalin's commitment to post-war co-operation.

The work of the Council of Foreign Ministers was not going to be a display of easy camaraderie. The CFM had been created to consider simultaneously the draft treaties for Italy, Bulgaria, Hungary, Rumania and Finland – in practical terms, this meant that each of the Big Three delegations sought to gain favorable, if limited, access to the respective strategic spheres created by the wartime lines of march. Or, as James L. Gormly has phrased it, each power had a 'double standard, discussing the other powers' spheres of influence but not its own'. Further, the first CFM session opened in London after a summer marked by the brooding air of Potsdam, the blue-white flash of atomic bombs, and new rumblings about the continued viability of the Grand Alliance – an interim period which Vojtech Mastny has labelled 'cramped détente'.[25] In the end, all Big Three CFM delegations accepted compromises which reified the division of Europe. The issue of colonies was a troublesome but minor aspect of East-West contention. Nevertheless, the discord over strategically placed Cyrenaica and Tripolitania went to the heart of the new (and old) dimensions of great-power rivalry in the Mediterranean and Near East.

PREPATORY WORK

Neither the new Labour foreign minister, Ernest Bevin, nor Secretary Byrnes began the London CFM talks with a firm notion of an acceptable settlement regarding Italy's colonies. As Byrnes had commented at a 4 September press conference, his mind was still open on the topic: 'I am looking for additional light and that condition of mind I will continue to have'.[26] Certainly there was no common Anglo-American policy beyond a shared desire to minimize Soviet influence in the region. It was in recognition of its geopolitical importance that CFM discussions about the fate of Libya were more frequent and more rancorous than those concerning either Eritrea or Italian Somaliland.

The interval between the conclusion of the Potsdam summit and the opening of the London talks in September provided an opportunity for British officials to assemble a Libyan policy. A Foreign Office paper of 5 August 1945 restated the familiar objective: securing Cyrenaica as a British trusteeship, to be used as a site for military bases and the stationing of reserve forces. On 21 August, responding to FO inquiries, the Joint Planning Staff similarly asserted a strategic imperative for British dominance in Cyrenaica. While the Egypt-Palestine area was the most suitable base for the bulk of British forces, Cyrenaica offered the best alternative site.[27] While Prime Minister Clement Attlee was free to argue the need for a re-evaluation of traditional British policy in the Middle East,[28] there was little value attached to such new approaches within either the military or civilian policymaking bureaucracy.

The reassertion of tried-and-true motifs was exemplified by a Cabinet paper jointly presented by Bevin and George Hall, the Colonial Secretary. Intended to serve as a guide for the British delegation to the upcoming CFM meetings, the policy paper asserted that the colonies had long been a bad investment for Italy and that their loss would not seriously affect the future economic health of the country. Still, given the desire to reintegrate Italy into the orbit of Western Europe, there might be good reasons 'for allowing Italy to retain a direct interest in certain of her colonies, provided that no direct interest of ours is thereby prejudiced and that the reactions of the inhabitants, who will not welcome the restoration of Italian rule, are not so violent as to provoke repercussions liable to threaten our position in the Middle East'. While annexation of any of the colonies was too problematic, Britain should ensure that the territories did not come under the sway of either a potentially hostile nation or a weak trustee unable to maintain order. Collective trusteeships were judged unworkable. None of the colonies was thought capable of self-rule. Hence, the paper advised (1) that Cyrenaica be placed under UN trusteeship with Britain as the trustee – this would be compatible with the wartime pledge to Sayed Idris; and (2) that Tripolitania be placed under a UN trusteeship with Italy as trustee, a system which could avoid 'the dangers inherent in the restoration of unqualified Italian rule'.[29]

However, Italian administration of Tripolitania could well founder on indigenous opposition even if approved by the big powers. Lieutenant Colonel R. J. Elles, a veteran of 16 years' service in the Middle East, protested to Bevin that renewed Italian control would be disastrous for British policy in the region. 'In the first place, Tripolitania is, whatever anyone may say to the contrary, an Arab country. The Italians only occupied it by force of arms, and their hold upon it was purely one of force; they did nothing to foster or encourage Arab progress; they exploited the country and the Arabs to their own advantage; and they were and are hated by the Arabs.' While the British government had made no promises to the Tripolitanians, wrote Elles, 'it has been tacitly assumed by everyone during the 2½ years that we have administered the country' that Italian rule would not be reinstated. There would be armed resistance if that happened. Elles sensibly asked: 'Are British soldiers to be used to enforce Italian occupation of a country which they so recently liberated from the Italians at the price of British lives?'[30]

Lieutenant Colonel Elles' views, while not particularly influential, were much like those already expressed by Brigadier Arundell. In addition, Elles' opinion was soon supplemented by reports from the Cairo office of the British Minister Resident: 'There is little doubt that the question of [the] disposal of Libya is assuming very considerable importance in the eyes of the Arab world and it will be looked on as a test of our intentions to give these smaller countries benefits which they think are secured to them under the United Nations Charter'. From within the Foreign Office, Lord Hood warned, 'This situation is becoming dangerous. Strong feelings in North Africa have been worked up and if an unpopular decision is reached at the Council of Foreign Ministers and made public, we shall have to face the music'.[31]

Such was the blessing and the burden of Britain's position in the Middle East. On the surface, extensive bases and occupation duties reflected the continued assertion of regional hegemony by a robust world power, and it was to such a theme which Molotov pointedly spoke during CFM sessions. However, Britain's grip on Middle East affairs was already fast failing by 11 September 1945 when the Council of Foreign Ministers began its deliberations. American and Soviet leaders intuited the veneer-like character of British claims to predominance in the Mediterranean and preferred to acknowledge England's previous great-power status only through perfunctory courtesies at the end of difficult meetings.

The American State Department had been unable to reach a consensus concerning the Italian colonies. The disagreement, not untypically, arose between the department's Europeanists and its analysts at the pertinent regional desks. In this case, the Office of European Affairs (EUR) and the Office of Near Eastern and African Affairs (NEA) held differing views of US security interests. Assistant Secretary of State James Dunn, who served as Byrnes' deputy throughout the CFM sessions of 1945–46, prepared a memorandum in mid-August which summarized the opposing viewpoints. While NEA favored a UN trusteeship for Libya, EUR preferred a restoration of Italian administration in that and other former colonies. NEA officials, wrote Dunn, believed that Arab leaders throughout the Middle East 'would feel that the retention by Italy of these colonies would be a barrier to the aspirations of the Arab and Moslem peoples to attain independence and to progress from the stage of being subject peoples to responsible communities able to deal with their own affairs'. Analysts within the Office of European Affairs, however, believed it essential to foster stable regimes along the Mediterranean and to guarantee secure access to Middle East oilfields; they felt that both goals could be imperiled by a mixed trusteeship regime in Libya. Dunn himself believed that a collective trusteeship arrangement was 'impracticable and unworkable'. In order to avoid 'having too many important countries projecting their control into territories bordering on the Mediterranean', he preferred to see all three dependencies retained by Italy either as colonies or trusteeships, subject to whatever necessary international restraints or safeguards.[32]

However, with its weak economy, Italy seemed poorly suited to resume such ambitious overseas administrative duties. As John E. Utter, wartime vice-consul in French North Africa, contended:

> A country in the pitiable state of Italy, impoverished and in need of restoring its economy, and protesting loudly that it is unable to pay reparations, is hardly one suited to take on the onerous and expensive responsibilities of non-paying colonies. Holding territories purely for prestige is an obsolete conception and contrary to all of the declarations of the United Nations; therefore the Italians should be made to face the issue and turn their energies to more profitable occupations at home.[33]

This was Byrnes' view. Further, he was unconcerned with shoring up British power in the region and intent rather upon providing the United Nations with an early trusteeship responsibility.[34] After all, what purpose did the new international organization serve if it could not handle low-rent issues and remove them from the agenda of big-power contention? An ambiguous trusteeship arrangement might provide the only basis for multilateral agreement, despite the fact that such planning posed what one British official termed a 'multitude of thorny problems'.[35] Molotov, on the other hand, was less concerned to throw such large bones to the United Nations and instead directed his gaze toward possible advantage in the eastern Mediterranean, where British decline and US disinterest might allow for enhanced Soviet influence. Or at the very least, a bold Soviet claim to a strategic coastal strip in North Africa might generate the requisite contention to create an opening for a favorable compromise on other issues.

THE FIRST SESSION

Delegations from China, France, Great Britain, the Soviet Union and the United States gathered in London for the opening session of the Council of Foreign Ministers.[36] It was soon apparent that, in Europe, the matters of

Trieste and the Italo-Yugoslav frontier would be among the most formidable to resolve. During the fourth and fifth meetings, it became clear that
the fate of Cyrenaica and Tripolitania comprised the nub of the colonial
question. As Byrnes later remarked, the Libyan issues became 'old friends'
to the negotiators.[37] The conferees found themselves, perhaps unexpectedly, facing questions laced with new complications:

1.   If Italy were forced to renounce its colonies, what impact would this
action have upon the Italian electorate – that is, would left-wing or
right-wing forces most profit? Or would popular disappointment with
treaty terms be little reflected in voting patterns?
2.   Despite the foreign ministers' agreement in principle that there
would be trusteeships for the Italian colonies, what kind of arrangements
should be instituted? There were several alternatives, including the
untried expedient of collective administration under the direction of the
UN Trusteeship Council. Should Italy be included in the ranks of the
trustees? The continued association of Rome with control of African
territories, directly or indirectly, might reduce Italian public dismay with
other controversial treaty terms. Yet, the restoration of Italian administration might well produce uprisings in the trusteeship territories and
possibly beyond.
3.   Should the colony of Libya be treated as a single, unified territory or
be divided into two separate administrative areas, with frontier rectifications to the southwest in recognition of French claims? For that matter,
the possible partitions of Eritrea and Italian Somaliland offered even
greater opportunity for imaginative gerrymandering.

The Italian government had voiced its own preferences before the first
CFM session began. American officials were told that a punitive peace
settlement would only hamper efforts to rebuild Italian political democracy
and heighten public unease about Italy's window to the West. Foreign
Minister Alcide de Gasperi argued that the colonies in question predated
the rise of fascist government and thus should not be an issue in the
Council's deliberations. De Gasperi contended that pre-fascist Italy 'never
considered colonies as a tool for imperialism, but rather as a means for
absorbing Italy's surplus manpower'.[38] Therefore, not only was Italian
colonization a virtuous enterprise, but also it was not a product of the
recent and unfortunate aberration in that nation's politico-military affairs.
Hence, Italy's colonial regimes should be restored. Similar representations
were made to other governments participating in the CFM discussions, not
without some effect. Yet, despite US concerns to strengthen pro-Western
sentiment in Italy – to avoid the emergence of a 'new totalitarianism'[39]
– Byrnes was not willing to champion conference proposals which
affirmed Italy's right to retain all of its pre-war colonies. He hoped that
Italian political leaders would be realistic and accept the loss of colonial

possessions as the price for their nation's full admission to post-war Europe.

Secretary Byrnes offered on 14 September a plan for establishing UN trusteeships in all three territories. His proposal stipulated a ten-year administration over a unified Libya, after which the country would become independent. For each colony, the Trusteeship Council would appoint a single administrator, who would be assisted by a seven-member advisory committee.[40] Meeting privately with the Soviet foreign minister, Byrnes argued his case: Arab peoples of the Middle East expected the victorious Allies to honor their wartime statements favoring self-determination; the creation of UN trusteeships would demonstrate to the world that the big powers truly were not seeking self-aggrandizement; and the composition of the advisory committees would ensure that concerned powers had a voice in the governance of the trusteeship territories. However, Molotov preferred having single nations serve as administrators, suggesting that perhaps the Soviet government, with its long experience in managing disparate nationalities, would be a good choice to direct the trusteeship regime in Tripolitania.[41]

Formal presentation of the US proposal came during the fourth meeting of the London session. Byrnes discussed the plan in much the same way as he had earlier with Molotov. Trusteeship and independence for Libya, he said, would 'give heart' to the world's peoples. While the Chinese foreign minister was supportive, the others offered predictable reservations. France, said Georges Bidault, must consider the security of its neighboring colonial territories; nor should Italy suffer confiscation of all its colonies. Bidault suggested that Italy had been a decent colonizer in the pre-fascist period, that the country had provided valuable assistance to the Allies in the latter phase of the war, and that Italy's need for renewed national prestige in the post-war era should be seriously considered. As such, Bidault spoke effectively to the French interest in maintenance of the colonial status quo.

Ernest Bevin, on the other hand, identified British interests with a refurbished status quo, one which accommodated Arab nationalism while retaining control of strategic sites in the Mediterranean and the Near East. As shown during the Levant crisis, only three months earlier, Britain's aims were no longer compatible with the old-style, belligerent imperialism of the past. Bevin therefore held that Italy deserved to lose its colonies and that Cyrenaica and Tripolitania should be administered separately. The conferees must acknowledge, he would frequently say, the British wartime pledge to Sayed Idris. Bevin agreed with Bidault, however, that the signal weakness of the American proposal was its reliance upon a new and untested system of international administration. Molotov then set forth his arguments, as he had earlier to Byrnes, in favor of a Soviet trusteeship over Tripolitania.[42]

When discussion resumed on the next day, at the ministers' fifth formal meeting, Bevin attacked the Soviet proposal and stoutly defended British interests in the region. Since Britain had supported Soviet claims for boundary adjustments in Europe, he expected the Soviets to recognize British interests in North Africa. As summarized in the minutes, Bevin remarked: 'The British claims in that area had been put forward on the same basis as had Russian claims in Eastern Europe, namely security – a perfectly legitimate basis'. Then, despite continuing reservations, Bevin abruptly offered to accept the US trusteeship plan as the basis for further discussions.

Molotov was unmoved. He would continue to press his claim to Tripolitania. He did this, he said, with no intent to impair British security interests; nor, he noted, would the Soviets transplant their Marxist-Leninist system to African soil. Molotov, like Byrnes, defended his proposal with reference to the United Nations Organization. But whereas Byrnes argued that responsibility for collective trusteeships would strengthen the organization, quickly providing the world with persuasive evidence of great-power acquiescence to high principle, Molotov averred that the experiment could easily fail and that an unsuccessful effort to govern the Italian colonies might do much harm to the UN's credibility. Then, as happened with all difficult issues, of which there were many, the ministers agreed to refer the matter to their deputies.[43]

This exchange during the fourth and fifth meetings represented the only substantive discussion of the Italian colonies during the first session of the Council of Foreign Ministers. The differing viewpoints offered little hope for easy reconciliation, though it was a procedural question which ultimately brought the conferees to an impasse and then adjournment on 2 October. The ministers had agreed in principle that trusteeship regimes should be created for the Italian colonies, but they had agreed on little else. Still resentful over recent conflict in the Levant, Bidault remained wary of British motives in North Africa. Bevin was concerned lest Britain incur the continuing costs of military administration in the Italian colonies, bear the burden of Arab protests against unfavorable turns in CFM negotiations, and in the end have gained nothing for its sacrifice. Byrnes wanted the Council to show strong support for the United Nations, but he remained open to new suggestions, preferring that disagreements over the fate of the colonies not disrupt conference consideration of other, more important issues. All three Western foreign ministers were united in opposing a Soviet trusteeship over any African territory.

Within the Foreign Office, a comment by J. G. Ward confirmed that the 'whole object of accepting the American proposal is to avoid putting the Soviet Government in control of an Italian colony'.[44] Given repeated representations from Near East governments in favor of either an Arab trusteeship or independence for Libya, Lord Hood observed that despite any disadvantages it might be preferable to pass the entire matter to the United Nations. 'Here everyone will at least have the satisfaction of expressing their views', he wrote, 'though many of them are bound to be dissatisfied with the results.' As Sayed Idris made clear, Libyan independence was a popular Arab cause.[45]

'The London meeting', noted Patricia Dawson Ward, 'was the first conference in recent memory to end without the usual glowing reports of unity and optimism, much less without a protocol.' Upon returning to Washington following the close of the session, Byrnes was cautious in his public remarks, emphasizing that while slowed, the peace treaty negotiations were not derailed. In recognition of the 'hard reality' that no single country could dictate terms to its allies, Byrnes insisted that he would remain committed to discovering the best 'intelligent compromise'. True, Soviet intransigence had marred the conference. But characterizing the meetings as 'exploratory', Byrnes pointed to many agreements in principle, especially with regard to the Italian treaty. He also reiterated American support for self-determination, for an 'interdependent, democratic world', and for a 'peoples' peace'. He would not allow 'procedural maneuverings' to obscure such fundamental matters and remained hopeful that future talks would achieve greater accord.[46] Yet, even mild-mannered boosterism would be difficult to sustain without an Allied rapprochement; though, to be sure, the divisions were not so serious as to preclude a return to diplomacy.

Privately, the secretary of state was more openly disappointed. A collapse of the Council of Foreign Ministers would nurture little public faith in the mechanics of international diplomacy and the efficacy of his tenure as helmsman of US foreign policy. The root of his problems lay with Molotov, and Byrnes was uncertain about the Soviet mood.[47] During a 16 October meeting with Secretary of the Navy Forrestal and Robert P. Patterson, the new secretary of war, Byrnes claimed that the Soviets wanted Tripolitania as an entrepôt to African uranium fields. According to the meeting minutes: 'Mr. Patterson inquired whether the Russians were really serious with regard to Libya and Mr Byrnes replied emphatically in the affirmative. He said it was the cause of all his troubles'. Instead of representing a forum for co-operation, the Council of Foreign Ministers was well on its way to becoming what Ward has called a 'showcase for Allied division'. However, as one journalist perceived, there was a 'residual reality' which would compel the big powers to resume their discussion.[48]

THE MOSCOW MEETINGS

The Council of Foreign Ministers was able to resume, in modified form, its work on the peace treaties following a Byrnes-Bevin-Molotov session in Moscow in late December 1945. This Christmastime tête-à-tête was a dramatic illustration of the instinctive unilateralism exhibited by the secretary of state: cabling Molotov to schedule a conference of the Big Three foreign ministers before securing the assent of Bevin. The referent for this gathering was Yalta rather than Potsdam, to the wartime *ad hoc* tradition rather than the more formal CFM structure. The Moscow meeting took place outside the Council but was designed to win a reaffirmation of the CFM's appointed task. As Byrnes explained it to British officials, the Moscow discussions were to be exploratory, to provide for a frank exchange; he believed that Molotov would be more 'pliable' on home ground. Byrnes assured British policymakers that he intended to travel to Moscow with or without their participation.[49] Bevin's determination that Britain remain an active partner in post-war planning and his desire for strengthened Anglo-American ties meant that he had little recourse but to accede, however reluctantly, to the meeting.[50]

Once together, the three diplomats ranged wide in surveying the international arena, discussing affairs in China, Iran, Korea and Indonesia. Nevertheless, the key issue was drafting the peace treaties and defining the scope and purpose of the peace conference to follow. Stalin did not lose the opportunity to press again for Tripolitania, but it was the matter of Soviet-Iranian relations which prompted his comment on the role of lesser powers. As reconstructed in an American memorandum, Stalin remarked:

> It is right to respect small nations and to safeguard their independence but the small nations are not always averse to attempting to promote friction between large powers. Some small nations come to the Soviet Government and charge that England and America are strangling and oppressing them. Others go to England and America with similar charges against the Soviet Union. It is necessary to take a skeptical view of such complaints from small nations who are very apt to stir up trouble.[51]

It was not long before the Soviet presence in Iran occupied center stage at the United Nations and became an explosive international drama. But in truth, all three powers tended to ignore or belittle protests from small powers which did not complement broad policy objectives. The Soviets were skeptical of Iranian and Turkish complaints. The British were skeptical of Iraqi and Egyptian complaints. The Americans were skeptical about the complaints of Central American nations. Small powers were, after all, small powers. This simple tautology carried great weight in big-power councils. Yet small powers could be helpful in providing an aura of virtue and legitimacy when properly assembled.

Byrnes' hope for the Moscow conference was that realpolitik and *quid pro quo* diplomacy might yet produce favorable results, that conflicting circles could be temporarily squared. And the meeting did produce an agreement which revived the moribund Council. The conference communiqué affirmed the so-called 4-3-2 Potsdam formula for preparing peace treaties with Germany's allies in Europe, such that the Italian treaty, for example, would be drafted by representatives of Britain, France, the United States and the USSR. Following the Council's approval of draft treaties, a peace conference would be convened, to include the five CFM-member nations as well as 'all members of the United Nations which actively waged war with substantial military force against European enemy states'. The conference would be advisory and could offer recommendations for revision of the draft accords; then those states 'signatory to the terms of armistice' would prepare the final treaty texts.[52] While this agreement effectively excluded China from the second session of the Council and legitimated the Soviet view of the CFM's terms of reference, it did provide for a peace conference of 19 nations (not counting the two USSR republics to be invited) free to discuss and offer advice on any aspect of the treaties. It had never been the intent of the Big Three that hard-fought compromises within the Council of Foreign Minsters would be reversed or rescinded by a vote of the general peace conference; but securing the views of a wider community of nations was at least a glance in the direction of international accountability. Whether it would benefit one power over another remained to be seen. 'The test of a successful peace,' commented Secretary Byrnes, 'is not in the form of its making, but whether it both commends itself to the nations concerned by its justice and wisdom and also commands the support of those nations whose unity is essential to preserve the peace.'[53] With the way thus cleared, the next session of the Council of Foreign Ministers began its formal meetings in Paris on 25 April.

THE SECOND SESSION, PART ONE

The Council reconvened without the deputies having made any meaningful steps toward consensus in the interim months.[54] Nor were the foreign ministers able to make quick progress toward agreement on any of the important issues. An exchange during the fourth meeting, on 29 April, revealed some adjustments regarding the Italian colonies. While Byrnes merely asked for reconsideration of his plan for UN-supervised trusteeships, both Molotov and Bevin offered revised proposals. Molotov suggested that a series of two-power trusteeships be established over the colonies, for a period not to exceed ten years, with Italy sharing administrative authority in each case with another Allied nation. For example, he said, Tripolitania might be assigned a joint Italo-Soviet trusteeship; Cyrenaica might become a joint Italo-American or Italo-British responsibility. However, Bevin countered with a new British position paper, calling for approval of two points: a decision in favor of Italy's renouncing sovereignty over its colonies and a vote in favor of immediate independence for a unified Libya. Both Molotov and Bidault spoke against independence, arguing that the people were unprepared for it. Byrnes predicted that no matter how often the ministers might discuss the issue, they simply would never agree on any method of parcelling out trusteeship responsibility amongst themselves. Ergo, a United Nations regime was the only feasible option.[55]

Several days later, Bidault called upon the American secretary of state and urged that the ministers begin scheduling informal meetings as a means to hasten agreement. Byrnes agreed that this might be useful and then recounted how US public opinion had recently taken a decidedly anti-Soviet turn; this new trend, he advised, would certainly prevent him from accepting concessions to the USSR on any substantive matters.[56] With heightened East-West tension in the spring of 1946, there was little doubt that pessimism reigned at the early gatherings of the second session, often boiling over into angry exchanges. A private meeting of the US and Soviet delegations on 5 May ended with joint tirades.

However, acceptance of the French proposal for a two-track approach – scattering informal discussions amongst the formal meetings – offered a better means for the delegations to measure their capacity for compromise. Yet progress was still slow. At the second informal meeting of the ministers, on 6 May, Brynes proposed that they agree upon Italian renunciation of colonial claims, begin drafting the pertinent treaty article, and designate the CFM as temporary trustee over the colonies while negotiations continued toward a long-range solution. If no accord could be reached after one year, he suggested, then the matter could be referred to the UN Trusteeship Council.[57] While the other three ministers were immediately critical of the idea, Byrnes' plan shortly resurfaced and found broader acceptance. In fact, the secretary's new proposal was not unlike the Foreign Office brief readied for the Potsdam Conference.

On the first anniversary of VE Day, hardly auspicious, James Byrnes pointed out that the Council had made little headway since the previous September. A report by the deputies, made the next day, confirmed his assessment. At the third informal meeting, on 10 May, Molotov indicated that he was willing to drop the Soviet claim to Tripolitania; this was an important concession, he said, and should be so noted. Then Bevin showed renewed interest in a British trusteeship over Cyrenaica, declaring that the Benghazi-Tobruk area had the same symbolic importance to Britain as Stalingrad did for the Soviet Union. Three days later, Byrnes again recommended postponing final consideration of the colonial issue for one year, but again he found no support and the matter was once more referred to the deputies.[58] After several more days of fruitless discussion, the ministers agreed on 16 May to recess until mid-June.

At the same time, information flowing from Libya to the British and US delegations was not encouraging. The British Military Administration (BMA) provided regular evidence of growing nationalist sentiment in Tripolitania. And popular opinion in Cyrenaica was already well known. General Bernard Paget, still commander-in-chief of British forces in the area, reported: 'If [a] decision on this territory involves reinstating Italian control in any part of it we are likely to be compelled to shoot up Arabs in the interests of Italians'. The War Office had previously advised that the BMA did not have the troop strength to handle widespread revolt. John Utter, attached to the US delegation for the CFM, arranged a brief visit to Tripoli in May 1946, and he reported that the entire Libyan population opposed a resumption of Italian rule. He also stressed the certainty of indigenous insurrection following unfavorable CFM action, noting that 'it is a common sight to see the Arabs circulating about town and country with guns slung over their shoulders'. He wrote:

> I firmly believe that some gesture should be made to these people by the conference to show them some consideration, for they as well as the whole Arab world are increasingly sensitive about being treated as inferiors in a cavalier fashion by Europeans. For the maintenance of good relations and the continuation of the high esteem in which the United States is held by Arabs, I feel that we should insist on some tangible demonstration of our convictions in the Atlantic and UN Charters. An arbitrary disposal of Libya will incur not only dissatisfaction among Libyans themselves but also among the entire Arab League.

In the State Department, the chief of the Division of African Affairs told a French diplomat that he feared serious disorders in Libya if Italy returned as administrator. 'It would be a strange situation', he recalled saying, 'if the United Nations had to help Italy keep order in the territory.'[59]

THE SECOND SESSION, PART TWO

The quick resumption of two-track diplomacy revealed new flexibility on the colonial issue. On 20 June, Molotov said that he might be willing to accept the new US proposal if a better agreement continued to elude them. Bevin advised that the suggested one-year's delay must not interfere with the work of the BMAs already installed in each territory.[60] In public and private conversations, the ministers recognized that Trieste and the Italo-Yugoslav border were now the chief stumbling blocks; by comparison, the colonies were no longer a major item of contention. On 26 June,

Molotov stated that he would not press for any change in the current administration of the colonies, though he favored the creation of an advisory council to provide the CFM with detailed reports about popular opinion in the territories. Bevin said that he could accept a study commission of some sort. That would be fine, replied Molotov.[61] On that basis, then, the British delegation prepared a draft treaty article, which was approved in principle during the thirty-third formal meeting, on 3 July. At the same time, the ministers moved quickly toward acceptance of a French proposal for the internationalization of Trieste, voted to convene the general peace conference on 29 July, and worked out a formula for providing Italian reparations to the USSR. The conference adjourned on 12 July.

THE LONG GOOD-BYE

'In retrospect', wrote William Taubman about the CFM sessions, 'all this talking seems a tedious sideshow to the onrushing Cold War.' At various points in the Council's labored dialogue, the participants certainly would have agreed. Molotov, noted Taubman, 'put on a bravura performance'. Patricia Ward likewise cast the Soviet foreign minister as a powerful, often dominant figure at the Council meetings. Yet, Byrnes was also effective during the second session, having learned much from his protracted encounter with the Soviet foreign minister.[62] But the Council's work was not finished in July 1946. Its long second session was followed by the Paris Peace Conference, then additional CFM meetings in December before the anticlimactic signing of the peace treaties in January 1947. In fact, the Council limped into 1947 before it fell full victim to cold war acrimony.

Discussion of the colonial question was essentially complete, however, when the Council adjourned in July. Italy would renounce all claims to its colonies; the territories would remain under British administration; final disposition of the colonies would be made by the four CFM powers within one year of the Italian peace treaty's coming into force. If the Council failed to reach agreement within that year's time, the future status of the colonies would be decided by the United Nations. In better times, the Council of Foreign Ministers would have had the opportunity to work out reasonable and possibly even realistic trusteeship arrangements. But the steely rhetoric of latter 1946 described a deeply divided world and left little room for intelligent compromise.

Initially a gesture toward post-war co-operation among the Grand Allies, the CFM's abortive session in September–October 1945 was not evidence that the gesture lacked meaning – rather that the political environment was fast changing. The Big Three had become the Big Two and a Fraction. The United States and the Soviet Union each had far-reaching aims for the post-war era. Both had filed claims to their respective spheres of influence, and neither was confident of the sincerity of the other. It was a difficult moment – the victors confronting each other across the scourged abyss of Europe, the seared landscape of Hiroshima and Nagasaki, and the rag-tag disorder of the colonial rimlands. The London conference was a false start. The Moscow meeting was a poor substitute for the wartime spirit, but it re-energized the CFM and established a vague but ultimately effective timetable. As well, the current of events and controversies through the first half of 1946 provided an impetus to complete the peace treaties before a complete breakdown in the negotiating process. For the major participants, having imperfect but suitable treaties was better than having none at all.

It may be that the second CFM session represented not only the tediousness of obstinacy and discord, but also a last lingering at the threshold of cold war. In a different day, the British would have received custody of Cyrenaica, Italian administration would have been restored in Tripolitania and likely elsewhere, and other powers would have contented themselves with gains closer to home. But in 1945–46, such comfortable metropolitanism was no longer possible. Additionally, the pace of global controversy forged new attitudes and new policies while the Council of Foreign Ministers struggled with its complex agenda.

Disposition of the Italian colonies was surely more difficult than US policymakers had imagined. There was surprise at Molotov's early insistence upon a Soviet trusteeship for Tripolitania. There was uncertainty created by Byrnes' desire for a unified Libya and a United Nations trusteeship regime. But for Bevin and Bidault, one plan was better than the other. Western leaders interpreted the Soviet proposal as a dangerous leapfrog beyond Turkey, across the Mediterranean, acquiring strategic port facilities and easy propaganda access to millions of colonial subjects – though a Soviet trusteeship sandwiched between the French and British, stretching southward into what de Gaulle called an 'ocean of stones and sand',[63] was less a real threat than a psychological bridgehead. If the Soviet claim were only a negotiating ploy, it was not a very effective one.

James E. Miller has observed that Molotov was able to use Italy 'to break American intrusion' into Eastern Europe. It was sphere for sphere. Increasingly, US plans for a lenient peace treaty, fuelled by the fear of Italian economic collapse, focused on continental Europe. As columnist James Reston had suggested shortly before the start of the first CFM session, the question of Italian colonies was 'essentially one of the relations among the great powers and how they intend to reorganize Europe'.[64] The settlement of colonial claims, if there were to be one, would be a spin-off from the resolution of broader issues. Because Europe represented the main theater of great-power struggle, colonial questions typically comprised a separate field of fire. Yet, in spite of the lengthy period of uncertainty, Cyrenaica and Tripolitania fared much better than other colonies, such as French Indochina or the Netherlands East Indies, where the immediate post-war years marked the beginning of bitter military struggle between native nationalists and colonial armies. While Libya and Italy's other former dependencies became, in a sense, loose change left over from the wartime expenditure – with diplomats turning only intermittently to the matter of their custody – the peoples of the French and Dutch territories in Southeast Asia could have profited from similar neglect. Instead, nationalist movements in Vietnam and on the islands of Java and Sumatra bore the full brunt of tragic but determined efforts to restore dispirited colonial regimes.

5 Struggle in the Rimlands: Southeast Asia, 1945–46

As the Council of Foreign Ministers began discussing the course of post-war Europe, first in London and then later in Paris, the sessions became a prototype for marathon diplomacy which tested the skill and stamina of all participants. The public and private jousting, the jostling and posturing, the numbing task of trying to string together disparate agreements which set boundaries, delimited reparations, redistributed military and economic assets, debated provisional governance, and considered options for colonial trusteeships – all this steadily bled the international forum of credibility and hope. 'Let not us who fought on freedom's side forget how near the shadows we came', said Secretary Byrnes at the Paris Peace Conference. 'We must never accept any disagreement as final.' Only through 'great co-operative effort', he said, could the nations assembled stamp out the virus of 'militant totalitarian nationalism', a stubborn organism which could still breed in a culture of 'famine, disease, and social disruption'.[1] Such phrases, while sonorous, played to inattentive heads by the time they were spoken in the summer of 1946. Who, after all, had fought on freedom's side? Surely not everyone. Was one totalitarian dictatorship as systemically distorted and dangerous as another? Was one capitalist system as exploitative, grasping and hegemonic as another? Disputes and stereotypes multiplied exponentially: naive Americans, weary and cynical Europeans, machine-like Soviet *apparatchiks*. Then came the metamorphosis: tough, newly street-smart Americans shoulder to shoulder with Western European allies who had sloughed off their existential despair. They stood together against the inscrutable 'Red Octopus'[2] which probed in all directions, reaching out its searing tentacles to grab hold of the lifeblood of democratic societies. Less cosmic problems proliferated also: bad weather, snarled finances, glacial self-doubt – with England and France caught between the two Goliaths of an unschooled yet crusading spirit.

By its final meetings, the Council of Foreign Ministers had become the new yardstick of deteriorating Soviet-American or, more broadly, East-West relations. It was a cliché, of course: victory did not bring peace. It brought instead new, durable intangibles to augment older conundrums. Obviously, there was going to be, as General Thomas T. Handy noted, 'a period of unsettlement and readjustment before the return of peaceful and orderly existence'. Or, as Secretary of War Patterson remarked, since it was inevitable that wartime decisions and strategies would be re-examined once the Axis powers were defeated, the military establishment should

117

expect 'to take a certain amount of post war banging around'.[3] Writ larger, there was quite a bit of post-war banging around yet to be concluded in the autumn of 1945, certainly in Europe but also in the Far East, where the Southeast Asia Command began its mopping up activities to secure the safe release of POWs and civilian internees and ensure the full capitulation of Japanese troops.

On 6 October 1945, General William J. Slim, commander-in-chief of Allied Land Forces in Southeast Asia, offered his analysis of what had become a major problem for SEAC as it carried out its reoccupation chores – nationalist ferment in both Indochina and the Netherlands East Indies. The situation in each colony, he wrote, was essentially the same, including the following common factors:

1. large colonies captured by Japanese forces 'after a very poor effort at defence by the responsible European power, with [the] resulting collapse of European prestige';
2. pre-war nationalist movements which further encouraged by the Japanese had 'increased in militant strength immeasurably . . . and which now . . . can with reason claim to be the only de facto government';
3. the fact that local nationalists were well armed, with considerable forces at their disposal;
4. the fact that most French and Dutch officials and resident Europeans did not realize 'the changed world attitude towards Colonial nationalism' and remained ignorant of the 'great local changes' which had taken place;
5. the presence of large Japanese armies throughout the territories which had yet to be disarmed;
6. the fact that no French or Dutch military forces 'of any real value or strength' were yet available for reoccupation duties, with little likelihood, because of logistical difficulties, of any soon arriving.

Already, there had been clashes between British troops and native nationalists, with casualties on both sides. More casualties would inevitably result from any effort to expand the limited zones of English control. SEAC was relying heavily upon Japanese troops to maintain order in both colonies; however, Slim advised that this policy offered 'many grave disadvantages'. To begin with, 'we cannot disarm the Japanese forces and have no prospect of doing so for a very considerable time, even if, as I think they would do, they are willing to disarm themselves'. Even in the areas patrolled by the Japanese, contended Slim, there remained little sense of personal security – which meant that SEAC simultaneously failed to provide adequate order and earned 'the opprobrium of the local inhabitants and to some extent of our Allies for employing the Japanese at all'. Another serious problem was the possibility that 'irresponsible French or Dutch elements' might provoke a large-scale native uprising resulting in great loss of civilian life and posing a threat to British forces as well. 'Should such a situation arise it would be extremely difficult to [for?] us to find in time either the reinforcements necessary or the shipping to carry them.'

General Slim then pointed to the difficulty which had dogged SEAC through its first month of reoccupation duties: ambiguous instructions about the purpose of its mission. 'Originally I understood that the main object was to disarm the Japanese and evacuate our prisoners without getting in anyway involved against nationalistic forces or movements. ... At the same time, we were to work in the closest accord with Dutch and French authorities and to make them responsible for the general internal security.' This strategy rested upon British forces holding only certain key areas, with French or Dutch forces controlling the remaining territory. But the small number of British troops in Southeast Asia, plus the lack of other effective European forces, required reliance upon Japanese units. Allowing French or Dutch colonial forces to go into action on their own would almost surely provoke widespread violence. If SEAC became responsible for internal security throughout Java, warned Slim, 'It should be understood that this means either that we co-operate with the only existing government, the Indonesian Republic, or we overthrow it and replace it'. In fact, he advised, the British could not hope to control more than the 'smallest areas'.

SEAC operations thus far, noted Slim, had alienated both sides: first the Vietnamese and Indonesians 'because we are regarded as re-imposing on them French and Dutch rule which they had already shaken off', and, secondly, French and Dutch authorities who expected the British more quickly and resolutely to restore full European sovereignty. 'The real and underlying danger is that the situation may develop so that it can be represented as a West versus East set-up.' Hence, Slim recommended that Britain 'hand over' the colonies to France and the Netherlands as soon as possible and then remove both areas from the Southeast Asia Command. He further advised: 'In order to enable us to tide over the period between now and the arrival of French and Dutch forces, every means should be used to impress on the, I fear, somewhat unrealistic Governments of France and Holland, the need for conciliation and for the honest offer of a reasonable measure of Self-Government.' Overall, wrote Slim, it was a 'rather confused situation ... frought [*sic*] with great danger'.[4]

General Slim's letter effectively capsuled the complex correlation of political and military forces which confronted Mountbatten's command as the initial fly-in of Indian troops to Saigon and Batavia began in mid-September 1945. The Combined Chiefs of Staff had given SEAC the task for which it was designed (in addition to killing Japanese soldiers): to provide a base for the resurgence of British power in the region and, to whatever extent possible, to assist France and the Netherlands in recovering their colonial territories. Informal memorandums were presented by the Foreign Office to the French and Dutch embassies in London on 14 August 1945. SEAC forces, it was announced, intended to secure only as much of the Saigon area as was necessary to ensure full control of the Japanese regional headquarters. 'So far as the rest of Indo-China is concerned, we suggest that as soon as the necessary French forces are available arrangements should be made to recognize Indo-China as a French military theatre and that every endeavor should be made to move French forces to the Far East for this purpose.' A civil affairs agreement would be drafted in short order so that French administrative control could be reasserted. Similarly, Mountbatten would order forces to Java to initiate RAPWI activity and to prepare the way for the restoration of Dutch civil administration. The primary function of SEAC commanders, nevertheless, was to manage the disarming of Japanese armies and advance the RAPWI effort.[5]

Upon their entrance into Saigon and Batavia, however, British forces were not stepping into a political vacuum. As Slim's letter acknowledged, indigenous nationalists had used their month's respite from external control to proclaim independent republics and establish bare-bones government ministries exercising authority over much of Vietnam and Java. The nationalists' task was twofold: (1) to convince Allied representatives that native regimes could and would protect life, property and the pursuit of public order, and (2) to demonstrate, somewhat paradoxically, that refusing to treat with them would result in widespread disorder and destruction. The Democratic Republic of Vietnam (DRV), formally proclaimed on 2 September and dominated by leftist Viet Minh leaders, had to contend with two occupying armies presenting two separate challenges: the need to discourage an extended Chinese occupation in the north and the need to win recognition from SEAC officers in Saigon. Unfortunately for Ho Chi Minh, the DRV administration in Saigon was weak, consisting of a city-wide committee buffetted by internal bickering, lacking the closer-knit cadre spirit of Tonkin Province. The British reoccupation army was commanded by Major General Douglas D. Gracey, a longtime colonial officer who had been with the 20th Indian Division since 1943. Elements of this division began arriving in Saigon on 11 September; and it was General Gracey who soon bore responsibility for gaining Japanese acquiescence to SEAC authority, for beginning the process of disarming and repatriating enemy troops, and for making crucial decisions about the legitimacy of local Viet Minh governance.

THE SEAC SAIGON MISSION

The city of Saigon was bedecked with Viet Minh and Allied flags. Banners written in English, draped on buildings or across the streets, proclaimed 'Down with French Imperialism', 'Independence or Death', and 'Welcome to the Allies'. Saigon was a deeply divided, polarized city: an imperial outpost of tree-lined streets filled with French shops, planted amidst peasant villages and dense jungle – redolent of fear, grief, hatred, outrage and violence. To the small OSS advance party which flew in at the beginning of September, Saigon was a confusing montage, alternately orderly and chaotic. The immediate task was to select a headquarters and begin preparing American POWs for evacuation. This was Operation EMBANKMENT, set up to reconnoiter the surrounding territory, gather information on the political-economic situation, and record evidence for possible war crimes trials as well as handling the release of captive Americans.[6]

Following a proper, courteous reception at the airstrip, Lieutenant Emile R. Counasse and his group were driven in Japanese staff cars to the Continental Palace Hotel in downtown Saigon. They were greeted there by enthusiastic French residents. 'Everyone crowded around us, trying to be the first one to touch the American flags we had on the backs of our jackets'. Despite the bedlam, the group snatched several hours' sleep; then, the lieutenant and others drove to a nearby POW compound for a preliminary survey of camp conditions. Returning to the hotel in the afternoon of 2 September, Counasse found in progress a street demonstration by thousands of Vietnamese. He reported that many participants were armed 'after a fashion' with Japanese swords, pistols and rifles, also with old flintlock shotguns' and 'long bamboo poles sharpened on one end'. Processions blocked all the main thoroughfares. By late in the day, 'the demonstration had turned into a violent mob scene. Shooting could be heard in all sections of the city'. Each side blamed the other for first blood. Counasse feared that the disorder would engulf the hotel, where hundreds of panic-stricken Frenchmen and their families had come for refuge. The lieutenant requested Japanese assistance, and troops shortly arrived to ring the hotel and its annexes.

The next day, Counasse encountered numerous Vietnamese-manned roadblocks as he attempted to visit additional American prisoners quartered outside the city. Treated roughly and held for two hours at one checkpoint, Counasse described his captors as 'a mob of savage barbarians, screaming at the top of their lungs'. Machineguns were placed at the hotel entrance that evening. It was an explosive situation. Long pent-up anger at French colonial rule seemed dangerously close to boiling over into wholesale anti-white violence. Germaine Krull, a French journalist, reported: 'I . . . had the strong impression of being in a city where I and my kind were detested. . . . [The Vietnamese] did not know whether I was French or English, but their reaction was not very encouraging. Not a smile, not a friendly glance anywhere'. In effect, a guerrilla army was

forming in and around Saigon – half-planned, half-spontaneously – without
the kind of discipline so evident in Hanoi. As one OSS sergeant put it,
Americans in Saigon found themselves in the middle of a 'drugstore
revolution'.[7] OSS personnel in Hanoi, whether or not they favored the
Viet Minh, could not dismiss the Tonkin regime as easily.

The main party for Operation EMBANKMENT arrived during 4–5 Septem
ber, commanded by Major A. Peter Dewey. The group included two able
officers who provided many of the most useful reports to emerge during the
final months of US intelligence activity in Southeast Asia: Captain Frank
M. White, Jr., and Captain Herbert J. Bluechel. Similarly, advance parties
of British personnel and French military and civilian officials arrived in
the city and set up their independent staffs. Jean Cédile was the desig
nated French commissioner for the southern province of Cochinchina,
having parachuted into the Saigon area in late August. It was Cédile
who would work closely with General Gracey, seeking to limit and
eventually subvert the political power of the local Vietnamese administra
tion. Initially, however, he floundered in the confusion of the city, with
little staff support, telling Krull: 'How can I tell what is true and what
isn't? People come to me all day long with various tales of an Annamite
uprising here or a plot there. These rumors are almost impossible to
confirm with the [French] population so undisciplined and in such a state of
panic'.[8]

What were the British going to do in the SEAC zone south of the 16th
parallel? How strong was their commitment to restore French rule over the
territory? Lord Mountbatten received orders from the British Chiefs of
Staff on 12 September 'that my authority, responsibility, and activities in
F.I.C. were strictly limited and temporary. This policy would have been
welcome if French forces had been on hand for supporting French
responsibilities; but adequate French forces, which had been promised to
me at Potsdam, were not yet available'. In fact, the only French force in
Asia, other than the troops interned by the Japanese or those which had
escaped to China, was the 5th Régiment d'Infanterie Coloniale (formerly
the Corps Léger d'Intervention) stationed on Ceylon. Consisting of only
about 1000 men, the 5th RIC could not by itself begin re-imposing French
rule in the southern countryside of Vietnam. Thus, General Gracey,
arriving in Saigon on 13 September, was left with the dilemma outlined by
Esler Dening, SEAC political adviser: effective implementation of the
RAPWI program required the maintenance of law and order; if the local
population were not co-operative, the only recourse was British military
action again dissident groups.[9] Dening might have added that the Vietna
mese would only be co-operative if they were convinced that the British
were not intent upon re-establishing colonial rule. Yet, the British govern
ment had already committed itself to the earliest possible return of
European dominance in Southeast Asia. Meanwhile, Japanese troops

remained armed and charged with police duties. John C. Sterndale Bennett, head of the Far Eastern Department, perceived that a conflict of one sort or another could hardly be avoided.

If the British forces endeavor to suppress anti-French activities on the part of the Vietnam party [that is, Viet Minh] or other groups we shall open ourselves to attacks from American anti-Imperialist opinion and no doubt from the Chinese, whereas a policy of complete non-intervention in domestic affairs will no doubt be interpreted by the French as a further step towards our alleged long-term objective of pushing them out of their colonial territories. ... Unfortunately it is probably true that the degree of difficulty which the French will experience in re-assuming control in Southern Indo-China will largely depend on the attitude which the British forces now adopt.[10]

Six days in Saigon convinced General Gracey that the Vietnamese administration 'constituted a direct threat to law and order' through its limited armed forces and its strongly anti-French press. On 19 September, Gracey informed Vietnamese officials that he was suspending publication of all Saigon-area newspapers and ordering all native police and other armed groups to remain in their barracks. On 21 September, he ordered a proclamation to be posted which prohibited all public demonstrations and meetings, forbade the carrying of weapons of any type, including the ubiquitous bamboo spears, 'except by British and Allied troops and such other forces and police which have been authorized by me'. Moreover, Gracey phrased the proclamation such that it apparently stretched British peacekeeping responsibilities to cover all of Indochina south of the 16th parallel. In his report to Mountbatten, Gracey explained: 'I would stress that though it may appear that I have interfered in the politics of the country I have done so only in the interests of maintenance of law and order and after close collaboration with senior French representatives'.[11]

Although Gracey had issued the proclamation on his own authority, Mountbatten advised the Chiefs of Staff that his subordinate 'acted with courage and determination in an extremely difficult situation together with as yet inadequate forces'. Fearing widespread riots, Gracey had chosen pre-emptive measures. However, Mountbatten did not favor SEAC becoming the guarantor for order throughout southern Vietnam; rather, he preferred limiting British authority to the Japanese Southern Army Headquarters. General Jacques Philippe Leclerc remained unwilling officially to assume jurisdiction over any territory until the equivalent of a division of French troops had been transported to the theater.[12]

Events in the field were soon again the locomotive of SEAC policymaking as General Gracey armed troops of the French 11th RIC – interned in their barracks since March – and allowed them to take over the Saigon government, roughly ejecting the Viet Minh from their offices during the early morning hours of 23 September. Anxiety about Vietnamese-initiated violence had been pervasive among the European residents; but now, what Germaine Krull described as an 'undisciplined horde' of angry French soldiers went on their own rampage through the city. She wrote: 'That night ... was the beginning of a ruthless war. Instead of regaining our prestige we had lost it forever, and, worse still, we had lost the trust of the few remaining Annamites who believed in us. We had showed them that the new France was even more to be feared than the old one'.[13]

Saigon thus became the seat of French efforts to renew their power in the region. As Peter Dennis has written, the coup was deceptively quick and easy. But Gracey's actions had enlarged the scope of British political-military responsibility while at the same time exacerbating the reigning mood of tension and fear. Gunfire spread throughout the city. Gracey had missed his chance to build a co-operative relationship with the Viet Minh, wrote Dennis. 'After the coup it was too late: Viet Minh distrust of British and French motives was irreversibly reinforced by Gracey's installation of the French and by his evident inability or unwillingness to restrain their excesses and brutality.'[14] Leaving Saigon on the 25th, Krull saw a city in flames. OSS agents reported 'that the Annamese were evacuating Saigon by the thousands. The city was without food, regular water supply, or electricity'. Vietnamese sought to isolate the city's residents, setting up hundreds more roadblocks.[15] Military posts and headquarters were attacked; sniping was constant. General Gracey issued instructions forbidding the display of national flags on all vehicles but his own. On 26 September, Major Dewey and Captain Bluechel, driving their jeep around a roadblock near the OSS house on Rue Paul Blanchy, were ambushed. Dewey was killed instantly. Grenades exploding, bursts from machineguns and the persistent crack of riflefire became the common nightsounds of Saigon. It was the language of empowerment for the colonial masses, and this guerrilla *lingua franca* did not recognize facile distinctions between Western flags. As columnist Arthur Krock commented, Dewey was 'one of the first American casualties in the bodeful era of peace-making that has released passions as violent as those of war'.[16]

Yet, Captain Bluechel continued to believe that Vietnamese viewed Americans as 'a separate people' – a people who were unlike Europeans in their attitude toward empire. 'The Viet Minh leaders were especially desirous of gaining our friendship', he wrote, 'and often expressed the hope that we would sponsor their bid for independence and thereby force the French to yield.' Bluechel was convinced that Dewey had been killed because he was mistaken for a Frenchman – had the jeep been flying the US flag, the 'shots would not have been fired'. Major Francis M. Small, however, disagreed. Anti-French sentiment was very strong, and the Vietnamese had come greatly to 'resent the British protection of French interests and inasmuch as the American military in Saigon regularly attend

British staff meetings, it is quite likely that the Annamese infer that the United States tacitly approves the British policy'. In the field, wrote Small, Vietnamese guerrillas did not distinguish between American and European soldiers. 'The road block and the machine gun emplacement appear to have been arranged with the intention of shooting at the next white man that came by.'[17]

Major Small would have agreed with Germaine Krull that General Gracey bore much of the blame for the spiralling violence in the aftermath of the Saigon coup. Gracey, observed Small, had blundered; his mishandling of the situation 'was the greatest single immediate contribution to the intensification of Annamese animosity toward all whites in Saigon'. Krull identified a greater, more emotive turn of the screw: 'Everything which happened thereafter can be directly traced to that date – women captured and mistreated, men and children assassinated, Dutch, English and American officers killed, shooting, burning factories, mysterious disappearances, all these and more happened'.[18]

If Krull's account was too apocalyptic, there was nonetheless rising pessimism among American and some British observers. Dening wrote to the Foreign Office: 'The clouds are rolling up in the Far East and I think that there is a very serious danger of the West being regarded as aligning itself against the East with incalculable consequences for the future'. British forces could not possibly suppress political unrest throughout the region. 'It follows from this that if we are to avoid trouble full sovereignty should be resumed in French Indochina and N.E.I. [Netherlands East Indies] as soon as possible.'[19] Here was the obvious solution: to get out and give the French and Dutch free rein to behave as well or as stupidly as they dared; but the 9th Régiment d'Infanterie Coloniale was not scheduled to arrive from the Mediterranean until the end of the year. The need to speed up the transport of French troops to Indochina clashed with another priority program: Operation PYTHON, the repatriation of British soldiers who had served long years in the Far East. As the Joint Staff Planning Committee noted, 'The effects of diverting British personnel shipping to accelerate the move [of French forces] at highest priority are unacceptable under existing Government priorities'. Ergo, the 20th Indian Division must remain the chief occupation army in Vietnam for several months. The joint planners suggested a strategy of securing the greater Saigon area and relying upon smaller forces, perhaps some of them French, for law and order in the remainder of the southern zone.[20] This was not good news for Mountbatten. Unrest continued in Vietnam and other occupied areas; there was growing public opposition in India to the use of Indian military forces for occupation duty in Southeast Asia; and the supreme commander would have to continue to deploy Japanese troops to maintain order. 'This means', he wrote, 'that I cannot begin to disarm them for another 3 months. By that time prisoners of war and internees will all have been removed and since it will be obvious that we could physically have disarmed the Japanese long before the end of December we shall have a less and less good excuse for retaining British/Indian forces here. In fact we shall find it hard to counter the accusations that our forces are remaining in the country solely in order to hold the Viet Namh Independence movement in check.'[21]

On 28 September, John Vincent, head of the Office of Far Eastern Affairs, proposed to his State Department colleagues that the US government sponsor a joint Allied investigative commission to look into Indochina affairs. Several days later, he reminded Under-Secretary Dean Acheson that the Vietnam situation had not improved appreciably since the Saigon coup. Abbot Moffat, head of the Division of Southeast Asian Affairs, added, 'Conditions in Indochina are very critical with the danger of a nationalist explosion which would have serious repercussions in all southeastern Asia'. He cited problems in the East Indies as well. However, the department's Europeanists were not so alarmed. H. Freeman Matthews, director of the Office of European Affairs, rejected Vincent's idea: 'I do not favor the proposed American initiative *at this time*. I should prefer to wait and see how the British and French work this out – at least until conditions grow worse'. Acheson agreed. James C. H. Bonbright, assistant chief of the Division of Western European Affairs, did not believe things would get much worse; further, he argued that the findings of such an investigative commission might well lend support to the 'ejection' of the French from the colony. The British 'are the ones who have the bear by the tail', Bonbright commented; if they wanted American help they could ask for it.[22]

For the department's European experts, US initiatives in colonial areas, such as Southeast Asia, were unnecessary intrusions into affairs which did not directly concern the American government. John F. Cady, an OSS analyst transferred to the newly created Division of Southeast Asian Affairs in the spring of 1945, later remarked that he and others of similar interests and expertise 'learned quickly that the Foreign Officer elite within the State Department were far more interested in preserving the European balance of power than in satisfying the nationalist aspirations of Southeast Asian peoples'. Or as John Hickerson, deputy to Matthews, said in an interview in 1979: 'Indochina was not in my consciousness at all at that time. I had other things to worry about'.[23]

While Mountbatten's reports made clear that nationalist resistance continued to be strong in some areas north of Saigon through October,[24] the British position was much eased by the arrival of additional Indian troops as well as the debarking of the French 5th RIC from the warship *Richelieu*. General Leclerc came to Saigon, and French units began to share in the task of pacification. On 9 October, an Anglo-French civil affairs accord, signed in London, provided the basis for the restoration of

French colonial rule. By the end of October, Admiral Georges d'Argen-lieu, recently appointed high commissioner for the colony, had reached Indochina and begun assembling his administrative staff. With Gracey's help, the French had made impressive strides toward reasserting their dominance in the south. In Tonkin Province, however, the Viet Minh remained a cohesive organization, led by a charismatic figure whose pragmatism and skillful diplomacy continued to leaven the more doctrinaire revolutionary-nationalist ethos of the movement. But the Democratic Republic of Vietnam had yet to receive international recognition, and the coming of the Chinese occupation army in early September offered at best a temporary shield from the kind of French intrigue which had advanced so quickly under SEAC auspices. Further, the Chinese posed dangers as well, descending upon a Vietnamese economy crippled by war-induced scarcity.[25]

In Hanoi, American OSS officers did not confront the same administrative disorder which prevailed in Saigon; also, they were in frequent contact with Ho Chi Minh and other authoritative DRV officials. The city was a colorful sea of Viet Minh flags and the usual spray of anti-French, pro-Allied banners. American soldiers were honored guests at the 2 September creation of the republic. Red dust hung in the air through the autumn, kicked up by the many marching feet of Viet Minh-organized processions and demonstrations. Arthur Hale, visiting for the US Information Service in October, reported that the DRV leadership 'wanted above all to ... prove itself mature and capable' to the Western world. Hale noted that many of the Vietnamese government workers were young and inexperienced. 'Yet, to an American observer, the freshness and hopefulness of the Annamite government and its people, the good faith behind its program for democratic self-government, make a welcome contrast with the rather effete, narrow and uncompromising attitude of the French population and official representation.' While there was obviously 'considerable' communist influence within the Viet Minh, Hale advised that there was 'ample evidence of an equally strong influence from the United States. The American experience in the Philippines has been brought to the people, down to the smallest village, by radio and newspaper'.[26]

Hale, like many others, noted the special friendship shown to American soldiers by the Vietnamese. The OSS city team for Hanoi, headed by Major Archimedes Patti, found a ready welcome from DRV officials, who actively though unsuccessfully sought a direct channel to US policymakers through such military missions. Along with Patti had come Jean Sainteny, commissioner-designate for Tonkin, who informally opened Franco-DRV discussions in late August. His first meeting with Ho came in mid-October, in the wake of the Saigon-area fighting. But Ho much preferred talking with Americans, whom he consistently told the same thing: that his demands were few; that he simply wanted independence, for which he was

willing to negotiate with the French; and that the Vietnamese had a long
history of resistance to occupiers and would fight to the death to be free.
He made no specific requests of the United States, except that it honor the
commitment to dependent peoples in the Atlantic Charter and show
goodwill toward Vietnamese nationalists. He frequently mentioned that an
independent Vietnam would look to the United States as a natural source
for investment capital and technical expertise.[27] But as Ho and Patti and
others spun benign scenarios in the charged atmosphere of post-war
Hanoi, the military power of the French continued to grow. First, though,
French authorities would have to deal with the Chinese, who showed every
sign of settling in with their 50 000-man occupation army.

THE SEAC BATAVIA MISSION

In a memorandum of 3 March 1943, S. Dillon Ripley – one of the first OSS
operatives sent to organize an intelligence network in Southeast Asia –
bemoaned the Allied failure to gather information about the situation in
the enemy-occupied Netherlands East Indies. It had been about a year
since the Japanese crushed the Dutch colonial army and subsequently
began to intern virtually the islands' entire European population. Ripley
remarked:

> We do not know the attitude of the Indonesians, not only towards the
> Japanese as conquerors, but also towards possible resistance. The only
> scrap of information about Indonesian public opinion is the fact that
> Soekarno and Mohammed Hatta, two well-known anti-Dutch Indone-
> sian nationalists, have both recently made pro-Japanese speeches. It is
> obviously difficult under present conditions to estimate the significance
> of those speeches.

Dutch efforts to leave behind a few special agents, with radio sets, had not
proven successful.[28] Seven months later, Ripley reported that few Dutch
officials were co-operative, and most were 'suspicious of an American
organization attempting to muscle in on their British-Dutch set-up [within
SEAC]'. The Dutch intended to use their own personnel to spearhead
special operations within their colony. 'This would all be very well', wrote
Ripley, 'if the Dutch could really run such an [intelligence] organization;
but I am afraid that they do not have the proper number of qualified Dutch
people.' Nor were the British moving quickly on any NEI infiltration
scheme. Thus, Ripley argued 'that it is up to [the] OSS to stand on its own
legs'. He envisioned an OSS office in Colombo, working in tandem with
but independent of British and Dutch agencies within the new Southeast
Asia Command.[29]

The OSS role within SEAC was never as secure as initially envisioned, and the rivalry between US and British intelligence agencies in Southeast Asia undercut the effectiveness of both. Still, OSS operatives were a source of valuable intelligence for much of the SEAC theater by war's end, and staff officers frequently portrayed themselves as looking out for America's interests on a far rim of the world – an area in which the United States would presumably want to be much more influential than during the pre-war years. However, no one seemed to know quite what was happening on the most populous East Indies islands of Java and Sumatra. OSS reports from French Indochina, for example, described widespread anti-French sentiment throughout the Vietnamese peasantry. No equivalent information was available from Dutch territories.

Pre-war analyses of the native population on Java and Sumatra had emphasized pervasive political immaturity and apathy. Thus, Walter A. Foote, the most experienced US diplomatic observer in Batavia during the 1930s, prepared a January 1944 report for General Douglas MacArthur which asserted that Indonesians remained little interested in politics. 'This is easily understood', he wrote, 'when it is realized that the natives of the East Indies, practically without exception, are polite, mild, docile, friendly, and possess a sense of humor somewhat akin to our own.' Indonesians' main interests in life, observed Foote, were simple: family, rice growing, raising a few chickens, 'a bamboo hut in a garden of banana and cocoanut trees', and an occasional movie, preferably an American 'Western'.[30] They hardly seemed a troublesome breed. Much the same thinking was reflected in an OSS Research and Analysis Branch profile of the East Indies situation in mid-August 1945. One report, titled 'Problems Arising from a Sudden Liberation of NEI', accurately pointed out that the Dutch could not restore their control over the archipelago without the co-operation of the native peoples. However, the authors then advised:

> It may be assumed that the general masses of Indonesians, who have come to hate the Japanese and who have suffered under them severe economic privations and restrictions, will welcome the prospects of greater stability and of better economic conditions under the returning NEI authorities. . . . It is not likely that at a time of transition and tense anticipation they will easily be persuaded to rally around leaders with exciting slogans who might try to whip them up to resistance.[31]

In fact, many Indonesians had indeed suffered severe privations during the Japanese occupation, such as those who endured forced labor or went hungry because of war-related distortions of the native economy. But the characteristic Indonesian response to the defeat of Netherlands forces in March 1942 had been one of elation. The Japanese, espousing 'Asia for Asians', announced the liberation of NEI from a malevolent West. 'The grasp of Europe was released', wrote Theodore Friend. 'Indonesians and Japanese shared a vision of triumph.'[32] Throughout much of the war, the leading native nationalists directly or indirectly collaborated with Japanese occupation authorities in the hopes of receiving genuine independence – or, failing that, with the intent to expand the mass base of their nationalist movement. For Javanese and Sumatrans, the Japanese offered an opportunity to short-circuit what the Dutch clearly intended to be a long-winded overlordship.

Freed by the conquering Japanese from their Dutch-imposed exile, the three most popular nationalist leaders – Sukarno, Mohammed Hatta and Sutan Sjahrir – reappeared in Java. Sukarno was the most charismatic of the three men and greatly widened his personal appeal through full co-operation with the occupation regime; Hatta was less enthusiastic but nonetheless saw distinct advantages to be gained through collaboration. Sjahrir disdained embracing the Japanese program; but he maintained his contacts with the other nationalists, and together during the war years they lobbied the Tokyo government for a grant of independence. Yet, Japanese political concessions to native nationalists in Southeast Asia were largely a product of military exigencies. 'Demands for independence by Indonesian nationalists were therefore hedged with Japanese equivocation', noted Joyce C. Lebra, 'attempting to sustain Indonesian hopes without ever granting them in substance.'[33]

Hence, a pre-surrender Japanese grant of political independence was not the chief legacy of the occupation. Instead, the more significant imprint for the post-war confrontation of colonizer and colonized lay in the training by Japanese military officers of Indonesian auxiliary forces. There were several paramilitary organizations established during the occupation, designed always to augment rather than to substitute for Japanese resistance to an Allied invasion. Last-minute, desperate training of such forces in 1945 even included the organization of local militias armed primarily with bamboo spears. But most important was the paramilitary group known as *Pembela Tanah Air*, Defenders of the Fatherland, abbreviated *Peta*. It remained an auxiliary force, never used by the Japanese; yet, by August 1945, Peta's more than 30 000 members were equipped with rifles and mortars, had ample ammunition, and were trained in guerrilla warfare tactics. Lebra pointed to this guerrilla training as the tool which gave Peta its revolutionary capability. Or as another historian put it, forces like Peta 'gave back to the Javanese the rudiments of what the Dutch had taken away: militant self-assertion and military capacity'.[34] In French Indochina, by contrast, revolutionary capability had been developed independent of and in opposition to the Japanese, pulled through the eye of the Viet Minh needle.

In Australia, Ceylon and London, Netherlands authorities were unable to develop effective intelligence-gathering operations during the war years and thus remained ignorant of the new burst of mass nationalism in Java and Sumatra. American and British planners tended also to assume that the native population had become so displeased with the Japanese that Allied armies would be welcomed as liberators. Western observers failed to realize that Japan's surrender was for Indonesians, as a former vice-consul put it, 'the beginning of *their* war and the end of a foreign war'. And further, most American policymakers believed that the Netherlands East Indies represented the kind of liberal colonialism which the United States intended to champion in the post-war era. As Stanley K. Hornbeck, a State Department Far Eastern expert, remarked: 'The Dutch gave to a vast group of scattered islands a political integration; they established throughout that area conditions of law, order and internal peace; they developed the area economically; they set its peoples on the roadway of social and political progress'. While no imperial regime was perfect in every way, Dutch authorities were credited with working steadily toward a better, more just colonial society. 'The United States is not the only country whose people have come to look with disapproval on the practices of the *old* imperialism', concluded Hornbeck.[35] In fact, the Dutch government-in-exile had negotiated in 1944 an agreement with Mac-Arthur's Southwest Pacific Area Command to exercise civil authority in the East Indies territory under US jurisdiction, most notably Java. For this reason, the shift of Java to SEAC after the Potsdam Conference was disappointing to the Dutch, despite their negotiating a similar arrangement with the British in September 1945.[36] Britain, of course, represented an imperial rival in Southeast Asia; and undoubtedly, SEAC did not have the military resources of MacArthur's command.

Dutch officials, both military and civilian, firmly believed that the close relationship between metropole and colony must continue well into the post-war period. Access to the raw materials and agricultural output of Java and Sumatra, which comprised 80 per cent of NEI exports, would be vital to Holland's economic recovery and reconstruction – and important further as a source of Dutch pride and sense of historical continuity.[37] Also of interest to Netherlands officials was the matter of Indonesian collaboration with the Japanese. In Europe, typically, collaborationists were not rewarded for their wartime activity. The bogy of Japan's lingering influence could conceivably be used to discredit such leading nationalist figures as Sukarno and Hatta. But it was not clear in late 1945, to either the French or Dutch, whether American audiences would respond better to accusations that Asian nationalists were Japanese stooges or to charges that they were communist dupes. Usually, to be safe, both allegations were made. The idea that nationalist groups were somehow alien-spawned was a convenient means to disparage mass movements whose tactics did not match Western expectations.

An OSS study issued in late August speculated that the Dutch decision to rely upon Japanese troops to maintain order until the arrival of Allied forces would lead to further loss of prestige for Europeans. Yet, there was little alternative, given that Java and Sumatra were last on the SEAC priority list. The new governor-general for NEI, Hubertus J. van Mook, born in Java, had broadcast to Indonesians a moderate exhortation to remain calm and orderly as the right step toward laying 'the foundations of that self-governing Indonesia which has been announced by Her Majesty and which is desired by all of us'. Van Mook was referring to a vague promise by Queen Wilhelmina, in 1942, that there would be a recalibration of the Holland-NEI relationship after the defeat of the Axis powers. Exactly what the new shape of empire might be had not been explained, nor was it now. The OSS paper pointed to Sukarno and Hatta as the key nationalist figures in the East Indies and downplayed their wartime collaboration: 'There is no reason to believe that Soekarno ever sincerely favored the cause and ideals of Japan'.[38]

On 17 August 1945, Sukarno and Hatta promulgated a brief declaration of independence for the Republic of Indonesia – or more appropriately, a republic of Java. Younger, militant nationalists had pressed for the early announcement. From the beginning, this new republic had at its disposal organized and reasonably well-equipped military forces, primarily through Peta but also evidenced by other paramilitary societies. A month later, a British convoy sailed into the harbor of Batavia ('Jakarta' to Indonesians). Ostensibly, the British task here was the same as elsewhere in the theater: Japanese disarmament/repatriation, RAPWI, and holding to the status quo. But the real status quo was quite different from the imagined one. And again, as in Indochina, good intentions would satisfy neither the concerned European power, reluctantly leaning on British military strength, nor the native nationalists, seeking recognition for their newly independent republic. Nor was the specter of endemic warfare any more appealing in Java and Sumatra than in Vietnam. As an OSS analysis noted, the British would be the first involved 'in the immediate quelling of any uprisings by militant Indonesians, though the Dutch when they arrive later may still be faced with considerable pacification problems'.

On 20 September, OSS operative Jane Foster reported from the Java capital: 'The red and white Nationalist flag is flying over all buildings where the Allies or Japanese are not actually in residence; it is the only flag of any kind in evidence. Slogans, advocating independance [*sic*], are painted in three foot letters in *English* (obviously for the benefit of the British occupation forces) all over downtown Batavia'. Foster described a city increasingly anxious and rumor-driven, with tales of late-night, fever-pitch jungle gatherings, caches of hidden weapons, barricades put up and sorties planned. 'Superficially, the following is responsible for the tension: the complete dependance [*sic*] of the Allies on the Japanese for the main-tenance of law and order with a resulting inferior position of the Allies in the eyes of the Indonesians; and the intransigence of the Dutch in regard to Indonesian demands.' On the 25th, she reported that the OSS team had spent the day in the Des Indes Hotel, 'waiting (like dopes) for all hell to break loose'. Nothing happened. 'All in all the thing is like a stage set by Dali, and I expect the Rockettes to dance out of Des Indes dressed as Kempei[tai, the harsh Japanese military police]. And we wouldn't be a bit surprised.' Foster suspected that the Japanese were 'playing the double game: promoting strife subversively and at the same time making sure they are not held responsible for it by cooperating to the fullest extent with the Allies and by obeying implicitly all allied demands'.[39]

Ambivalence about the Japanese role in the immediate post-war scene of Southeast Asia was common. Enemy troops, in defeat, behaved very correctly, quite unlike the evocative imagery of Japanese fanaticism so prevalent among Westerners. But there was little doubt that the Japanese had successfully conspired to overturn the European colonial system in Asia. Native nationalists had received from Tokyo open (if nonetheless qualified) encouragement of their aspirations for independence and now relied upon Japanese arms (and, in Indonesia, training) for defense. Thus, there were reservations among some military personnel about the integrity of Southeast Asian nationalist movements. For instance, General Elliot Thorpe, from MacArthur's headquarters in Tokyo, charged that the Japanese had sown 'intellectual landmines' throughout the region. 'The Japanese General-Staff is well aware of the American weakness for sympathizing with the underdog', he said, 'particularly races fighting for supposed independence, and undoubtedly the indoctrinated students will make full use of that weakness in post-war operations.'[40] However, once in the field, American observers were typically quick to realize the indigenous wellsprings of native nationalism.

'Even though the maintenance of law and order may be the exclusive aim of the British, it hinges almost exclusively on [the] Allied attitude towards and treatment of Indonesian nationalists', concluded an OSS analyst. Mountbatten sought to avoid direct conflict with the Indonesian republic. On 28 September, he urged Dutch official Charles O. van der Plas, a former governor in Java, to open negotiations with the nationalist administration.[41] The local British commander, Lieutenant General Philip Christison, arrived on the 29th – by which time British forces were emplaced in Batavia – and immediately displayed a tolerant attitude toward the local nationalists. Dutch officials, however, refused to admit that conciliatory gestures were necessary; instead, Mountbatten was told that native resistance would collapse in the face of an Allied show of arms. Netherlands officials asserted that Sukarno was a 'tool and puppet' of the Japanese, that he had 'fascist tendencies' and had 'preached hatred against the Allies', and that he was a 'mere opportunist' with 'certain demagogic gifts'. Alexander Loudon, the Dutch ambassador to Washington, told Under-Secretary Acheson that the Indonesian republic represented a communist foothold in the Far East. Loudon complained that 'the British did not have the forces, or apparently the will, to do anything about the Indies or to help the Dutch do anything. . . . The Ambassador felt that the Dutch people felt that they had been abandoned by their allies after having behaved well and with sacrifice to themselves in the Far East'.[42]

But the English had their own grievances against the Dutch, as evidenced in an October 'run over the Far East' by Esler Dening, writing to Sterndale Bennett of the Foreign Office. Reviewing affairs in Thailand, French Indochina and the Netherlands East Indies, Dening felt that many problems could be resolved by patience and tact – largely by other powers emulating the British example. He did not believe, for example, that Vietnamese nationalism represented an insoluble problem, though Dening contended that the Japanese bore a heavy responsibility in both Indochina and NEI for encouraging 'half-baked independence talk'; and he wondered if they were still providing behind-the-scenes assistance. While Dening complained of the 'badness' of the Chinese and the Americans north of the sixteenth parallel and contended that their actions would likely 'make life difficult for some time to come', he felt that the Gaullist French were generally behaving rather well. Indochina was a troubled spot, to be sure, but the situation might yet be salvaged.

It was rather the East Indies which prompted a bout of despair, as Dening wrote: 'All through the war people used to say – and indeed I was one of them – that the Dutch were the only Ally who never gave one a moment's trouble. They would, of course, choose to wait until the end of the war to behave badly'. He was especially angry at the Dutch government for its sharp criticism of General Christison on the basis of unsubstantiated press reports. Dening himself thought that Christison tended to speak too frankly to reporters, but the Dutch were much overreacting.

> I think the Dutch are being stupid. For, as in the case of Indo-China, I do not believe that the independence movement in the Netherlands Indies is an insoluble problem, nor do I believe that shooting is the cure. . . . I have little confidence in the ability of the Dutch to tackle this situation with common sense. If they don't, that is their business once we have left, but it is very much our business now. . . . These independence movements in Asia must be treated with sympathy and understanding. Otherwise they will become really serious. As I have indicated, they are half-baked and treated in the proper way they should not be very terrifying. But treated the wrong way they may well, in the end, spell the end of Europe in Asia.

Since British forces were handling the initial reoccupation, Dening advised against taking any 'nonsense' from either the French or Dutch. 'In the end, they may well have cause to be grateful to us – though gratitude is not a very marked feature of international relations.' Instead, the Dutch ambassador to Britain complained to Prime Minister Clement Attlee that the

British were purposefully dragging their feet in the reoccupation of the East Indies.[43]

Meanwhile, American officials were objecting to the use of lend-lease trucks, clearly stenciled as US vehicles, to transport Dutch and British soldiers through the streets of Batavia. This had already been a problem involving French military operations in the Middle East. Thus, Secretary Byrnes remarked at a news conference in latter October that 'where any lend-lease property is used in the post-war period in any way that has a political connotation ... it should not bear the emblem of the United States'. This represented, he said, a 'general policy that has been applied elsewhere'. Byrnes refused to say whether his comments indicated approval or disapproval of the use of American military equipment in colonial theaters. Rather, he suggested that the key issue was the specific language of the various contracts negotiated with the English and Dutch governments, about which he knew little and therefore could hardly discuss.[44] This legalistic approach did not disguise American embarrassment, and requests had already been made that US 'emblems' be removed from all lend-lease arms, equipment, vehicles and uniforms.

In Batavia on 9 October, not far from their compound, OSS personnel watched Dutch troops evict Indonesians from a building across the street from the offices of Lieutenant General L. H. van Oyen, the local commander of Netherlands forces. In particular the Americans wanted to see if the Indonesians would be hauled away in trucks with US markings. Instead, about 25 people were 'herded' at bayonet point into the rear of Van Oyen's headquarters. A short time later, the same OSS group was startled as Dutch troops opened fire on a car sporting a nationalist flag on its windshield. In fact, American observers were soon themselves in the line of fire, with machinegun bullets thudding into their building. The car's driver was killed, and the vehicle crashed nearby. 'The conclusions drawn by members of this detachment who ... observe[d] the whole incident', wrote Jane Foster, 'were that the Dutch ... opened fire out of sheer panic.'[45] It was a dramatic demonstration of the anxiety of Dutch troops and the volatility of the local situation. Americans in the midst of such turmoil were themselves at risk, as shown two weeks earlier by the killing of Major Dewey in Saigon. If the Dutch were as stupid as Dening portrayed them, then more shooting was on the way.

As Jane Foster described the mood in Batavia in her reports of late September, she had just been told that the Office of Strategic Services would cease to exist as of 1 October. 'We are slightly confused as to where our stuff will eventually land', she wrote to the head of her section. 'This is the point, much of the material we are sending you is of interest only to the State Dept.'[46] It was in anticipation of the agency's breakup that higher-echelon planners like Lieutenant Colonel John Coughlin had begun addressing the need for maintaining US listening posts in Southeast Asia and other colonial areas. During the eventful last days of the Pacific war and the subsequent SEAC reoccupation efforts, OSS teams had been the government's only reliable source of information in the region. Policymakers in Washington as well as legation staffers actively sought out OSS officers for briefings. Acting Secretary Joseph Grew acknowledged the State Department's dependence upon military intelligence in mid-July 1945 as he addressed letters to the head of the OSS and the secretaries of navy and war seeking additional information about French Indochina.

In late September, Don S. Garden, chief of the Southeast Asia Section within the Special Intelligence (SI) Branch of OSS, wrote to his colleague in the India-Burma Theater, W. Lloyd George, that the political and economic reporting from the Far East remained of great importance to the State Department. He had heard many 'laudatory' comments about the performance of OSS teams. 'In one case, our information reached them as much as twenty-four hours ahead of an Army communication and, since they told us they were making decisions hourly, this time lapse would have been not only a handicap, but might have changed the course of important events.' Looking ahead to sharp personnel cutbacks and the heavy workload placed upon skeleton staffs during liquidation of the wartime agency, Garden told Lloyd George, 'I'm not wishing you any hard luck, but I hope the SI people will be the last out, so they can squeeze the last drop of intelligence from the area'.[47]

US WITHDRAWAL FROM SEAC

Visiting the State Department in mid-September 1945, French diplomat Francis Lacoste spoke with James Bonbright, chief of the Division of Western European Affairs, about the possibility of a Franco-American civil affairs agreement in northern Indochina. Bonbright replied that such matters were more properly a concern of French and Chinese diplomats. Lacoste responded that this attitude did not surprise him; and, as Bonbright recorded, Lacoste observed 'that, speaking entirely personally, he understood that we were following a completely hands-off policy in Indo-China. I intimated, also personally, that he was entirely correct but at the same time assured him that this negative attitude did not mean that we were opposed to the return of this territory to French control'. Thus, Stanley Hornbeck could accurately remark nearly two years later that the United States had followed a general policy of 'acquiescence and absten-tion' with regard to colonial problems in Southeast Asia. This was not the result of any neo-isolationist stance; rather, such aloofness was a natural outgrowth of several policy decisions. First and foremost, the timely transfer of colonial territories from the Southwest Pacific Area Command to SEAC, agreed to at Potsdam, relieved US military forces of the

responsibility for reoccupation duties in such troubled waters as the East
Indies. In this case, there was a sweet harmony between political and
military goals.[48] Secondly, the trusteeship accord reached at Yalta had
wrung any sense of immediacy from Roosevelt's far-flung scenarios for
stimulating indigenous self-rule.

The convergence of political and military policy priorities likewise
argued, by October 1945, for an early US exit from the Southeast Asia
Command – a joint Allied endeavor, to be sure, and one which ultimately
thinned Japanese forces in Asia by some 130 000 soldiers. But SEAC too
openly ranged Western European powers (and by implication, the West
generally) against native nationalist movements. Following Japan's surrender and the president's decision to disband the OSS, it was logical for the
Joint Chiefs to argue that American participation in SEAC was no longer
required or even useful. In mid-October, a note proposing the earliest
practicable US withdrawal from SEAC was sent to the Combined Chiefs of
Staff.[49]

Here, as in other areas, the liquidation of war-related affairs was more
cumbersome than it initially appeared. The British Chiefs requested that
no publicity be attached to the US departure from SEAC: otherwise
Mountbatten's ability to deal effectively with French and Dutch officials
would be undercut. The British viewpoint was given support by FE chief
John Carter Vincent, who wrote that 'widespread publicity . . . smacks too
much of announcing that we are withdrawing from any interest in
Southeast Asia'. He had no objection to a 'routine release' which State
Department officials and field personnel could explain as a product of
military demands. Subsequently, in a memorandum of 5 December 1945,
Brigadier General A. J. McFarland advised the British Chiefs of Staff that
the JCS had agreed to terminate the American role in SEAC with a
minimum of publicity. United States representation within the command
was limited to inter-theater liaison by the end of the year.[50]

The months of October through December 1945 comprised a twilight era
for America's wartime presence in Southeast Asia. The number of US
military observers steadily dwindled in the face of European complaints
about continued intelligence reporting. The war was over, and the US
government obviously wanted to quit its SEAC responsibilities. Why were
American agents still operating in the theater? Brigadier General Thomas
S. Timberman, head of the US Army liaison staff with SEAC, felt it
necessary to write to Mountbatten and list the tasks which personnel of the
newly designated Strategic Services Unit (SSU) were performing. The
head of India-Burma Theater intelligence operations, Lieutenant Colonel
William C. Wilkinson, affirmed that contacts between Americans and
native nationalists had been much restricted and that the quality of new
information was correspondingly reduced. 'In actual fact', wrote Wilkinson, 'our present "intelligence coverage" in South East Asia consists

principally of furnishing information nearly all of which is available from the press associations, and from other government agencies, such as Foreign Economic representatives and the State Department.' He argued nonetheless that SSU teams in Indochina and Java (typically composed of the same people who were there as OSS agents) continued to funnel vital data to US policymakers and performed 'valuable leg-work for the State Department'.[51]

Reports from on-the-spot observers continued to reinforce familiar themes. For instance, Mountbatten's reservations about using Japanese troops to maintain order in the East Indies were borne out: Indonesians much resented SEAC's reliance upon ex-enemy forces. As Major Robert A. Koke, SSU, observed, 'Apparently it has been one of the worst blows against the white-man's prestige that could have been made. It also has been very effective in convincing the Indonesians that the white men have no new ideas but merely wish to reestablish the old order'. Koke spoke with several officials of the native republic in early December and reported: 'There appeared a complete lack of faith in the Netherlands intentions. It was considered certain that if the Dutch are eventually given a free hand they will only be satisfied if they can dictate their own terms. Since the nationalists have no intention of submitting to dictation, it is expected that the Dutch will resort to a bloody campaign of military suppression'. Koke also noted growing nationalist resentment of official US aloofness from NEI affairs.[52]

In a separate memorandum, dated 21 December 1945, Major Koke and Lieutenant R. Stuart affirmed that while Indonesians continued to look toward the United States as the leader of the post-war world, that attitude surely would change if American officials remained indifferent to the restoration of colonial empires in Southeast Asia. 'Silence will be interpreted as meaning that the United States is in agreement with Dutch and British policy.' Further, they advised:

> That America is superficially conscious of trouble in Indonesia, and in South East Asia, is seen ... in Secretary Byrnes' statement that lend-lease equipment and weapons bearing the marking USA must not be used for 'political purposes, as in the Far East'. Indonesians recognize this statement for what it is – a measure which hurts no one, helps no one, and clarifies nothing.
>
> America's failure to take a stand in the controversies of South East Asia and Indonesia is, however, doing more than harming United States prestige. ... Re-imposition of colonial rule in Indonesia will not crush the Nationalist movement; the seeds of World War III may well germinate in a society which is returned to the status quo ante bellum.

Both men were suspicious (unfairly as it turned out) of British motives in the archipelago, sensing an effort to use the SEAC-sponsored military occupation to wrest economic and possibly territorial advantage from the Netherlands. Meanwhile, they argued, US policy remained 'purely negative'. If the United States were doing anything to assist the Indonesian republic, no one knew about it. Koke and Stuart were adamant:

> America, to retain her prestige in Indonesia and exercise the leadership she is capable of in the Far East must restate and implement the ideals which millions of soldiers and the population of the East think that World War II was fought for. The importance of South East Asia and Indonesia to the future peace of the world is certainly sifficient [*sic*] to warrant the formulation of a definite, positive, policy toward these areas.[53]

While all such comments certainly did not reach the desks of appropriate State Department officials, staffers in the Office of Far Eastern Affairs were well aware of the risks and dangers which American acquiescence entailed. The colonial ghetto continued openly to totter toward conflict and conflagration. For others within the department, primarily the Europeanists, the risks and dangers in Southeast Asia and other colonial rimlands were neither so certain nor so important.

YEAR'S END

During the war, a British officer interned in the Dutch East Indies recalled a fellow prisoner saying 'that one of our gravest dangers was that we were imprisoned at a moment when not just the chickens but all the *pterodactyls* of our history in the Far East had come home to roost'. It was an apt metaphor, pointing to the extraordinary metamorphosis which had taken place in the attitudes of native peoples in the region. As bluntly acknowledged by war correspondent Martha Gellhorn: 'The tall white men had been conquered and debased by short yellow men; why should anyone accept the white man as master again?'[54] Major Robert Koke's reports echoed such sentiments. By the end of September 1945, the French were tentatively restored in southern Vietnam courtesy of a co-operative British commander; however, their future role in Tonkin was not at all certain. In Java, Dutch representatives remained, in effect, shunned by both native nationalists and the reoccupation command. General Philip Christison, with the support of his theater commander, sought to accommodate the republic and to force Netherlands officials to begin meaningful negotiations with local nationalists. As Sukarno had requested in a 30 September letter to Mountbatten, 'We do not ask the Allied Military Forces to recognize the Republic of Indonesia. We only ask you to acknowledge facts, namely that to the feelings of the people there exists a Republic of Indonesia with a government'. More to the point were Sukarno's remarks in a newspaper interview of the same day: 'We have established a republic and are determined to stand on that'.[55] Failure to recognize the nationalists' claims, at least in a *de facto* manner, promised to hinder greatly the RAPWI effort, to delay the departure of Commonwealth troops from the East Indies, and to threaten the well-being of the thousands of European and Eurasian internees scattered throughout the islands.

A Research and Analysis Branch paper of 5 October 1945 noted: '[The] British experience in southeast Asia so far has demonstrated that it is not to Britain's advantage to play the role of hard-fisted policeman promoting prewar imperialism'.[56] As it turned out, this was nowhere more fully realized by the British themselves than in Java, where Sukarno and other leaders of the Indonesian republic could lay claim to genuine mass support. It seemed clear to Mountbatten that Dutch authorities must negotiate with the nationalists. Dening's advice against taking any 'nonsense' from the Dutch held sway. General William Slim, commander of Allied Land Forces in Southeast Asia, sent his chief of staff, Major General H. E. Pyman, to report on the Java situation in early October. Much like the Batavia portrayed in Jane Foster's reports of late September, Pyman found a city on the edge of explosive violence, with Netherlands forces only heightening the tension. He recorded in his diary: 'Dutch troops can go nowhere except in strength, and they are like red rags to a bull'.[57] However, Netherlands authorities refused to deal with Sukarno, and the British remained locked into an indefinite stay amongst a hostile population by, firstly, their initial commitment to restore Dutch rule in NEI, and secondly, their obligation to repatriate hard-to-reach POWs and civilian internees.

Native military resistance to the extension of the British bridgehead came with the landing of two Indian battalions at the northeastern port of Surabaya in late October. Before the bitter, weeks-long struggle for the city could be won, Mountbatten was forced to authorize the landing of a full Indian division and the use of air attacks and naval bombardment. As OSS officer Edmund Taylor later remarked, the Surabaya encounter was 'one of the decisive colonial engagements of our day, for the fierce resistance of the ... Indonesians removed the last doubts in the minds of most British, Dutch and French colonial soldiers that the old imperialist way was gone forever. If empire meant fighting full-scale battles with modern weapons, then imperialism was no longer profitable'. On the other hand, if full-scale battles could be won, then imperial rule might still be restored. Hence, the impact of Surabaya was less conclusive than some may have supposed. For the British, however, the message was clear: there must be greater pressure placed upon the Dutch to reach a reasonable settlement with the republic, and there must be a better, working *modus vivendi* between General Christison and Indonesian officials.[58] The first meeting between Netherlands officials and Sukarno took place on 31

October but entailed little in the way of genuine dialogue. The Dutch viewed Sukarno's wartime collaboration as a betrayal of the colonial administration, and they resented his bold, assertive nationalism. Even more so, the Dutch hated their own impotence, which Sukarno (and in a different way, the British) so obviously symbolized. Still, with continuing pressure from Mountbatten and British diplomats, the frequency of Dutch-Indonesian contacts increased through the remainder of the year.

In French Indochina, affairs moved superficially in a more orderly way toward an end to British reoccupation duties and a restoration of the French regime, at least in the southern zone. On 12 December, Mountbatten reported that 'the policy of gradual handover to [the] French continues. In the Saigon area the situation has been generally more quiet'. French forces were conducting mopping up operations through the Mekong River delta and elsewhere south of the 16th parallel, still meeting stiff resistance in some areas.[59] Colonel Chapman-Walker toured both occupation zones in Indochina during the final weeks of the year and authored a lengthy report. Arriving in Hanoi on 17 December, he found adequate electricity and water, with telephones operating 'no more erratically than in provincial France'. He praised the efficiency and discipline of Chinese troops, noting that the disarmament of Japanese forces was proceeding well. French troops remained concentrated in the local fortress, the 'Citadel'. Chapman-Walker was skeptical of French claims that the transport of a small number of additional troops from China would provide the means to overthrow Viet Minh control. Yet, he was sympathetic to the situation facing many French residents. 'The greater majority of the pure Annamites obviously detest the French and regard them as fair game from the point of view of murder and spoilation. It is now quite impossible for any French family to employ an Annamese cook, as every evening there are cases of French families being poisoned under particularly agonising circumstances.' Like other observers, Chapman-Walker catalogued a series of economic problems worsened by the Chinese occupation. In particular, he pointed to a grave rice shortage in the north.

While affirming that Ho Chi Minh 'in every way is a most remarkable man', the colonel stressed the communist character of the Viet Minh regime in terms of its emblem and political program. Its assemblies and marches resembled the Hitler Youth, and its uniforms were like those worn by Tito's troops in Yugoslavia. The Viet Minh, he said, were an effective fighting force, with the leadership core consisting of 'the old militant nationalists and revolutionary Annamites, who have given the French considerable trouble for years'. Chapman-Walker described what appeared to be well-planned efforts to move 'organized units and arms dumps' outside Hanoi into the countryside, presumably in expectation of a 'general uprising'. As in previous conversations, Ho Chi Minh promised to lead a guerrilla war against the French if recognition of Vietnamese nationalism were denied. 'His magnificently intelligent face made me believe that such resistance would be effectively directed, and his sincerity assured me that it would be fanatical.'

In Saigon a week later, Chapman-Walker spoke with General Gracey's chief of staff, who outlined the planned evacuation schedule for British troops. The colonel confirmed Mountbatten's description of a relatively orderly transition, though he criticized the attitude of French forces:

> The guerrilla activities of the Annamite troops in this area consist only of sporadic sniping and the placing of homemade anti-vehicle mines on the road at night. However, owing to the French troops' unwillingness to undertake any operations on their feet, their sole activities appear to be confined to the main Saigon-Hue road and the hinterland is left to the Viet Minh.

In his conclusion, Chapman-Walker advised that the Potsdam decision on Indochina may have served the French better than they realized. He asserted, 'In my opinion, had European troops undertaken the military occupation of North F.I.C., they would have encountered savage resistance from the Tongkinese'. The Chinese, however, had entered Tonkin peacefully and carried out their occupation tasks in a 'workmanlike manner'. But some sort of conflict in the north appeared inevitable unless French officials were prepared 'to negotiate with Ho-chi-min[h] on the latter's terms'.[60]

To many observers, the situation in Southeast Asia remained obscure: an untidy, cruel, ironic, tragic endnote to the Pacific War. Was it really necessary that, having recently suffered such hardship, the native peoples of Vietnam, Java and Sumatra must enroll in new struggles? Was it appropriate that the families of Frenchmen and Dutchmen should be so vulnerable to pains inflicted by their former servants and coolies? Was it right that the promise of new uprisings would again pit Asians against Europeans? The role of ideology, terror and mass mobilization sharpened the struggle but blurred the issues at stake. World opinion had tired of grim violence.

The analyses and commentaries of US intelligence teams in Southeast Asia during the latter half of 1945 had emphasized the following themes:

1. the local nationalist movements were strong and durable;
2. the promise of independence to the Philippines was widely known and had done much to generate a favorable US image among colonial peoples;
3. there was considerable but not necessarily overwhelming communist influence in the Viet Minh, and DRV leaders were determined to exercise self-rule or launch a protracted guerrilla struggle;

4. Indonesian nationalists were equally determined to achieve independence and wielded considerable military strength;
5. the forcible reimposition of colonial regimes would lead to disruptive conflict throughout the region and further undermine Western (and particularly American) prestige; and
6. Southeast Asia should be an important factor in post-war American political and economic planning.

The ebb of wartime goodwill toward the United States throughout the Asian rimlands could hardly fail to excite comment among the State Department's Far Eastern experts. Yet, John Carter Vincent's remarks on 20 October 1945 outlined the limits of post-war American idealism. In the groggy afterlight of war, he commented, there was no room for 'foreign policy for fun or as a luxury'. Problems abounded in East Asia, with 'a defeated and so far unregenerate Japan' opposite a China plagued by serious political and economic disorder. 'In southeast Asia a situation has developed to the liking of none of us, least of all to the British, the French, the Dutch, and, I gather, to the Annamese and Indonesians.' While the US government acknowledged the sovereignty of the European power in both Indochina and NEI, it was hoped that early, mutually beneficial settlements could be reached in both areas. 'It is not our intention', said Vincent, 'to assist or participate in forceful measures for the imposition of control by the territorial sovereigns, but we would be prepared to lend our assistance, if requested to do so, in efforts to reach peaceful agreements in these disturbed areas.' Vincent assured his listeners that America remained committed to the goal of self-government for colonial peoples after appropriate tutelage. 'We can be sentimental as well as practical – as long as we *are* practical.' Two days later, Vincent explained to Matthews and Hickerson of EUR that his suggestion of a US mediative role in Southeast Asia was nothing new, that it was designed to offset the 'negative statement' about the American unwillingness openly to assist in the forceful restoration of colonial controls, and that it did not constitute a formal offer of US good offices.[61]

Abbot Moffat, director of the Division of Southeast Asian Affairs, was troubled by the drift of American policy. On 12 October 1945, he had advised Vincent that it would not serve American interests 'to give long-range support with military supplies to the administrations of Indochina or the NEI. It would seem important to avoid any entanglement in the colonial problems of western powers in Southeast Asia unless essential to protect American security interests from some threat not presently visible'. However, avoiding entanglement was not the only challenge to US policymakers. In a 9 November memo titled 'Inventory of Foreign Policy Problems', Moffat pointed to US-British haggling over the post-war status of Thailand (Siam) as well as the long-term impact of the 'hands-off' policy toward Indochina and Indonesia. He continued to be concerned about French and Dutch use of 'lend-leased' equipment. Moffat implicitly questioned the department's continued advocacy of imperial restoration in Southeast Asia in view of, among other things, (1) the unpredictable character of French and Dutch policy in the region; (2) the possibility of prolonged military struggle and 'economic paralysis' in FIC and NEI; (3) 'the rapid decline in recent months of American prestige among all colonial peoples and particularly those of Southeast Asia who, whether we wished it or not, looked to us for leadership and support and whose friendliness will be essential in the case of future trouble in Asia'; and (4) the apparent rising prestige of the Soviet Union among peoples of the region. In addition, he asked, what was the likelihood of a regional open door following the re-establishment of 'preferred economic positions' by the imperial powers? Moffat was emphatic in this and later memorandums that American policy toward the Philippines must remain firmly wedded to the promise of self-government in 1946. 'Philippine independence is the one tangible application of the lofty ideals which the United States has proclaimed', he wrote. 'The effect of our failure to carry out our pledge . . . would be disastrous on our position throughout Southeast Asia.'[62]

But the articulation of problems and the listing of options were no substitute for policymaking. War's end meant that American military involvement and intelligence-gathering in Southeast Asia would soon be over. No influential US official planned otherwise. While hardly substantive enough to affect the outcome of the complex struggles under way, American operations in Indochina and the Netherlands East Indies had generated much useful information and, equally important, valuable insights into local politics and the broader issues of colonialism and nationalism. Unfortunately, with regard to Vietnam, it was information largely ignored. As one historian noted, American policy toward Indochina by late 1945 had demonstrated a 'dual character': the initial *de facto* recognition of the DRV regime by OSS officers coupled incongruously with Vincent's October endorsement of continued colonial rule. According to Robert McMahon, it was this recognition of the European sovereigns – along with the substantial lend-lease aid which flowed into the colonial theaters of Southeast Asia – which 'belied any official professions of American "neutrality" [in the metropole-nationalist struggle]'.[63]

In addition, events in Southeast Asia were easily overshadowed by US concerns about the stability and recovery of Western Europe. This was an unsurprising policy event. In fact, it was Ho Chi Minh who told an OSS officer in December 1945 that while the United States was Vietnam's best hope for a benefactor, it was unlikely that such a relationship would develop. Captain Frank White later recalled: 'He said he felt that the US Government would find more urgent things to do. He said something to the effect that, after all, Vietnam is a small country and far away. Vietnam could not be expected to loom large in the preoccupations of the United States'. Meeting with journalist Harold Isaacs in November, Ho averred that Vietnamese nationalists would simply have to rely upon themselves.[64] He was right. For the short-term, the gaze of those who dominated American policymaking was directed toward the huddled, hungry peoples of Western Europe, and then secondarily toward the different but interwoven problems of China and Japan. For US policymakers, the simplest course regarding colonial territories was to issue statements of virtuous principle and uncertain application, to remain aloof from the actual struggles which might emerge, and to urge upon all parties a moderate course and continuing dialogue. The breakdown of reasoned dialogue among the big powers, however, evident in early 1946, was the harbinger of an ever more Eurocentric American foreign policy which inexorably reduced affairs in Southeast Asia to shadowy, enigmatic morality plays. On Christmas day, 1945, Sutan Sjahrir wrote to President Truman: 'Sporadic fighting is taking place all over the country but, ill-armed as my people are, they die in thousands rather than submit to having the Dutch foisted on them'.[65] Yet, at the same time, there appeared on the horizon several *modi vivendi* which seemed to offer both Vietnamese and Indonesians the opportunity to practice self-rule in deed if not entirely in name.

COLONIAL DIPLOMACY

In a cable of 1 December 1945, Stanley Hornbeck, ambassador to the Netherlands for slightly more than a year, offered a hagridden interpretation of recent events in the East Indies. Fearful that the collapse of Western influence in NEI would 'invite an influx' of possibly Chinese or (more likely) Japanese intrigue, Hornbeck launched into a cautionary tale. He put forward a kind of vague domino theory, positing a widening ripple effect – through southern Asia and into parts of Africa – to harmful trends in Indonesia. An Asian expert but not, it appeared, an Asianist, Hornbeck sounded decidedly metropolitan. 'More and more', he wrote, 'the evidence which becomes available indicates that the present situation in the Netherlands East Indies is a product of Japanese inspiration and a projection of the Japanese war effort.' Despite Japan's defeat, 'Japanese armed forces, through and with elements in the native population [in NEI] whom by various procedures they have made their dupes and agents, are still engaged in activities which might well be described as "vicarious guerrilla warfare"'. It was important to frustrate such enemy 'machinations'. American interests, Hornbeck warned, were being threatened by recent developments in the East Indies, and he advised that US policymakers adopt a more 'positive' policy toward affairs in the archipelago.[66] There was little doubt that, for Hornbeck, a positive policy meant greater support for the metropole. In fact, he seemed to be suggesting that defeat of an Indonesian nationalist movement sponsored and succored by the Japanese represented merely an extension of the wartime struggle against the Tokyo regime.

While such arguments surely reinforced the views of the powerful Europeanist clique within the State Department, Hornbeck's gloss bore little resemblance to the complex reality in the Southeast Asian colonial theater. He had learned nothing from Surabaya. Lieutenant Colonel K. K. Kennedy, recently returned from Batavia, reported to a group of department Asianists in early December and confirmed the opinion of OSS observers that nationalist feeling was widespread among the Indonesian peasantry. As Abbot Moffat recalled: 'He felt that a fully equipped Dutch division could probably penetrate Java and proceed wherever it wished to go, but that immediately after the army had passed a given point the revolution would close in behind it'. The Dutch officials he met with, said Kennedy, remained oblivious to the power and appeal of native nationalists.[67] Such had been the common complaint of British policy-makers, applied to both the French and the Dutch. Hostile, sullen native populations did not ease the 'handover' to previous sovereigns, nor did widening guerrilla conflict promise the rapid restoration of normal trade.

A 19 December 1945 press release from the State Department expressed concern at the continued conflict in the Netherlands East Indies, especially in view of the collapse of Dutch-Indonesian negotiations. Accordingly, because of the international impact of events in the region, 'Our sole desire is to see such peaceful settlements achieved as will best promote world stability and prosperity and the happiness of people. Such a settlement can be attained only through a realistic, broad-minded and cooperative approach on the part of all concerned and a will to reconcile differences by peaceful means'. Therefore, American policymakers urged the resumption of talks with the nationalists in accord with the charter of the United Nations and the wartime goals of the Grand Alliance.[68] There was no mention of the Atlantic Charter. Vague and nonjudgmental, the press release reinforced the image of the United States as a neutral government. British military actions in the final days of the year expanded the zone of SEAC control around Batavia. Subsequent high-level Anglo-Dutch talks appeared to promise renewed efforts to reach a reasonable settlement in the East Indies. The US consul general in Java, Walter Foote, demonstrated little change from his pre-war views of Indonesians, avowing: 'Ninety-eight percent of [the] people are apathetic towards politics and want peace above all'. While decrying the role of native extremists, Foote characterized Sjahrir and others of his cabinet as 'moderate, thoughtful men who will agree with [the] Dutch when Batavia and other large cities are cleared of trouble-makers and their lives made safe'.[69]

Sympathetic to the goals of their European allies, British officials remained skeptical of the ability of either the French or the Dutch to restore intact their colonial administrations. In Saigon, General Gracey's consistent support of French restoration laid the groundwork for British withdrawal from southern Indochina by year's end. In Java, however, Netherlands representatives continued to balk at substantive negotiations with the nationalist regime. Hence, Mountbatten authorized more extensive British-Indonesian contacts in order to hasten completion of the RAPWI mission. Otherwise, things seemed to be going well. 'Outside Java', he later wrote, 'the state of affairs in South-East Asia gave no cause for anxiety'.[70] On 1 February 1946, experienced diplomat Archibald Clark Kerr (Lord Inverchapel) arrived in Batavia to offer his good offices as part of a co-ordinated British effort to move the Dutch and the nationalists toward agreement. Mountbatten had meanwhile assuaged wounded Dutch pride by removing General Christison from the SEAC theater and replacing him with another commander.[71] It was in Vietnam, though, that what appeared to be a new, more liberal colonial diplomacy first bore fruit.

By the end of January 1946, the French had assumed full responsibility for Indochina military affairs below the 16th parallel. On 28 February, a Sino-French agreement cleared the way for French reoccupation of northern Vietnam pending some kind of understanding with DRV officials. While nationalist sentiment in Tonkin was obviously very strong, the ability of the Viet Minh to resist a concerted French military offensive was uncertain. General Philip E. Gallagher, overall commander of American personnel in Tonkin during latter 1945, believed that two fully equipped French divisions could retake the north. The Viet Minh were well organized and well supplied with small arms, said Gallagher, but he doubted that nationalist forces could match French firepower.[72] From Paris, US Ambassador Jefferson Caffery reported that the French government favored a conciliatory approach toward the DRV. The assistant chief of SEA, Kenneth P. Landon – visiting both Hanoi and Saigon – was not as optimistic. Nevertheless, he was able to report that negotiations continued between Jean Sainteny, the French commissioner for Tonkin, and Ho Chi Minh. An agreement could be beneficial to both sides if it accorded the DRV at least *de facto* recognition as an autonomous regime and if it provided France with the means to expand its military presence in the north. French altruism, however, was an unreliable element at best. As Sainteny later recalled, his countrymen were determined to return in force to Hanoi, 'the administrative and spiritual capital' of the colony and 'the nerve center of this turbulent peninsula'.[73] As it happened, the French had everything to gain by an ambiguous settlement, and the Viet Minh had everything to lose.

Thus, for several months, Sainteny and Ho regularly met to discuss the fate of the Viet Minh republic and France's future in the region. Sainteny blamed American OSS personnel for making his job more difficult: for legitimizing the DRV regime and fuelling Ho's aspirations for independence. Finally, however, as French warships neared the port of Haiphong, on 6 March 1946, a Franco-Vietnamese accord was signed. France recognized the DRV as a 'free state having its own government, parliament, army, and finances', forming a part of the newly conceived, ostensibly commonwealth-like French Union. With regard to Ho's strongly held view that the three provinces of Tonkin, Annam and Cochinchina should comprise one unified republic, the French pledged to respect the results of a plebiscite. In return, DRV officials agreed to allow French military forces into northern Vietnam for the purpose of relieving the Chinese occupation army and completing the task of repatriating Japanese troops. An annex to the agreement stipulated that as many as 15000 French soldiers might re-enter the north but that virtually all of them would evacuate DRV territory within five years. Further 'frank and friendly negotiations' would be scheduled to flesh out the accord's generalities. The day before the agreement was signed, southern Indochina was officially removed from SEAC. 'French administration has been restored in most [southern] provinces and Annamites are returning to work', reported Mountbatten.[74] In Java, the Franco-Vietnamese agreement appeared to offer a workable framework for Dutch-Indonesian negotiations.

France, wrote Sainteny, was rescued 'from an abyss'. For the short term, both sides – the Viet Minh as well as the French – were spared a bitter, costly military confrontation. Lauristan Sharp, formerly of the Division of Southeast Asian Affairs, believed that the March accord might represent an important turning point in Franco-Vietnamese relations, serving as an 'indication that Indochinese may be permitted some real degree of control over their own destiny in friendly collaboration with one of the major western democracies'. However, the situation soon deteriorated. One journalist who accompanied French Legionnaires sailing for Indochina, during the winter of 1945–46, reported that the humiliation of German defeat and occupation was still fresh – and that the troops were eager for battle. 'Now they wanted to wash away the stigma of defeat in the waters of the Mekong and the Red River', he wrote. Yet, many of the soldiers aboard were German recruits who idled away their evening hours singing Wehrmacht songs.[75] The same month marked the reintroduction of Dutch forces into Java. The sense of impending crisis in Indochina was heightened by continuing Franco-Vietnamese clashes below the 16th parallel. As Ellen Hammer noted in her pathbreaking study of post-war Vietnam, the 6 March agreement was never applied to Cochinchina. Native nationalists in the south remained divided amongst themselves; and the French relied upon military operations to retain control.[76]

The status of southern Vietnam remained the greatest obstacle to further interim understandings between the French government and the DRV.

The Viet Minh leadership insisted that the March accord implicitly recognized the unity of the three provinces. Further, as Lauristan Sharp pointed out, a truncated DRV, shorn of Cochinchina, could hardly hope to build a viable national economy. The French obviously much valued the southern area for its rice and rubber production; as well, Cochinchina contained the largest share of French investments in the colony.[77] At the end of May, Ho Chi Minh departed for France, for a new round of negotiations. In Paris in late June, he was properly received as a head of state. By that time, however, the high commissioner in Indochina, Admiral d'Argenlieu, had already undercut the March accord by recognizing an independent republic in Cochinchina. The Viet Minh could never accept this *fait accompli*. In the East Indies, discussions between Dutch officials and Indonesian nationalists, at an impasse through the spring and summer, began anew in the fall.

MISTRESS OF THE SEAS AND AIR

On 13 May 1946, Admiral Mountbatten surrendered to the French all his remaining responsibilities for Indochina. The withdrawal of British troops from NEI did not start until very late in the year, by which time it had become apparent that the 6 March accord was a major diplomatic victory for the French. The Dutch and Indonesians would have to work out their own model. But even as French forces moved more boldly against Vietnamese nationalists and the Dutch anticipated the use of military force in Java and Sumatra, the fist-in-the-glove formula for European empire was very nearly an empty vessel. It was another casualty of the Second World War. Here was the real *fait accompli*. Illusions lingered; the war's grey twilight concealed as much as it revealed. The British government carried out the thankless task of formally restoring its allies' colonial rule in Southeast Asia with little enthusiasm. It was more duty than passion. The effort reinforced the realization in London that British military power was essentially spent, that Britain had fallen far and fast from the top ranks of global power.

An estimate of Britain's post-war capabilities produced by the War Department's Joint Intelligence Committee did not offer much hope for a revitalized English prowess. Pointing to the preponderance of Soviet power on the continent, the rapid shrinking of British offensive forces, the economic toll of war, and the new military vulnerability of the home island amidst weakening imperial ties, the report advised: 'Britain is now facing one of the most critical periods in her history'. While sea power had been in the past Britain's chief tool for both offensive and defensive action, it would not be effective against the USSR. 'Against that nation, a long-range air or guided missile offensive directed at important targets in the interior appears to offer the greatest promise as the principal means of offensive action, at least until the Soviet capabilities of resisting other forms of offensive action have by that means been greatly reduced'. Anticipating the more public expressions of Anglo-American solidarity which would soon follow, the JIC study observed: 'The mutual interests of the United Kingdom and the United States preclude the possibility of an Anglo-American conflict. Thus it is in relation to the U.S.S.R. that the military capabilities of the British Empire should primarily be considered'.[78]

While the JIC's discussion of 'chief problem areas' reflected outdated strategic thinking – viewing Mediterranean and Far Eastern affairs essentially in terms of Anglo-Soviet rivalry – the committee's conclusion was sound: such that 'the economic and military limitations of British capabilities, with the U.S.S.R. predominant in Europe and the United States mistress of the seas and air, already restrict Britain's power of initiative'. Further, the continued viability of the British Empire 'depends to a high degree on the friendship or sufferance of the United States'. Partnership with the United States would 'at all times be the cornerstone, in fact the paramount need, of British policy. Commercial rivalry may sometimes strain this policy but will never avoid it'. While British leaders and their public would find it difficult to accept England's decline and loss of world leadership, the trend was irreversible. For this reason, the British government would seek US assistance in countering the Soviet position on the continent. In Southeast Asia, noted the committee, events were moving at a fast pace. It appeared that the long-range objective of Britain was 'the settlement of the controversies between the French or Dutch Governments and "nationalist" groups on a basis sufficiently short of outright independence to forestall serious repercussions in India, Burma, and Malaya, which would affect British interests and prestige adversely throughout the East'. Thus, while seeking 'constructive' settlements in FIC and NEI, the British would probably resist any offers of UN-sponsored or other third-party mediation as an unhealthy precedent in colonial territories.[79]

American interest in Southeast Asian affairs was soon overwhelmed by the press of events in Western Europe, the Mediterranean, and the Middle East. Colonies only rose to the top of the international agenda – as typified by the Council of Foreign Ministers discussions – when they whetted great-power competition. The list of international crises through 1946 and early 1947 was crammed with alternate specters of European collapse and US-Soviet confrontation. In this atmosphere of big decisions to be made, worlds to be won or lost, and seas to be made lakes, the colonial rimlands sometimes emerged as flashpoints but never occupied center stage for long. The European heartland was exactly that: the centerpiece of Soviet-American rivalry.

6 Erring on the Safe Side: The Cold War and the Politics of Colonialism, 1946–47

Strange climes, alien cultures, the human eddies of withered imperial systems – such was the confusing, colorful backdrop for the unfolding of a cold war triggered by heartland-inspired ambitions, ambivalence and anxieties. Around southern Eurasia, the rimlands curled crescent-like from atoll's edge to craggy ridges, from the scrub and sand of North Africa to the broadleaf jungles of Southeast Asia. 'Cargo cults' had been seeded on Pacific islands: quasi-religious doctrines based on the divinely ordained appearance of food and other provisions attached to parachutes. Decades later, cult enthusiasts would still await the blossoming of new goods from the skies. All along the distant marches of empire, it seemed, black, brown and yellow peoples crouched in anticipation of the dramatic change sure to come on the wings of war. Westerners saw the colonial world alternately glistening in naive beauty, then pulsing with primitive energy alongside atavistic tradition and fatalistic neglect. Such shifting perspectives were common among US intelligence officers who savored their wartime role of gathering background material for the *pax americana*. The colonial theaters provided compelling, even romantic tales of fading glory, sahibs in decline: from the pampered, servant-ridden OSS quarters in New Delhi, through tense jungle intrigue and tough guerrilla warfare, through new bonds of comradeship between Southeast Asians and Americans, to the tattered, half-pathetic disarray of colonial administrations in such cities as Tripoli, Beirut, Damascus, Hanoi, Saigon and Batavia. The war left in its wake debris of all kinds – physical, personal and political. Cast-off myths, loose cannons, assaults on the old order – the masses were astir, arising.

By the end of 1946, the ongoing struggles in colonial spheres offered an extraordinary *mise-en-scène* for history-in-the-making. Onlookers could choose their reigning metaphor from among several appealing options: the thrilling, inexorable heartbeat of mass empowerment; the cleansing imagery of peasant virtue triumphing over decadent, Old World cynicism and injustice; or, more darkly, the fearsome portraits of ancient apathy and murderous passion manipulated by self-appointed demagogues of uncertain wisdom and affiliation. Americans did sympathize with the underdog, as was often said; but foreign affairs was no baseball game. The struggle which began in the colonial rimlands was for hearts and minds, not points or medals. And from the beginning, the conflict was marked by fierce ambiguity.

Even those observers accustomed if not inured to human suffering were pessimistic about the fruits of anticolonial warfare. Visiting Vietnam at the war's end, journalist Harold Isaacs recorded his dismay at the continuing misery and hardship among the people. Peace had not broken out. 'Instead there were the small wars of the aftermath, the many shadows of more and greater wars to come.' Paradoxically to many, the mass rigor and excitement of war seemed, retrospectively, more ennobling than the self-interested pursuits of peacetime. Elizabeth P. MacDonald, an OSS operative in the India-Burma Theater and China, gazed wistfully out over the war's dénouement:

> I was glad, like everyone else, that it was over, because the people who might have been killed tomorrow in action would be alive now for the rest of their natural lives. But there was a sudden vacuum which peace had brought. Up to now there had been purpose, urgency, importance in doing what we were doing. Now things suddenly had no meaning. The jeeps outside were relics of a former age. The men in uniforms were now suddenly just civilians who would go home and try to find lost threads of an earlier life. They would never go out again and blow bridges or count Japanese convoys rolling along the dusty roads of China.[1]

Correspondent Martha Gellhorn likewise found peace 'uneasy and unconvincing'. But she was equally discouraged by 'the postwar new-style little war' she soon saw while reporting from Java. The situation was a 'pathetic murderous mess', and her sympathies lay with the emaciated Dutch internees now confronted, after their release from prison camps, with angry, combative Indonesians. British officer Laurens van der Post, held prisoner in Java for three years, similarly was dismayed by the island's continued strife, believing nationalist objectives to be 'confused and dubious' compared to the surety and virtue of the Allied campaign against Japan. Moreso than other observers, Isaacs believed that Asians deserved a better life, that the aftermath of war should offer opportunities for self-government. Even so, the picture was grim. 'Peoples everywhere were caught in the writhing postures of perpetual conflict', he recalled.[2]

Except for Greece, the fighting in Europe was largely over by VE Day. There were yet gruesome ghosts to exhume, but the day-to-day grittiness and uncertainty of life was a product of shell-shock, the threat of prolonged deprivation, and the danger of stormy political intrigue. Tumult in the colonial world was only one aspect of the global dissonance which confronted American policymakers. The attractive power of grand strategy was quite genuine in the midst of so many puzzle pieces piled in such masterful disarray. Where were the connective threads, the dovetail joints, the guiding lights? As veteran diplomat Stanley Hornbeck wrote: 'World politics and international relations are a chain-woven fabric. Effective conducting of foreign relations calls for constant and skillful correlating of many strands and links'.[3] Priorities must be established. All things could be contemplated, but for now only a select few could be achieved – those which had direct, immediate impact on the ability of the United States to solidify its wartime economic growth and to expand its political reach. Horizons of new hegemony beckoned, neither cynically nor conspiratorially, nor always by invitation. It was to be a new hegemony of know-how, engineering, mass production and profligate enthusiasm. It was the flexing of new muscle: the proud, confident New Worlder, occasionally benevolent, always intrusive. Principles counted, as did virtue, but a mature pragmatism shaped much of the early post-war period. Self-determination was reserved for those who could handle the rigors of independence. Race had something to do with it: pervasive stereotypes of bush savages, slick Arabs, esoteric cults, and oriental desuetude all suggested that aspirations ran well ahead of talent and capability. Colonial peoples appeared childlike, well-meaning but too unschooled to understand the arc of power politics and the dialectical clash of complex, canny ideologies.

In August 1946, Italian leader Alcide de Gasperi addressed the delegates to the Paris Peace Conference, remarking, 'Do not linger on the steps of transient expediency. Do not deceive yourselves that with a mere truce or an instable compromise you can achieve your ends'.[4] His referent, of course, was the peace treaty's impact upon the fragile economy and volatile polity of Italy. But it was a fair comment. 'Transient expediency' was the hardy perennial of big-power politics, no less so in the weary world of 1946. Correspondent William Attwood had reported the listless first-anniversary rites of VE Day in Paris only a few months earlier.[5] Still, Europe was the grand gridiron upon which the immediate post-war order would be shaped. True, it was a battered landscape, over which staggered hungry people whose fear and anxiety might paralyze reason and vindicate brutality. Had Hitler won after all: denigrating democracy, undermining optimism and faith, obliterating all sense of hope and security? This was what some observers feared. American exuberance was tempered by the enfeeblement of Europe.

The Americanization of international affairs was not meant to be underwritten by economic grants or substantive military commitments. To begin with, it would be too costly.[6] Further, demobilization of the wartime armed services proceeded at a pace which promised thinly manned fleets, squadrons, divisions and depots. Military leaders fought vainly to staunch the cutbacks in funding and personnel. On 19 March 1946, Admiral Chester Nimitz cautioned the House Naval Affairs Committee: 'During this war our country has reached a position of preeminence in world affairs. That position of preeminence carries with it great responsibility. If we exercise that responsibility and maintain our strength it will tend to stabilize world conditions during a postwar period where they are not yet stabilized'. While he would not essay the exact level of naval strength needed, Nimitz said, 'I do know, however, that our stake, by virtue of our country's position in the world, is so great that if we are going to err it would be better to err on the safe side and have a navy big enough'.[7] Ever more consistently, in fact, this became the judgment of the Truman administration. It was either convenient or necessary to err on the safe side – to affirm the value of order, to encourage restoration over revolution, to exaggerate danger in order better to enforce consensus. The United States would be, in Secretary Forrestal's words, the 'great stabilizer' in international relations.[8] The mistress of the seas and air was steady but less inspiring as advocate and protector of the *status quo*. Evolutionary paths could not accommodate revolutionary dreams.

THE IRON CURTAIN

In 1943, columnist Walter Lippmann had written, 'If there is no peace after this war, it will be soon apparent'. It was. He believed that 'the return from a state of total war to a state of peace which no one trusts will raise catastrophic issues in our midst'. In particular, he worried about the domestic political polarization which would greet the failure of America's leaders to frame a sound, reasonable foreign policy for the post-war era. In international affairs, Lippmann advised, the United States must become 'solvent': commitments must accurately reflect the national interest, and there must be adequate means to sustain those commitments. This was not simply a business ledger.

> The items on both sides of the account include incommensurables and intangibles. Nevertheless, there is a grim accounting if the budget of foreign relations is insolvent. The accounting is in war. Insolvency in foreign policy will mean that preventable wars are not prevented, that unavoidable wars are fought without being adequately prepared for them, and that settlements are made which are the prelude to a new cycle of unprevented wars, unprepared wars, and unworkable settlements.

Lippmann's solution to this dilemma was close Anglo-American co-operation; if necessary, he favored the creation of a bloc which would form the nucleus of a two-ocean security network. This partnership would tie together dual, compatible commonwealths: the British with their world-girdling association of dominions and the United States with its sister republics in the Western Hemisphere. Lippmann's Anglo-America represented 'a community of interest and not a plan of domination or a scheme of empire'. Humankind faced a 'shrunken' world, possibly soon again to be strife-torn; much depended upon US-British co-operation.[9] Lippmann's thesis was akin to Winston Churchill's fond planning, if not Roosevelt's.

Although the triumphant transatlanticism of 1948–49 was several years away, the complementarity of Anglo-American interests had been widely recognized in US planning circles by the war's end. An OSS analysis written in April 1945 had warned that Soviet behavior in Eastern Europe revealed an aggressive, expansionist purpose, one which could only be countered by the formation of a 'Western-European-Mediterranean-American bloc'. Sumner Welles, former Roosevelt confidant, wrote comfortably of the need for British-American partnership, to serve the two nations' parallel global interests and to speed the United Nations on a successful voyage. Applause filled the room when General Dwight Eisenhower told a House committee, in November 1945, 'There will never be a war between Great Britain and the United States'. The War Department's Joint Intelligence Committee produced in February 1946 a strong (if somewhat patronizing) affirmation of intertwined Anglo-American strategic and economic interests.[10] The Combined Chiefs of Staff remained operative in Washington as a vestigial expression of wartime unity. There was a visceral Anglo-American impulse among civilian and military leaders of both nations.

In a speech of 28 February 1946, Secretary of State James Byrnes adumbrated the pervasive uncertainty in world affairs. While America had 'pinned' its hopes 'to the banner of the United Nations', the initial session of the General Assembly had witnessed considerable discord. Though not directly identified, the obvious transgressor was the Soviet Union. 'I should be lacking in candor if I said to you', remarked the secretary, 'that world conditions today are sound or reassuring. All around us there is suspicion and distrust, which in turn breeds suspicion and distrust.' It was a familiar theme for Byrnes. 'If we are to be a great power', said Byrnes, 'we must act as a great power'. He declared:

> It has never been the policy of the United States in its internal affairs or in its foreign relations to regard the *status quo* as sacrosanct. The essence of our democracy is our belief in life and growth and in the right of the people to shape and mould their own destiny. ... Our diplomacy must not be negative and inert. ... Though the *status quo* is not sacred and unchangeable, we cannot overlook a unilateral gnawing away at the *status quo*. The Charter forbids aggression, and we cannot allow aggression to be accomplished by coercion or pressure or by subterfuges such as political infiltration.

A year later, such references to external pressure and fifth-column subversion would be the bedrock of the Truman Doctrine.

Secretary Byrnes promised that the United States would not remain aloof from challenges to the integrity of the United Nations. The closing passages of his speech clearly represented an indictment of the Soviet Union: for threatening its neighbors, stationing troops overlong in Iran, obstructing the 'making of peace', and conducting a 'war of nerves' against other powers. Yet, none of this need be permanently disruptive. 'We must get back to conditions of peace', said Byrnes. 'We must liquidate the terrible legacy which the war has left us. We must return our armies to their homelands. We must eliminate the breeding grounds of suspicion and fear. ... To avoid trouble we must not allow situations to develop into incidents from which there is no retreat. ... Great states and small states must work together to build a friendlier and happier world.'[11] His remarks were all things to all people. The world community could accommodate diversity; problems could be resolved, even big ones; and peace, if not at hand, might still be achieved. But aggression would not be tolerated, and the United Nations provided the requisite legitimacy to challenge those powers which gnawed at the fiber of an even-keeled world. Here was the new imperial ethos: so afraid of slippage, of erosion. Also, Byrnes' speech, as Fraser J. Harbutt has observed, foreshadowed the harsher, more pessimistic analysis offered by Winston Churchill at Fulton, Missouri, a few days later.[12]

Much has been made of Churchill's 'iron curtain' speech of 5 March 1946. The imagery was not new, nor were the former prime minister's sentiments. But the official sanction given his remarks represented a new willingness publicly to excoriate the USSR and build toward big-power confrontation. Churchill quickly drew attention to Truman's having 'travelled a thousand miles to dignify and magnify our meeting here today and to give me an opportunity of addressing this kindred nation, as well as my own countrymen across the ocean, and perhaps some other countries too'. Times were 'anxious and baffling', as he had before frequently commented. Offering the obligatory caveat, Churchill noted that he spoke only for himself. 'There is nothing here but what you see.' What Americans saw, of course, was a grand old man, an admired curmudgeon, a heroic wartime leader, a legend yet recently minted. And he was speaking, as he had so powerfully during the struggle against Nazi Germany, about clear and present dangers. The United States, said Churchill, stood 'at the pinnacle of world power'; but this 'primacy' was the harbinger of both opportunity and dread – the chance to provide genuine security for the West's common people in their 'myriad cottage or apartment homes', coupled with anxiety over the return of the 'two giant marauders, war and tyranny'.

The United Nations stood as a tool for peace, but its future was less certain than the ringing rhetoric of its inception. As well, said Churchill, the secret of the atomic bomb must remain in Anglo-American hands. Can you imagine our fear, he asked, if such a secret were monopolized by 'some Communist or neo-Fascist State'? Tyranny, as epitomized by totalitarian states, was the shrewd enemy of American and British freedoms. While the future might well promise abundance for the world's peoples, this 'sad and breathless moment' forced upon Britain and the United States a special responsibility. Here was the crux of his message, remarked Churchill: 'Neither the sure prevention of war, nor the continuous rise of world organisation will be gained without what I have called the fraternal association of the English-speaking peoples. This means a special relationship between the British Commonwealth and Empire and the United States'. Such a relationship required continued close military co-operation, in both strategic planning and weapons procurement. As both Lippmann and Welles had counselled, Churchill contended that close Anglo-American ties would only enhance the stature and strength of the United Nations. For another global war would surely result in awesome destruction: 'The dark ages may return, the Stone Age may return on the gleaming wings of science'. Yet, even as people shuddered at such imagery, there was a new threat to peace, said Churchill. That threat was the Soviet Union – the nation which had rung down across Europe 'an iron curtain'.

The metaphor was so compelling that the phrase was still in limited use decades later. 'Iron curtain' (or 'steel curtain', in the words of General Eisenhower) expressed perfectly the growing consensus among US policymakers that the Soviet government represented a malevolent purpose. Further, said Churchill, there were additional, related dangers. In front of the iron curtain lay embattled Italy and France, where communist parties yoked themselves to Soviet objectives. Everywhere but in the British Commonwealth and the United States, communism was on the march – 'a growing challenge and peril to Christian civilisation'. It was indeed a 'sombre' picture, with problems as well in the Far East. However, there was hope in resolute action. 'I do not believe that Soviet Russia desires war', remarked Churchill.

> What they desire is the fruits of war and the indefinite expansion of their power and doctrines. . . . From what I have seen of our Russian friends and Allies during the war, I am convinced that there is nothing they admire so much as strength, and there is nothing for which they have less respect than for weakness, especially military weakness. . . . If the Western Democracies stand together in strict adherence to the principles of the United Nations Charter, their influence for furthering those principles will be immense and no one is likely to molest them.

Churchill's message was quite clear. Divided, Britain and America would falter; their democratic traditions would be overcome by the insidious pressure of communist conspiracy. Together, the British Empire and the United States, well armed, could confidently walk the 'high-roads of the future'.[13] But there were still the low-roads of the present to be navigated; and while adept at stirring anxiety, Churchill's words did not outline specific policies. This was not unexpected. No longer prime minister, no longer the same influential arbiter of the fate of foreign peoples, Churchill – like England – sought to accomplish more by persuasive argument than middling action.

Whether or not Winston Churchill was as influential as some historians have suggested, February and March of 1946 remained a pivotal moment, marking the redirection of Truman administration policy toward the Soviet Union. It was a policy based now on shared sentiments about Soviet expansionism and the strategic importance of the Mediterranean basin as well as a new realization of the decline of British power.[14] The fading of omnipotent Albion was evident worldwide. In the Far East, the war itself had marked the turning of the tide. The phasing out of SEAC during early 1946 was welcomed by both British and American military leaders. Mountbatten's relief at having completed a complicated, difficult task – alternately coddling and prodding recalcitrant allies, treating irregularly with native nationalists – was evident in his final report. There had never been much American affection for SEAC – it was a sop to Anglo-American solidarity; it was needed because US priorities lay elsewhere. Mountbatten's command was not fondly recalled. But SEAC had nonetheless performed workmanlike stabilizing duty much in accord with the cautious US policy toward colonial territories. Closer to Europe, at the base of the Balkans and around the eastern arc of the Mediterranean, British military strength was likewise waning. As American Ambassador Lincoln Mac-Veagh had written to Roosevelt in October 1944: 'Militarily speaking, the British Empire is anachronistic, perfect for the eighteenth century, impossible for the twentieth. Every day brings its evidence of weakness and dispersion . . . and dependence on America's nucleated strength'.[15]

Walter Lippmann had believed in 1943 that Anglo-America would rub shoulders with the USSR in central and eastern Europe and that it was in those 'borderlands' that West-East conflict would most likely erupt.[16] This seemed the logical conclusion, and there was no doubt that Europe remained the centerpiece of US, British and Soviet post-war strategic planning. However, it was along the periphery of Europe that trouble spots proliferated during 1945–46: civil war in Greece, Soviet-Turkish unpleasantries, Anglo-French discord in the Levant, escalating violence in Palestine, Anglo-Egyptian wrangling, an uncomfortable 'standfast' British Military Administration in Cyrenaica and Tripolitania, and nationalist agitation in French North Africa. Chief among the Near East crisis points was northern Iran, where the continued presence of Soviet troops intensified Western fears that Stalin sought to establish a puppet Azerbaijani regime within easy reach of Persian oilfields. And to the east of Iran lay India, where the pre-war nationalist movement had ignited widespread protest against continued British rule – discontent only somewhat subdued by the exigencies of war, now again strongly on the rise. The UN showdown over Iran very successfully engaged the anti-Soviet impulse in American political life, but it did nothing to clarify US goals toward the colonial world, except to reinforce the official mood of circumspection and conservatism.

COMMUNISM, COLONIALISM, AND FRENCH NORTH AFRICA

In his 'Long Telegram' of 22 February 1946, George Kennan, chargé in Moscow, set forth his enduring analysis of the Soviet worldview and the necessary US response. Kennan very effectively articulated the emergent consensus in Washington in favor of stronger countermeasures against perceived Soviet aggressiveness. Kennan surely sought to rally American policymakers against more than simple Russian expansionism. His references to the 'Kremlin's neurotic view of the world', the Soviet passion for 'total destruction of rival power', and the underground work of 'a concealed Comintern' underscored the views of the sternest hard-liners within the Truman administration – how else to respond to a ruthless, amoral, maniacal doctrine?

Yet, Kennan also addressed another important issue: the extra-European appeal of communism, 'with its honeyed promises to a desperate and war torn outside world'. He wrote, 'Toward colonial areas and backward or dependent peoples, Soviet policy ... will be directed toward [the] weakening of [the] power and influence and contacts of advanced Western nations, on [the] theory that in so far as this policy is successful, there will be created a vacuum which will favor Communist-Soviet penetration'. Kennan was not much concerned with official Soviet interest in trusteeship responsibilities, which he considered largely an effort 'to complicate and inhibit exertion of Western influence ... rather than to provide [a] major channel for [the] exerting of Soviet power'. Instead, his major worry was Soviet sponsorship of violent class struggle in Western Europe, exacerbated by the enervation of imperial ties. 'Mistakes and weaknesses of western colonial administration will be mercilessly exposed and exploited. Liberal opinion in Western countries will be mobilized to weaken colonial policies. Resentment among dependent peoples will be stimulated. And while [the] latter are being encouraged to seek independence of Western Powers, Soviet dominated puppet political machines will be undergoing preparation to take over domestic power in respective colonial areas when independence is achieved.'[17] Kennan offered hope that the strength of American institutions and traditions would guide US policymakers toward ultimate victory over the Soviet adversary, but his picture of a grim, dystopian communist juggernaut left little room for maneuvering and experimentation.

Kennan's thesis of a Soviet effort to strike at Western Europe through the soft underbelly of its colonial empire was not new to State Department policy planners. In fact, an internal debate was already under way regarding the extent of communist influence in emergent areas – especially, in early 1946, along the southern rim of the Mediterranean, in French North Africa. The State Department's interest in 1946 was similar to its wartime concerns about Arab attitudes toward the Allies, except that the United States was then directly involved as an occupying power. However, the limits of the US wartime role were amply demonstrated by the tardy and ineffective American protests over the French assault against Arab nationalists at Sétif in May 1945. Equally revealing was a departmental memorandum of 11 June 1945 titled 'North African Wheat Crisis'. Livingston T. Merchant of the War Areas Economic Division noted that a projected wheat famine in French North Africa could not be averted by greater American efforts to supply foodstuffs to the territories. Raising assistance levels to that desired by the French government would mean, wrote Merchant, diverting nearly all US shipping from Western Europe and significantly modifying military planning for Japan's final defeat. Hence, in his division, Merchant observed, 'We do not regard North Africa, shipping- and supply-wise, as a problem separable from France. We have also taken the position that, if [a] choice must be made, our interests in Western Europe are greater than in North Africa'. The French would have to decide what amount of their designated tonnage could be spared for the North African colonies.[18] As before, Europe was the first priority.

Edward Lawton, the US consul general in Algiers since October 1944, toured the arid southern zone of Algeria following his reassignment to Washington in August 1945. He saw little opportunity for any significant American economic role in post-war Algeria; but, like other contemporary observers, Lawton affirmed the strategic value of the Sahara for future 'air communications'. United States policies toward North African Muslims, he advised, would have wide repercussions throughout the Middle East. To Arabs, said Lawton, the official US attitude toward their region seemed one of 'disinterested friendship'. Nine months later, the new consul general, Harold Finley, reported continuing food and clothing shortages in Algeria but no political disturbances. The first anniversay of the Sétif uprising was not marked by renewed violence. Finley noted that the French Communist Party was actively recruiting Muslim adherents, though with limited success: a 'considerable number' of Algerian Arabs had joined the party, but 'chiefly, it is believed, with their tongues in their cheeks'. Finley doubted 'that any permanent, long-range alliance between Communist and Moslems is possible because of their marked difference in ideology and doctrine'.[19] The incompatibility of Islam and Marxism-Leninism was common currency in the State Department.

Finley's summary of Algerian affairs also demonstrated his lack of enthusiasm for native nationalist leaders, whom he viewed as extremists. To him, it was 'unthinkable' that a viable Muslim state could be established. 'As one observer recently remarked, "Where would they get the stenographers?"' The comment likely came from one of the local French officials, with whom Finley maintained close relations. The governor-general, Yves Chataigneau, was portrayed as 'an intelligent, kindly, hard-working' official who was pro-American and always co-operative. Finley believed that once there were available greater stocks of food and clothing, there would be little Arab unrest. Virtually the same viewpoints had been aired earlier in a *New York Times* article by Clifton Daniel, who stressed the geographical and psychological remoteness of French North Africa 'from the political turbulence at the other end of the Arab world'. The influence of the Arab League, he averred, 'appears to diminish with every mile west of Cairo'. The French, observed Daniel, were confident of their control and emboldened to contemplate both economic and political reform. With Moscow apparently uninterested in dabbling amongst the region's Arabs and with muted communist criticism in France, North Africa slumbered as crises rose and fell elsewhere. 'The critical period of post-war change and confusion has passed', wrote Daniel. 'The United States and Britain now have bigger fish to fry.' Such optimistic views of Algerian affairs were disputed, however, by the US ambassador in Paris, Jefferson Caffery, who feared a Soviet plan to weaken Western Europe and communize the Mediterranean littoral by posing as the friend of colonial peoples.[20]

As soon became clear, the State Department lacked consensus on Soviet/communist strategy toward European colonies and protectorates in the Mediterranean. For France, there seemed to be two alternatives: either (1) French communists would continue to uphold imperial ties with North Africa in the hopes of winning control in Paris and subsequently overseeing the establishment of leftist colonial regimes, or (2) French communists would aggressively ally themselves with Arab nationalists and connive to sever imperial ties as a prelude to rebellion in North Africa and the creation of party-led revolutionary directorates. The discussion was opened to a broader audience in July when the department instructed its consulates in Algiers, Casablanca, Rabat and Tunis to begin sending fortnightly airgrams reporting on communist propaganda and political activity directed at Arabs. Copies of the instructions were sent to the American embassies in Paris and Moscow as well as the legations at Tangier and Cairo. In his cover memorandum, Acting Secretary Joseph Grew wrote:

The Department is led to believe that, so long as the Soviets still have hopes of gaining control of France by peaceful means, their policy will only be one of establishing friendly relations between Arab nationalist leaders of North Africa and the Communist party, rather than 'actually weakening their ties with France'; and that not until the Communists are convinced that they have little or no chance of gaining control of France, and with it North Africa, will their program be aimed at breaking the North African communities away from the mother country.[21]

The message to Algiers and other North African consulates acknowledged that the scale of communist activity among North African Arabs remained small. Nevertheless, wrote Grew, 'it is possible that the Nationalist groups in North Africa might conceivably come to feel that there is something to be gained by a temporary alliance with the Communists, especially if the impression grows on them that they can expect nothing from France, and little more from the Western Powers'. At present, though, it appeared reasonable to assume that French communists would not conduct an 'open campaign' for Arab independence. The department was quick to stress, however, that any communist gains among Arabs would be harmful to US interests.[22] American apprehension over Algerian affairs had increased following elections in early June which brought Ferhat Abbas and ten *Manifeste* supporters into the new French Constituent Assembly. While debating the form and substance of the Fourth Republic's new constitution, the assembly could logically consider North African issues as well. It was not known to what extent Abbas and his supporters would use the assembly as a forum for militant nationalist views, or to what degree Abbas' presence would foster a nationalist-communist alliance which might enhance the party's appeal in Algeria.

Ambassador Caffery responded to the department's analysis with a combative counter-estimate, asserting that there was indeed an urgent communist threat in French North Africa. While he agreed with others in the State Department that the Soviets *pro forma* cultivated good relations between communist parties and Arab nationalists, Caffery added a worrisome caveat.

> In this connection, however, the Embassy would like to express its belief that it is extremely difficult in such relatively backward countries as Algeria, Tunisia and Morocco, to distinguish between Communists, autonomists and those natives advocating full independence. It would seem, on the contrary, that these various movements, *which should in theory be quite separate and distinct, are on the contrary confused and interwoven at the base*, with a few leaders at the top giving the appearance of separate and distinct movements.

Caffery did not believe that the obvious contradictions between communist ideology and Islamic precepts were a major obstacle to the spread of Soviet influence among Arabs.

The Embassy, viewing the situation from Paris, believes that Communist doctrine in North Africa *is purposely kept exceedingly fluid, ill-defined, and that according to Leninist-Stalinist theory it has been tailored to adapt itself to the loose and as yet uncrystallized nationalist aspirations* of these areas and towards the exploitation of the misery and subnormal standards of living which for several years have prevailed in North Africa, due to a series of dry years and to the war.

Communism, argued Caffery, wore 'a cloak of nationalism and local autonomy in North Africa'. Thus, the election of Abbas to the Constituent Assembly was an 'indirect Communist success'. Thus, the French Communist party was already pursuing policies which abetted the spread of nationalist sentiment in North Africa and thereby weakened imperial ties.[23]

Caffery's argument was well tuned to Truman administration concerns regarding the troubled landscape of Western Europe as well as the global communist threat. Specifically, the image of a ruthless conspiracy, tailoring its doctrine to fit the audience – with potentially explosive results in colonial areas – complemented Kennan's brooding protrait of the Kremlin's imperialist drive. Political underdevelopment or naïveté invited communist exploitation. The conclusions expressed in the State Department's July circular to its Mediterranean-area embassies had been tentative, and Caffery's bare-knuckles analysis strengthened the hand of departmental hard-liners. In a memorandum of 21 August, Harry H. Schwartz of the Office of Near Eastern and African Affairs (NEA), claimed that communists remained a formidable force in French politics and were now more openly espousing Arab nationalist aims. In his margin comments, NEA Director Loy Henderson agreed with Schwartz that the United States should take more direct steps to discourage Arab-communist co-operation. Such efforts should include the select pooling of information with the British government and discreet efforts to warn North African nationalists that, in Schwartz's words, 'it is dangerous to play with communists'. A week later, Ambassador Caffery summarized a Constituent Assembly debate which raised fundamental questions about Algeria's future. 'Blunt remarks' by Ferhat Abbas and other nationalists 'stirred up resentment which at times spread to all but the Communist benches'. Only the communist deputies, said Caffery, consistently supported the nationalists. 'Frenchmen now realize for the first time in decades that a potentially critical Algerian problem exists, and they are beginning to be disturbed at its implications.'[24]

Thus, although estimates of Marx's appeal to North Africans would continue to vary, the department's dialogue with Caffery had sharpened anxiety about Soviet solicitousness toward nationalist groups and concern about the domino-like momentum of communist gains in colonial areas. The rimlands appeared to offer ample opportunity for communist subversion or trickery, for new threats to US plans for a global network of open doors reinforcing Western (especially American) dominance. It was also apparent that colonial peoples exuded a self-conscious linkage, at least of the heart, among the disparate nationalist efforts at autonomy or independence. Ferhat Abbas spoke out in support of the Viet Minh during the summer of 1946. The Arab League emerged as a strong proponent of Libyan independence during the 1945–46 sessions of the Council of Foreign Ministers. Nehru put pressure upon the British viceroy to remove Indian troops from reoccupation duties in Indochina and the East Indies. Any movement which cut across the imaginary but discrete boundaries between world regions was viewed with suspicion by American policymakers.

As 1946 wore on toward 1947, the tide of rimland nationalism became more violent in response to determined metropole efforts to restore imperial authority. While the myopic, stubborn diplomacy practised by the French and the Dutch ostensibly protected Western interests in Southeast Asia – and indeed, they unfailingly argued that this was so – American and British officials were well aware of the dangers posed by a hostile, alienated colonial world. Troublesome allies could cause long-term damage to image and prestige – the same allies who were dependent upon a nurturing United States for their recovery in Europe. Yet, the leverage suggested by the obvious inequality of US-Western European ties was not real. Or, to put it a bit differently, the advantage was not quite realizable. France was a good example, its society so bruised and frayed by defeat, occupation and collaboration. France suffered so openly from 'maladies' arising from the war, wrote correspondent Harold Callender: 'physical disorganization and moral depression'. The French people, he said in June 1946, have been 'overwhelmed by disillusionment which has put their faith in themselves and in the world to a severe test'.[25]

State Department officials had made similar observations. For instance, at the time of the Yalta conference, Acting Secretary Joseph Grew had written of the stark dismay of the French people: they were cold and hungry; they lacked the necessary machinery to rebuild their factories; millions of Frenchmen remained in prison camps. Their country's liberation had of course been the source of further devastation. Despite the rapid inflow of American aid to civilians as well as the use of US *matériel* to re-equip the French army and overhaul French naval vessels, serious problems remained. State Department official Camden H. McVey advised in October 1945 that the French were recovering not only from physical destruction but also 'deep emotional wounds'. He commented:

I do not believe that the American people, individually or collectively, could even approach the depths of shame and humiliation which the French have suffered, and from which, in ways scarcely understandable to us, they are trying to recover. . . . Because great things were expected of France, France took the disappointment of the world deep into her soul as her personal shame and humiliation. Her behavior, both national and individual, has been plainly conditioned by this psychological depression ever since.

It was not simply lost honor which must be redeemed; there was also the undeniable 'war-borne economic retrogression' which stifled any hopes of quick reconstruction. Yet, French economic renewal was critical to the stability of the American and the world economy. McVey was more restrained when estimating the ability of France to remain a great power. 'Essentially, the leadership that France can . . . best provide is political. scientific, and cultural. Our own close ties with France had always been based on these intellectual attributes rather than on her military or economic strength.'[26]

This was metropolitan France that Grew and McVey were talking about. Goodwill toward French recovery was genuine because economic growth was so important to the US-European trade relationship. But the tendency of French officials stubbornly to resist any external suggestions for reform within the empire was annoying. As American diplomatic agent Paul H. Alling observed (from Tangier) in early 1947:

Although Arabs here are naturally friendly [to] our country, I do not entirely discount [the] possibility that if [the] French hold them in check too tightly or too long, nationalists may reluctantly accept aid from Communist sources in [the] mistaken idea that [such a] course would give them real freedom. In my opinion it is [in the] interest [of] France and [the] US that progress toward self-government be quickened.[27]

But the French had no interest in promoting self-rule in their colonies.

Meanwhile, Great Britain faced numerous perplexing problems along the shores of the Mediterranean. In Libya, British officials focused upon upgrading the understaffed military regime in both Cyrenaica and Tripolitania. A special 'working party' was set to tour the territories by the end of 1946 for the purpose of recommending administrative reforms which would 'predispose the native in favor of the long-term solutions' desired in London – primarily, an Anglo-Cyrenaican alliance granting Britain the base rights being lost elsewhere in the region. It was self-interest to be sure, but Americans were less critical than they might have been. As US diplomat John Utter noted, 'The British want bases in Cyrenaica, and quite openly say so, but have long since passed the stage where they wish to obtain them by undertaking the colonial rule of a vast territory'.[28] Hence, Perfidious Albion was much less a threat to American policy priorities than insecure and imprudently assertive Gaul. Southeast Asia posed the problem quite clearly.

WARFARE IN VIETNAM

Writing more than a year after VE Day, former State Department official Rupert Emerson observed: 'The notorious iron curtain obscures not only Eastern Europe, but much of Southeastern Asia also despite the fact that no accusation can be made that the latter area is in the grip of the Soviet Union'. It was rather American policy, he seemed to suggest, which was in the grip of iron curtain fever. The ideological enemy stood poised at every door of the global house – to use another Churchill metaphor. Like other Asianists, Emerson pointed to the disappointment of native peoples in the colonial territories of the Far East – dramatic changes had been promised but had not come. Imperial reforms announced from Paris were little more than a 'sugar coating'. Likewise historian Ellen Hammer commented sardonically about 'the fondness of liberated France for new and more acceptable labels' while French colonial dominance was to continue unchallenged and unbroken.[29]

Americans appeared to have adjusted to the resurgence of colonial powers with relative equanimity. However, remarked Emerson, 'the readiness of the Western world to forgive and forget was not matched by an equal complacency on the part of the Southeast Asians who well remembered that a new world was supposed to be in the making'. United States policy remained cautious and conservative, such that it 'does not go far enough to endear it to the harassed imperial powers, nor does its unofficial liberal tradition produce enough concrete results to win it the trust of the native nationalists.' American policymakers must recognize, said Emerson, that the situation in Southeast Asia was 'shot through with complexities, incalculables, and uncertainties'. While pre-war communist doctrine and methodology had left an 'imprint' upon regional nationalist movements, native leaders were nonetheless 'building on local foundations and were responding to the increasingly vocal needs of their own people. Lacking responsive friends elsewhere, it can be no matter of great surprise that many of the nationalists should have accepted gratefully the aid which came to them from Communist sources'. Looking ahead, Emerson was not optimistic about the fate of the region. 'If there are any who expect utopias to arise as empires are dissolved, they are doomed to grave disappointments.' The United States had an important role to play, its own imprint to leave; but action and inaction would be equally influential – there was no way to remain aloof from or neutral toward events in Southeast Asia.[30] Still, US leaders were reluctant to accept the idea that nationalist upheaval could bear the marks of Marxism-Leninism and yet be the product of a genuinely indigenous movement – OSS claims notwithstanding. Observers like Jefferson Caffery argued forcefully that unrest in French North Africa and similar colonial situations was a chaotic mosaic of naive local nationalists and dedicated, pernicious communists.

The notion of a predatory world communist movement was again well rooted in the State Department by early 1946. It colored the department's collective judgment about the character of people and events in Vietnam and other colonial areas. Certainly no one familiar with the inner history of the executive branch during the years 1945–46 could accuse US policy-makers of friendship toward Ho Chi Minh and the Democratic Republic of Vietnam (DRV). President Truman was uninterested in Indochina issues. Top-ranking officials were primarily concerned with restoring France's voice in European councils. Also important, American diplomats abroad were highly suspicious of the Viet Minh's leftist leadership – for the same reason argued by Caffery: that communists sought to manipulate anti-colonial movements and deceitfully wore a 'cloak' of nationalist sympathies.

Ambassador Caffery had reported in early February 1946 that French officials would likely pursue a 'conciliatory and moderate' policy toward the DRV. He attributed this new liberalism to the new political ascendancy of the socialists in Paris. 'This does not mean, however', he cautioned, 'that they are thinking in terms of independence for Indo-China[,] for no Frenchmen appear to be thinking in such terms.'[31] Kenneth P. Landon, assistant chief of the Division of Southeast Asian Affairs (SEA), visited both Saigon and Hanoi and spoke with French, Chinese and Vietnamese officials the same month. While the shape of a Sino-French agreement for the evacuation of Chinese occupation troops was fairly clear, Landon reported continued confusion in Franco-Vietnamese talks. Jean Sainteny, commissioner for Tonkin, contended that residents of Cochinchina would likely seek continued French rule. Ho Chi Minh, on the other hand, argued forcefully that the southern province must be joined with Annam and Tonkin in a unified, independent Vietnam. The two positions were irreconcilable.

From Ho, Landon received copies of letters to the governments of Britain, China, the USSR and the United States. As in previous efforts to attract the attention and support of the big powers, Ho emphasized the positive wartime record of the Viet Minh, the proclamation of independence in September 1945, and the fact that France's former sovereignty had been overthrown. 'The new republic of Vietnam, thus legally constituted, is in the reconstruction of the world a factor of peace and progress. She is entitled for her safeguard to refer to the most sacred principles of [the] SAN FRANCISCO and ATLANTIC Charters.' The French, said Ho, remained aggressive, their troops committing atrocities against the Vietnamese population, north and south, while DRV leaders struggled to restore administrative and educational services and create a new political system. 'Foreign correspondents and members of the Allies Missions who have come to the country can bear witness to the new life in regenerated Vietnam, to our capacity to self-government, our desire to live free and

independent.'[32] Since foreign governments had no official relations with
the DRV, the only people who *could* bear witness to Viet Minh sincerity
and popular support were largely journalists and military observers – and a
few interested State Department officials. The information to substantiate
DRV claims was available; it was simply ignored by top-level American
policymakers, who continued to assert a studied neutrality which worked
to the advantage of France.

Despite its failure to deal decisively with the status of Cochinchina, the 6
March 1946 accord was proclaimed the first step toward Franco-Viet Minh
rapprochement; and it appeared to be so as further negotiations were
scheduled for the summer. Ho Chi Minh arrived in France in June and
spent ten days in the coastal town of Biarritz, escorted by Sainteny,
awaiting the consolidation of a new cabinet in Paris. The Vietnamese
leader fished in the Bay of Biscay, sampled local restaurants, and relaxed
on the beach while French politicians arranged their affairs. Years later,
Sainteny commented: 'I wonder if France has ever appreciated the extent
of the homage Ho Chi Minh paid the French by such trust [as he
demonstrated in 1946]. He agreed to travel to a country that still exercised
protectorate powers over Indochina, a powerful nation that had pursued
him for almost thirty years and had condemned him to death!'[33] In fact,
since the March accord had not resulted in any significant improvement in
the international status of the DRV, Ho Chi Minh was compelled to accept
France's invitation as the only alternative to immediate warfare in Vietnam. After his official reception in Paris on 22 June, Ho awaited the
beginning of negotiations in Fontainebleau, about 40 miles to the south.

The results were meager, perhaps predictably. On 1 April, the US
consul in Saigon, Charles S. Reed, had expressed little hope for a resolution
of Franco-Vietnamese differences. 'One might hope that both sides [will]
take no steps during [the] period of negotiation which might jeopardize [a]
final peaceable outcome but [there is] every likelihood [of a] stormy period
ahead, particularly so far as concerns [a] mature status [for] Cochin China.'
Nor were American officials particularly interested in such problems.
Secretary of State Byrnes acknowledged on 10 April 'the reversion of all
Indo-China to French control'.[34] On 13 May, Mountbatten tendered his
official departure from Indochina; by the end of the month, the bulk of
Chinese military forces had withdrawn from northern Vietnam. On 1 June,
the Saigon colonial regime announced the establishment of the independent republic of Cochinchina. Consul Charles Reed reported: '[It is]
Believed there will be [a] strong reaction in [the] north and it is possible
that [the] French may have endangered continued peaceable negotiations
with Viet Nam. However, [the] French may feel strong enough now to risk
[an] open break'.[35] Sporadic violence crackled throughout Vietnam as the
discussions opened at Fontainebleau on 6 July; and from the beginning,
the talks were embittered by the controversy over Cochinchina – an area

which a former OSS operative called the 'agricultural keystone' of Vietnam.[36] Without Cochinchina, all parties seemed to realize, the DRV was indeed a precarious economic and political entity. In Paris, Ambassador Caffery met with Philippe Baudet, director of the Asiatic Division of the French Foreign Ministry, who seemed to confirm Reed's analysis of an emboldened France. 'Baudet ... indicated', Caffery reported, '[that] French officials are not particularly anxious to speed up [the] work of [the] Fontainebleau conference and are quite willing for relations with Viet Nam to continue under [the] present agreement [that is, the 6 March accord] until the pacification of Indochina and particularly Cochin China is completed.'[37]

As the Paris Peace Conference painstakingly surveyed the political climate of Europe, the French government stumbled toward a military confrontation in Southeast Asia. This was the conclusion of a thoughtful memorandum of 9 August, by Abbot Moffat, SEA director. The French, he said, were maneuvering 'to confine and weaken Viet Nam i.e., the DRV'. They were doing this by seeking to build an Indochinese federation without DRV participation under the cover of plodding negotiations at Fontainebleau. 'Annamese leaders had long emphasized', Moffat noted, 'their view that the inclusion of Cochinchina in Viet Nam was a matter of life and death to their country.' Evidence gathered by SEA supported the Viet Minh contention that no French-administered referendum on the future status of Cochinchina would be conducted fairly. Moffat believed that 'the conclusion is inescapable that the French are endeavoring to whittle down Viet Nam and to settle the future form of organization of Indochina with those who may be expected to be amenable to French influence'. He wrote: 'In conclusion, it is SEA's view that the Annamese are faced with the choice of a costly submission to the French or of open resistance, and that the French may be preparing to resort to force in order to secure their position throughout Indochina'.[38]

The discussions at Fontainebleau ended ineffectively, as many had come to expect, on 14 September 1946, although a *modus vivendi* was initialed by Ho Chi Minh and Marius Moutet, the French Minister of Overseas Territories. Sainteny himself called it a 'pathetic' document, considering what the Vietnamese delegation had initially hoped to achieve. The 6 March accord had held out the hope of autonomy if not independence; French diplomacy of the summer had sought to circumvent and vitiate the Viet Minh republic. The *modus vivendi* preserved diplomatic contact between the parties, but without resolving any major issue. It was merely a preliminary to armed struggle. Before sailing for Hanoi, Ho portrayed his signing such an inconclusive document as proof of his conciliatory disposition.[39] Further Franco-Vietnamese negotiations, tentatively scheduled for early 1947, never took place.

Before leaving France, Ho Chi Minh had told Moutet, 'We will fight.

You will kill ten of my men while we kill one of yours. But you will be the ones to end up exhausted'. The party line was a promise of tough, indefinite resistance. Ho had spoken similarly to nearly every OSS officer and US diplomat he had met during and shortly after the war: French intransigence would be met by Vietnamese intransigence. Yet in discussions with State Department officials, including SEA staffers, Brigadier General Philip Gallagher of the Chinese Combat Command had belittled the capacity of the DRV to resist a French military offensive. He was asked: were Viet Minh leaders realistic about their vulnerability? Gallagher answered that yes, they likely were. 'They are strong on parades and reiterate their willingness to "fight to the last man", but they would be slaughtered and they have been told that and probably know it', he is recorded as saying. Vietnamese troops could not, he believed, fight effectively against a modern, well-equipped French army.[40] While Gallagher was later proven wrong, the tenacity of Viet Minh guerrilla warfare had yet to be ably demonstrated to the world.

Ho Chi Minh arrived at Haiphong on 21 October 1946, his first return to native soil since the previous May. As Franco-Vietnamese relations worsened, defined by spiralling streetfighting, the State Department showed new interest in the possibility of a behind-the-scenes Soviet role in Indochina affairs. On 9 October, Acting Secretary Dean Acheson had sent a note to the consulate general in Saigon complaining about the Viet Minh flag, with its gold star on a red background. Such an arrangement, he said, 'will inevitably lead nationals of other countries to form conclusions which the Vietnam Government [DRV] would apparently not wish them to form'. Sûreté staffers in Saigon unsurprisingly hinted at a resurgence of communist activity within the colony. James O'Sullivan, US vice-consul in Hanoi, cautiously reported apparent contacts between DRV leaders and Chinese communists.[41]

Still, both O'Sullivan and Reed doubted allegations about direct links between Vietnamese leaders and Moscow or Peking. The former advised, 'French concern over Communism may well be devised to direct [the State] Dept's attention from French policy in Indochina'. Nonetheless, Acheson was firm in his belief that the 'least desirable eventuality would be [the] establishment [of a] Communist-dominated Moscow-oriented state [in] Indochina'. Ho Chi Minh, said Acheson, had a 'clear record' as a communist agent. In a note of 17 December, Secretary Byrnes stated that the DRV regime was controlled by communists who were 'possibly in indirect touch with Moscow and direct touch with [the Chinese Communists in] Yenan'. While some Viet Minh leaders, like Ho, were apparently willing to co-operate with France, others were not. Byrnes then asserted, in a somewhat contradictory statement: 'Nationalist sentiment runs deep among the Vietnamese as does opposition to the French, and they might easily turn against all whites. French influence is important not only as an antidote to Soviet influence but to protect Vietnam and SEA from future Chinese imperialism'. Both sides bore responsibility for the breakdown of negotiations, said Byrnes; but it was clear that the secretary had been much influenced by French representations of the Viet Minh as a group of childish, ruthless, doctrinaire left-wing nationalists.[42]

In making such comments, Byrnes believed he was summarizing the most recent intelligence from the Indochina territories. Abbot Moffat, the chief spokesman for Southeast Asian nationalism within the State Department, visited Vietnam during the last few weeks of 1946, arriving in Saigon on 3 December. Impressed with the calibre of recently appointed French officials, he noted: 'They are really superior individuals; but I gather that even they are pretty badly hamstrung by their subordinates who are the same seventh rate functionaries who were here before the war'. A round of official dinners kept Moffat off Saigon streets as local administrators nervously sought to maintain public order. After three days, Moffat flew to Hanoi, where heavy fighting had erupted for several days in late November over control of the port of Haiphong. Moffat wrote:

> This was my first experience in visiting an area under tension, with warfare anticipated anytime. . . . It was quite a shock to have to drive into the city with ditches cut across all but narrow spots in the road; to see fox holes excavated in the sidewalks; and barricades . . . erected at certain points, also holes for mines dug at various street intersections. . . . Even the market places are not crowded and after sunset the streets are deserted as much of the native population has left the city and many more go away at night.[43]

Moffat's instructions from the State Department, signed by Acheson, had unfortunately arrived in Saigon after his departure. However, there was little which would have been helpful. Moffat was advised to urge a co-operative stance upon both French and Vietnamese officials. '[You] May say [that the] American people have welcomed [the] attainments [of the] Indochinese in [their] efforts [to] realize [such] praiseworthy aspirations [as] greater autonomy [with]in the framework [of] democratic institutions and it would be regrettable should this interest and sympathy be imperilled by any tendency [among the] Vietnamese administration [to] force [the] issues by intransigence and violence.' Moffat could inform Ho Chi Minh that similar comments were being made to the French government, designed to encourage restraint and moderation. Caffery would tell French officials that the United States did not desire that 'perpetual foment' in Vietnam become a source of instability throughout the region. Moffat was told: 'Avoid [the] impression [that the] US Govt [is] making [any] formal intervention [at] this juncture. Publicity [of] any kind would be unfortunate'.[44]

Such general and unobtrusive instructions were unnecessary as Moffat toasted French officials and carefully maneuvered, once in Hanoi, for a conversation with Ho. Speaking first with Vo Nguyen Giap, the Viet Minh military commander, Moffat did not like his 'dead-pan face' and semi-fanatical communist demeanor. When Moffat suggested that warfare would harm many more Vietnamese than Frenchmen, Giap only commented that independence would require sacrifice. 'Later he did say that the Vietnamese might not win', recalled Moffat, 'but that in any event the French would not win. In this I think he epitomized well the situation, because the French are really through in the Annamese countries; they cannot afford a straight military reconquest which would in any case be an enormous task.' It was a disheartening conversation for Moffat, who realized better than in Saigon the deep rift between the colonial administration and DRV leaders. 'After leaving Giap we drove around the city. Every exit was barricaded; but more symptomatic yet was the fact that in the time I was in Hanoi, I raised a responding grin (a little tentative at that) in just one child; one smile at a foreigner in three days!'[45] It was not the summer of 1945 when Americans were jubilant co-partners in victory. It was over a year later, when the Viet Minh stood alone and apparently outgunned.

While in Hanoi, Moffat arranged a brief meeting with Ho Chi Minh, on 14 December; it was the last official talk between a State Department officer and the veteran revolutionary. Ho was 'obviously weak and his voice was often very feeble'. As he had done consistently for two years, Ho described his own aims in poignant, moderate tones. As Moffat recalled:

> He spoke of his friendship and admiration for the United States and the Americans he had known and worked with in the jungle ... and how they had treated the Annamese as equals. He spoke of his desire to build up Vietnam in collaboration with the French so that his people might be better off, and to that end they wanted independence to seek friends among other countries as well as France and to secure the capital needed to develop their country, which France was too poor to give them. He said he knew that the United States did not like communism, but that that was not his aim. If he could secure their independence that was enough for his life time.

Moffat could not remember the exact words of the conversation.

> The intent, at any rate was a smiling, and friendly 'Don't worry' – which coincides with the ablest French views (not the popular view) that the group in charge of Vietnam are at this stage nationalists first, utilizing their party techniques and discipline to that end; that an effective nationalist state is a prerequisite to any attempt at developing a communist state – which objective must for the time being be secondary. ... I confined my remarks to expressing a hope for a peaceful settlement and my very genuine pleasure at meeting him.[46]

Moffat's analysis was more subtle than Byrnes' cable had indicated. Yet, he had stressed both the improved character of the French colonial regime and the unwavering communism of the Viet Minh leadership. On 19–20 December, large-scale conflict broke out between French and Vietnamese forces in Hanoi and quickly spread throughout Tonkin. Jean Sainteny lay wounded on the rough pavement after his vehicle hit a mine. 'I knew only one thing: the Indochinese war had begun', he wrote. 'And in the darkness, ripped open by flashes of gunfire, all our efforts and hopes were swallowed up.'[47]

The full tragedy in Vietnam was better captured by *New York Times* correspondent Foster Hailey, who was working with his colleague Robert Trumbull to gather information about Southeast Asian turmoil. In a lengthy private letter, dated 31 December, Hailey began, 'The last day of the painful year of 1946 is an appropriate time to write of Indo-China. For it is one of the more painful spots of Asia'. The French were deluding themselves, wrote Hailey. 'The French can no more hold Indo-China than a straw house can stop a whirlwind. They haven't enough Frenchmen, even in France, to hold it. That is, unless we are willing to give them the atom bomb and let them utterly destroy the most attractive little people I have seen anywhere, and the most appealing.' He recounted tales of terror and torture perpetrated by the Saigon Sûreté, of drunk, ex-Wehrmacht Foreign Legionnaires tromping through the streets of Hanoi. He described a stubborn resistance movement in the south. The provisional native government of Cochinchina, sneered Hailey, 'is a puppet if I ever saw one, with French "advisors" running the show from fine buildings and the Cochin Chinese officials twiddling their thumbs in bare offices halfway across town'.

Like Moffat, Hailey and Trumbull found Hanoi to be an armed camp, with trenches and barbed wire stretching through much of the city. On meeting Ho Chi Minh, whom they thought to be dying of tuberculosis, both journalists were favorably impressed. They believed, as Sainteny said he did also, that Ho was sincere in wanting a peaceful settlement. 'Ho Chi Min[h] is undoubtedly the former Comintern leader of Southeast Asia', noted Hailey. 'But in an hour and a half talk he used no Communist dialectics, his followers deny any ties with Moscow – which I believe, because the Russian officials in Saigon have absolutely nothing to do and apparently never even see anyone – and I believe Russia in Indo-China, as elsewhere in the Far East, is keeping strictly hands off while the democracies make hay for them.' Hailey believed the Viet Minh to be primarily a nationalist party, not an arm of Soviet intrigues. He wrote further: 'I believe we should take a very critical view of French colonialism in Indo-China. ... For some day these people of Asia are going to have their freedom. There are a lot of them to kill. It is up to us to say whether the transition will be peaceful or bloody. If it is the latter, then all Asia undoubtedly will someday be Communist'.[48] It was a common theme by year's end: the United States would play a major role, one way or the other – through action or inaction – in Southeast Asia. And the failure to identify American interests with those of native nationalists would have far-reaching consequences for US-Soviet cold war rivalry. Hailey's next stop was Java.

INDONESIA: THE LINGGADJATI AGREEMENT

The Netherlands East Indies and French Indochina had been so much alike: colonial backwaters teeming with native resentment amid the flotsam of Japan's abortive campaign for empire. Little peoples, with delicate features, like children to Western eyes – they wanted independence. They demanded it. In Saigon, the British commander had simply overridden the poorly organized nationalist opposition. In Hanoi, Viet Minh stamina triumphed over the disorder of Chinese occupation. In Indonesia, the British won little admiration for an admirable performance: preserving the face of imperial rule by initiating contacts with the *de facto* native republic – contacts strengthened after such sobering battles as Surabaya. The Dutch returned, to be sure, but never with the same self-confidence and upper hand of the past. Leaning heavily and uncomfortably upon the British – and dependent upon American lend-lease *matériel* – the Netherlands could no longer project the lean, fearsome countenance of the conqueror. Arrogance was brought low. Bright veils were pierced, and pretence was not redeemed. Thus, it seemed natural for correspondent Robert Trumbull to write, in December 1946, 'The Dutchman knows he has lost this country [Indonesia] and that he is an alien on the streets he built'.[49] But, as had been noted by OSS observers and English officers in Batavia, Dutch authorities were not at all reconciled to the loss of their East Indies jewel. Moreover, the same political instability which plagued the post-war French republic, complicating colonial affairs, also affected the ability of the Netherlands government to thrash out a policy toward Indonesia.

The reasonable course for Dutch officials was diplomacy. The same held true for the leaders of the Indonesian republic. General Philip Christison had tried to sponsor a negotiated settlement; Mountbatten had consistently encouraged Dutch moderation. American policymakers likewise favored a face-to-face dialogue between Dutch and Indonesian representatives. A State Department memorandum of 26 December 1945 foreshadowed Secretary Byrnes' comments of two months later by asserting that it was proper for the United Nations to concern itself with what might appear to be internal issues. Despite what Netherlands representatives would surely argue, 'the United Nations cannot fail to be deeply interested in the solution of problems that are of vital importance to the entire world, and that any problem relating to the maintenance of international peace and security would clearly be within the competence of the United Nations'.[50] The scope of UN concerns was theoretically quite broad.

Such was to be the official US position if the matter came before the UN Security Council. It would be much better, however, if the dispute were resolved locally – though a quick settlement of Dutch-Indonesian contention appeared unlikely. Ambassador Alexander Loudon continued to complain to the State Department about British policy in the East Indies, charging that Mountbatten's command had 'pampered' the nationalist leaders and persistently undermined the authority and prestige of Netherlands officials.[51] As usual, such complaints were brought to high-placed Europeanists within the department – those who most regretted the distracting character of colonial disturbances and most favored a diplomatic solution founded upon continued metropole sovereignty. But aside from stressing that the US government disapproved of extremist actions by anyone and that it hoped for an early, effective resolution of Dutch-Indonesian differences, there was little else American policymakers were prepared to do. The imbroglio was not of their making, rather, it was a European affair, with the British playing the lead role. The American withdrawal from the Southeast Asia Command, formally announced in early January 1946, underscored US reserve.

In late January, British diplomat Archibald Clark Kerr (later Lord Inverchapel) was sent to Batavia to foster renewed Dutch-Indonesian exchanges. He was told to seek a 'speedy solution' to the East Indies problem in order to facilitate the completion of SEAC's reoccupation duties, to minimize the further loss of life among British troops and civilian internees, and to accelerate British evacuation of the archipelago. From Batavia, the American consul general, Walter Foote, reported that General Christison had been relieved of his command. 'Members [of the] British General Staff informed me ... this means [a] firmer attitude towards Indonesians and stern methods to break [the] present hopeless impasse, [and] restore law and order. ... [Christison's] soft attitude and gentle methods in dealing with Indos allegedly led to much of [the] present chaos.' Foote noted that the Dutch were likewise 'cleaning house' by transferring local commanders who seemed to stand in the way of a settlement. Foote retained his pre-war disbelief in the reality of Indonesian nationalism and typically pictured the republic as a floundering enterprise, staffed by simple-minded leftists, which would be hard-pressed to sustain itself through difficult times.[52]

His work supplemented by high-level Anglo-Dutch discussions in London, Clark Kerr's presence in Batavia stimulated the re-opening of Netherlands-Indonesian talks on 10 February 1946. Hubertus van Mook, acting NEI governor general, spearheaded Dutch efforts, while Sutan

Sjahrir represented the republic. As in Indochina, realists on both sides found themselves close to agreement, at least for the short-term. Van Mook believed that Sjahrir was a moderate who offered the best hope for a reasonable agreement. The interim compromise character of the 6 March accord in Indochina provided a model for both sides in the Indonesia dispute, with Van Mook taking the initiative. As Robert McMahon has summarized:

> At the heart of Van Mook's plan lay his willingness to recognize the de facto authority of the republic and his offer to the republic to become a partner in a federative Indonesian Free State. In turn, the republic would have to cease all hostilities and to join in general deliberations with representatives from all parts of the East Indies, and with minority groups, to determine the political structure of the future Indonesian state and its relations with the Netherlands.[53]

It was the same basic concept as the Franco-Vietnamese agreement: temporary, *de facto* recognition would be granted the native nationalists in return for their commitment to an amorphous federation of dependencies. Underlying the arrangement was the promise of further negotiations to flesh out the ambiguities. It was the type of diplomatic sleight-of-hand which allowed for the co-existence of mutually exclusive points of view while holding out the possibility of eventual reconciliation. Such was an affirmation of the diplomatic *process* without, as it happened, effectively resolving specific issues – and, of course, specifics insistently rose to the surface of colonial diplomacy. Most difficult was the scope of the republic's *de facto* sovereignty. Was it to include only parts of Java, as the Dutch favored, or was it to include Sumatra as well – as desired by Indonesian nationalists? Here was the fundamental contradiction little obscured by diplomatic maneuvers: Netherlands authorities hoped to contain the Indonesian republic by surrounding it with weak dependencies, all parts of an archipelago-wide federation dominated from The Hague. Leaders of the republic, on the other hand, wanted first to guarantee the survival of their fledgling regime, and, secondly, to achieve *de facto* sovereignty over as much island territory as possible so as to lay the groundwork for eventual hegemony over the archipelago.

American priorities were consistently expressed in the vaguest terms to Indonesian officials – much as Ho Chi Minh, on the eve of general warfare in northern Vietnam, had been told by Abbot Moffat that the United States desired peace and prosperity for all. As Walter Foote reported from Batavia, he explained the US position as one of neutrality, 'that our Govt and [the] American people wish well for all peace-loving people; that we desired [that the] Indo[nesian] people gain peace, [a] good standard of living, better education and general advancement'. The United States, said Foote, was trying [to] change from war to peace production and ... 140 million Americans need raw materials which now [were] held up by [the] strife in [the] Netherlands East Indies. I added that [the] US [was] ready to buy great quantities [of] all goods which would assist rehabilitation [of the] Netherlands East Indies industries and make possible [the] supply of consumer goods needed here but that I feared continued strife would result in great delay and further chaos, deterioration, hatred, famine, disease, bloodshed and losses to all.[54]

By the end of March 1946, both sides appeared close to an agreement. Foote cabled on the 31st, 'Clark Kerr, Van Mook and Sjahrir dined with me last night and all were in a happy mood'. Unfortunately, Dutch domestic politics were unsettled, and a provisional government was unable to move decisively toward an agreement with Indonesian nationalists.[55] The optimism was premature. On a secondary diplomatic front, Admiral Mountbatten continued effectively to work for an understanding which would permit the withdrawal of British forces by year's end.

The collapse of Dutch-Indonesian talks in April and the departure of Clark Kerr were followed by several months of on-again, off-again discussions: new position papers, counter-proposals, angry huffs, consultations with respective cabinets, low-level armed conflict in both Java and Sumatra, renewed contacts. Walter Foote interrupted the tedious pace of such exchanges in July by asserting, 'I am convinced beyond a doubt [that the] British have some ulterior motive re NEI'. British military forces, he contended, did little to preserve order; English diplomats and military officers provided advice to Sjahrir and other Indonesian leaders concerning their response to Dutch proposals. Further, the British military actively obstructed Dutch efforts to enlarge the zones of Netherlands control. Foote was especially suspicious of London's plans for Sumatra, an island which abutted Malaya and which could greatly enhance Britain's economic position in Southeast Asia. 'British control [of Sumatra] would pass to their hands [the] world's most important rubber and palm oil areas plus [the] Sumatra market for imported goods.'[56] It was a provocative analysis without any foundation, a spasm of Anglophobia. Shortly, there was another breakthrough in the negotiations, marked by the new readiness of the Netherlands government to accept the republic's authority over Sumatra.

The new British mediator in Batavia was Lord Killearn, formerly British proconsul in Egypt, appointed special commissioner for Southeast Asia. His arrival in August was a convenient trigger for a new flurry of diplomatic activity. Foote, however, was pessimistic. Articulating a theme he would return to at the end of the year, the consul general advised: [The] Better classes [of] Indos and [the] masses of people want [a] truce and final peace but Indo authorities like Sjahrir [are] unable [to] implement agreements since hundreds [of] parties, bands led by fanatical or ambitious men will not permit [a] truce or peace unless [it] suits them. Any goodwill shown by [the] British or Dutch is regarded as [a] sign of weakness and used as political capital [by such fanatics]'. He again criticized British 'appeasement' and averred that when given a free hand, Dutch forces easily restored order 'without serious fighting because of [the] natives' desire for peace'. Foote warned: 'If [the] British interfere in Dutch-Indo negotiations and go beyond [the] quality of [an] intermediary, no one can foresee what [the] future holds'.[57]

Nonetheless, a truce arrangement of 14 October was followed by discussions in the city of Linggadjati which produced a draft Dutch-Indonesian accord on 15 November. The agreement recognized the republic's *de facto* authority over the islands of Java, Madura and Sumatra; as well it posited the creation of a federation, the United States of Indonesia – including also Borneo and the Great East – in which the republic would play a key, but not dominant, role. A State Department memorandum prepared by John Carter Vincent (FE) and John Hickerson (EUR) outlined the provisions of the so-called Linggadjati Agreement and advised making favorable remarks to the Dutch ambassador. 'From the outset', they wrote, 'this Government had been concerned lest the continued political disturbances in the Netherlands East Indies should develop into a full-scale war, and had on several occasions urged upon the Netherlands Government the necessity for a prompt and peaceful solution.' While parts of the accord were vague and obviously would require elaboration, the Linggadjati Agreement represented 'an equitable and workable compromise'. However, Vincent and Hickerson warned, failure quickly to ratify the agreement 'will lead to a deterioration in good will so severe as to render impossible the resumption of negotiations. In this latter event, it seems likely that open warfare will break out and that in any case the most radical elements in Indonesia will seize power. Such a situation would provide the most favorable conditions for communist infiltration'.[58]

The agreement appeared to be a significant accomplishment. As one historian has commented, 'In contrast with the rapidly deteriorating situation in nearby Indochina between the French and the Vietnamese nationalists, Linggadjati indeed seemed to represent a hopeful and rational precedent for other imperial powers to follow'. Continuing guerrilla attacks in NEI were downplayed by both sides, with the Dutch military describing them as 'normal scrimmages'. Yet, Foote remained pessimistic about the disorder which he saw as endemic to NEI. 'My opinion', he reported, 'is [that] with [the] exception of [a] small group [of] moderate leaders, [the] Indonesians have no intention [of] living up to [the Linggadjati] agreement and will circumvent it in every way possible. Even if [the] agreement is ratified, struggle will continue with armed clashes and increased chaos for at least two years.' Moderate Indonesians, he said, were outnumbered 'ten to one' by extremists. 'On [the] other hand', Foote added, '[the] unexpected often happens here.'[59]

Formal ratification of the Linggadjati Agreement came on 25 March 1947, by which time, ironically, its flaws had become more apparent. In particular, noted Leslie Palmier, differing interpretations of such key terms as 'co-operation' and 'federal' foreshadowed heightened contention:

> The Dutch assumed that co-operation with the Republic nevertheless implied a continuation of Dutch sole responsibility until the United States of Indonesia was formed; the Republic interpreted the term to mean joint responsibility and mutual consultation in the setting up of the projected federation. The Dutch took 'federal' to mean equal states with equal voices tuned in key with that of the Netherlands; the Republic understood that it did not deny the Republic primacy or its position as co-equal with the Netherlands in sponsoring the United States of Indonesia.

An American intelligence estimate was also pessimistic about the prospects for peace in the archipelago. While the Linggadjati accord had climaxed months of difficult negotiations, the report concluded, 'Remaining differences in interpretation of the agreement ... are so deep and fundamental that orderly progress toward [a] final adjustment of Dutch and Indonesian aspirations in the islands cannot be expected'.[60]

During the months between November 1946 and April 1947, US policymakers continued to affirm Dutch sovereignty in NEI, to encourage a reasoned, voluntary resolution of Indonesian-Dutch disagreements, and to press the American vision of a post-war open door world. Acting Secretary Dean Acheson noted on 12 March 1947, after a visit by two Dutch representatives, 'Dept stated that this Govt is deeply interested in [the] prompt economic rehabilitation [of] N.E.I. and ... it considers that immediate free and unhampered trade and commerce between N.E.I. and [the] rest of the world is one of [the] most essential steps to world rehabilitation as well as to [the] economic rehabiliation of the N.E.I.; that it believes that [the] "open door" policy is an essential predicate of such free and unhampered commerce'. American political, strategic, and economic interests coalesced more powerfully in the East Indies than was typical in other colonial areas. As Gary Hess has observed, 'Political stability and the open door in Indonesia were essential if the United States and its European allies were to have access to its vital resources'.[61]

On 3 April 1947, the United States recognized the Republic's *de facto* jurisdiction over areas specified in the Linggadjati Agreement. It was agreed that the Netherlands Foreign Ministry would deliver notice of this recognition to Sutan Sjahrir; but, afterward, the State Department would 'expect any of its consular officers in the territory under the *de facto* authority of the Republic to follow [the] usual practice of dealing directly with local authorities on local matters within their competence such as [the] protection [of] U.S. nationals, property, shipping and commerce'. Other countries likewise accorded the Republic limited recognition: Australia, Great Britain, China, Egypt, India, Iran and Syria. Thus, concluded Evelyn Colbert, the Indonesians began to gain 'powerful friends outside the circle of great powers'. By way of contrast, the DRV regime in Vietnam 'had neither an accepted international status nor determined friends . . . and the view took root at this time that the United Nations had no role in Vietnam'.[62]

It was not certain, however, what role the United Nations might play in the East Indies until the late summer of 1947. American goals for the archipelago remained the same: stability, the open door, and expanding ties with a moderate nationalist regime. These points were repeated to The Hague again in mid-May, indicating that Southeast Asia remained an area of 'special concern' to the US government. 'Strong nationalist movements throughout [the] area are not isolated phenomena of concern to [a] few colonial powers only. [The] outcome will have [a] profound effect on [the] future [of the] world. [The] Area [is] strategically located athwart [the] Southwest Pacific and [is] of [the] greatest economic importance.' Unless a co-operative relationship developed between colony and metropole, nationalists might drift toward a 'pan-Asiatic or totalitarian philosophy'. And, while not offered in a 'spirit of interference', the secretary of state was clear that inauguration of the open door offered the 'first and most imperative step in stabilizing political and economic conditions and in rehabilitating [the] Indonesian economy'.[63]

Netherlands proposals for a united Western front in Southeast Asia were not well received by American policymakers, even when Dutch diplomats posed the specter of 'a Communist stronghold situated between Singapore, the Philippines and Australia'. Instead, State Department officials Hugh Cumming and Abbot Moffat advocated full, patient elaboration of the Linggadjati Agreement combined with efforts to advance economic recon- struction in NEI. 'With respect to the danger of Communist domination of the Netherlands East Indies, we feel that Communist influence at the present is neither widespread nor effective.' Current Indonesian leaders were judged 'to be Socialist and not Communist, Nationalist and not Soviet-controlled'. Therefore, 'a joint Western Power approach' might be 'interpreted by the Indonesians as a threat to their national aspirations and thus result in defeating our purpose of stabilizing the present Indonesian regime'. Several months later, Moffat expressed American objectives in much the same way: 'to secure a settlement of the present Indonesian situation which will meet the natural aspirations of Indonesian nationalism and, at the same time, preserve so far as possible for the Netherlands the economic strength which she derives from association with the Indies'. Any resort to military force by the Dutch, he advised, would diminish Western strength in the region and aid the growth of Soviet influence.[64]

Nonetheless, with nearly 110000 troops in the East Indies by the beginning of July, Netherlands authorities were prepared for a military showdown with the republic. Charles Wolf, the US vice-consul in Batavia, talked with a number of Dutch officers and enlisted men. Their morale, he reported, was high. Wolf recalled, 'Their theory was that fighting had to come sooner or later: the sooner it began the sooner it would be over, and the sooner they could return home. Without exception, they felt that the military issue would be settled within a few weeks by the complete destruction of the Indonesian forces. The confidence of the Dutch army just prior to the outbreak of hostilities was boundless'. Walter Foote continued to argue that Indonesian leaders were 'stalling' and did not intend to carry out their responsibilities under the Linggadjati Agreement. Anarchy reigned. 'Further delay in [the] restoration [of] law and order', he wrote on 19 June, 'which the Republic [is] unable to accomplish, may lead to bloodshed among [the] Indos themselves and misery untold among [the] poorer classes of Indos who form 95 percent of [the] population [and] who [are] apathetic towards politics and [who] desire only [the] right to return to work in peace.'[65] Foote did not waver in his antipathy toward the republic's leadership and his belief that Dutch policy in NEI was enlightened and reasonable.

The awaited Netherlands military offensive against the Republic began on 20 July. It greatly complicated NEI affairs, generating a sense of a region aflame, the triumph of old politics – a meager, tattered colonial power acting out of desperation, hopelessly enmeshed in a potentially disastrous imbroglio. The Dutch police action in the East Indies and French military efforts in Vietnam both posed difficult problems for US policymakers who wanted to demonstrate clear distinctions between the actions of 'democratic' Western governments and those of the 'totalitarian' communist world. The use of diplomatic talks and negotiated accords as a cover for imperial restoration, for instance, was not dissimilar to the perceived unprincipled tactics of the Soviet Union and communist parties in general. In a discussion with Secretary George C. Marshall, the new Netherlands ambassador, Eelco van Kleffens, explained that negotiations would be resumed once a more representative group of Indonesians had been found. The Dutch government, according to the memorandum of conversation, 'had no desire to reimpose a colonial system upon the Indonesians but ... felt that the present Indonesian government was dominated by a minority group of extremists unrepresentative of the real sentiments of the Indonesian people'. Van Kleffens, it was noted, 'stated and restated this thesis at great length'.[66]

PANCHO VILLAS AND ADOLF HITLERS

When Secretary of War Robert Patterson appeared before the House Committee on Military Affairs on 8 November 1945, he offered a sobering scenario for future warfare. The next time, he said, the United States would be the first nation attacked. 'The attack may come with lightning speed and may make use of weapons of great power and guided missiles launched at great distances from our coasts and sighted with electronic devices of extreme accuracy'. Survival of the United States as an independent nation would require an immediate counterattack. Response time would be very important, Patterson emphasized. 'In the war just ended a quarter of a million American fighting men gave their lives on foreign battlefields. If war comes again more than that number of men, women and children may be wiped out in a single day in their own homes.' Atomic weapons had 'made war more terrible and more total than ever before. There would be no noncombatants in a future war; every man, woman, or child would be in the danger zone'. Patterson reminded his audience, 'I do not make these statements to be melodramatic'.

The secretary appeared before the committee to speak in favor of the Truman administration's proposal for Universal Military Training (UMT) – a program which would require that all young males complete a year of military service. Patterson portrayed Universal Military Training as necessary to create the trained reserve of 'citizen-soldiers' to cope with atomic attack: a wide-ranging group to organize relief services, to restore basic utilities, to rally the population, and to provide the requisite military force, in short order, to take offensive action and seize enemy launch sites. 'As I see it', he commented, 'the military position of the United States will determine the maintenance of world peace.' It was a common statement by government officials in the immediate post-war years: it must be the burden and the glory of the US government to patrol the Pacific, to gird Western Europe, to defend the forces of freedom in a beleaguered world. General Dwight Eisenhower, commander of US forces in Europe, also spoke to the committee, addressing much the same topic, though less apocalyptically. He averred neither that another world war was inevitable nor that the USSR necessarily posed a dangerous threat to American security. In response to friendly questioning from Congressman Thomas E. Martin of Iowa, Eisenhower denied that UMT would encourage the growth of militarism in America and affirmed that the program might prevent the country from slipping back into its sleepy, pre-Second World War unpreparedness. Martin remarked: 'I recall how we were looked upon with disdain by Pancho Villa, and I know how little he respected our ability in the Mexican campaign, and if we were to go back to the old days of 1914, or thereabouts, we could encourage an outcropping of future Pancho Villas and future Hitlers?' 'That is my conviction', replied Eisenhower.[67]

Martin's comment generated an apt image. The twin dangers of the post-war world were frequently viewed as an aggressive, totalitarian Soviet Union – with Stalin typically equated with Hitler – fuelling a worldwide conspiracy to challenge and attack the roots of Western power at every impasse. Kremlin masterplanners, robotlike communist party activists, dedicated Comintern-style subversives, fanciful and fanatical revolution-aries, bandits and opportunists: they were all enemies of decency, order and stability. They were all threats to American hegemony. Insurgent movements, especially armed rebellions, could be captured by native communist parties whose aim was to exploit uncertainty and suffering in accord with Soviet directives. Adolf Hitlers and Pancho Villas abounded, it seemed, in the crisis-ridden world of 1945–47. They peered with hungry, predatory eyes at the war-blighted democracies of Western Europe.

Military leaders appearing before the House Committee on Appropria-tions in the early months of 1947 waxed on the importance of forward bases and air power; the continued viability of naval forces; the need for well-financed, long-range research and development; and the urgency of eternal vigilance throughout a shrunken globe. They denigrated what James Forrestal termed 'the seductive appeal of push-button warfare'. As before, the theme was America's new vulnerability, with the enemy now clearly identified. 'If global war comes to us again', said General Eisenhower, 'the first blow will be struck not at Warsaw but at Washing-ton; not at London but at Los Angeles; not even at Pearl Habor but at Pittsburgh.' 'Ruin and defeat' might come to the United States 'in an appallingly few hours'. Army Air Force General Carl Spaatz talked about the 'Arctic frontier': 'While none of us, of course, know when war may come, we can with reasonable assurance tell from whence it will come'. The Secretary of War, in April, tied together the vestiges of America's role in the Second World War with new security exigencies. 'En route from the occupation areas to the United States', said Patterson, 'one passes through a cordon of defensive positions which form a perimeter about the continental United States and provide us with a cushion of distance in case of attack. . . . When occupation is ended, these bases will be our outposts of defense. If war should come, they would also be the springboards of our counterattack.'[68]

The greatest danger to American national security was believed to be societal collapse in Western Europe. Everything else – all the chaotic, disturbing trends in East Asia, Southeast Asia and Afria – took second place to the hard-bitten pattern of US-Soviet rivalry in Europe. This was true for both Moscow and Washington. 'Inexorable events force high responsibilities of leadership upon America in this restless, trembling world at this critical hour', remarked Senator Arthur H. Vandenberg in early March 1947.[69] There was, it seemed, a vicious cycle of unrest and uncertainty. The best place to stem the red tide, to put a fist in the dike, to

restore a sense of normality was undoubtedly Western Europe. It was a
historically durable workshop and the wielder of a venerable common
heritage. Only in Western Europe, it was judged, was there the necessary
physical infrastructure and proper ethic for sound economic and political
reconstruction. Once the heartland was rescued, then the outlying areas
could be more effectively secured – this was the view shared by virtually all
State Department officials, regardless of their area of specialization. As
Henry L. Deimel of NEA later commented, 'I think Europe first was
necessary, because a world without Europe would be a world dead for us, a
world in Russian hands'.[70] Until the consolidation of a non-communist
Western Europe was assured, the attention of American policymakers was
only intermittently and fitfully turned toward unrest in rimland areas. The
only exception to this generalization lay along the flank of Europe, through
the Mediterranean basin and the Near East, where Western fears of
possible Soviet gains suggested a nascent, generic domino theory attuned
to an increasingly Manichean, zero-sum worldview.

TO THE TRUMAN DOCTRINE

At the beginning of December 1946, a *New York Times* headline proclaimed: OUTLOOK FOR COMING WINTER IS DARK FOR MOST OF EUROPE. Hard
times had not been appreciably eased during the 20 months since Germany's surrender. The newspaper article began:

> As winter closes in on Europe millions are looking with mingled hope
> and anxiety toward the United States, whence emanated the promise of
> freedom from want. The blight of war is still upon many countries,
> liberated and conquered. . . . The peoples of large areas of the Continent
> are living from hand to mouth, dependent upon weekly deliveries of
> supplies from America and to a lesser extent from Britain and Russia.

It appeared likely that public dissatisfaction about the availability of food,
clothing, and fuel had played a role in recent electoral gains by communist
parties in France, Italy and Austria.[71] Was this what Walter Lippmann had
feared: a peace which no one trusted? War-spawned misery was too little
alleviated. Distrust of procrustean capitalism was common; the Labour
government in London was not the only Western regime planning to
overhaul its economy. While factories were not idle, industrial production was generally below pre-war levels. Exports suffered, and
imports ballooned or were held in check only by government-imposed
austerity.

On 28 January 1947, a British Foreign Office despatch to its Washington
embassy stressed that close co-operation with the United States remained a
'fundamental tenet' of Britain's policymaking. The two nations, for

instance, had parallel interests in the Middle East and would find it mutually advantageous to pursue policies designed to limit 'the social unrest which provides fertile ground for communist propaganda and Soviet penetration'. In the Far East, 'The United States recognises our particular strategic interest in South-East Asia. Here nascent nationalisms look to us both for help and guidance. Unless we help they will look to Russia'. Britain's greatest problem derived from its weak economy. 'Above all, the United States must appreciate our financial difficulties and particularly our shortage of dollars. This shortage conditions all our economic and political thinking; it has a vital bearing upon the decisions we must take about our domestic programme as well as upon our foreign policy.'[72] Indeed, the decline of British power, worldwide, was never more evident than during the early months of 1947, as England reeled before the fury of a crippling winter storm. The entire country was blanketed with snow beginning on 24 January, accompanied by harsh, bitter-cold winds, and there was little relief until mid-March. It was, as one writer put it, 'a unique aggregate of climatic malevolence'.[73] Nor, of course, were the blizzards and severe cold restricted to England – much of Europe suffered through the hard winter, only to experience a summer of drought.

It was in the midst of record snowfalls and domestic food and fuel rationing that the British government announced its inability to continue financial assistance to Greece beyond 31 March.[74] Previously, Churchill and then the Labour cabinet had sought to preserve Greece as a British client by discouraging the powerful communist guerrilla army from seizing power after the German evacuation of Athens. However, even with 75 000 troops in the country by early 1945, British policymakers could neither stabilize the Greek economy nor engineer an effective non-communist governing coalition. Elections in March 1946 did not produce a unity government; instead, by the end of July, there was renewed warfare between right and left throughout the Greek countryside. 'Extremism will beget extremism', wrote Ernest Bevin, 'and Greece will be in a vortex of violence to the advantage only of the communists within and without.'[75] It was a theme picked up by American officials in February 1947 as the British government notified Washington of its inability to continue military and financial support of non-communist forces in Greece. State Department officers worked feverishly to prepare policy papers documenting the need for rapid American intervention to bolster both Greece and Turkey in the face of apparent Soviet subversion and aggression.

It was Dean Acheson, then under-secretary, who co-ordinated this policymaking activity. In his memoirs, he reconstructed a 26 February White House discussion with congressional leaders, who needed to grasp quickly the geopolitical urgency of affairs in the eastern Mediterranean. 'Never', he wrote, 'have I spoken under such a pressing sense that the issue was up to me alone.'

No time was left for measured appraisal. In the past eighteen months, I said, Soviet pressure on the Straits, on Iran, and on northern Greece had brought the Balkans to the point where a highly possible Soviet breakthrough might open three continents to Soviet penetration. Like apples in a barrel infected by one rotten one, the corruption of Greece would infect Iran and all to the east. It would also carry infection to Africa through Asia Minor and Egypt, and to Europe through Italy and France, already threatened by the strongest domestic communist parties in Western Europe.[76]

There was no better illustration in 1947 of the simplicity and power of the domino metaphor. The enemy was strong, ruthless, self-assured, poised for action. The enemy was not only a tough, totalitarian state, but also a diseased, evil ideology which could *infect* a progressively expanding circle of societies, *penetrating* new continents and cultures. It was a formidable picture indeed.

President Truman would need to address a joint session of Congress: to rally public opinion, to explain the cold war policies of the past year, to dramatize the Soviet threat (much as Acheson had done), to justify greater expenditures. Thus, the speech would have a wider scope than just Greece and Turkey; there was a new global context in which such policy choices logically unfolded. Loy Henderson, head of NEA, later recalled his support for a broad-ranging statement of cold war purpose, though he did not directly suggest the need to scare people. 'We used Department of State language like "tell them the truth about the situation".'[77] But polemic was also on the agenda.

On 12 March 1947, Harry Truman delivered his special message to Congress, calling for $400 million in emergency assistance for both Greece and Turkey. The main focus of his remarks was upon the turmoil in Greece, where 'a militant minority' had created 'political chaos' and impeded economic recovery. 'The very existence of the Greek state', said Truman 'is today threatened by the terrorist activities of several thousand armed men, led by Communists, who defy the government's authority at a number of points, particularly along the northern boundaries.' The Greek army, by itself, could not cope with this insurrection. Great Britain no longer had the funds to sustain its military involvement in Greece, and the United Nations could not act quickly enough. While the Greek government was not a perfect democracy, remarked Truman, it was still more representative than a self-appointed band of communist partisans. Turkey also required American help – largely financial assistance to maintain and modernize its armed forces in order to continue to resist Soviet encroachment.

Truman acknowledged, then, that there were 'broad implications' to extending this kind of aid. 'One of the primary objectives of the foreign policy of the United States is the creation of conditions in which we and other nations will be able to work out a way of life free from coercion.' This had been a major reason for establishing the United Nations. But this objective could not be realized if totalitarian regimes were permitted to impose their will upon free peoples, as has already been done in Poland, Rumania and Bulgaria. Then, in the sentence which became the root of the so-called Truman Doctrine, the president declared: 'I believe that it must be the policy of the United States to support free peoples who are resisting attempted subjugation by armed minorities or by outside pressures'.

Like Roosevelt telling Americans about the distant but important fronts of war in 1942, Truman said, 'It is necessary only to glance at a map to realize that the survival and integrity of the Greek nation are of grave importance in a much wider situation'. Here, Truman warmed to Acheson's domino (or 'rotten apple') imagery. If Greece fell to communism, he suggested, there would be an immediate negative impact on Turkey. 'Confusion and disorder might well spread throughout the entire Middle East.' In fact, throughout the tricontinental region, peoples struggling against totalitarianism would be dismayed and discouraged. 'The seeds of totalitarian regimes,' said Truman, as had Byrnes similarly at the Paris Peace Conference, 'are nurtured by misery and want. They spread and grow in the evil soil of poverty and strife. They reach their full growth when the hope of a people for a better life has died.' The United States must keep hope alive. 'Great responsibilities have been placed upon us by the swift movement of events', concluded the president.[78] Truman was able to sign the authorization bill on 22 May.

The Truman Doctrine speech was based on sweeping assertions. The arguments were convincing. The background logic seemed historically sound: appeasement led to war; dictators were insatiable; the Soviets only understood firmness; the 'swift movement of events' required the same global American initiative as had the Second World War. Times had changed. A former ally was now the principal (and implacable) foe. The battle had to be joined with greater energy. Truman's speech capsuled nearly all of the assumptions which became key to the American approach to the cold war for a number of years: monolithic communism, falling dominoes, a worldwide watch on the Soviet Union.

As has been frequently pointed out in recent years, the inherent globalism of the Truman doctrine was not immediately reflected in changes in American foreign policy. The priority area remained Europe – as was soon evidenced by the Marshall Plan. Truman's 12 March speech explored for public consumption what had already become basic themes of State Department thinking.[79] Nonetheless, the Truman Doctrine remains what Robert McMahon has called 'a landmark in postwar U.S. foreign policy'. It remains so partly because it typified what George Kennan later called the 'neurotic self-consciousness and introversion' of American foreign policymaking – characterized by 'universalistic and pretentious' pronouncements largely directed toward a domestic constituency. Truman's remarks were also critical, as Bruce Kuniholm has noted, because the analysis 'encouraged a misleadingly simplistic view or model of the world'. It was myth-making of a new and vigorous kind. Subsequently, 'the State Department's task of continuously redefining the international situation would be discouraged. Instead, abstractions would justify security interests and impose themselves on a world which had changed, a world for which those abstractions were increasingly irrelevant'. In a similar way, Theodore Draper has scored the Truman Doctrine as the origin of what became a common 'abstract, generalized mode of domino theorizing ... without asking how or why, ... [functioning] as a substitute for thought'. Thus was 'codified' an illusion: that American power, at the appropriate time, would be sufficient to shoulder the global commitments implied by Truman's universalistic rhetoric. [80]

There emerged, then, fresh models for US foreign policymaking during the years 1946–47. First, the outcome of the Iranian crisis of 1946 argued for continued firm opposition to perceived Soviet expansionism. Secondly, the civil war in Greece and the American response to British withdrawal in 1947 offered again a picture of resolute action, within a redefined international arena, defending intertwined strategic-economic interests. In the end, Greece itself was not nearly so important as what it symbolized: resistance to Soviet subversion. Hence, Lawrence S. Wittner and others have discussed the importance of the 'Greek model' as a milestone regarding anti-guerrilla efforts in outlying locales. [81]

Lincoln MacVeagh, the long-time US ambassador to Greece, stressed the different character of post-war political turmoil during executive session testimony before the Senate Foreign Relations Committee on 28 March 1947. The collapse of Western interests in Greece, he said, would 'bring the country into the satellite orbit of the Russian Empire'. The Balkan peninsula had become 'a frontier between the Western world and the expanding eastern Communist-dominated world ... where you have a situation like oil and water, where they do not mix'. MacVeagh described the growth of the Greek communist movement during the war: 'The whole thing was a social revolution, and not one of the nice old revolutions we used to have in the old days'. Even after the British had arranged a cease-fire in the civil war, 'the nigger in the woodpile was still there': dedicated communists whose ultimate aim was 'to turn Greece into a totalitarian state'. MacVeagh pointed to what he called a 'critical crescent'. 'It went from Afghanistan to Finland, and along that crescent the Soviet [Union] has bulged and bulged and bulged.' [82]

Like the hoe and other implements, containment was invented simultaneously and independently throughout the different geopolitical desks and offices of the Truman administration. In his 'long telegram' and then later in his 'X' article for *Foreign Affairs*, George Kennan had given a reasonable, historically versed voice to a policy consensus already established. Kennan's thesis of messianic Marxism-Leninism coupled with traditional Russian expansionism was especially convenient, uniting all strands of anticommunist, anti-Soviet sentiment in the State Department and executive branch, whether predominantly emotional, ideological or pragmatic in nature. Ideologues and realpolitikers could comfortably embrace containment, presented as it was in the guise of a purely defensive tactic, one adopted reluctantly against a monster menace which would respond only to tough talk and the threat of military force. Years later, Kennan summarized his late-1946 policy views this way:

> Don't make any more unnecessary concessions to these people [the Soviets]. Make it clear to them that they are not going to be allowed to establish any dominant influence in Western Europe and in Japan if there is anything we can do to prevent it. When we have stabilized the situation in this way, then perhaps we will be able to talk with them about some sort of a general political and military disengagement in Europe and the Far East – not before. [83]

But once containment was acknowledged and shaped by the rhetoric of the Truman Doctrine, it was far easier to expand perimeters than contract them. The 12 March speech had put the United States 'on the line', said Senator Walter F. George. 'Call it communism, totalitarianism, or whatever you want to call it, it is there.' Washington was going to stay on the line. There was inspiring purpose in Kennan's words to students at the War College in June 1947: 'Today we Americans stand as a lonely, threatened power on the field of world history'. The United States was shedding its adolescence and turning, in the words of James Reston, 'to the frontier of a cynical and melancholy world'. [84]

THE WORLD PIANO

Brigadier General George A. Lincoln of the War Department General Staff spoke before the Senate Foreign Relations Committee, in executive session, on 2 April 1947. 'It happens', he said, 'that we are having a little trouble about Greece and Turkey at the present time, but they are just one of the keys on the keyboard of this world piano that is being played at the present time.' The peoples of Western Europe, the Middle East, and 'clear around into the Pacific' were 'watching what the United States is doing [in Greece and Turkey]. They are watching what Russia is doing; they are watching which way the peoples move, and we recognize that if the countries of the world lose confidence in us they may in effect pass under the Iron Curtain without any pressure other than subversive pressure being put on them.'[85] General Lincoln was among the last group of administration representatives to appear before the Foreign Relations Committee on behalf of S. 938, the legislation authorizing American assistance to Greece and Turkey. The bill's approval in late May 1947 was the prelude to heightened American involvement in the Mediterranean – now as a replacement rather than a prop for the visibly fading British Empire.

The European priority remained sacrosanct, but a sense of roving crisis in colonial areas also continued to attract attention. Nothing could be completely ignored. In French North Africa, communist recruitment efforts appeared stymied by nationalist fragmentation and cultural conservatism, though NEA officials still worried about militant Arab leaders. In British East Africa, nationalist sentiment was apparently on the rise, though as yet poorly co-ordinated. Along the coastal zones of Libya, pro-independence groups had quickly found a voice during the deliberations of the Council of Foreign Ministers. Soviet interest in the Tripolitanian trusteeship appeared to be lost amidst the flood of reports and other paperwork generated by the CFM deputies during and after their laborious preparation for a tour of the ex-Italian colonies in 1947–48.

At the eastern end of the Mediterranean, the blade of perennial crisis was being honed in Britain's Palestine mandate – the heir to a confused imperial agenda, a rebirth of militant Zionism in the wake of the Holocaust, and a long-standing opposition by Palestinian Arabs to the creation of a Jewish settler theocracy in their midst. The mandate was a catspaw for too many unbending desires, only some of which were colonial in origin. Palestine was a tragedy awaiting its inevitable fulfillment, and American policy only exacerbated the rising tide of tension and violence in the territory. Across the Dead Sea and the Persian Gulf, around Iran's southern coast, Pakistan and India took shape as independent nations after bloody fighting flared between Hindus and Muslims. The conflict bore out British predictions as surely as it indicted an imperial rule which had so long stoked such religious bitterness and division.

Across the Bay of Bengal, in Southeast Asia, the Franco-Vietnamese struggle became ever more violent, more determined; but it was a war little followed by the leading powers. In the Netherlands East Indies, on the other hand, the Dutch military offensive of July 1947 precipitated the first major UN-sponsored mediation effort of the post-war years – forcing US policymakers more resolutely to address the colonial drama in Indonesia than elsewhere. Along the rim of East Asia floated American-occupied Japan; China was once again locked in civil war. Korea was split into competing US and Soviet zones, and a nominally independent Philippines was fast becoming an arsenal of autocracy. The 91 000 residents of Micronesia remained under the jurisdiction of the Navy Department. 'We govern the mandated islands through international law, by reason of having captured them', said Captain William F. Jennings to the House

Appropriations Committee.[86] What were the continuities in these and other colonial scenes? What was important to American security and what was not? Potentially, everything was important: that was the lesson of the Second World War. The world piano was there to be played, not simply looked at. If America did not play it, another power would – one less generous, less freedom-loving, less humane. In the immediate post-war era, US policymakers struggled with the need to gather information and make decisions about the colonial world. At the same time, the obvious priority of European issues and problems generated a dynamic which consistently pigeonholed the affairs of dependent peoples. But not all the news was bad.

In early February 1947, consul Harold Finley reported from Algiers that local communists were relatively inactive. Events in Vietnam, however, 'have been much in the limelight', he noted, primarily because several battalions of troops, including Foreign Legionnaires, had recently embarked for Saigon. Two months later, Finley happily wrote: 'There is [a] growing awareness in Algiers of the Communist threat. In a large measure, President Truman's message to the Congress on the Greek and Turkish loans has been responsible for pointing this up'. Even Ferhat Abbas, said Finley, had good things to say about a 'Franco-Moslem entente' and the possibility of resolving the Algerian question within the bounds of a Paris-sponsored federalism. In June, additional reports confirmed that the communists were 'losing ground here in Algeria'.[87]

A 16–19 June meeting in Paris brought together American diplomats from US missions to Algeria, Morocco, Tunisia and Egypt. A few days earlier, Secretary Marshall had expressed concern about the pattern of French colonialism in the region. Some resolution of Franco-Arab contention, he wrote, was a 'matter of urgency lest [the] situation in North Africa developed into one comparable to that now existing in Indochina' and possibly come before the United Nations at its September 1947 meeting. Such had already been the case with Indonesia. Marshall advised that the French approach 'leading Nationalist elements' with a long-term plan for the 'gradual but sure evolution' of dependencies toward dominion status under 'benevolent tutelage'. North African states should become 'friendly partners' of France rather than 'weak and unwilling vassals'. The United States, said Marshall, had no interest in becoming a dominant power in North Africa and would be willing – after the announcement of French reform efforts – to encourage Arab leaders to reduce their demands and co-operate with the French government. Thus, Marshall could envisage the North African colonies and protectorates 'developing into prosperous self-governing "associated states"'.[88]

The recommendations of the Paris conference echoed the ideas contained in Marshall's cable. France, it seemed clear, should develop an evolutionary program for its North African dependencies of Morocco and

Tunisia. Algeria should be treated separately, due to the size and politico-economic importance of its French settler population. For Algeria, the conferees advised simply administrative reform and the 'elaboration of an economic program'. Neither Tunisia nor Morocco was judged ready for self-government. The conference report concluded, in what had become a common refrain, 'Premature and hasty achievement of theoretical independence under present-day world conditions, instead of achieving true sovereignty, could well lead to new and sterner bondage'. The consuls agreed that American efforts to moderate the demands of Arab nationalists should be conditioned on France's willingness to pursue a realistic, comprehensive reform of its colonial policy. [89]

The discussions about French North Africa well expressed the growing State Department consensus regarding US policy towards colonial areas where there was no open alliance between nationalists and communists. The concept of a liberal colonialism – initiating meaningful reforms, training native cadres for self-rule, and announcing a definite timetable for local autonomy was the paradigm usually envisaged by US diplomats as the basis for their recommendations to foreign governments. Often, such advice was linked to pressure for the establishment of 'nondiscriminatory' trade practices – a routine euphemism for the open door. However, France was not a liberal colonial power seeking (as was Britain) to maintain its yet extensive commercial and security network through a rejuvenated, more co-operative commonwealth. Rather, France was intent upon retaining unquestioned supremacy within its empire. This was clear to observers of the Indochina struggle, which was increasingly the worst-case scenario against which other situations were measured and worsening portents more easily identified.

Thus, only a short time after the series of optimistic reports from Algiers, Henry S. Villard (NEA) believed the local political situation to be 'serious', a threat to US strategic interests. 'The nationalist movement in North Africa is gaining in strength and determination', he wrote. Nationalist leaders wanted independence from France, and communists were trying to exploit this sentiment – though Villard appropriately noted that communist parties in France and North Africa were reluctant to support full native independence and tended rather to lobby for greater autonomy. The Moroccan and Tunisian nationalist leaders had, for instance, refused to associate themselves with the communists. But there was a leadership vacuum in Paris, contended Villard.

Due to the post-war confusion in France, French psychopathic reaction caused by the humiliation of 1940 and by fear of losing her Empire, the blocking tactics of the communists, and the lack of unified direction due to successive provisional and coalition governments, France has not evolved a long-range colonial policy designed successfully to meet the changed political situation in her Empire. The French have been inconsistent and misdirected in their use both of force and concessions vis-à-vis their dependent peoples, and, as a result of all of these factors, France would appear to be in a very poor position to solve the political problems facing her in North Africa.

Unless the French government and Arab nationalists could soon reach some accord on a long-term solution to their disagreements, continued Villard, 'this area will suffer increasingly from political tension and may even burst into violence in the not too distant future'. Sudden independence 'might well result in chaos and eventual communist control'. Nonetheless, concluded Villard, there was little expectation of widespread revolt among Arabs in the next 12 months.[90]

Reports from the field continued to provide evidence of a wide gulf between Algerian nationalists and the metropolitan-dominated communist parties. A new edition of *La Nation Algérienne*, the militant newspaper of the Parti Populaire Algérien (PPA), quoted remarks by Messali Hadj, who ridiculed the slogans and program of the French communists. He also denounced the idea of a Franco-Muslim entente:

> There can be no union between masters and slaves. It will be necessary first to free the people from constraint and then abolish in practice the odious colonial regime so that the natives ... can freely express themselves and thus prepare themselves in accordance with their national aspirations. ... The colonialists, those suckers of the blood of oppressed peoples under the tri-color[,] have not acquiesced in the creation of the French Union and will not do so unless they have assurances that the Union will guarantee their domination based on crime and depredation.

The newspaper also declared PPA solidarity with the peoples of Indonesia and Vietnam.[91]

NEA Director Loy Henderson remained concerned about possible communist gains. His 6 October 1947 memo to Acting Secretary Robert Lovett was titled 'Unsatisfactory Political Situation in French North Africa'. Henderson favored a more active US effort to bridge the gap between the French government and Arab nationalists 'if we are not to be faced with another impasse comparable to that in Indo-China and Indonesia'. Yet, other analysts questioned the need for worry about recreating Vietnam in Africa. On the surface, wrote Joseph Palmer, assistant chief of the Division of African Affairs, it did indeed seem reasonable to fear communist advance in North Africa and the rise of armed resistance. Then he observed:

> We are beginning to wonder if this danger has not been over-emphasized and, in fact, whether the Moslems, once having gained independence,

would not be able to dispose of the Communists, and therefore the Communist danger, quickly and rather efficiently. The best comparable example which we have been able to study is Indo-China; and there the Communists have control of the nationalist movement in a country not contiguous to the USSR. If the French are driven out or voluntarily get out in the not too distant future, there is a grave danger that, for a while at least, Indo-China will be under the indirect control of the Kremlin. Can the same thing happen in North Africa? We feel inclined to doubt that it would because of the absence in North Africa of the principal factors which account for communist influence in Indo-China.

For example, continued Palmer, 'The outstanding Viet-Namese in Indo-China, Ho Chi Minh, is a Moscow-trained man who was known long before the war as a Nationalist and who is widely hailed among the Viet-Namese as having always devoted all his selfless energies to the unification and freedom of his country'. There was no such outstanding personality in North Africa. Secondly, 'Ho Chi Minh basks in the glory of a Resistance record gained during the Japanese occupation'. But the circumstances of wartime North Africa did not provide the opportunity for such anti-fascist legitimacy to be conferred on any native group. Thirdly, wrote Palmer, 'The non-Communist Viet-Namese are, by and large, indifferent to Stalinist communism. Their religion does not make communism abhorrent to them. Most of them do not seem to be fully aware of what it means or of the danger that it entails. They are intent upon the eviction of the French and everything else, including communism, is completely secondary'. The same was not true in French North Africa, said Palmer, where most leading nationalists were anticommunist and feared the growth of organized communist groups. Fourthly, 'There is no unified completely non-communist Nationalist party in Indo-China. The only unified party is the Communist party'. In North Africa, on the other hand, there were many, even competing, nationalist organizations.[92]

French North Africa was not Vietnam. But anticolonial fervor could nonetheless rock the imperial boat across several continents. From British East Africa, the US consul in Nairobi, Joseph I. Touchette, reported increased nationalist agitation through the spring and summer of 1947, with heightened racial division in the colony. The potential for political disorder was another inducement, he believed – in addition to strategic considerations – for a military base in the colony. 'Two divisions of British troops would outnumber the total East African white population. Bayonets might keep [the] natives in order.'[93] In late July, Touchette noted: 'There is no doubt that, as a result of the war, a new role is being assumed by Africa. ... The Africans of British East Africa have become politically conscious and are demanding increased representation as well as greater educational opportunities. Important changes are underway on the

African continent and those taking place in East Africa are not the least'. Touchette felt that the British government recognized the continent's new role in the post-war world and was committing substantial resources to its East African sphere. 'That Kenya is bound to become a strategic base, due to recent events in Egypt, India and Palestine, seems assured', he wrote. 'Air bases strung across Central Africa from the west to the east coast, which played such an important part in the war, appear not to be ignored.'[94]

In 1947, the Mediterranean littoral and the Near East comprised 'inescapable entanglements' for the United States. There were many dangers, many opportunities. Most obviously, of course, there were the Saudi Arabian oilfields, which Dean Acheson had previously termed 'one of the greatest material prizes in world history'.[95] There had been the 1946 contretemps over Iran which marked the opening of the cold war. As suggested by the phrase 'Middle East', broadly defined, the region emerged as – if not a 'hinge of fate' – a linchpin for the expanding doctrine of containment. The Middle East's border with three continents – Europe, Asia and Africa – had been the basis for the 'rotten-apple' (or falling-domino) arguments which underlay the Truman Doctrine.

The Soviet threat, the British ally: such were the themes of a Joint Chiefs of Staff memorandum of 3 July 1947. The Soviet Union, said the JCS, 'is engaged in improving its strategic position and increasing its military potential by attaching to itself states, peoples and areas to which it has no legitimate claim and to the great military disadvantage of the United States and our potential allies'. Hence, American interests would suffer if the Soviet Union acquired control – even via joint trusteeship – over any former Italian colony. An intelligence report of 25 July argued that 'Soviet capabilities for creating instability in the Middle East depend to a considerable extent on the opportunities arising from the disposition of the Italian African colonies'. In any war with the USSR, contended the JCS, Great Britain would be America's most important ally; therefore, the Joint Chiefs urged strong US support for British strategic goals in the Middle East – including English base rights in Cyrenaica. 'However, there is doubt that the British can, within the next ten years, deploy sufficient land, sea and air forces in the area to insure, with a reasonable degree of certainty, adequate protection of Anglo-American strategic interests in the Middle East and the Eastern Mediterranean.'[96]

Not long afterward, on 30 July, Secretary of State Marshall was notified that the British government was compelled 'on financial and manpower grounds' to withdraw its troops from Greece and reduce its military forces in Italy. Privately, Marshall objected to 'our thorn-pulling operations on the British lion' and claimed that the British were 'far too casual or freehanded in passing the buck of the international dilemma to [the] US with little or no consideration for the harmful results'.[97] But this was more a complaint about the *speed* of Britain's collapse as a Mediterranean/ Middle East military power than about the collapse itself. The United States was waxing, England was waning – that was certainly clear before 30 July 1947. The basic congruence of US-British strategic interests in the region was reaffirmed in October during secret bilateral sessions called the 'Pentagon Talks'. A preconference memorandum prepared by the State Department explained: 'We now take full cognizance of the tremendous value of this area as a highway by sea, land and air between East and West; of its possession of great mineral wealth; of its potentially rich agricultural resources. We also realize the serious consequences which would result if the rising nationalisms of the peoples of the Middle East should harden in a mould of hostility to the West'. The memorandum noted that 'the implications of recently and clearly demonstrated Soviet expansionist aspirations in the Middle East obviously need no elaboration'. [98]

Central to understanding and accommodating the 'rising nationalisms' of the world's southern rimlands, however, was what one OSS officer had called the 'communist bogy'. He was referring to the Viet Minh. His advice had been to ignore ideology and to assess the legitimacy of the nationalist movement on the basis of a fresh, accurate appraisal of its goals and popular support. [99] Writ larger, his comments pointed to important questions: How influential were communists within anticolonial movements? Was there such a thing as 'national' communism? Or, to put it another way, could communists be genuine nationalists? From Paris, Ambassador Jefferson Caffery – always eager to uncover the hidden hand of the 'Stalintern' [100] in colonial affairs – argued persuasively that the primitive polity in overseas dependencies obscured at ground level any differences between well-meaning nationalists and dedicated communists. In effect, a search for fine distinctions would inevitably be frustrated. Better to trust the metropole, shore up Western Europe, and then gently pressure the imperial powers to liberalize their colonial regimes. Undoubtedly, the methodology of Soviet control in Eastern Europe fostered an easy-to-come-by sense of the communist monolith – Stalin Allee – and its willful, cynical manipulation of people and parties. Yet, Joseph Palmer's memorandum comparing anticolonial groups in Vietnam and French North Africa had shown an awareness of the fusion of communism and nationalism personified by the Viet Minh.

There were other questions raised. John Davies of the newly established Policy Planning Staff argued, for instance, that 'the Far Eastern communist picture is not the same as that in Europe', that 'applying mechanistically the European pattern' to Asian politics was a mistake. Favoring what he called an 'Asiaticized approach', Davies believed: 'Communism in the Far East is a synthesis and perhaps therefore the most subtle and misleading political phenomenon on the world scene today'. [101] But the cold war did not celebrate subtlety. On both sides, the rhetoric fed simplistic analyses and rewarded those with easy access to deterministic scenarios.

The Far East offered numerous opportunities for 'applying mechanistically' the fundamental cold war assumptions about Soviet subversion. The battlefront extended over many miles of rugged terrain, rough seas and arbitrary lines of demarcation. On 20 May 1947, Dean Acheson told the Senate Foreign Relations Committee, 'As you know, the difficulty is that at the 38th parallel there is now a complete Iron Curtain'. Southern Korea had become another spoon-fed client. Large quantities of food and fuel were imported to sustain the American zone. Lieutenant General John R. Hodge, head of the occupation regime, warned that the Soviet Union wanted to add Korea to its collection of satellites. The Korean situation, Hodge commented, 'affects very greatly our position in the whole Oriental picture'. The Japanese, for instance, were watching closely the direction of American policy in Korea. It was thus, wrote Russell D. Buhite, that the US occupation began to accumulate certain 'imponderables' which went beyond questions of mere strategic significance.[102]

Only a short distance eastward lay the grander and more active American occupation regime in Japan. General Douglas MacArthur functioned as an American satrap while State Department and military planners ambitiously plotted the economic resurgence of the Home Islands through 1947–48. Tokyo could once again be the industrial center of East Asia, drawing its nutrients from the agrarian fields of Southeast Asia. As Kennan noted in his memoirs, 'Japan, as we saw it, was more important than China as a potential factor in world-political developments. It is ... the sole great potential military-industrial arsenal of the Far East'.[103] A rebuilt Japan, reflecting Western priorities and functioning as a well-manned outpost along the US security perimeter, could overcome the disadvantage of a communist victory in China. State Department analysts were not optimistic about the corrupt, haphazard military campaign of Chiang Kai-shek.

Hence, southern Korea was fast becoming symbolic of the expansion of American power and the commitment to hold distant zones of possible conflict – much as was divided Berlin. Occupation authorities in Japan epitomized the 'can-do' spirit of the United States, planning the political and economic rebirth of what had so recently been a much despised enemy. In the Philippines, a conservative elite was placed in power; pre-war US economic and military hegemony was effectively recreated via new treaties and base agreements. American policymakers, observed Russell H. Fifield, liked to believe that Philippines independence was a beacon to colonial peoples of Southeast Asia. 'The beacon, however, was often dim.'[104] Even so, the beacon appeared stable, and the Philippines stood as tangible proof that self-determination, of one sort of another, was feasible.

An August 1947 memorandum by Kenneth Landon of the Division of Southeast Asian Affairs sought to clarify American policy toward dependent areas 'and to put the United States in a positive and assertive position, where heretofore our attitude has appeared to be weak and negative'. His main theme followed 'the line that the United States supports the principle of ultimate freedom for all peoples but that it also supports the principle of individual freedom; and that it believes that the attainment of independence by a country unready for it will jeopardize the chances of the individual's also attaining freedom'. Landon believed that he could reconcile the contradictions in American colonial policy 'by emphasizing that the right of men to be free is at least as valid as the right of nations to be free. ... It seems to me that this is the only line we can follow which, without committing us to the unqualified support of the aims of such people, will regain us the initiative and deprive the USSR of it'.

Still, it was a difficult balancing act. Expressing the American policy as one rooted in concerns for human rights did not really make it any more flexible or helpful to dependent peoples. Landon's memorandum, in effect, put forward the same arguments already advanced by US diplomats: the metropoles should pursue a more progressive, benevolent tutelage and begin training native peoples for independence in the not-so-distant future. The colonizer and the colonized should recognize 'a common goal and strive together for a continuing, permanent relationship of voluntary association'. The United States government, wrote Landon, should continue to urge evolutionary change in imperial relationships in order to create the 'freely collaborative partnership' so necessary for world stability. Somewhat more prophetically, Landon noted: 'Force and violence as instruments of policy are not easy to set aside and to disown even when their purpose has been served, even when the objective is national independence'.

For the United States, the important short-term goal was stability. 'The world is desperately in need of a respite from stress and strain', commented Landon. 'The nervous and physical stamina of the human race has worn thin. What the peoples of every country require is tranquility and a breathing spell.'[105] Landon was right. Stress and strain *were* widespread; a breathing spell *would* be good news to hard-pressed societies in Europe and Asia; and people living at the edge of famine, worn down by long years of unrelenting poverty, *were* in need of reliable governance. But colonialism remained an enduring aim of European powers. This was quite clear in Indochina and Indonesia, where the State Department's careful exposition on liberalism, orderliness, and voluntarism did not leave a lasting mark. 'War in Indonesia would be self-defeating to Dutch purposes', wrote Kenneth Landon on 18 July 1947, two days before the Netherlands offensive began. French military forces had been fighting for 22 months in Indochina. 'The only results', said Landon, 'have been to weaken the

French in France, to destroy the economy of Indochina, and to create a hatred of the French among the Annamese that may endure for genera-tions'. An *ad hoc* group of the State-War-Navy Coordinating Committee advised that 'the military pacification of Indochina would probably require a French army at least three times the size of the present French forces'. [106] The Dutch-Indonesian dispute was brought before the UN Security Council in July. By the end of August, the United Nations had created an investigative commission and, as it turned out, become a major player in the internal politics of the East Indies.

As it happened, then, American policymakers by the fall of 1947 were giving more systematic attention to colonial unrest than ever before; but it was within an ideological context which identified colonies via the light reflected from the metropoles. Soviet-American contention mandated an examination of the political economy of Western dependencies in order to anticipate troublespots, to identify and dampen leftist tendencies among native nationalists, and to buttress wherever possible pro-American attitudes. While there was intermittent sentiment among US officials in favor of a more sophisticated analysis of anticolonial unrest – considering even the possibility of communist-nationalist fusion outside the Stalinist mold – the more simplistic cold war theses always prevailed. Upheaval in the colonial rimlands was a toothsome complication which diverted re-sources from the European vortex. Shrugging off its wartime rhetoric in favor of self-determination, the United States became instead an exemplar of the new 'imperial' ethos: promoting evolutionary change through the maintenance of colonial ties, based on local systems fathered or midwifed by the metropole and run by moderate, pro-Western nationalists who often represented the least progressive sectors of indigenous society. While there were squabbles among State Department Europeanists, Africanists, Asianists, and so forth, such disagreements were not, essentially, about the Europe-first strategy.

The major paradigms of US diplomacy remained (1) the open door, (2) a resurgent unilateralism, and (3) the concept of an indivisible peace – or indivisible national security, depending upon the perspective. The rationale seemed clear-cut: the open door was regularly and routinely offered as the best and fairest means to effect world economic recovery and enshrine principles which would not only benefit American industry but democratize access to global resources and markets. Second, the internationaliza-tion of problem-solving through the United Nations, which had once seemded a safe, stabilizing concept (and still could be periodically useful), had become something of a liability with the onset of the cold war and the need for quick action in faraway places without the comfortable dialogue of deliberative assemblies. The United Nations was judged too slow and cumbersome to deal with the Greek-Turkish crisis in 1947. A creative defense of American unilateralism came from State Department analyst

Benjamin Cohen, who, responding to criticism of the Marshall Plan for bypassing the UNO, argued that the United Nations 'was not a totalitarian institution and everything need not be done through it'.[107] Thirdly, the essential conservatism of the indivisible peace was merely a variant of the domino theory: everything could be important, depending upon what happened and how it happened. Societies devastated by war, unable to climb out of numbing poverty, might well follow, in the words of George Marshall, a 'grim progression' toward the tyranny of communist domination. 'Every dismembered economy is a potential threat', said Senator Vandenberg. Western security, read a CIA study, was 'manifestly indivisible'. Or as Secretary of Defense Louis Johnson would later say, 'Security is multiple'.[108] The politics of orderliness inspired a status quo globalism which offered much to the few and little to the many. It was better to err on the safe side.

Conclusion: The World Deployed

In January 1950, William L. Clayton, former assistant secretary of state for economic affairs, spoke about the troubled legacy of the Second World War. 'Hitler failed, it is true', said Clayton, 'but as he went out he slammed the door so hard it jarred the universe, as he promised he would do.' In the aftermath of victory over the Axis, the United States was forced to make desperate choices in a new struggle, facing a shrewd ideological foe. The enemy was guided by 'Oriental cunning', using the technique of 'boring from within' to subvert freedom and undercut American power. The challenge and the danger could be easily depicted: one had only to 'watch the map'.

> If we had before us here today a map of the world, drawn to outline the progress and developments in the cold war – black for communism and white for freedom, this is what it would show: Most of continental Asia in black and the rest of it resting under a very dark shadow; most of the European Continent in black right up to and west of Berlin and much of the rest of it sustained by subsidies from the United States; the United States still in white, of course, but caught midway between Europe and Asia in a sort of huge economic vise or pincers, the pressures of which are fast becoming unbearable. Those pressures will grow and grow.

Because the threat was not direct armed attack against the United States or its allies, the United Nations could be of little assistance. The 'economic problem', said Clayton, was 'the heart and soul of the cold war': 'One of Stalin's most effective weapons is the fear which he instills into the ranks of democratic governments, causing them to spend excessively for armaments, and the fear which he instills into private people, causing them to withhold the capital upon which free enterprise depends'. Americans *should* fear communism, Clayton advised, because Stalin was winning the cold war. 'The Communists are closing in on us. . . . The truth of the matter is that communism is catching on in the world. It feeds on cold, hunger, and hopelessness. There is entirely too much of that kind of food in the world today and too little of the kind that nourishes the body, the heart, and the spirit.' In the two-camp competition for hearts and minds, the Western world was too uninspiring. 'The Communists are awakening the masses', said Clayton, 'and make no mistake about it, the masses are listening.' The world's peoples were restive. 'In the old days the masses suffered in silence, in isolation and in ignorance but in our modern world they are no longer silent, their isolation is gone forever, and their

201

ignorance is fast disappearing. . . . It does little good to preach democracy
to a man who has to see his wife and children go to bed cold and hungry
every night.'[1]

The theme of the 'awakening masses' was among the most powerful
call-to-arms imagery of the era, especially as it referred to non-European
territories. It was as if much of the world's population had been sleeping
and now in unison, like a sprawling single cell, millions of people were
sitting up, rubbing their eyes, and wondering where they would find their
next meal. As they flailed about, semi-conscious, they were insidiously
courted by communist casuists. Joseph Palmer, assistant chief of the
Division of African Affairs, voiced a typical State Department sentiment in
October 1947 when he referred to 'the strategy long since drawn up by
Lenin . . . namely, use the Nationalists in a dependent area to gain
separation from the mother country, then turn the masses against the
Nationalist leaders, institute universal franchise, parliaments, etc., in such
a way that the disciplined Communist party can gain an effective control
over the undisciplined and less well organized opposition'.[2] But it was not
only Africans or Asians who responded to the Soviet clarion. Hard times in
France and Italy were reflected in the growing electoral strength of their
respective communist parties. 'The condition is uneasy, very uneasy',
noted Lewis W. Douglas, US ambassador to Britain. George Romney,
managing director of the Automobile Manufacturers Association, described his August–September 1947 travels through Western Europe:

> Like most Americans, I thought the main problems in Europe were the
> economic rehabilitation of agriculture and industry, the political prob-
> lem of working out the peace treaties, relocating displaced persons,
> stabilizing currencies, and reducing international trade barriers. But
> everywhere I went I found the most urgent problem was to avert
> starvation and freezing for millions of people in Europe this [coming]
> winter. . . . All countries that I visited were still suffering from a severe
> drought in the summer of 1946; harsh, cold, freezing weather last winter
> that froze some crops; floods this spring; and a worse drought this
> summer. . . . The fields of England were parched and brown. In
> Denmark and the other Scandinavian countries . . . dairy cattle were
> being killed due to the lack of forage. The same was true in France. . . .
> In every country I visited, agricultural output was off from 30 to 40
> percent.

Senator Arthur Vandenberg worried 'lest the strains become too great and
result in an expanding economic depression which would engulf western
Europe and, eventually, spread over much of the rest of the world'.[3] While
it was assumed that Americans would always place high ideals above a full
stomach, others – even Europeans unfortunately – could not do the same.
There remained the oft-expressed fear among US analysts that the world's

masses would abandon any commitment to democracy for the promise of square meals (or more accurately, the illusion of square meals) at the table of totalitarianism. Yet, this view of a passive, reactive, possibly cynical and opportunistic world populace co-existed with a more positive, romantic view: the rising up of the downtrodden to throw off the shackles of imperialism and backwardness to reach out for the freedoms, the opportunities, and the know-how of the American system. What did the future hold? As George Marshall commented in May 1947, 'In my own experience in campaigns we have a very hard time and we seldom settle them the first week, and they get worse and worse, and finally they get better – I hope'.[4]

AMERICAN ANTICOLONIALISM

War's end in 1945 revealed a world of diverse and bewildering opportunities within a transformed political and technological landscape. There was good reason for optimism but ample evidence of deep-rooted, continuing hardship and struggle: to fill power vacuums, to restore markets, to regenerate dignity and hope, to adjust to the collapse of old systems, to assert and realize goals of national self-determination. Superpowers loomed. Philosophies of discontent flowered. The seasons of discontent promised to be many. Moving southward and eastward from the ruins of Europe, into the rimlands of empire, was to witness the pervasive malaise of a decrepit colonialism, a tottering superstructure no longer based on any firm and convincing display of racial or military superiority. The war's impact had been profound throughout the colonial areas of Africa, the Middle East, South and Southeast Asia – where British, Dutch and French empires faced strong challenges from indigenous nationalist groups.

Weakened empires, exhausted allies and distant, restive colonial populations promised difficulties for American policymakers who surveyed the post-war horizon. The Second World War had done many things, but it had not resolved very basic problems regarding great-power relationships, the structure of the world economy, and the legitimacy and timetable of self-determination. The quick resurgence of ideological contention, the collapse of the wartime camaraderie (however exigency-driven its roots), the sharp tones of diplomatic exchanges – these things made the recrudescence of suspicion and hostility regular features of international discourse. For Western colonial empires, the end was in sight, though the character of the penultimate days was less clear: the systems shaken but not razed, the peoples stirred but not always in open rebellion. Overtures from indigenous nationalist leaders were often ignored and just as often suppressed. Only Britain, it seemed, was willing to accept the changed imperial environment of the latter 1940s. However, wide application of the principle of self-determination was not acknowledged by either of the two major anticolonial powers: the United States or the USSR. Their anticolonialism was circumspect and circumscribed by expanding notions of self-interest and strategic necessity, coupled with a Eurocentric view of the post-war balance of power.

Franklin Roosevelt, because he so often expressed his distrust of and opposition to imperialism, appeared to embody a hardy species of American anticolonialism. For Europeans, it was a species characterized by a superficial knowledge of international affairs; a vague, impractical, and likely harmful sentimentality; and blatant opportunism in trying to parlay dime-store idealism into tangible benefits for the American economic system abroad.[5] British policymakers further discerned a visceral Anglophobia operative within the ranks of the Roosevelt administration, the Congress, the Joint Chiefs, and the American public. For many US officials, FDR's anticolonialism bespoke a post-war world system revolving around a benign America. For them, self-determination was not an empty slogan; it was international justice. Roosevelt's vision of colonial self-determination rested upon a global open door energized by the prodigious US productive capacity and its pragmatic goodwill. America would serve as a father figure with its potent mixture of altruism and business acumen.

However, Roosevelt was anticolonial in everything he said and in little that he did. He apparently believed what he said and was genuinely moved by the plight of colonial peoples caught in iron laws of want and subjugation. Yet, he showed little inclination to press allies for concessions to native nationalists in areas where the American troop presence was substantial – for instance, the British in India or the French in North Africa. The notion of imposing an isolated trusteeship in Indochina after the war was always rhetorical doodling. Roosevelt never tried systematically to mobilize the strong anticolonial sentiments of State Department officials through specific policy proposals.

After Roosevelt's death and the onset of cold war, American anticolonialism became, in the words of Robert C. Good, a 'complex verbal alchemy'.[6] It was a mixture that evoked little immediate interest in the aspirations of colonial peoples for autonomy or independence. Placed alongside the bigger picture of superpower hostility and conflict – which challenged, it was said, the fundamental tenets of the American way of life – the hopes of the colonized were a negligible factor. The wartime bloodletting, both exotic and grisly, had seemed mercifully temporary; but it was shortly followed by a bitter rivalry of unknown duration. Initially less harrowing perhaps, the cold war became steadily more disturbing amidst a new sense of American vulnerability at the hands of an evil, basilisk enemy. As John Dower has pointed out, the hate-images of the Second World War, from the Pacific front, proved readily adaptable to the cold war: 'deviousness and cunning, bestial and atrocious behavior, homogeneity and monolithic control, fanaticism divorced from any legitimate goals or realistic perceptions of the world, [and] megalomania bent on world conquest'.[7]

English diplomat Ivone A. Kirkpatrick, visiting the US offices of the British Information Service in late 1946 and early 1947, described America as 'a nation where people are apt to live on word spinning'. He observed: 'No country has abused us more than America for Imperialism; in no country is the conception of our Commonwealth more misunderstood or disliked. Yet our efforts to move with the times now seem to arouse some misgiving and regret'. Public opinion was not yet ready to assign Britain the status of an expired, second- or third-rate power. In fact, said Kirkpatrick, there was quite a bit of interest in British affairs. Asking why, he answered, 'The Americans are thrilled by strife. Strife is news'.[8] And strife remained news. In particular, though, Kirkpatrick's phrase 'word spinning' became a fitting description for the increasingly barren, formulaic American invocation of its anticolonial heritage.

In his memoirs, Harry Truman maintained: 'I had always been opposed to colonialism. Whatever justification may be cited at any stage, colonialism in any form is hateful to Americans. America fought her own war of liberation against colonialism, and we shall always regard with sympathy and understanding the desire of people everywhere to be free of colonial bondage'. The proof was an independent Philippines. Americans, continued Truman, had always endorsed the 'undeniable right of a people to determine its own political destiny. . . . There could be no "ifs" attached to this right, unless we were to backslide on our political creed. *But the real problem, as I saw it in its application to immediate events, was not one of principle*. We accepted the principle of political freedom as our own and believed that it should apply elsewhere as well. *The real problem was that of procedure and method*'.[9]

Such statements well illustrated the gradualist American program for colonial self-rule. A hurly-burly approach, fraught with uncertainty and prone to fanaticism, was to be rejected in favor of moderate demands, reasonable expectations, and nondiscriminatory trade. A more ambitious, aggressive anticolonialism was suspect, brimming over with naïveté, demagoguery, and opportunities for communist manipulation. In his March 1947 speech on behalf of Greek-Turkish aid, Truman had said, 'The world is not static, and the *status quo* is not sacred'.[10] But the only status quo about to change radically was Western Europe's, via economic revitalization, not the status quo of overseas dependencies. In fact, amidst the reddening world map of the cold war, imperial ties were recast as spokes of stability rather than routes to despair. Colonial peoples should be patient and await percolative gains from restored metropoles.

The Marshall Plan was for Western Europe. What of Asia? Secretary Marshall explained: 'The very magnitude of the world problem as a whole

requires a careful direction of our assistance to the critical areas where it
can be most immediately effective'. Such an investment was 'in one
important sense a world recovery program. The delay in European
recovery has created a serious problem for many countries which normally
supply the European market with raw materials and other commodities'.[11]
Europe was reconstructable. There was no similar assurance for China,
with its corrupt, splintered Guomindang oligarchy. What about Southeast
Asia, where America's Eurocentrism collided with the most radical and
best equipped of the rimland nationalist movements?

Former Secretary of State James Byrnes was still elaborating the
wartime theme of colonial peoples' love for America when his memoirs
were published in 1947. 'In our approach to the myriad troubles of Asia',
he wrote, 'we should always remember that we start with a tremendous
reservoir of good will. The fulfillment of our promise of independence to
the Philippines and our acts of friendship toward the independent Kingdom of Siam stand as beacon lights to millions of Asiatics who are looking
toward an expansion of their political and economic freedom'. He did
sound a cautionary note: 'In all the change that inevitably lies ahead in
Asia, we must make sure our actions do not drain this reservoir of good
will. Our own safety and security, as well as the peace of the world, depend
upon our being on the side of progress in Asia'.[12] Unfortunately, Byrnes'
portrait was already out of date. His statements contrasted sharply with the
views of Harold Isaacs, a journalist who travelled through Southeast Asia
during the stormy weeks after Japan's surrender.

Isaacs' book also appeared in 1947, and he offered a poignant, pessimistic analysis – emphasizing the vast disappointment among Southeast
Asian nationalists that the Atlantic Charter did not constitute a real policy
goal for the major powers. The United States, in particular, was the focus
of this disappointment, which soon had become angst and bristling
hostility. 'It was the most spectacular fact of the first postwar months',
recounted Isaacs, 'the puncturing of the American myth, the rude
destruction of hopes that never had any foundation in the first place.
Watching it happen, in country after country following Japan's
collapse, was like witnessing the crumbling of castles in the sky.' Asian
nationalists 'discovered that America placed a higher premium upon
its bloc with the Western powers than upon upsetting the colonial
system'.[13]

THE THREAT OF SELF-DETERMINATION

The United States was a moody nation indeed as it stood mired in
anticommunist anxiety, uncertain of its friends and too certain of its

enemies. Patricia Ward's detailed study of the Council of Foreign Ministers concluded that 'the fragility of American-Soviet relations did not withstand the threat of peace'.[14] Another threat was the eruption of uninstructed independence movements – that is, self-determination which was wholly the product of indigenous forces and unconcerned about US sensitivities and policy agendas. American officials only looked with favor upon nationalist efforts which envisioned an evolutionary road and anticipated close co-ordination with Western economies. Further, US dicta became increasingly arbitrary and inflexible as the cold war intensified.

To Harold Isaacs, chaotic international affairs represented the triumph of irrationality. 'It is difficult to wander anywhere on the face of the earth', he observed, 'without being assailed by a sense of being in a madhouse where delusions govern amid hopeless and needless suffering, where myopia and fear have obscured the most elementary demands of true self-interest'. There was no such thing anymore as a local problem.[15] Certainly he was not the first journalist to score the character of empires or curse the dark. The imperial systems had outlived persistent critics. Colonialism remained a resilient dying enterprise in 1943, when General Patrick Hurley, who frequently undertook fact-finding missions for Roosevelt, wrote: 'In all the nations I have visited, I have been told, usually by British and Americans, that the principles of imperialism already have succumbed to the principles of democracy. From my own observations, however, I must say that if imperialism is dead, it seems very reluctant to lie down'.[16]

In seeking official commitments to the principle of ultimate self-government for colonies and the open door-initiated devolution of empires, Roosevelt had foreseen something of the shape of the post-war international system. As former diplomat Philip C. Jessup commented, FDR 'anticipated the Third World in his eagerness to end or curtail colonialism'. Clearly, rising nationalism among dependent peoples would become an important factor in big-power relationships. Millions of Asian, African and Arab peoples could neither be ignored nor much longer suppressed. As former vice-consul Charles Wolf commented in 1948:

> It is no longer visionary to speak of the awakening and incipient consolidation of an area stretching from the Philippines in the Northeast and Indonesia in the East, to Egypt in the West. Recent events – especially those in Indonesia and India, but also in the Philippines, Indo-China, Burma, and Egypt – have demonstrated the vitality of these tendencies. The West can work with them in a spirit of acceptance and constructive help, or it can try to undermine them. The former course may earn rich economic and social rewards. The latter can only cause resentment and bitterness.[17]

TRIAL FLIGHT

There were colorful phrases to describe the colonial world. As Lord Inverchapel (Clark Kerr) remarked in October 1947, 'There lies between the western countries and the countries which are Communist or Communist controlled, a kind of crescent of middle lands stretching from Scandinavia through Europe, the Middle East and South East Asia to the Far East, whose orientation will either be towards Western ideas or towards Communism'. Michael Schaller has discussed the view among American policymakers that the fate of Japan and Southeast Asia comprised 'linked sectors on a "great crescent" that stretched in an arc from the Kurile Islands to the borders of Iran and Afghanistan'. Foreign Service officer George McGhee called it the 'middle world'.[18] Middle lands, middle worlds, and crescents – such Tolkienesque precursors to the term 'Third World' all bore the same geopolitical stamp. There was always the implicit acknowledgment of an expanding East-West competition throughout the world's belt of disparate rimland societies.

During 1947, there occurred the trial flight of American containment as an integrated, global doctrine. It was directed primarily against the threat of Soviet expansionism in Europe – either through direct aggression or, more commonly, cagey, fifth-column activities. The same year also marked the trial flight of a colonial policy which had been previously an *ad hoc* agglomeration of presidential declarations, wartime initiatives, strategic considerations, and State Department infighting. By 1947, the Rooseveltian glimmer was gone, and the stark demonology of the cold war had emerged. Containment dictated a *realpolitik* which mocked ritual assurances that the United States was inherently and unabashedly anticolonial. Nationalist movements in the colonial world had to prove their non-communist bona fides before receiving even limited US encouragement – and the State Department's preferred rate of movement on colonial issues was glacial at best. Moreover, where native nationalists were led by communists, as in Vietnam, American policy hardened into unequivocal hostility. Veteran Comintern agents need not apply for US assistance. It mattered little how often Ho Chi Minh sought to reassure American representatives of his essentially pragmatic course. France stood as the keystone in the American security frontier in Europe.

On the other hand, where provisional regimes demonstrated their moderation, showed a willingness to negotiate in good faith, and could effectively mobilize world opinion on their behalf – as in Indonesia – there the US position was more flexible. But the basic policy guidelines for colonial areas held firm: the rimlands contained peoples of obscure and enigmatic purpose, peoples who could be best schooled and upgraded by the same European powers which had colonized them. The need for enlightened tutelage was a lasting lesson which American officials had learned from their Philippine encounter. If there were to be independent republics carved out of the colonial crescent, the process should be slow and deliberate, possibly through UN-sponsored arrangements. Above all, US policymakers sought to avoid the sudden appearance of untested, unpredictable, and likely unstable regimes in the colonial world.

NEW MYTHS

H. Stuart Hughes, a former OSS officer and self-described middle-level State Department staffer, wrote in 1969 that 'something of the feel and taste of the late 1940's has slipped into oblivion'. His service with the department during 1946–47 marked, he said, 'the period of ... incipient cold war ... during which our country and the Soviet Union together reached the point of no return'. For Hughes, the historians of post-war American diplomacy had not captured 'the quality of bewilderment and moral untidiness it had at the time'. He perceived the cold war as 'the result of a cumulative, mutually reinforcing series of mistakes and mis-understandings – an elaborate counterpoint in which our government and that of the Soviet Union seemed almost to be working hand-in-hand to simplify the ideological map at the expense of minor political forces, intermediate groups, and nuances of opinion'.

It was a new era of myth-making – not necessarily sound myths, but durable and useful ones nonetheless. American officials chose images and metaphors which strengthened the appeal of globalism as well as drawing upon older elements of the US self-portrait: the city upon a hill, the revolutionary republic, the homeland of liberty, the advocate of the downtrodden. But as Sally Marks has observed, the world simply did not behave in the ways that American policymakers hoped or expected, 'partly because its realities were not what American planners assumed them to be'.[19] Rhetoric substituted for analysis. Mistaken assumptions bred flawed analogies and fuelled muddled doctrines. Such was to be the character of the cold war.

The latter 1940s was a qualitatively different era for virtually everyone. For American leaders, there were wider responsibilities to assume and a vaster knowledge to assimilate and master. For Western Europeans, it was the end of stubbornly held myths confirming that European society was the most civilized, the most creative in the world, and therefore the linchpin of a well-oiled global system that nurtured a basically humane order. Such was the *mission civilisatrice*, slightly misty, always gratifying. Years later, European writers would still be arguing that the intervention of thick-headed American sentimentalists had doomed what were yet viable colonial systems, especially in Southeast Asia. Hugh Tinker, however, was more correct in his assessment: 'The toppling of the Europeans came not from American pressure but from the forces of Asian nationalism pitted against powers no longer strong enough to enforce their rule upon their subjects'.[20] Even US policymakers tended to forget the strength of nationalist armies. Perhaps the British, who fought limited engagements in both Vietnam and Indonesia during 1945–46 while awaiting the arrival of French and Dutch troops, remembered best the determination of their native opponents.

For colonial peoples, the years after 1945 marked the beginning of a new age of historical memory – or more to the point, a time when, to borrow a phrase, 'memory turned into pining, keening myth'.[21] Linked to older, even ancient, accounts of national or supranational (in the case of Islam) splendor, the new myths focused upon the heroism of the anti-imperialist struggle and the unity and high purpose of nationalist movements. For a short time, the United States had been able to stand outside the Western imperialist stream, perceived as a nation and people apart from Europe, endowed with certain inalienable attitudes – for one, a belief in freedom. Thus, Ho Chi Minh and Sukarno had addressed their articulate appeals to the American government. Thus it was that American intelligence operatives typically found a friendly reception in colonial areas. Thus it was that Ho Chi Minh, on the eve of open warfare in northern Vietnam in December 1946, reminded Abbot Moffat of the respect with which OSS operatives had treated their Viet Minh allies.

But the sense of American uniqueness was soon superseded – nearly everywhere in the colonial world – by the angry identification of the United States as the last avatar of the imperial ethos. America appeared as the essential behind-the-scenes support to the obviously weakened European colonial powers. American lend-lease equipment was freely used by French forces in Damascus and Saigon as well as Dutch troops in Batavia. American financial assistance underwrote the French and Dutch military efforts in North Africa and Southeast Asia. Thus became rooted the image – expressed in mythic style – of an insensitive, arrogant, exploitive United States. What had been perceived as a bountiful, generous culture was now seen instead as a selfish, materialistic giant – a threat to the integrity of smaller societies.

THE UNITED STATES AND THE THIRD WORLD

In the years after 1950, colonial societies began to enter, in Edmund Taylor's words, 'the maelstrom of twentieth-century history'. Governments representing newly independent countries joined the United Nations. They were courted by both the Americans and the Soviets. They were sought for the growing rosters of the cold war teams. Yet, it was a problem-laden emergence, in many ways: weak economies, political personality cults, bloated military budgets and ethnic conflict. As American leaders surveyed the world landscape two decades after the Axis surrender, it seemed that the ex-colonies had coalesced into 'a surly and disobedient Third World'.[22] What had happened?

For the reasons discussed in this book, the immediate post-war years remain the seedbed for the crystallization, spread, and institutionalization of anti-Americanism as a lasting if not permanent feature of Third-World culture – a ritualistic denunciation of the pervasive and alien influence of Western materialism and capitalism. While the ritual character of the criticism has served to devalue the tendency – as if it were simply a case of a powerful nation being castigated for its accumulation of wealth – the initial source of the dislike and disappointment lay in those actions taken and not taken by American policymakers during the years 1945–47. It was in the heady months of latter 1945 that the United States was expected to lead the way in the dismantling of empires and the coming of redemption and independence. The redemption would have been elusive in any case; but having been denied self-rule except through great struggle and sacrifice (and surely this process warped many good intentions), nationalists characteristically came to view America as the great deceiver, the prop of reaction. They wanted their former futile hopes and expectations of American largesse thoroughly exorcised, root and branch. It was an anti-Americanism based both on real and imagined injustice – on real and imagined US complicity in the perpetuation of stifling colonial or neocolonial regimes. Unfortunately, American foreign policy fed the illusion as well as the reality.

Even if there had been no cold war, the relationship between the United States and dependent areas would have been far from predictable. As Christopher Thorne has pointed out, during the war years America represented 'an essentially Western and white order, political and economic'.[23] Such would have continued to be the case even if Roosevelt had lived through his fourth term. But of course there *was* a cold war, with long-range implications for the balance of power and terror, for state mobilization of vital physical and human resources, and for the attitudes of policymakers toward what promised to be a disorderly process of decolonization. The policy complications engendered by Soviet-American competition undermined, distorted, and ultimately destroyed whatever genuine anticolonial sentiment had existed among upper-echelon American officials. The zero-sum vision of US-Soviet struggle – with good guys, bad guys and nothing in between – left no room for any policy of sustained criticism of and sanctions against Western European colonial powers.

However, while cold war doctrine for the European theater was the product of a wide consensus in American government, the same strategies applied mechanistically (and even sloppily) in other, nonanalogous areas of the world resulted in pursuits which became, over time, steadily more unreasonable and untenable. Containment writ large, carried out as a global campaign, bore less and less resemblance to the true correlation of forces as the major arena of US-Soviet competition began to shift away from Europe and toward the Third World. The rise of Third-World nationalism confronted American policymakers with accelerating contradictions as well as burgeoning and unrealistic commitments. The holistic imprint of imperialism was poorly understood through the latter 1940s and remained so.

Ernest May has drawn attention to the tendency among US policymakers toward a systematic misunderstanding and misuse of history, especially in the promulgation of false and simplistic analogies.[24] Indeed, given the range and survival rate of falling-domino scenarios, there seemed to be a multiplier effect at work in the State Department and among the Joint Chiefs. Third-World regimes, caught in the ideological and military crossfire of the cold war, often withered in the face of systematic disruption and intervention. Once-proud nationalists became puppet rulers for the East or West. Indigenous movements were undermined and thwarted, or they achieved victory only after disastrous sacrifice. The toll of bitterness was difficult, even years later, to estimate. Colonialism was dead, but great powers continued to impose themselves upon dependent peoples – continued to prowl the rimlands in hopes of discovering better formulas for dominance and control. In a world deployed, violence flared throughout the colonial theaters. The globalization of Third-World issues and crises was a poor substitute for self-determination.

Notes

Chapter 1

1. Arata Osada (comp.), *Children of Hiroshima*, ed. Yoichi Fukushima for the English-language edition (New York: Harper Colophon, 1980), pp. 119–20, 124, 132 and *passim*; Luis W. Alvarez, *Alvarez: Adventures of a Physicist* (New York: Basic Books, 1987), p. 7. The first book consists of brief recollections written by those survivors of the Hiroshima bombing who were generally of elementary school age in August 1945; the accounts were assembled in 1951. The quoted words 'rain of ruin . . .' are from a prepared statement released in Washington, DC after the Hiroshima bombing; Truman was then at sea, aboard the USS *Augusta*, returning from the Potsdam Conference; quoted in Harry S. Truman, *Year of Decisions*, vol. 1 of *Memoirs* (Garden City, NY: Doubleday, 1955), p. 422.
2. Bradley F. Smith, *The War's Long Shadow: The Second World War and Its Aftermath; China, Russia, Britain, and America* (New York: Simon and Schuster, 1986), p. 138.
3. Counasse, 'Saigon Mission', folder no. 85, Box 25, Entry 110, Record Group (RG) 226, Military Reference Branch, National Archives and Records Administration, Washington, DC (hereafter cited as MRB).
4. 'U.S. at War', *Time*, 20 August 1945, pp. 19–20; Raymond B. Fosdick, 'The Challenge: One World or *None*', *New York Times Magazine*, 2 September 1945, p. 8; 'Atomic Age', *Time*, 20 August 1945, p. 29.
5. Attlee to Truman, 25 September 1945, folder: Attlee, Clement R. – Miscellaneous, Box 170, President's Secretary's Files, Harry S. Truman Papers, Harry S. Truman Library, Independence, Missouri.
6. Bush to Robert P. Patterson, 3 January 1947, Vannevar Bush folder, General Correspondence Files, Robert P. Patterson Papers, Library of Congress, Washington, DC; Bateson to Gen. William J. Donovan, through Col. John G. Coughlin, 18 August 1945, folder no. 2131, Box 118, Entry 154, RG 226, MRB.
7. Sumner Welles, *Where Are We Heading?* (New York: Harper, 1946), p. 334.
8. John Lukacs, *1945: Year Zero* (Garden City, NY: Doubleday, 1978), p. 150, has concluded: 'Had the atomic bomb not been invented, the history of the world in 1945 and after would have been largely the same. Japan would have capitulated sooner or later. A Third World War with Russia was unthinkable, atomic bombs or not'.
9. Adam B. Ulam, *Expansion and Coexistence: The History of Soviet Foreign Policy, 1917–67* (New York: Praeger, 1968), p. 413; Bateson to Donovan, 18 August 1945, folder no. 2131, Box 118, Entry 154, RG 226, MRB; Theodore Draper, 'American Hubris: From Truman to the Persian Gulf', *New York Review of Books*, 16 July 1987, p. 42; Barton J. Bernstein, 'Roosevelt, Truman, and the Atomic Bomb, 1941–1945: A Reinterpretation', *Political Science Quarterly* 90 (Spring 1975): pp. 59–60. The theme of a hidden agenda behind American use of the atomic bombs against Japan was, of course, the thesis of Gar Alperovitz, *Atomic Diplomacy: Hiroshima and Potsdam* (1965), reprinted in 1985 by Penguin Books with a new introduction. While Alperovitz was principally concerned with the broad impact of the atomic bomb project (as it neared completion) upon Truman-administra-

tion diplomacy during the spring and summer of 1945, his book has often been read as asserting that the *primary* reason for the use of atomic bombs was the desire to secure political advantage over the Soviet Union. In fact, Alperovitz does suggest the primacy of political factors (see, for example, pp. 158–61, 165, 287–8), but his new introduction stresses the theme of atomic-*influenced* diplomacy in the early months of the Truman presidency. A more deterministic approach is reflected in Norman Cousins, *The Pathology of Power* (New York: Norton, 1987), pp. 47–8.

10. William D. Leahy, *I Was There* (New York: McGraw-Hill, 1950), p. 438. Leahy had opposed using the atomic bomb against Japan: 'The Japanese were already defeated and ready to surrender because of the effective sea blockade and the successful bombing with conventional weapons' (p. 441). Barton Bernstein, 'Roosevelt, Truman, and the Atomic Bomb', p. 51, has pointed out that Leahy's opposition to using the atomic bomb was not influential in policymaking circles because he was regarded as an old-line military leader who had never believed the Manhattan Project would produce a working device.

11. Smith, *The War's Long Shadow*, pp. 129–30; Robert L. Messer, *The End of an Alliance: James F. Byrnes, Roosevelt, Truman, and the Origins of the Cold War* (Chapel Hill: University of North Carolina, 1982), p. 184.

12. Robert M. Hathaway, *Ambiguous Partnership: Britain and America, 1944– 1947* (New York: Columbia University Press, 1981), p. 45.

13. See, for instance, Hathaway, *Ambiguous Partnership*, p. 22; Messer, *End of an Alliance*, pp. 83–4; Patricia Dawson Ward, *The Threat of Peace: James F. Byrnes and the Council of Foreign Ministers, 1945–1946* (Kent, OH: Kent State University Press, 1979), p. 6; Vojtech Mastny, *Russia's Road to the Cold War: Diplomacy, Warfare, and the Politics of Communism, 1941–1945* (New York: Columbia University Press, 1979), p. 108.

14. Philippe Devillers, *Histoire du Viêt-Nam de 1940 à 1952* (Paris: Editions de Seuil, 1952), p. 8. Albert Memmi, the Tunisian writer, has described the development of colonial systems in terms of the need to legitimize myths of racial and cultural superiority, asserting that over time the colonized partially accept and begin to internalize the roles and precepts they have been assigned; *The Colonizer and the Colonized*, trans. Howard Greenfield (New York: Orion, 1965). Systematic dehumanization of the colonized was the basis for Franz Fanon's classic study, *The Wretched of the Earth*, trans. Constance Farrington (New York: Grove, 1968). For Fanon, this internalization of racial and cultural myths could only be overcome through violent anticolonial revolution, 'the terrible stone crusher, the fierce mixing machine' (p. 50).

15. Personal interview with John D. Hickerson, 26 June 1979, Washington, DC.

16. Julius W. Pratt, 'Anticolonialism in United States Policy', in Robert Strausz Hupé and Harry W. Hazard (eds), *The Idea of Colonialism* (New York: Praeger, 1958), p. 114.

17. See, for instance, Assistant Secretary William L. Clayton, 'The Foreign Economic Policy of the State Department', *Department of State Bulletin* 12 (27 May 1945): pp. 979–80 (hereafter cited as *DSB*); memorandum of conversation by the assistant chief of the Division of Near Eastern Affairs, 10 March 1945, *Foreign Relations of the United States, 1945* (Washington: GPO, 1969), 8: p. 1054 (hereafter cited as *FRUS* followed by the appropriate year); address by John A. Loftus, chief of the Petroleum Division of the Office of International Trade Policy, *DSB* 15 (11 August 1946): pp. 276–80; and remarks by Abbot Low Moffat, former chief of the division of Southeast

Asian Affairs, 10 May 1972, in Senate Committee on Foreign Relations, *Causes, Origins, and Lessons of the Vietnam War, Hearings*, 92d Cong., 2d sess., 1973, p. 204.

18. The phrase is from Robert C. Good, 'The United States and the Colonial Debate', in Arnold Wolfers (ed.), *Alliance Policy in the Cold War* (Baltimore: Johns Hopkins Press, 1959), p. 233.

19. For instance, Robert J. McMahon, *Colonialism and Cold War: The United States and the Struggle for Indonesian Independence, 1945–49* (Ithaca: Cornell University Press, 1981), p. 45, has concluded that anticolonialism 'was never an overriding principle of American foreign policy' before or during the Second World War. 'The need to balance other interests always tempered American anticolonial inclinations.' Akira Iriye, *Power and Culture: The Japanese–American War, 1941–1945* (Cambridge: Harvard University Press, 1981, paperback), pp. 191–2, has noted that US policymakers were more interested in assuring the integration of colonial areas into a multilateral global system than in 'espousing indigenous causes for immediate autonomy or independence'. For discussions of British colonialism in India and American policymaking and public opinion, see Gary R. Hess, *America Encounters India, 1941–1947* (Baltimore: Johns Hopkins Press, 1971); Kenton J. Clymer, 'The Education of William Phillips: Self-Determination and American Policy Toward India, 1942–45', *Diplomatic History* 8 (Winter 1984): pp. 13–35; and Anita Inder Singh, 'Decolonization in India: The Statement of 20 February 1947', *International History Review* 6 (May 1984): pp. 191–209.

20. The text of the Atlantic Charter is included in Samuel I. Rosenman (comp.), *The Public Papers and Addresses of Franklin D. Roosevelt*, 14 vols (New York: Harper, 1950), 10: pp. 314–15.

21. Quoted in Lord Hailey, 'The Colonies and the Atlantic Charter', *Journal of the Royal Central Asian Society* 30 (1943): pp. 234, 237.

22. 'The President Reports to Congress on His Atlantic Meeting with Prime Minister Churchill', 21 August 1941, in Rosenman, *Public Papers ... of Franklin D. Roosevelt*, 10: p. 334; the quoted phrase is from FDR's press conference of 16 August 1941, ibid., 10: p. 321.

23. 'We Must Keep on Striking Our Enemies Wherever and Whenever We Can Meet Them', in ibid., 11: pp. 105, 107–8, 109, 114–15.

24. Sumner Welles, 'The Realization of a Great Vision', address at the Arlington National Amphitheater, 30 May 1942, in *The World of the Four Freedoms* (New York: Columbia University Press, 1943), pp. 72, 75. See Julian G. Hurstfield, *America and the French Nation, 1939–1945* (Chapel Hill: University of North Carolina Press, 1986), p. 156, for an illustration of the popularity of the phrase 'people's war' among administration spokesmen.

25. Quoted in Elliott Roosevelt, *As He Saw It* (New York: Duell, Sloan and Pearce, 1946), pp. 74, 115–16.

26. Robert Dallek, *Franklin D. Roosevelt and American Foreign Policy, 1932–1945* (New York: Oxford University Press, 1979), p. 358.

27. Wendell Willkie, *One World* (New York: Simon and Schuster, 1943), pp. 158, 161.

28. Walter LaFeber, 'Roosevelt, Churchill, and Indochina: 1942–45', *American Historical Review* 80 (December 1975): p. 1279; Halifax to Eden, 18 January 1944, CAB 122/812, Public Record Office, London, England (hereafter PRO); William Roger Louis, *Imperialism at Bay: The United States and the Decolonization of the British Empire, 1941–1945* (New York: Oxford University Press, 1978), p. 113. See also Foster Rhea Dulles and Gerald E.

Ridinger, 'The Anti-Colonial Policies of Franklin D. Roosevelt', *Political Science Quarterly* 70 (March 1955): pp. 1, 18.

29. Donnelly minute, 23 March 1945, file FO371/44574, item AN929/22/45, PRO (Foreign Office documents are hereafter cited file/item, PRO); Frederick Puckle, Adviser on Indian Affairs to the British embassy in Washington, to P.J. Patrick, India Office, 25 April 1945, FO371/44561/AN1561, PRO.

30. Terry H. Anderson, *The United States, Great Britain, and the Cold War, 1944–1947* (Columbia: University of Missouri Press, 1981), p. 85.

31. Butler minute, 21 January 1945, FO371/44595/AN154, PRO; and Cadogan minute, 22 January 1945, ibid. See also comments by B. E. F. Gage, North American Department, summarized in Balfour (Washington) to Foreign Office, 2 August 1945, FO371/44574/AN2438, PRO; C. R. Attlee, *As It Happened* (New York: Viking, 1954), p. 254; and C. L. Sulzberger, *Unfinished Revolution: America and the Third World* (New York: Atheneum, 1965), pp. 13–14. Roger Makins, former British ambassador to the United States, commented: 'One often had the feeling that some Americans always saw a budding George Washington in every dissident or revolutionary movement [in the colonies]'; oral history interview, 10 August 1970, Truman Library.

32. Lord Hailey, 'The Colonies and the Atlantic Charter', pp. 238–9, 243.

33. 'British and American Views on the Applicability of the Atlantic Charter to Dependent Areas (Particularly British Africa)', 30 August 1944, Research and Analysis Branch report no. 1972, Office of Strategic Services, RG 59, Department of State records, National Archives (hereafter cited as DSNA).

34. Anthony Eden, *The Reckoning* (Boston: Houghton Mifflin, 1965), p. 592; Charles Bohlen, *Witness to History, 1929–1969* (New York: W. W. Norton, 1973), p. 172.

35. The term is from FDR's press conference of 19 August 1941, in Rosenman, *Public Papers ... of Franklin D. Roosevelt*, 10: p. 327.

36. Bohlen, *Witness to History*, p. 131; Charles de Gaulle, *The Complete War Memoirs of Charles de Gaulle, 1940–1946*, 3 vols in one (1967; reprint, New York: Da Capo Press, 1984), p. 230. For another reference to the Yalta photographs, see Robin Edmonds, *Setting the Mould: The United States and Britain, 1945–1950* (New York: W. W. Norton, 1986), p. 40. Anthony Eden, *The Reckoning*, p. 594, recalled, 'Churchill liked to talk, he did not like to listen, and he found it difficult to wait for, and seldom let pass, his turn to speak. The spoils in the diplomatic game do not necessarily go to the man most eager to debate'. Herbert Feis, *Between War and Peace: The Potsdam Conference* (Princeton University Press, 1960), p. 189, used the phrase 'rainbow discourse' to refer to Churchill's penchant for rambling conversation at the Berlin summit.

37. Cadogan to Lady Theo, 6 February 1945, in David Dilks (ed.), *The Diaries of Sir Alexander Cadogan, 1938–1945* (New York: G. P. Putnam's, 1972), p. 704.

38. Messer, *The End of an Alliance*, p. 41. Russell D. Buhite has suggested that the Yalta summit should not have been held at all, that the course of the war had placed Roosevelt and Churchill at too strong a disadvantage in early 1945; *Decisions at Yalta: An Appraisal of Summit Diplomacy* (Wilmington, DE: Scholarly Resources, 1986), p. 133.

39. FDR comment, 3d Plenary Meeting, 6 February 1945 (Bohlen Minutes), and remarks made at a tripartite dinner meeting, 8 February 1945 (Bohlen Minutes), *FRUS: The Conferences at Malta and Yalta, 1945* (1955; reprint, Westport, CT: Greenwood, 1976), pp. 661, 798–9.

40. Ibid., pp. 770–1, 844, 856, 858–9, 947.
41. Ibid., p. 977; Joseph Grew to American embassy, Chungking, 7 June 1945, State Department Decimal Files, 851G.00/6-745, RG 59, DSNA.
42. Donnelly minute, FO371/44595/AN154, PRO; Stimson entry for 3 March 1945, *Henry Lewis Stimson Diaries* (New Haven: Yale University Library Microfilm Edition, n.d.), reel 9, vol. 50: p. 160.
43. Forrestal testimony, 14 March 1945, House Committee on Appropriations, *Navy Department Appropriation Bill for 1946, Hearings before the Subcommittee of the Committee on Appropriations*, 79th Cong., 1st sess., 1945, part 1: p. 25.
44. For Stimson remarks, see entries 3 March and 30 March 1945, *Stimson Diaries*, reel 9, vol. 50: pp. 160, 211. The Joint Chiefs of Staff had urged that, since the Pacific mandates were vital to American security, the islands be under the 'sole sovereignty' of the United States: 'Their conquest is being effected by the forces of the United States and there appears to be no valid reason why their future status should be the subject of discussion with any other nation'. JCS to secretary of state, 11 March 1944, *FRUS 1944*, 5: p. 1201.
45. For a detailed description and analysis of the work of State Department committees in post-war planning, see Louis, *Imperialism at Bay, passim*; also Akira Iriye, *Power and Culture*, chaps 2–3.
46. Benjamin Gerig, 'Significance of the Trusteeship System', *The Annals of the American Academy of Political and Social Science* 255 (January 1948): pp. 42–4; Ralph J. Bunche, 'Trusteeship and Non-Self-Governing Territories in the Charter of the United Nations', *DSB* 13 (30 December 1945): p. 1044. Bunche was acting chief of the Division of Dependent Areas, Office of Special Political Affairs at the time the article appeared.
47. Bunche, 'Trusteeship', p. 1044; Thomas remark, Senate Committee on Foreign Relations, *The Charter of the United Nations, Hearings*, 79th Cong., 1st sess., 1945, p. 584.
48. *Charter of the United Nations, Hearings*, p. 221 (Stettinius), p. 315 (Connally). See ibid., pp. 3–33, for the text of the Charter.
49. House Committee on Naval Affairs, *Sundry Legislation Affecting the Naval Establishment, 1945, Hearings*, 79th Cong., 1st sess., 1946, pp. 1010–11, 1014. The committee's 19-day inspection tour took place from 14 July to 2 August 1945.
50. Stewart C. Easton, *The Rise and Fall of Western Colonialism* (New York: Praeger, 1964), p. 152.
51. Donovan to Truman, 5 May 1945, containing enclosure, 'Problems and Objectives of United States Policy', 2 April 1945, folder: OSS, Chronological File April–May 1945, Box 15, Rose Conway File, Truman Papers, Truman Library.
52. Lloyd C. Gardner, *Approaching Vietnam: From World War II Through Dienbienphu, 1941–1954* (New York: W.W. Norton, 1988), p. 22; Dallek, *Roosevelt and American Foreign Policy*, p. 429; LaFeber, 'Roosevelt, Churchill, and Indochina', p. 1285. Joseph M. Siracusa, 'FDR, Truman, and Indochina, 1941–1952: The Forgotten Years', in Joseph M. Siracusa and Glen St Barclay (eds), *The Impact of the Cold War: Reconsiderations* (Port Washington, NY: Kennikat Press, 1977), p. 166, made the same point as Gardner. William H. Chafe, *The Unfinished Journey: America Since World War II* (New York: Oxford University Press, 1986), p. 35, noted that FDR was 'never afraid of inconsistency'.
53. John J. Sbrega, 'The Anticolonial Policies of Franklin D. Roosevelt: A

Reappraisal', *Political Science Quarterly* 101 (1986), observed that 'the sweeping idealism of Roosevelt's concept of trusteeship was shattered' by the Yalta formula. Nonetheless, he wrote, FDR continued to think that his ultimate goals could be reached through the United Nations. 'Roosevelt undoubtedly died believing dependent peoples everywhere were already on the path to independence in the sense that his leadership had marked out the inevitability of that political process for the postwar era' (pp. 76–7). See also *idem*, 'The Anticolonial Views of Franklin D. Roosevelt, 1941–1945', in Herbert D. Rosenbaum and Elizabeth Bertelme (eds), *Franklin D. Roosevelt: The Man, the Myth, the Era, 1882–1945* (Westport, CT: Greenwood Press, 1987), pp. 191–201.

54.   Warren F. Kimball, 'Naked Reverse Right: Roosevelt, Churchill, and Eastern Europe from TOLSTOY to Yalta – and a Little Beyond', *Diplomatic History* 9 (Winter 1985): pp. 15–16.

55.   Timothy Garton Ash, 'From World War to Cold War', *New York Review of Books*, 11 June 1987, p. 44. This piece was a review essay of books by Hugh Thomas, Martin Kitchen and Fraser J. Harbutt.

56.   See, for instance, Joyce and Gabriel Kolko, *The Limits of Power: The World and United States Foreign Policy, 1945–1954* (New York: Harper & Row, 1972), p. 6; McMahon, *Colonialism and Cold War*, p. 11; S. Neil MacFarlane, *Superpower Rivalry and Third World Radicalism: The Idea of National Liberation* (Baltimore: Johns Hopkins University Press, 1985), p. 1.

57.   Matthew J. Just, 'The Great Dilemma of American Foreign Policy', *Virginia Quarterly Review* 34 (Spring 1958): p. 228.

58.   Edward R. Stettinius, Jr., *Roosevelt and the Russians: The Yalta Conference*, ed., Walter Johnson (Garden City, NY: Doubleday, 1949), pp. 25–6; Nicholas J. Spykman, *America's Strategy in World Politics: The United States and the Balance of Power* (1942; reprint, Hamden, CT: Archon, 1970), p. 154.

Chapter 2

1.   House Committee on Foreign Affairs, *To Create a Department of Peace, Hearings*, 79th Cong., 1st sess., 1945, pp. 32–3.

2.   Proclamation 2660, 16 August 1945, *Public Papers of the Presidents of the United States: Harry S. Truman*, 1945 (1961), p. 223; *New York Times*, 2 September 1945.

3.   Harry Truman to Bess Truman, 10 August 1946, in *The Letters from Harry to Bess Truman, 1910–1959*, ed., Robert H. Ferrell (New York: W. W. Norton, 1983), p. 530.

4.   Sumner Welles, *The Time for Decision* (New York: Harper, 1944), p. 299; idem, 'Problems of Dependent Peoples', *Washington Post*, 28 March 1945; idem, 'Britain's Empire', *Washington Post*, 8 August 1945.

5.   H. A. Wieschhoff, *Colonial Policies in Africa* (Philadelphia: University of Pennsylvania Press, The University Museum, 1944), pp. 73–4, 101; Rupert Emerson, 'Nationalist Movements in Southeast Asia', in John Carter Vincent *et al.* (eds), *America's Future in the Pacific* (New Brunswick: Rutgers University Press, 1947), p. 136.

6.   John Carter Vincent, 'Our Far Eastern Policies in Relation to Our Overall National Objectives', in *America's Future in the Pacific*, pp. 5–6; Philip Jessup to Joseph Ballantine, 14 October 1949, Box 47, General Correspondence 1919–1958, Philip C. Jessup Papers, Library of Congress, Washington, DC. Like many Western observers, Jessup was fond of using the obstetrical

metaphor regarding Third World areas; see his *The Birth of Nations* (New York: Columbia University Press, 1974).

7. Finley to secretary of state, 23 May 1946, State Department Decimal Files, 851R.00/5-2346, Record Group (RG) 59, Department of State records, National Archives and Records Administration, Washington, DC (hereafter cited as DSNA).

8. Cordell Hull, *The Memoirs of Cordell Hull*, 2 vols (New York: Macmillan, 1948), 2: p. 1478; Mundt remark, 9 November 1945, Committee on International Relations, *Selected Executive Session Hearings of the Committee, 1943–50*, vol. 2: *Problems of World War II and its Aftermath*, pt. 2: p. 453; Edward R. Stettinius, 'The Economic Basis for Lasting Peace', *Department of State Bulletin* 12 (8 April 1945): pp. 599, 596–7.

9. 'The Future of the Philippines', September 1949, booklet prepared for the visit of the congressional Far Eastern Survey Mission, folder 17: State Department Correspondence 1949, Box 35, White House Files, Harry S. Truman Papers, Harry S. Truman Library, Independence, Missouri.

10. 'Radio Address on the Seventh Anniversary of the Philippines Commonwealth Government', 15 November 1942, in Samuel I. Rosenman, *Public Papers and Addresses of Franklin D. Roosevelt*, 14 vols (New York: Harper, 1950), 11: p. 475.

11. William A. Hoisington, Jr., *The Casablanca Connection: French Colonial Policy, 1936–1943* (Chapel Hill: University of North Carolina Press, 1984), pp. 190, 194.

12. William L. Langer, *Our Vichy Gamble* (1947; reprint, Hamden, CT: Archon Books, 1965), p. 112; Julian G. Hurstfield, *America and the French Nation, 1939–1945* (Chapel Hill: University of North Carolina Press, 1986), p. 143.

13. Langer, *Our Vichy Gamble*, p. 135; the text of the Murphy-Weygand agreement is included in ibid. as Appendix I.

14. Robert Murphy, *Diplomat Among Warriors* (Garden City, NY: Doubleday, 1964), p. 92.

15. Kenneth Pendar, *Adventure in Diplomacy: Our French Dilemma* (New York: Dodd, Mead & Company, 1945), pp. 10, 20–22; Hurstfield, *America and the French Nation*, p. 24. Regarding Arab attitudes, Pendar noted: 'They loved America and, like most unsophisticated foreigners, had a touching idea that we were all-good and all-powerful' (p. 39).

16. Murphy, *Diplomat Among Warriors*, p. 123.

17. See FDR's press conference of 28 December 1943, in Rosenman, *Public Papers . . . of Franklin D. Roosevelt*, 12: pp. 569–75.

18. See Langer, *Our Vichy Gamble*, p. 333, for the text of Murphy's letter to Giraud; though Murphy used the term 'United Nations' it was clear that US policy was his referent. For FDR's remarks, see 'The President Broadcasts to the French People on the Day of the North African Invasion', 7 November 1942, in Rosenman, *Public Papers . . . of Franklin D. Roosevelt*, 11: p. 452. In a message to Marshal Pétain the next day, Roosevelt referred pointedly to the 'greedy eyes' cast by Germany and Italy upon French North Africa and assured the Marshal that the United States sought no territorial gain. 'My clear purpose', wrote FDR, 'is to support and aid the French authorities and their administrations. That is the immediate aim of these American armies.' In Ibid., pp. 455–6.

19. Memorandum for the president, by Capt. John L. McCrea, 17 January 1943, US, Department of State, *Foreign Relations of the United States: The Conferences at Washington, 1941–1942, and Casablanca, 1943* (Washington: GPO, 1968), p. 610. Additional volumes of this series will hereafter be

cited as *FRUS* followed by the appropriate year, volume number and page.

20. Ibid., pp. 695–6.

21. Murphy, *Diplomat Among Warriors*, pp. 145, 168–9. Murphy recalled that FDR told him: 'You overdid things a bit in one of the letters you wrote to Giraud before the landings, pledging the United States Government to guarantee the return to France of every part of her empire. Your letter may make some trouble for me after the war' (p. 168).

22. See Hoisington, *Casablanca Connection*, pp. 207–8, and R. T. Thomas, *Britain and Vichy: The Dilemma of Anglo-French Relations, 1940–42* (New York: St Martin's Press, 1979), p. 108.

23. James J. Dougherty, *The Politics of Wartime Aid: American Economic Assistance to France and French Northwest Africa, 1940–1946* (Westport, CT: Greenwood Press, 1978), pp. 5, 7 (quote), 68, 103, 118; Mohamed Khenouf and Michael Brett, 'Algerian Nationalism and the Allied Military Strategy and Propaganda during the Second World War: The Background to Sétif', in David Killingray and Richard Rathbone (eds), *Africa and the Second World War* (New York: St Martin's Press, 1986), pp. 268–9.

24. Arthur Layton Funk, *The Politics of* TORCH: *The Allied Landings and the Algiers* Putsch, *1942* (Lawrence: University Press of Kansas, 1974), p. 254.

25. This summary is based on a reading of the following: 'French Policy Toward Arabs, Jews and Italians in Tunisia', 23 December 1943, Research and Analysis (R&A) Branch report no. 1469, Office of Strategic Services (OSS), RG 59, DSNA; 'Native Nationalism in French North Africa', 20 May 1944, R&A report no. 1693, ibid.

26. 'French Policy Toward Arabs, Jews and Italians in Tunisia', 23 December 1943, R&A report no. 1469, p. 1, OSS, RG 59, DSNA.

27. Stettinius to the consul general at Casablanca (H. Earl Russell), 1 December 1943, *FRUS 1943*, 4: pp. 745–6.

28. Murphy to secretary of state, 26 June 1943, ibid., p. 742.

29. Arthur H. Vandenberg, Jr., ed., *The Private Papers of Senator Vandenberg* (Boston: Houghton Mifflin, 1952), p. 134; the remarks were made as part of Vandenberg's Senate speech of 10 January 1945 announcing his new-found internationalism.

30. The first quoted phrase is from 'Manifestations of Anti-American Sentiment in Selected African Areas', 27 January 1944, R&A report no. 1471, p. 4, OSS, RG 59, DSNA; Khenouf and Brett, 'Algerian Nationalism', p. 269. Edward Behr, *The Algerian Problem* (New York: W. W. Norton, 1961), p. 50, noted that American troops 'spread their own native brand of orthodox American anti-colonialism'.

31. Mayer to secretary of state, 5 January 1944, *FRUS 1944*, 5: pp. 527–8. After this interview, Mayer quickly relayed his information to the Resident General.

32. Childs to secretary of state, 28 December 1943, ibid., p. 526; Childs to secretary of state, 14 January 1944, ibid., pp. 533–4. For Childs' views about his tenure in North Africa, see his *Diplomatic and Literary Quests* (Richmond, VA: Whittet & Shepperson, 1963), esp. pp. 19–20, 24, 40, 44–5.

33. Hull to Mayer, 31 January 1944, *FRUS 1944*, 5: p. 536.

34. 'Manifestations of Anti-American Sentiment in Selected African Areas', 27 January 1944, R&A report no. 1471, pp. 1, 5, OSS, RG 59, DSNA. The report found a similar pattern of French resentment and native optimism in French West Africa.

35. 'Native Nationalism in French North Africa', 20 May 1944, R&A report no. 1693, p. 42, OSS, RG 59, DSNA.

36.   Lawton to secretary of state, 24 March 1945, 851R.00/3-2445, RG 59, DSNA. Vis-à-vis rumors of US encouragement of local nationalists, Lawton complained to the State Department that there were people attached to the consulate over whom he had no control and that possibly some of them, such as an OSS operative, had made contact with Arab leaders. 'Another possibility is that certain social contacts which I know to have taken place between nationalist leaders and United States Army officers attached to the local office of the Joint Intelligence Collection Agency (JICA) were exaggerated and misinterpreted.'

37.   Lawton to secretary of state, 14 April 1945, 851R.00/4-2745, RG 59, DSNA; Woodruff memorandum, dated 3 April 1945, enclosed in Jefferson Caffery (US ambassador to France) to secretary of state, 4 April 1945, 851R.00/4-545, ibid.

38.   Lawton to secretary of state, 11 May 1945, no. A-143, 851R.00/5-1145, RG 59, DSNA; Lawton to secretary of state, 11 May 1945, no. 453, 851R.00/5-1145, ibid.; 'Moslem Uprisings in Algeria, May 1945', 30 May 1945, R&A report no. 3135, p. 1, OSS, RG 59, DSNA. French authorities sought but were refused permission to use American aircraft to ferry troops to the Sétif area; for a discussion of that issue, see the following: memorandum of conversation, James C. H. Bonbright, 11 May 1945, 851R.00/5-1145, RG 59, DSNA; acting secretary of state (Joseph Grew) to American Consulate Algiers, 12 May 1945, 851R.00/5-1145, ibid.; Caffery (Paris) to secretary of state, 13 May 1945, 851R.00/5-1345, ibid.; Lawton (Algiers) to secretary of state, 14 May 1945, 851R.00/5-1445, ibid.; Charles W. Lewis, Jr., US consul general Casablanca, to secretary of state, 15 May 1945, 851R.00/5-1545, ibid.

39.   Lawton to secretary of state, 11 May 1945, no. A-143, 851R.00/5-1145, RG 59, DSNA; Lawton to secretary of state, 11 May 1945, no. 453, 851R. 00/5-1145, ibid.; Caffery to secretary of state, 11 May 1945, 851R.00/5-1145, ibid.

40.   Lawton to secretary of state, 23 May 1945, 851R.00/5-2345, RG 59, DSNA; 'Moslem Uprisings in Algeria, May 1945', 30 May 1945, R&A report no. 3135, pp. 6–7, OSS, RG 59, DSNA. The PPA circular attacked the Algerian Communist party as an accomplice to French colonialism, referring to the group as 'imperial-communists'. Paul J. Zingg, 'The Cold War in North Africa: American Foreign Policy and Postwar Muslim Nationalism, 1945–1952', *The Historian* 39 (November 1976): p. 51, noted: 'The European character of the [Algerian] Communist party, Marxist atheism, and the frequent association of the Communists with French colonialist policies all influenced Algerians to favor Muslim leadership and Muslim political parties'.

41.   Central Committee, Parti Populaire Algérien, to the president of the United States, n.d., enclosure in American Consulate General Algiers to secretary of state, 3 July 1945, 851R.00/7-345, RG 59, DSNA.

42.   Tuck to secretary of state, 21 June 1945, 851R.00/6-2145, RG 59, DSNA. From Algiers, Edward Lawton reported that a usually reliable source averred that a minimum of 30 000 Arabs had been killed in the Sétif disturbances; Lawton to secretary of state, 25 May 1945, 851R.00/5-2545, ibid.

43.   Acting secretary of state (Grew) to the American embassy in Paris, 30 July 1945, 851R.00/7-3045, RG 59, DSNA. Caffery reported: 'The information . . . was at once brought by me to the attention of [Foreign Minister Georges] Bidault, who took note of it, sought to minimize the entire affair, gave the usual explanations, expressed understanding of our motives and so forth'.

Text included in acting secretary of state (Dean Acheson) to the American legation in Cairo, 5 October 1945, 851R.00/10-545, ibid.

44. Acting secretary of state (Dean Acheson) to the American legation in Cairo, 5 October 1945, 851R.00/10-545, RG 59, DSNA.

45. This was the conclusion of 'Moslem Uprisings in Algeria, May 1945', 30 May 1945, R&A report no. 3135, p. 7, OSS, RG 59, DSNA, which noted: 'The present French difficulties in Syria and Lebanon have overshadowed the Algerian crisis. A reverse for France in the Near East will, however, diminish her prestige in all Moslem lands, including Algeria'.

46. Edward Grigg, 'Imperial Security in the Middle East', n.d., pp. 1–2, circulated to the Cabinet as C.P. (45)55, 2 July 1945, CAB 66/67, Public Record Office, London, England (hereafter cited as PRO). The memorandum had been previously considered and approved by the Middle East Defence Committee. A paper prepared by the Post Hostilities Planning Staff (PHPS) closely parallelled Grigg's analysis concerning British strategic interests in the Middle East. The PHPS study noted the deep-rooted character of unrest throughout the region, the difficulty of implementing any peaceful solution to the Palestine problem, and the need, therefore, to cultivate Arab goodwill. It would be to Britain's advantage to promote greater US interest in the region. Annex II, 'Internal Security', outlined the three main threats to Mideast stability: (1) Arab nationalism, with hostility and distrust directed primarily at Zionism and French policy in the Levant; (2) Jewish nationalism and Zionism; and (3) Egyptian nationalism. See 'Security in the Eastern Mediterranean and Middle East', report by the Post Hostilities Planning Staff, 27 March 1945, P.H.P. (45)10(O)(Final), CAB 79/31, PRO; the paper was signed by C. C. A. Allen, F. C. Curtis, and R. Sorel-Cameron.

47. 'Future of the Italian Colonies', Attlee memorandum, 1 September 1945, C.P. (45)144, enclosure in FO371/50792/U6968, PRO.

48. Hood minute, re C.P. (45)144, in ibid. Viscount Hood was a member of the Reconstruction Department of the Foreign Office, the division overseeing negotiation of the peace treaties, disposition of the Italian colonies in Africa and related matters.

49. Roosevelt to Churchill, 3 March 1944, R-485, in Warren F. Kimball (ed.), *Churchill & Roosevelt: The Complete Correspondence*, 3 vols (Princeton University Press, 1984), 3: p. 14; Churchill to Roosevelt, 4 March 1944, C-601, ibid., p. 17.

50. Roosevelt to the American Director of Economic Operations in the Middle East (James M. Landis), 6 March 1944, *FRUS 1944*, 5: pp. 1–2; memorandum of conversation between King of Saudi Arabia and President Roosevelt, 14 February 1945, *FRUS 1945*, 8: pp. 2–3; Minister in Saudi Arabia (William A. Eddy) to secretary of state, 3 March 1945, ibid., p. 8. Eddy quoted FDR as saying, 'The English ... work and sacrifice to bring freedom and prosperity to the world, but on the condition that it be brought by them and marked "Made in Britain"'.

51. 'General Catroux and the French Colonial Empire', 3 March 1944, R&A report no. 1487, pp. 9, 6, OSS, RG 59, DSNA.

52. A. B. Gaunson, *The Anglo-French Clash in Lebanon and Syria, 1940–45* (New York: St Martin's Press, 1987), p. 6.

53. 'General Catroux and the French Colonial Empire', 3 March 1944, R&A report no. 1487, p. 17, OSS, RG 59, DSNA.

54. 'Proclamation du Général Catroux', 8 June 1941, in 'Statements of Policy by His Majesty's Government in the United Kingdom in Respect of Syria and

the Lebanon, 8th June–9th September, 1941', enclosure in FO371/45561/
E1667, PRO; a simultaneous statement by Miles Lampson (later Lord
Killearn), British ambassador in Cairo, formally associated Britain with the
Free French pledge to recognize Syrian and Lebanese independence, ibid.

55.   Lyttelton to de Gaulle, 25 July 1941, enclosure in FO371/45558/E959, PRO;
see this same folder for the full terms of the Lyttelton-de Gaulle exchange.

56.   Gaunson, *Anglo-French Clash in Lebanon and Syria*, pp. 24, 78. The official
historian of British policy in this period noted that as of late June 1941, 'It
was ... clear that General de Gaulle regarded the Free French as full
inheritors of the rights exercised by the Vichy authorities and that, in view of
the unpopularity of the French régime, his unwillingness to recognise the
existence of an Arab problem might have serious consequences'; Llewellyn
Woodward, *British Foreign Policy in the Second World War* (London: Her
Majesty's Stationery Office, 1970), 1: p. 569.

57.   Lebanese leaders demanded the following: (1) the transfer to the Syrians and
Lebanese of administrative control of the 'common interests', referring to
customs, patents and other revenue sources which the French highly valued;
(2) the transfer of French administrative personnel to advisory positions with
the local governments; (3) the substitution of a regular French diplomatic
staff for the colonial officals; and (4) the modification or annulment of those
constitutional provisions granting governing power to the French; 'General
Catroux and the French Colonial Empire', 3 March 1944, R&A report no.
1487, p. 51, OSS, RG 59, DSNA.

58.   Quoted in ibid., p. 58. 'This was wishful thinking', concluded the OSS
report. General Catroux had saved face for France, but the French position
in the Near East 'had been irreparably damaged' (p. 58). There was a new
agreement signed between the FCNL and the Syrian and Lebanese governments on 23 December 1943, such that certain 'common interests' would be
shared equally by Syria and Lebanon, reserving 20 per cent of the total
revenue for a common fund; this responsibility would be transferred to the
local governments as of 1 January 1944. Thus, the OSS study concluded:
'The full implementation of Syrian and Lebanese independence ... promises
to be effected without further delay or difficulty. It is certainly to be hoped
that the French will not permit French prestige to be further damaged by
continued temporizing' (p. 59). By November 1943, Jean Helleu had
succeeded Catroux as delegate general in the Levant, but Catroux was
returned to Lebanon to handle the crisis. Gaunson, *Anglo-French Clash in
Lebanon and Syria*, p. 127, contends that the 1943 crisis was probably not
planned by the FCNL but rather by 'the resentful clique of old Vichy
colonialists in Beirut'.

59.   'Crisis in Lebanon', 15 November 1943, R&A report no. 1511, pp. 6–7,
OSS, RG 59, DSNA.

60.   One of the main themes in Charles de Gaulle's memoirs was the British
desire for hegemony through the Middle East; *The Complete War Memoirs
of Charles de Gaulle, 1940–1946*, 3 vols. in one (1967; reprint, New York:
Da Capo Press, 1984), pp. 167, 183, 524, 532, 878–9. British diplomat
Reader Bullard, *Britain and the Middle East: From Earliest Times to 1950*
(London: Hutchinson's University Library, 1951), p. 146, wrote: 'The
mutual suspicions of France and England are old, and they die hard'.

61.   Commander-in-Chief, Middle East, to the War Office, 27 December 1944,
enclosure in FO371/45556/E40, PRO; a similar warning came from Edward
Grigg, British Minister Resident, in Shone (Damascus) to Foreign Office, 16
January 1945, FO371/45556/E403, PRO. For Shone's quoted comment, see

Shone to Foreign Office, 30 December 1944, FO371/45556/E8, PRO. Shone had replaced the controversial Major General Edward Spears earlier in December; for a discussion of Spears' role in intensifying Anglo-French friction in the Levant, see Gaunson, *Anglo-French Clash in Lebanon and Syria*, chap. 4 and pp. 147–57.

62. For conversations with Ostrorog, see Grigg (Cairo) to Foreign Office, 30 December 1944, FO371/45556/E211, PRO, and Shone to Foreign Office, 4 January 1945, FO371/45556/E251, PRO. Butler's minute, 13 January 1945, appears in ibid.

63. Shone (Damascus) to Nevile Butler (Foreign Office), 17 January 1945, FO371/45557/E728, PRO; Foreign Office to British embassy, Paris, 27 January 1945, FO371/45556/E403, PRO. For a good summary of Duff Cooper's pro-French perspective on the Levant dispute, see his cable to the Foreign Office, 5 February 1945, FO371/45558/E862, PRO.

64. Hankey comment on cover page of FO371/45556/E403, PRO; Foreign Office to British ambassador in Cairo, for Shone, 16 February 1945, FO371/45559/E1113, PRO; Churchill quoted in Gaunson, *Anglo-French Clash in Lebanon and Syria*, p. 147.

65. Eden to Shone (Damascus), 26 January 1945, FO371/45556/E276, PRO, and Eden to Duff Cooper (Paris), 26 January 1945, ibid.; Grigg, 'Imperial Security in the Middle East', n.d., pp. 2, 11, CAB 66/67, PRO.

66. The word 'undertaking' is from a minute by R. M. A. Hankey, 16 March 1945, FO371/45561/E1726, PRO; Lord Killearn (Cairo) to the Foreign Office, 6 February 1945, FO371/45558/E926, PRO; Churchill minute, 11 January 1945, FO371/45557/E696, PRO.

67. Butler minute, 27 February 1945, FO371/45559/E1227, PRO.

68. Hankey minute, 28 February 1945, FO371/45561/E1776, PRO; Hankey minute, 28 March 1945, FO371/45561/E1884, PRO.

69. 'American Economic Policy in the Middle East', 2 May 1945, *FRUS 1945*, 8: pp. 35–7.

70. British embassy to the Department of State, aide-mémoire, 1 February 1945, *FRUS 1945*, 8: p. 1037; British embassy to the Department of State, aide-mémoire, 9 February 1945, ibid., pp. 1039–40; British delegation at Yalta to the secretary of state, 11 February 1945, ibid., p. 1041.

71. 'Record of Conversation with the President of Syria at the Minister Resident's Villa, Cairo, on 17th February, 1945', FO371/45560/E1415, PRO. The next day, in a personal minute, Churchill expressed his thoughts this way: 'Put more shortly, we neither guarantee the States their independence nor the French their privileges, but we should like to see both objects achieved'. Churchill minute, 18 February 1945, FO371/45559/E1113, PRO.

72. Acting secretary (Grew) to Wadsworth, 16 February 1945, *FRUS 1945*, 8: p. 1043; Acting secretary (Grew) to Caffery, 16 February 1945, ibid., pp. 1044–5. For the US statement in recognition of Syrian and Lebanese independence, see *Department of State Bulletin* 11 (24 September 1944): p. 313.

73. Memorandum of conversation, 10 March 1945, *FRUS 1945,* 8: pp. 1053–4.

74. Duff Cooper to Foreign Office, 1 February 1945, FO371/45557/E745, PRO; Bidault quoted in Duff Cooper to Foreign Office, 11 February 1945, FO371/45559/E1001, PRO.

75. For Bidault's comment, see Caffery to secretary of state, 21 February 1945, *FRUS 1945*, 8: p. 1049; and for Catroux's remarks, see Lord Killearn (Cairo) to Foreign Office, 12 February 1945, FO371/45559/E1060, PRO.

76. British Consul General Algiers (J. E. M. Carvell) to Foreign Office, 16

March 1945, FO371/45562/E1980, PRO; Duff Cooper to Foreign Office, 5 April 1945, FO371/45562/E2261, PRO.

77. Acting secretary (Grew) to Caffery, 30 April 1945, *FRUS 1945*, 8: p. 1061; first secretary and consul at Damascus (Satterthwaite) to the secretary of state, 30 April 1945, ibid., p. 1062; Shone to Eden, 30 April 1945, p. 8, FO371/45564/E3122, PRO; Shone (Damascus) to Foreign office, 27 April 1945, FO371/45563/E2706, PRO.

78. Churchill to de Gaulle, 4 May 1945, enclosure in British Minister (John Balfour) to the director of the Office of Near Eastern and African Affairs (Loy W. Henderson), 5 May 1945, *FRUS 1945*, 8: p. 1067.

79. Shone (Beirut) to Foreign Office, 10 May 1945, FO371/45563/E3007, PRO.

80. Acting secretary (Grew) to Wadsworth, 11 May 1945, *FRUS 1945*, 8: p. 1073; Shone (Beirut) to Foreign Office, 14 May 1945, FO371/45563/E3061, PRO; Lebanese Minister (Charles Malik) to secretary of state, at San Francisco, 12 May 1945, *FRUS 1945*, 8: p. 1074.

81. The text of the French aide-mémoire is in Wadsworth to secretary of state, no. 138, 18 May 1945, *FRUS 1945*, 8: p. 1080; Wadsworth to secretary of state, no. 137, 18 May 1945, ibid., p. 1079; Shone (Beirut) to Foreign Office, 18 May 1945, FO371/45355/E3197, PRO. A Foreign Office telegram to its Washington embassy noted: 'It will not be possible for Mr. Shone and his United States colleague to restrain local Governments much longer unless they can point to some initiative which offers a prospect of escape from the present impasse'. In ibid.

82. Wadsworth to secretary of state, 20 May 1945, *FRUS 1945*, 8: p. 1083; Shone (Beirut) to Foreign Office, no. 379, 21 May 1945, and Shone to Foreign Office, no. 380, 21 May 1945, FO371/45564/E3291, PRO.

83. Henderson Memorandum to acting secretary of state, 23 May 1945, *FRUS 1945*, 8: pp. 1093–5. See also Brian Gardner, *The Year that Changed the World: 1945* (New York: Coward-McCann, 1963), p. 169.

84. Consul in Damascus (Young) to Foreign Office, 25 May 1945, FO371/45565/E3377, PRO; memorandum of conversation by the acting secretary of state (Grew), 26 May 1945, *FRUS 1945*, 8: pp. 1103–4; text of Foreign Office press release in FO371/45565/E3333, PRO; Commander-in-Chief, Middle East, to the War Office, CIC728, 26 May 1945, FO371/45566/E3524, PRO; Eddy to secretary of state, 26 May 1945, 890D.01/5-2645, RG 59, DSNA; Azzam Bey statement in Lord Killearn to Foreign Office, 27 May 1945, FO371/45565/E3421, PRO.

85. The text of the French press release is in Caffery to secretary of state, 29 May 1945, *FRUS 1945*, 8: pp. 1111–12; Shone (Beirut) to Foreign Office, 28 May 1945, FO371/45566/E3456, PRO; Lord Killearn (Cairo) to Foreign Office, 29 May 1945, FO371/45566/E3530, PRO; memorandum of conversation by Foy D. Kohler, 29 May 1945, *FRUS 1945*, 8: pp. 1110–11.

86. Wadsworth to secretary of state, 29 May 1945, *FRUS 1945*, 8: pp. 1114–15; Beirut Legation to Foreign Office, 30 May 1945, no. 453, FO371/45567/E3560, PRO, *bracketed section in original*; Beirut Legation to Foreign Office, 30 May 1945, no. 438, FO371/45566/E3533, PRO, *bracketed section in original*; Grigg (Cairo) to Foreign Office, 30 May 1945, FO371/45566/E3547, PRO; Satterthwaite comments in Wadsworth (Beirut) to secretary of state, no. 165, 30 May 1945, 890D.01/5-3045, RG 59, DSNA; Quwatli quote from a message to the secretary of state, 30 May 1945, included in text of Henderson memorandum, 31 May 1945, *FRUS 1945*, 8: p. 1118. For the text of similar notes sent by Quwatli to Truman and Churchill, respectively, see Wadsworth to secretary of state, 31 May 1945, *FRUS 1945*, 8: p. 1125 and

Beirut Legation to Foreign Office, 31 May 1945, no. 462, FO371/45567/ E3614, PRO.

87.	Churchill to Truman, 30 May 1945, *FRUS 1945*, 8: p. 1117; Conclusions, cabinet meeting of 31 May 1945, C.M. (45), CAB 65/53, PRO. For de Gaulle's version, asserting that there were repeated, wanton attacks against French forces, see his *War Memoirs*, pp. 882–6.

88.	Wadsworth to secretary of state, 2 June 1945, *FRUS 1945*, 8: pp. 1131–2; statement by Syrian foreign minister, in Beirut legation to Foreign Office, 1 June 1945, FO371/45568/E3687, PRO; British delegation, San Francisco, to Foreign Office, 1 June 1945, FO371/45568/E3635, PRO; Grew memorandum, 1 June 1945, 890D.01/6-145, RG 59, DSNA.

89.	For a summary of de Gaulle's remarks, 2 June 1945, see Duff Cooper to Foreign Office, 3 June 1945, FO371/45568/E3710, PRO; also de Gaulle, *War Memoirs*, p. 889. Noting that the British government had consistently explained its concern about Levant disorders in terms of its regional responsibilities, de Gaulle argued, 'Conversely events in Arab states such as Palestine, Iraq or even Egypt evidently interest France and not only France'. The phrase 'to have her foot firmly ...' comes from a comment in Caffery to secretary of state, 3 June 1945, *FRUS 1945*, 8: p. 1134.

90.	Forrestal comment, 30 July 1945, in Walter Millis (ed.), *The Forrestal Diaries* (New York: Viking, 1951), p. 81.

91.	Mundt comment, 9 November 1945, in *Selected Executive Session Hearings, 1943–50*, 2: p. 455.

92.	De Gaulle, *War Memoirs*, p. 928.

93.	Caffery to secretary of state, 8 July 1945, *FRUS 1945*, 8: p. 1156; memorandum by the assistant chief of the Division of Western European Affairs (J. C. H. Bonbright) to Loy Henderson, 30 August 1945, ibid., p. 1162; memorandum of conversation, by Henderson, 3 December 1945, ibid., pp. 1175–9. According to the British, the phrase 'leading role' did not appear in the final text of the Anglo-French agreement because of Henderson's objections: see ambassador in the United Kingdom (John G. Winant) to the secretary of state, 13 December 1945, ibid., p. 1182–3, and British embassy to the Department of State, message from Bevin, 18 December 1945, ibid., p. 1183.

94.	Henderson to Brig. Gen. H. H. Vaughn, military aide to President Truman, 10 November 1945, ibid., pp. 10–11; Henderson memorandum for the secretary of state, 13 November 1945, ibid., pp. 11–18.

Chapter 3

1.	Escott Reid, *On Duty: A Canadian and the Making of the United Nations, 1945–1946* (Kent, OH: Kent State University Press, 1983), p. 35.

2.	John W. Dower, *War Without Mercy: Race and Power in the Pacific War* (New York: Pantheon Books, 1986), pp. 9–10, 19–21, 28, 36–7, 81–7, 92, 294.

3.	Reid, *On Duty*, pp. 24, 25–6, 31, 34, 42, 50.

4.	Leonard Woolf, *Imperialism and Civilization* (New York: Harcourt, Brace, 1928), p. 20; V. G. Kiernan, *From Conquest to Collapse: European Empires from 1815–1960* (New York: Pantheon, 1982), p. 213.

5.	Robert M. Blum, *Drawing the Line: The Origin of the American Containment Policy in East Asia* (New York: W. W. Norton, 1982), p. 104.

6.	Gabriel Kolko, *Anatomy of a War: Vietnam, the United States, and the Modern Historical Experience* (New York: Pantheon, 1985), p. 4.

7.   George E. Taylor, *American in the Pacific* (New York: Macmillan, 1942), pp. 4, 5, 6, 17, 22, 29, 93, 107, 110–11, 146, 149. In a similar vein, Julius Pratt, 'Anticolonialism in United States Policy', wrote that the United States practised colonialism 'with an uneasy conscience and a more or less steady purpose of return to the paths of virtue'; in Robert Strausz-Hupé and Harry W. Hazard (eds), *The Idea of Colonialism* (New York: Praeger, 1958), p. 114.

8.   John Carter Vincent, 'The Post-War Period in the Far East', *Department of State Bulletin* 13 (21 October 1945): p. 648; emphasis in original.

9.   Draft declaration, 9 March 1943, *Foreign Relations of the United States: The Conferences at Washington and Quebec 1943* (Washington: GPO, 1970), pp. 718–19. Additional volumes of this series will hereafter be cited as *FRUS* followed by the appropriate year, volume number and page.

10. Hull-Eden meeting, 21 August 1943, State Department minutes, ibid., pp. 926–7; Sterndale Bennett minute, 5 April 1945, in FO371, folder 46325, item F2144/127/G61, Public Record Office (hereafter cited as FO371 and file/item, PRO); Sterndale Bennett to Horace Seymour, Chungking, 24 April 1945, FO371/46325/F2263, PRO.

11. Christopher Thorne, *Allies of a Kind: The United States, Britain, and the War Against Japan, 1941–1945* (New York: Oxford University Press, 1978, paperback), pp. 396, 456, 468–9, 538, 724–5.

12. FO brief, 28 March 1945, FO371/46325/F2663, PRO.

13. JCS memorandum, 'Specific Operations in the Pacific and Far East, 1943–44', 9 August 1943, *FRUS: Conferences at Washington and Quebec 1943*, pp. 426–32; memorandum to the Joint Staff Planners, 9 August 1943, ibid., pp. 432–3.

14. Marshall comments, Combined Chiefs of Staff (CCS) meeting, 14 August 1943, ibid., pp. 857–8; Marshall comment, CCS meeting, 18 August 1943, ibid., p. 883; FDR comment, CCS meeting with Roosevelt and Churchill, 19 August 1943, ibid., pp. 901–2.

15. Memorandum by the British Chiefs of Staff, 15 August 1943, CCS 308, pp. 968–71; CCS to Roosevelt and Churchill, 24 August 1943, ibid., pp. 1129–30. The South West Pacific Command, under General Douglas MacArthur, retained responsibility for the remainder of the Netherlands East Indies and offensive action in the Philippines. As Christopher Thorne, *Allies of a Kind*, p. 614, points out, American officials shifted Thailand to the India-Burma Theater in latter 1944, though it was restored to SEAC during the Potsdam Conference in the summer of 1945.

16. See Philip Ziegler, *Mountbatten* (New York: Alfred A. Knopf, 1985), pp. 219–21, for a discussion of the politics of Mountbatten's appointment. The complicated command structure in the region following SEAC's creation is discussed in Charles F. Romanus and Riley Sunderland, *Stilwell's Mission to China* (Washington: Department of the Army, 1953), p. 364.

17. Davies memorandum, 'Anglo-American Cooperation in East Asia', 15 November 1943, pp. 1, 4–5, 7, 9, 10–11, Box 48, Entry 99, RG 226, Military Reference Branch, National Archives and Records Administration (hereafter cited as MRB). Similar views had been expressed earlier; see memorandum by the chief of the Division of Near Eastern Affairs (Paul H. Alling), 19 June 1943, *FRUS 1943*, 4: p. 239. Alling quoted from a Davies memo (n.d.) to the effect that US and British psychological warfare interests in SEAC did not coincide and that the United States must not be identified by Asians as simply another imperial power. Alling noted that his division 'heartily concurs' with Davies' analysis. See also John Paton Davies, Jr., *Dragon by*

the Tail: American, British, Japanese, and Russian Encounters with China and One Another (New York: W. W. Norton, 1972), p. 304.

18. Davies, *Dragon by the Tail*, p. 315; Edmund Taylor, *Richer by Asia*, 2d edn (Boston: Houghton Mifflin, 1964), p. 32; Edmund Taylor, *Awakening from History* (London: Chatto & Windus, 1971), p. 279.

19. Davies, *Dragon by the Tail*, p. 315. See also Taylor, *Richer by Asia*, p. 29, who noted that this 'reasonable argument over strategy [for the theater] led to endless confused, petty bickering over trivial issues'.

20. OSS/SEAC Mission Report, July 1944, enclosure in Heppner to Donovan, 1 August 1944, Box 47, Entry 99, RG 226, MRB; OSS/SEAC Mission Report, September 1944, enclosure in Heppner to Donovan, 4 October 1944, ibid. In the words of another OSS staffer, relations between the two agencies became 'marked by pathological suspicion'; Taylor, *Richer by Asia*, p. 75. See also Heppner to Donovan, 4 October 1944, folder 2222, Box 127, Entry 154, RG 226, MRB. British intelligence was plagued with internal bureaucratic conflicts as well; see Charles Cruickshank, *SOE in the Far East* (New York: Oxford University Press, 1983).

21. See Matthews memorandum, 26 August 1944, and attached aide-mémoire, *FRUS: Conference at Quebec 1944*, pp. 247–9; Hull to Roosevelt, 26 August 1944, ibid., p. 249; Roosevelt to Hull, 28 August 1944, ibid., p. 252.

22. 'Indochina and Southeast Asia', memorandum for the president, 8 September 1944, ibid., pp. 261–3. The memorandum was authored under the guidance of Abbot Low Moffat, chief, Division of Southwest Pacific Affairs; James C. Dunn, director, Office of European Affairs; and Joseph C. Grew, director, Office of Far Eastern Affairs.

23. Hull to Roosevelt, 8 September 1944, ibid., pp. 264–5.

24. Asked about the 'political aspect' of US military operations in Indochina, State Department adviser John K. Emmerson (in the CBI theater) could do little but repeat the same vague guidance. While admitting he was 'uninformed' about current policy, he stated: 'However, I do believe that as long as the operations contemplated do not involve the United States Government politically there would be no objection. In other words, the State Department would not wish to be committed politically to any French or other group, or to any particular post-war settlement for Indo-China'. See Emmerson to Col. F. B. Hayne, 25 September 1944, folder 664, Box 144, Entry 148, RG 226, MRB.

25. OSS/SEAC Mission Report, July 1944, enclosure in Heppner to Donovan, 1 August 1944, Box 47, Entry 99, RG 226, MRB.

26. Bishop memorandum, 'South East Asia Command', 4 November 1944, enclosure with Robert L. Buell, consul at Colombo, to secretary of state, 10 November 1944, folder 'S.E.A. 1944–46', Box 4, Records of the Philippine and Southeast Asia Division, Lot Files, National Archives (State Department files hereafter cited as DSNA); Heppner to Donovan, 4 October 1944, folder 2222, Box 127, Entry 154, RG 226, MRB. Ziegler, *Mountbatten*, pp. 279–80, noted that the Kandy headquarters 'soon became a byword for elegance and luxury'; however, he contended that while overstaffed the Kandy complex was not overluxurious, did operate efficiently, and 'was a superbly effective piece of public relations' vis-à-vis communicating a new sense of pride and purpose to Allied forces in Southeast Asia. Former OSS operative Elizabeth P. MacDonald, *Undercover Girl* (New York: Macmillan, 1947), p. 121, noted that Americans also jokingly referred to SEAC as 'Save England's Asiatic Colonies'; her book contains a description of the Kandy headquarters by colleague Jane Foster (p. 132).

27. The quoted phrase is from a Foreign Office memorandum of 21 March 1944, 'The Essentials of an America Policy', in Terry H. Anderson, *The United States, Great Britain, and the Cold War, 1944–1947* (Columbia: University of Missouri Press, 1981), pp. 12–13; see also Robert M. Hathaway, *Ambiguous Partnership: Britain and America, 1944–1947* (New York: Columbia University Press, 1981), p. 52.

28. Dening to Foreign Office, 5 March 1945, in FO371/46325/F1417, PRO.

29. Ziegler, *Mountbatten*, p. 313.

30. Minute by L. H. Foulds, Far Eastern Department, 5 March 1945, quoted in Peter Dennis, *Troubled Days of Peace: Mountbatten and South East Asia Command, 1945–46* (New York: St Martin's Press, 1987), p. 26; see also the discussion in John J. Sbrega, ' "First Catch Your Hare": Anglo-American Perspectives on Indochina during the Second World War', *Journal of Southeast Asian Studies* 14 (March 1983): pp. 71–2.

31. JCS memorandum, 17 July 1945, CCS 890/1, *FRUS: Conference of Berlin (Potsdam), 1945*, 2: p. 1314; see also Marc S. Gallicchio, *The Cold War Begins in Asia: American East Asian Policy and the Fall of the Japanese Empire* (New York: Columbia University Press, 1988), pp. 30–32.

32. See CCS to Truman and Churchill, 24 July 1945, enclosure to CCS 900/3, *FRUS: Conference of Berlin (Potsdam), 1945*, 2: p. 1465. When initially asked about this division, Mountbatten responded favorably, though he noted that the French were not likely to be happy with it; CCS meeting minutes, 24 July 1945, ibid., p. 377.

33. Taylor, *Richer by Asia*, p. 378; Dennis, *Troubled Days*, p. 14.

34. Raoul Aglion, *Roosevelt and de Gaulle, Allies in Conflict: A Personal Memoir* (New York: Free Press, 1988), pp. 180–81; Albert Camus, *American Journals*, trans. Hugh Levick (New York: Paragon House, 1987), p. 31. The French edition was copyright 1978. Camus was less impressed after debarking, characterizing Manhattan as a 'desert of iron and cement' (p. 51). See also Charles de Gaulle, *The Complete War Memoirs of Charles de Gaulle, 1940–1946*, 3 vols in one (1967; reprint, New York: Da Capo Press, 1984), p. 907.

35. 'Use of Indo-China Resistance Forces: Clarification of Policy with Respect to French Participation in the War in the Pacific', report by the *ad hoc* committee, 13 March 1945, folder: ABC 384 Indo-China Sec. 1-B, Box 427, ABC Decimal Files 1942–8, RG 319, MRB.

36. Evelyn Colbert, *Southeast Asia in International Politics, 1941–1956* (Ithaca: Cornell University Press, 1977), p. 42.

37. OSS/SEAC Mission Report, September 1944, enclosure in Heppner to Donovan, 4 October 1944, Box 47, Entry 99, RG 226, MRB.

38. 'Problems and Trends in FCNL Colonial Policy', 25 September 1944, pp. v, 26, Research & Analysis (R&A) Branch report no. 2374, OSS, RG 59, DSNA; French embassy in China to American embassy in China, 20 January 1945, *FRUS 1945*, 6: p. 295–6.

39. 'Situation in French Indo-China', 26 December 1944, enclosure in Glass to Major David Hunter, 8 January 1945, headquarters, OSS, India-Burma Theater, Box 24, Entry 110, RG 226, MRB. By early 1945, the OSS/SEAC group had been restructured as OSS/IBT (India-Burma Theater), still headquartered at Kandy, with Heppner promoted to colonel and designated Strategic Services Officer (SSO), China Theater; see Archimedes L. A. Patti, *Why Viet Nam? Prelude to America's Albatross* (Berkeley: University of California Press, 1980), pp. 26–7.

40. Cruickshank, *SOE in the Far East*, p. 132. 'The French army', wrote the

author, 'caught off guard, was no match for the Japanese. Morale was low, security poor, equipment out of date, and the loyalty of the natives suspect' (p. 135). The arrival of the Corps Léger d'Intervention, Cruickshank averred, might have made it possible to prolong French resistance; he blames both Churchill and Roosevelt for the failure to transport additional French troops to Southeast Asia before the Japanese coup (pp. 123–4, 136). The US War Department reported that during 12-28 March a total of 34 missions were flown by the 14th Air Force, based in China, to assist French forces. 'These missions represent 98 aircraft sorties of which 23 were bombing, 24 offensive reconnaissance, and 51 regular reconnaissance. Of the total sorties flown, 28 were in compliance with direct requests by the French'; Maj. David Sommers to Department of State (Attention: H. Freeman Matthews), 4 April 1945, 851G.00/4-445, RG 59, DSNA.

41.   Roosevelt to Hull, 1 January 1945, *FRUS 1945*, 6: p. 293; phrase 'Outer Perimeter' from comment by Col. Dean Rusk, attached to the American staff of SEAC, as reported in a memo by Col. John G. Coughlin, SSO/IBT, 14 March 1945, folder 228, Box 20, Entry 110, RG 226, MRB; Lincoln to Robert A. Lovett, assistant secretary of war for air, 7 April 1945, folder: ABC 384 Sec. 1-B, Box 427, ABC Decimal File 1942–8, RG 319, MRB.

42.   See for example, Bonnet to secretary of state, 12 March 1945, *FRUS 1945*, 6: pp. 297–9; Caffery to secretary of state, 13 March 1945, ibid., pp. 300–1; memorandum of conversation by the assistant secretary of state (James C. Dunn), 19 March 1945, ibid., pp. 301–2; Bonnet to secretary of state, 14 April 1945, ibid., pp. 304–6; Fenard memorandums to the Combined Chiefs of Staff, 26 March, 27 March and 5 April 1945, enclosures to CCS 644/21, folder: ABC 384 Indo-China Sec. 1-B, Box 427, ABC Decimal Files, RG 319, MRB; Lovett to John J. McCloy, 2 April 1945, ibid. Charles de Gaulle, *Complete War Memoirs*, p. 855, recalled his feeling that 'French blood shed on the soil of Indochina would constitute an impressive claim [to restored sovereignty over the colony]'. See also 'De Gaulle Appeals for Indo-China Aid', *New York Times*, 15 March 1945, p. 15.

43.   CCS Combined Secretariat memorandum for the Chief of the French Naval Mission, 22 April 1945, folder: ABC 384 Indo-China Sec. 1-B, Box 427, ABC Decimal Files, RG 319, MRB.

44.   SWNCC meeting minutes, 13 April 1945, ibid.; Gary R. Hess, *The United States' Emergence as a Southeast Asian Power, 1940–1950* (New York: Columbia University Press, 1987), p. 150.

45.   Draft memorandum, 'Suggested Reexamination of American Policy with Respect to Indo-China', n.d., Department of Defense, *United States-Vietnam Relations 1945–1967*, 1971, vol. 8, pt. VB2: pp. 6–8; the memorandum was transmitted from EUR in Matthews to Dunn, 20 April 1945, ibid., p. 5.

46.   Edwin Stanton to James Dunn, 'Memorandum for the President Regarding Indochina', 21 April 1945, ibid., pp. 9–12; Moffat comment, 10 May 1972, Senate Committee on Foreign Relations, *Causes, Origins, and Lessons of the Vietnam War, Hearings*, 92d Cong., 2d sess., 1973, p. 166 (hereafter cited as *COLVW*).

47.   Moffat to James Bonbright and Edwin Stanton, 6 March 1945, Box 7, Records, Philippine and Southeast Asia Division, RG 59, DSNA; memorandum for the president, 'American Policy with Respect to Indochina', n.d., *US-Vietnam*, vol. 8, pt. VB2: pp. 19–21.

48.   Acting secretary (Grew) to the ambassador in France (Caffery), 9 May 1945, repeating Stettinius' report, *FRUS 1945*, 6: p. 307. It was also the belief of

the British Foreign Office that the US government had committed itself 'to the hilt' to recognize French sovereignty over Indochina; Annex IV, FO brief of 28 March 1945, FO371/46325/F2663, PRO.

49. 'An Estimate of Conditions in Asia and the Pacific at the Close of the War in the Far East and the Objectives and Policies of the United States', 22 June 1945, *FRUS 1945*, 6: pp. 556–80.

50. Patti, *Why Viet Nam?*, p. 137.

51. 'Indochina's War-Time Government and Main Aspects of French Rule', 10 July 1945, p. 10, R&A no. 1715, RG 59, DSNA.

52. Berno to Brig. Gen. Thomas S. Timberman, 9 July 1945, folder 228, Box 20, Entry 110, RG 226, MRB; Patti, *Why Viet Nam?*, pp. 30, 65, 86. Timberman was head of the Liaison Staff of the Commanding General, US Army Forces, India-Burma Theater. William R. Langdon, US consul for Kunming and Yunnan, dismissed reports of any ongoing French resistance effort in the colony, asserting that such claims were merely made for propaganda purposes 'and to whiten the French sepulchre in Indochina'. Langdon to secretary of state, 3 August 1945, 851G.00/8-345, RG 59, DSNA.

53. Deer Report no. 1, 17 July 1945, in *COLVW*, p. 244; Thomas, 'Report on Deer Mission', 17 September 1945, in ibid., pp. 256–7. Many OSS teams were named after animals; see MacDonald, *Undercover Girl*, p. 230.

54. Deer Report no. 1, 17 July 1945, in *COLVW*, p. 246, emphasis in original; Thomas to Wampler, 20 July 1945, in ibid., pp. 248–9.

55. Thomas, 'Report on Deer Mission', 17 September 1945, in *COLVW*, pp. 258–61. Following desultory military action in Thai Nguyen, Viet Minh officials and the local Japanese commander arranged a cease-fire. On 26 August, there were parades in the town, with many buildings flying Viet Minh flags, to celebrate the end of the war. After his short stay in Hanoi, Thomas departed Vietnam for Kunming, China, on 16 September; ibid., pp. 262–4.

56. Coughlin, SSO/IBT, to Donovan, 18 August 1945, folder 228, Box 20, Entry 110, RG 226, MRB.

57. Patti, *Why Viet Nam?*, p. 141; Coughlin, SSO/IBT, to Donovan, 'Future Plans', 18 August 1945, folder 228, Box 20, Entry 110, RG 226, MRB (note that this is a different memo than the one cited in the previous footnote; the memorandums are not numbered); see also Coughlin cable, 29 August 1945, folder 2302, Box 136, Entry 148, RG 226, MRB. The Saigon team was to be headed by Maj. A. Peter Dewey, the Singapore team by Maj. R. A. Koke, the Batavia team by Maj. Crockett and the Hanoi team by Maj. Patti.

58. George Weller, 'Can France Hold her Eastern Empire?', *Saturday Evening Post*, 30 November 1946, p. 143.

59. Gabriel Kolko, *Anatomy of a War*, p. 23, refers to Ho's 'self-effacing style' as a factor in his ability to provide creative leadership for the communist party apparatus in Vietnam, noting that Ho encouraged the growth of 'alternative ideas and strategies' which generated a more flexible party doctrine than elsewhere. Kolko characterizes Ho 'as the only important true organizational Leninist to emerge from the international communist movement'.

60. *New York Times*, 13 January 1946, p. 4.

61. Patti, *Why Viet Nam?*, p. 86.

62. Thomas, 'Report on Deer Mission', 17 September 1945, in *COLVW*, p. 264; Thomas, 'The Vietminh Party or League', appendix to his report, in ibid., pp. 266–7, 270. See also René J. Defourneaux (as told to James Flowers), 'A Secret Encounter with Ho Chi Minh', *Look*, 9 August 1966, pp. 32–3;

Raymond P. Girard, 'City Man Helped to Train Guerrillas of Ho Chi Minh', *Evening Gazette* (Worcester, MA), 14 May 1968; and idem, 'Ho is Described as Clever, Yet Naive', ibid., 15 May 1968.

63.   Taylor, *Awakening from History*, p. 280; Hale report, in Senate Committee on Foreign Relations, *The United States and Vietnam: 1944–1947*, staff study no. 2, 92d Cong., 2d sess., 1972, pp. 26–8, 31. Taylor later wrote that the anticolonial views spawned in Southeast Asia caused him to take a new view of racial segregation in American society upon returning home, perceiving it as 'the most serious, the most difficult, and the most disgraceful colonial problem in the world' (*Richer by Asia*, p. 102). In a later interview, Patti emphasized that Ho prized his American contacts for the moral support they gave his cause, rather than expecting any sort of direct US aid beyond the war. 'He did use us, and I know it', said Patti. 'I knew he was using us, and I didn't mind frankly because the use he made of us was more one of image rather than substance.' Michael Charlton and Anthony Moncrieff, *Many Reasons Why: The American Involvement in Vietnam* (1978; reprint, New York: Hill and Wang, 1989), pp. 9–10.

64.   Bluechel to commanding officer, OSS Detachment 404, Headquarters SEAC, 30 September 1945, in *COLVW*, p. 284.

65.   Ho Chi Minh to President Truman, 17 October 1945, in *US–Vietnam*, vol. 1, pt. C: pp. 73–4. Ho's telegram was referred to the State Department, where Abbot Moffat, chief, Division of Southeast Asian Affairs, advised that no action be taken with regard to it; ibid., p. 71.

66.   Ho Chi Minh to secretary of state, 22 October 1945, in ibid., pp. 80–1.

67.   'Address on Foreign Policy at the Navy Day Celebration in New York City', 27 October 1945, *Public Papers of the Presidents of the United States: Harry S. Truman*, 1945 (1961), pp. 431–4.

68.   Charles Cheston, acting director, to Truman, 25 September 1945, folder: Chronological File, OSS, September 1945, Box 15, Rose Conway File, Truman Papers, Harry S. Truman Library, Independence, Missouri. Cheston's memo included the following statement by Ho Chi Minh: 'The Republic [of Vietnam] was brought to power by the overwhelming will of the Annamese people on 25 August. The Annamese people have expressed their unanimous desire to live under a free and independent democratic regime. They hope sincerely that the great American republic, having fought to defend the liberty of the world, will support and receive Indo-China in its independence movement. The Annamese firmly rely on the sympathy on the part of the American proponents of justice and liberty'.

69.   Moffat comments, 10 May 1972, in *COLVW*, pp. 187, 166. Moffat, however, did believe that France should have granted independence to the Vietnamese in 1945–6 (pp. 165–6). Gary R. Hess, *The United States' Emergence as a Southeast Asian Power*, has pointed out that staffers in the Office of European Affairs took the initiative in implementing a policy of filing and not answering letters from Ho Chi Minh and other Viet Minh leaders (fn. 44, p. 396). See folder 203F, Official File, Truman Papers, Truman Library, for cross reference sheets noting referral to the State Department of Ho's letters to Truman.

70.   See, for example, Gabriel Kolko, *The Roots of American Foreign Policy* (Boston: Beacon Press, 1969), p. 92.

71.   See Jean Sainteny, *Ho Chi Minh and His Vietnam: A Personal Memoir*, trans. Herma Briffault (Chicago: Cowles, 1972), p. 60. He considered Maj. Archimedes Patti a 'rabid anticolonialist' who 'regarded with a jaundiced eye anything that remotely resembled a return of French colonialism in Indochina'

(p. 47). Sainteny nonetheless had great respect for Ho Chi Minh, with whom he had much contact. Peter M. Dunn, *The First Vietnam War* (New York: St Martin's Press, 1985), has offered the most extreme version of the seduction theme, referring to Patti as 'a virulently anti-Allied, pro-Viet Minh OSS officer' (p. 22) and asserting that the actions of OSS personnel in Vietnam in 1945 'ensured the survival of the Communists in Indochina' (p. 49).

72. See also Gary R. Hess, 'United States Policy and the Origins of the French-Viet Minh War, 1945–46', *Peace and Change* 3 (Summer–Fall 1975): p. 25; and idem, *United States' Emergence as a Southeast Asian Power*, p. 178.

73. The phrase is from Oliver E. Clubb, *The United States and the Sino-Soviet Bloc in Southeast Asia* (Washington: The Brookings Institution, 1962), p. 143.

74. Taylor to Donovan, 25 April 1945, folder 2092, Box 115, Entry 154, RG 226, MRB.

75. Benjamin Rivlin, *The United Nations and the Italian Colonies* (New York: Carnegie Endowment for International Peace, 1950), p. 3.

Chapter 4

1. Maj. A. W. Schmidt, Acting Divisional Deputy, African Division, SI, OSS, to Lt. W. T. M. Beale, Executive Officer, SI, OSS, 7 September 1944, 'Report of Field Conditions', pp. 7–8 for quotes, folder 140d, Box 29, MEDTO Africa Division, Entry 99, RG 226, Military Reference Branch, National Archives and Records Administration, Washington, DC (hereafter cited as MRB). Schmidt noted: 'Although Africa is a newly discovered continent for millions of Americans as a result of the present war, it has nevertheless been very much a going concern for a hundred years. Most Americans are greatly surprised that the coasts of Africa are dotted by substantial cities with many modern facilities, that trade and commerce with the hinterland have been organized for many years by well established companies and that life under European direction is organized on a high scale.' For a map of the Benguela railroad, see 'Railroads of Angola', 13 August 1942, Geography Division, Office of Strategic Services, OSS-824-A, RG 226, Cartographic and Architectural Branch, National Archives.

2. George F. Kennan, 'The Sources of Soviet Conduct', as reprinted in *Foreign Affairs* 65 (Spring 1987): p. 861. Kennan wrote of the USSR: 'Its main concern is to make sure that it has filled every nook and cranny available to it in the basin of world power'.

3. J. R. R. Tolkien to Christopher Tolkien, 30 January 1945, in Humphrey Carpenter (ed.), *The Letters of J. R. R. Tolkien* (Boston: Houghton Mifflin, 1981), p. 111; Stettinius diary entry, 1 February 1945, *The Diaries of Edward R. Stettinius, Jr., 1943–1946*, ed., Thomas M. Campbell and George C. Herring (New York: New Viewpoints, 1975), p. 233; Albert Camus, *American Journals*, trans. Hugh Levick (New York: Paragon House, 1987), p. 25; Christopher Thorne, *The Issue of War: States, Societies, and the Far Eastern Conflict of 1941–1945* (New York: Oxford University Press, 1985), p. 322.

4. John Colville, *The Fringes of Power: 10 Downing Street Diaries, 1939–1955* (New York: W. W. Norton, 1985), p. 607; 'Radio Report to the American People on the Potsdam Conference', 9 August 1945, *Public Papers of the Presidents of the United States: Harry S. Truman*, 1945 (1961), pp. 203, 211.

5. The phrase is taken from a State Department memorandum of 2 January 1945, *Foreign Relations of the United States, 1945* (Washington: GPO, 1967), 2: p. 1411 (hereafter cited as *FRUS* followed by the appropriate year).

6. Vernon McKay, 'The Future of Italy's Colonies', *Foreign Policy Reports* 21 (1 January 1946): p. 270. This article offers a useful guide to pertinent newspaper and magazine commentaries regarding State Department and CFM discussions about the Italian colonies.

7. William Roger Louis, *The British Empire in the Middle East 1945–1951: Arab Nationalism, the United States, and Postwar Imperialism* (New York: Oxford University Press, 1984), p. 23; Scott Fox to Maj. Gen. A. V. Anderson, 21 September 1946, file FO371/53518, item J3852/640/66, Public Record Office, London, England (Foreign Office documents hereafter cited file/item, PRO).

8. Lord Rennell, *British Military Administration of Occupied Territories in Africa during the Years 1941–1947* (1948; reprint, Westport, CT: Greenwood Press, 1970), pp. 283, 291, 455–7. In fact, wrote Lord Rennell, 'It is probable that the Cyrenaican Arabs had never been happier in a generation' (p. 468).

9. E. E. Evans-Pritchard, *The Sanusi of Cyrenaica* (London: Oxford University Press, 1949), p. 229.

10. Eden statement quoted in Adrian Pelt, *Libyan Independence and the United Nations: A Case of Planned Decolonization* (New Haven: Yale University Press, 1970), p. 41; Anderson, Civil Affairs Branch, GHQ Middle East, 'Sayed Idris El Senussi', 21 December 1944, FO371/50788/U1031, PRO. The Libyan Arab Force, created by the British in 1940, wore as its badge the Senussi emblem of a white crescent and star upon a black field; Lord Rennell, *British Military Administration*, p. 25.

11. Arundell, 'Future Policy in Cyrenaica: Note by C.C.A.O.', 13 November 1944, Appendix B of ORC [Overseas Reconstruction Committee](45)9, 13 July 1945, FO371/50790/U5520, PRO.

12. 'Future of Cyrenaica and Tripolitania: Note by Chief Civil Affairs Officer, Middle East', 10 July 1945, DC(45)7(Revised), Appendix I: 'Cyrenaica', pp. 8, 9, and 5 for quotes, FO371/50790/U5577, PRO.

13. Ibid., Appendix II: 'Tripolitania', pp. 3, 2, 4 for quotes, FO371/50790/U5577, PRO. Arundell considered the French claim to the Fezzan essentially untenable and believed the territory should be part of Tripolitania. He believed that the 'Fezzanese themselves' were clearly anti-French: 'They do not like the methods of French administration which they allege to be oppressive, and there is little doubt that they would opt for British suzerainty in preference to any other' (p. 5). Arundell's recommendations were approved 'in general' by the Middle East Defence Committee, which asserted: 'The territory of Cyrenaica should remain under British protection as a Senoussi principality fitted in as might be most appropriate to the Trusteeship clauses of the United Nations Charter'; J. W. Evans, secretary, Middle East Defence Committee, to the secretary, War Cabinet, 12 July 1945, ibid.

14. Hood minute, 22 June 1945, FO371/50790/U4860, PRO; Baxter minute, 27 June 1945, ibid. Ronald I. Campbell noted that Azzam Bey, secretary general of the newly formed Arab League, 'w[oul]d have strong views & try to interest the League in the question because he had fought with the Senussi for the freedom of "Tripolitania" ... & considered himself a hero of that struggle'. Azzam Bey would oppose either Italian or French administration of the area, said Campbell; minute of 27 June 1945, ibid. Campbell was referring to the role played by Azzam Bey in a short-lived Tripolitanian

Republic during 1918–23; see Pelt, *Libyan Independence*, pp. 14–27. Pelt observed that this brief effort to establish a Muslim regime to counter expanding Italian influence represented 'a precedent of fundamental importance for the ultimate establishment of the Libyan State' (p. 15).

15. Coverly-Price minute, 29 June 1945, ibid.; Hoyer Millar minute, 7 July 1945, ibid.; Broadmead minute, 10 July 1945, ibid. Broadmead wrote: 'I fully agree ... that we must avoid giving the Americans the impression that we want any of these Italian possessions for ourselves. If we do that there will be cries of British "imperialism" which will be liable to complicate matters in other fields'.

16. Hood minute, 18 July 1945, FO371/50790/U5497, PRO; 'Future of the Italian Colonies and the Italian Mediterranean Islands', Foreign Office brief, n.d., ibid. As a practical matter, continued the brief, 'It may be desirable to make some frontier rectifications in favor of France who has aspirations to the Fezzan and the Oases near the Tunisian frontier'. The brief advised partition along ethnic lines for Eritrea and unification of 'all Somali inhabited territories' into a greater Somalia with a single administrating power, possibly the United States (or Britain).

17. Hull memorandum, 3 August 1944, *FRUS: The Conference at Quebec 1944*, pp. 408–10; the memo is also available in FO371/50789/U2844, PRO. With regard to southern Libya, Hull wrote that 'limited frontier rectifications in the Fezzan area favoring the French would not appear objectionable, but any outright cession of territory in violation of the Atlantic Charter would be undesirable'. Hull favored the absorption of Eritrea by Ethiopia; and the State Department would support, he indicated, a plan for a unified Somali state. Hull noted that his memo was the product of close study by the department's experts: 'While the conclusions drawn are in no sense final, they represent long and careful study'; Hull to Roosevelt, 11 September 1944, *FRUS: Conference at Quebec 1944*, p. 408.

18. *FRUS: Conference of Berlin (Potsdam)*, 2: pp. 305–6; see also the original briefing books, 'The Berlin Conference: Background Information for the Meetings of Heads of Government', 6 July 1945, vol. 3, tab 9, Naval Aide Files, Harry S. Truman Papers, Harry S. Truman Library, Independence, Missouri.

19. Cadogan to Lady Theo, 15 July 1945, in David Dilks (ed.), *The Diaries of Sir Alexander Cadogan, 1938–1945* (New York: G. P. Putnam's Sons, 1972), p. 761; Cadogan to Lady Theo, 16 July 1945, ibid., p. 762; for other comments about the devastation of Berlin, see William D. Leahy, *I Was There* (New York: McGraw-Hill, 1950), p. 396, and Robin Edmonds, *Setting the Mould: The United States and Britain, 1945–1950* (New York: W. W. Norton, 1986), p. 59. For Acheson's remark of 10 July 1945, see Committee on International Relations, *Selected Executive Session Hearings of the Committee, 1943–50*, vol. 1, *Problems of World War II and its Aftermath*, pt. 1: pp. 106–7. Acheson was addressing the need for additional US assistance through the United Nations Relief and Rehabilitation Administration (UNRRA). William Clayton, assistant secretary of state for economic affairs, seconded Acheson's view of the critical situation in Italy (p. 117).

20. Robert L. Messer, *The End of an Alliance: James F. Byrnes, Roosevelt, Truman, and the Origins of the Cold War* (Chapel Hill: University of North Carolina Press, 1982), p. 184.

21. Herbert Feis, *Between War and Peace: The Potsdam Conference* (Princeton University Press, 1960), p. 184.

22. Thompson minutes, 22 July 1945, *FRUS: Conference of Berlin (Potsdam)*, 2: pp. 244–68; quote from p. 265.

23. 'On Trust Territories: Russian Proposal Presented to the Foreign Ministers', 20 July 1945, ibid., p. 632.

24. State Department minutes, 23 July 1945, ibid., pp. 276–89; State Department minutes, 1 August 1945, ibid., pp. 550–1. Section XI of the final conference communiqué affirmed that disposition of the Italian colonies would await conclusion of the peace treaty; ibid., p. 1510.

25. James L. Gormly, *The Collapse of the Grand Alliance, 1945–1948* (Baton Rouge: Louisiana State University Press, 1987), p. 60; Vojtech Mastny, *Russia's Road to the Cold War: Diplomacy, Warfare, and the Politics of Communism, 1941–1945* (New York: Columbia University Press, 1979), p. 288.

26. Byrnes press conference, 4 September 1945, *Press Conferences of the Secretaries of State, 1922–1973* (Wilmington, DE: Scholarly Resources, n.d.), microfilm edition, reel 10.

27. 'Note on Cyrenaica', Foreign Office brief, 5 August 1945, FO371/50791/ U6051, PRO; 'Future of Cyrenaica', 21 August 1945, report by the Joint Planning Staff, J.P.(45)195(Final), enclosure in FO371/50791/U6443, PRO. The JPS was responding to a Foreign Office inquiry of 5 August, Hood to Maj. Gen. L. C. Hollis, FO371/50791/U6051, PRO.

28. See the Attlee memorandum, 'Future of the Italian Colonies', 1 September 1945, FO371/50792/U6968, PRO, discussed in chap. 1. Attlee was opposed to Britain's taking responsibility for any of the Italian colonies. 'They involve us in immediate loss. There is no prospect of their paying for themselves. The more we do for them the quicker we shall be faced with premature claims for self-government. We have quite enough of these awkward problems already.' As well, there were economic limits on what and how many new responsibilities British military forces could assume; see Hugh Dalton to Bevin, 6 September 1945, FO371/50793/U6970, PRO.

29. 'The Future of the Italian colonies and the Italian Mediterranean Islands', 25 August 1945, ORC (45)21, FO371/50792/U6540, PRO. The proposal also advocated (1) the partition of Eritrea between Ethiopia and the Sudan, and (2) a combining of several territories on the Horn of Africa, including British and Italian Somaliland, into an international trusteeship under British direction.

30. Elles to Bevin, 25 August 1945, FO371/50792/U6822, PRO. At the end of his letter, Elles noted: 'You cannot, obviously, be expected to take any very violent action on a mere letter from someone of whom you have never heard. But the facts that I have stated can be verified, and I myself hope to be posted home shortly'.

31. Minister Resident's Office, Cairo, to the Foreign Office, 11 September 1945, FO371/50792/U6907, PRO; Hood minute, 13 September 1945, ibid.; for a comment similar to Lord Hood's, see R. D. J. Scott Fox to Maj. Gen. A. V. Anderson, 21 September 1946, FO371/53518/J3852, PRO. Brigadier Arundell emphasized that a return to Italian rule was unacceptable to Tripolitanian Arabs; however, he believed that there could be fashioned a workable trusteeship arrangement under UN auspices in which Italy might participate. He restated his earlier viewpoint: 'For reasons of which you are aware trusteeship for Cyrenaica must be British and not international'; Chief Civil Affairs Officer, Middle East, to War Office, 13 September 1945, OET/ 45977, FO371/50792/U7805, PRO. However, a different viewpoint was expressed by Field Marshal Harold Alexander, Supreme Allied Commander in the Mediterranean, who believed that Italy should have certain of its colonies returned as a means to foster pro-Western sentiment and aid

economic recovery; see Alexander C. Kirk to secretary of state, 31 July 1945, *FRUS 1945*, 4: pp. 1013–15.

32. Dunn to Byrnes, 16 August 1945, Box 6, Records of the Office of African Affairs, RG 59, DSNA. Dunn had little to say about either Eritrea or Italian Somaliland.

33. John E. Utter, adviser to the US Delegation to the Paris Peace Conference, to Henry S. Villard, 15 August 1946, Box 5, ibid.

34. See Byrnes' discussion in *Speaking Frankly* (New York: Harper, 1947), pp. 92–3. A memo by British official Gladwyn Jebb, dated 26 June 1946, reported a conversation with Byrnes' adviser Benjamin V. Cohen, who suggested that if the British 'had said from the start that Cyrenaica was essential to us strategically, everything would have been much easier, since the Americans only put forward their proposal for collective trusteeship for Libya on the assumption that we were going to stay in Egypt'. FO371/53519/ J4322, PRO.

35. Minute by James Marjoribanks, of the Reconstruction Department, 7 November 1945, FO371/50796/U8840, PRO.

36. The foreign ministers and their deputies for the first session of the CFM were as follows: China: Wang Shih Chieh and Wellington Koo; France: Georges Bidault and Maurice Couve de Murville; Britain: Bevin and Ronald I. Campbell; the USSR: Molotov and Fedor G. Gusev; the United States: Byrnes and James C. Dunn.

37. Byrnes, *Speaking Frankly*, p. 94.

38. See Ferruccio Parri, president, Italian Council of Ministers, to Truman, 22 August 1945, *FRUS 1945*, 4: pp. 1022–4; De Gasperi to secretary of state, 22 August 1945, ibid., pp. 1024–9, quote from p. 1028. A note from the Italian embassy in Washington claimed: 'The ancient African colonies of pre-fascist Italy are bound by indissoluble ties to Italian minds: they are poor territories inhabited by a small native population composed mostly of nomads, where Italy has achieved a great work of civilization and where large Italian communities have established their homes'; Italian embassy to the Department of State, received 4 September 1945, ibid., 2: p. 107.

39. The phrase is from acting secretary of state (Joseph Grew) to Truman, 30 June 1945, ibid., 4: pp. 1009–10; it appears again in Appendix A, Report on Military, Naval, and Air Clauses of the Treaty of Peace with Italy by an Ad Hoc Committee of the State-War-Navy Coordinating Committee (enclosure to SWNCC 155/1, dated 6 September 1945), ibid., p. 1037.

40. It was the proposed advisory committee which prompted correspondent Herbert L. Matthews to write: 'One overwhelming factor that this plan for Italy will automatically bring into effect is the entrance of Russia . . . into the regulation and control of territories on the Mediterranean and Red Seas and the Indian Ocean, not to mention the African continent'; *New York Times*, 16 September 1945, p. 1. The specter of Soviet involvement in collective trusteeships had caused similar objections from James Dunn, as noted supra.

41. Memorandum by the US delegation, 14 September 1945, *FRUS* 1945, 2: pp. 179–81; memorandum of conversation, by Charles Bohlen, 14 September 1945, ibid., pp. 164–5.

42. Record of the Fourth Meeting of the Council of Foreign Ministers, London, 14 September 1945, ibid., pp. 166–75; see pp. 168–72 for the comments summarized.

43. Record of the Fifth Meeting of the Council of Foreign Ministers, 15 September 1945, ibid., pp. 186–94; see pp. 189–92 for the comments

summarized; the quote is from p. 189. Several months later, Bevin told Stalin that he had supported the American proposal with the understanding that it posited a four-power trusteeship; United Kingdom Delegation [to the Moscow Conference] Record of a Conversation at the Kremlin, 24 December 1945, *FRUS 1945*, 2: p. 775.

44.　Minute by J. G. Ward, 19 September 1945, in FO371/50794/U7574, PRO. Ward was a member of the Reconstruction Department. With regard to the US proposal that Libya and possibly Eritrea be granted independence within ten years, he wrote: 'This is an absurd suggestion, and with regard to our unhappy experience with a much more advanced country like Iraq, which had fifteen years under British tutelage, obviously a very dangerous one to any colonial power'. The American Joint Chiefs of Staff similarly commented in May 1946 that the idea of an independent Libya was 'a political fiction', though by that time the official British position had shifted in favor of Libyan independence; JCS to military attaché, US embassy, Paris, 2 May 1946, folder 092.3 Paris, Box 101, ABC Decimal Files 1942–48, RG 319, MRB.

45.　Hood minute, 13 September 1945, FO371/50793/U7314, PRO; Sayed Idris, in a letter to Gen. Bernard Paget, 21 September 1945, FO371/50794/U7952, PRO, expressed his determination to address the CFM if there were no agreement on Libyan independence. For examples of comments by Arab governments, see the statement by the Iraqi minister to Egypt, forwarded by the British embassy, Cairo, FO371/50793/U7468, PRO; a conversation with the Syrian president, Young (Beirut) to Foreign Office, 24 September 1945, FO371/50793/U7396, PRO; a note from the Lebanese government, Young (Beirut) to Foreign Office, 26 September 1945, FO371/50793/U7453, PRO; and a note from the Egyptian ambassador in London, 12 September 1945, in FO371/50793/U7314, PRO.

46.　Patricia Dawson Ward, *The Threat of Peace: James F. Byrnes and the Council of Foreign Ministers, 1945–1946* (Kent, OH: Kent State University Press, 1979), p. 43; Byrnes, 'Report on First Session of the Council of Foreign Ministers', 5 October 1945, *Department of State Bulletin* 13 (7 October 1945): pp. 507–8, 511–12 (hereafter *DSB*).

47.　Robert L. Messer has written: 'Like Roosevelt, Byrnes clung to the hope that somehow the realpolitik of big power diplomacy and the idealistic expectations of the domestic foreign-policy publics could be reconciled, or at least not allowed to conflict so openly and violently as to destroy the postwar peacekeeping structure'; *The End of an Alliance: James F. Byrnes, Roosevelt, Truman, and the Origins of the Cold War* (Chapel Hill: University of North Carolina Press, 1982), p. 81. Edmonds, *Setting the Mould*, p. 72, has suggested that the 'logical sequel' to US use of the atomic bomb against Japan was for Molotov to be 'as difficult as possible' during the London meetings. William Taubman, however, believed that the breakdown of the London Conference 'was a blow to Soviet hopes' and that Stalin thus favored by late in the year 'a species of détente' with the Western powers; *Stalin's American Policy: From Entente to Détente to Cold War* (New York: W. W. Norton, 1982), pp. 120, 122.

48.　Minutes of a meeting of the secretaries of state, war and navy, 16 October 1945, *FRUS 1945*, 2: pp. 60–1; Ward, *Threat of Peace*, p. 17; Anne O'Hare McCormick, 'Council Split on Principles Not Procedures', *New York Times*, 3 October 1945, p. 18. In his memoirs, Byrnes reiterated his claim that the Soviets sought military advantage through a Tripolitanian trusteeship; *Speaking Frankly*, p. 92.

49. Memorandum of conversation [with Lord Halifax], by the secretary of state, 29 November 1945, *FRUS 1945*, 2: pp. 590–1; Byrnes to Winant, 3 December 1945, ibid., p. 593; memorandum of conversation [with Michael Wright] by the secretary of state, 4 December 1945, ibid., p. 595.

50. The course of US-British relations in the immediate post-war years has been analyzed in a series of recent monographs. The authors point to a realization within the Foreign Office that Britain's post-war decline required Anglo-American partnership to counter the threat of Soviet expansionism in Europe and the Middle East. However, US policymakers initially vacillated between compromise with and hardline opposition to Soviet aims, pursuing *ad hoc* policy goals while rejecting any overt collaboration with England until well into 1946 or early 1947 – despite the fact that the two nations frequently had similar and parallel policy goals. See Terry H. Anderson, *The United States, Great Britain, and the Cold War, 1944–1947* (Columbia: University of Missouri Press, 1981), pp. 7–8, 12, 80–5, 92, 103, 119; Elisabeth Barker, *The British Between the Superpowers, 1945–50* (University of Toronto Press, 1983), pp. x–xi, 20, 46–7, 53, 62, 90; Robert M. Hathaway, *Ambiguous Partnership: Britain and America, 1944–1947* (New York: Columbia University Press, 1981), pp. 5–6, 42, 142, 171–2, 180, 209, 211, 228, 250–3.

51. Memorandum of conversation, by the US Delegation at the Moscow Conference of Foreign Ministers, 19 December 1945, *FRUS 1945*, 2: p. 686. Stalin then said that the Soviet government would not withdraw its troops from northern Iran until the current regime effectively demonstrated its friendship.

52. The final communiqué of the Moscow meeting is contained in Harriman to the acting secretary of state, 27 December 1945, *FRUS 1945*, 2: pp. 815–24; quotes from pp. 816–17. The peace treaties with Rumania, Bulgaria and Hungary were to be drafted by delegations from Britain, the United States and the USSR; the treaty with Finland would be prepared jointly by Britain and the Soviet Union. See p. 816 for a list of nations to be invited to the peace conference.

53. Byrnes, 'Report by the Secretary of State on the Meeting of Foreign Ministers', *DSB* 13 (30 December 1945): p. 1033.

54. For this session, the deputies were Maurice Couve de Murville (France), James Dunn (US), Gladwyn Jebb (UK) and Andrei Y. Vyshinsky (USSR).

55. US Delegation Record, CFM, 2d Sess., 4th meeting, Paris, 29 April 1946, *FRUS 1946*, 2: pp. 156–63; see also a memorandum by the British delegation, CFM (46)22, 30 April 1946, 'Peace Treaty with Italy: Italian Colonies', ibid., p. 194. Bevin also outlined his plan for merging all Somali peoples into a British trusteeship covering a substantial portion of the Horn of Africa. Several days later, Molotov typically asserted that Britain simply wanted to control all the Italian territories. 'He thought it might be difficult for England to digest these additional colonies.' Britain had enough colonies, he remarked. 'Mr. Bevin answered with some heat that it was a strange statement for a representative of a country which by its own admission covered one-seventh of the earth's surface.' See US Delegation Record, CFM, 2d sess., 1st informal meeting, 2 May 1946, ibid., pp. 221–2.

56. Memorandum of conversation, by the director of the Office of European Affairs (H. Freeman Matthews), 1 May 1946, ibid., pp. 203–6. Bidault spoke very directly to his concerns about the security of French Tunisia: 'He referred to the tranquility existing in French North Africa, to its vital importance as a source of manpower and resources for France, and to the

inflammatory effect which he anticipated should a territory immediately adjoining Tunisia be granted immediate independence or even promised early independence.' While he had no love for Italy, he explained, he did not care for the uncertainty of collective trusteeship, nor did he want either the British or Soviets abutting Tunisia. 'He spoke bitterly of British activities in Syria and the Lebanon, and said he did not want any repetition in Libya' (p. 205). In the State Department, Francis Lacoste of the French embassy told Henry Villard, chief of the Division of African Affairs, that France did not want either the British or the Soviets next door to Tunisia and that Italy was the only acceptable trustee for Tripolitania; memorandum of conversation, by Villard, 9 April 1946, Box 4, Records of the Office of African Affairs, RG 59, DSNA.

57. US Delegation Record, CFM, 2d sess., 2d informal meeting, 6 May 1946, *FRUS 1946*, 2: pp. 253–4.

58. US Delegation Record, CFM, 2d sess., 13th meeting, 8 May 1946, ibid., p. 305; US Delegation Record, CFM, 2d sess., 3d informal meeting, 10 May 1946, ibid., p. 335; US Delegation Record, CFM, 2d sess., 5th informal meeting, 11 May 1946, ibid., p. 349; US Delegation Record, CFM, 2d sess., 6th informal meeting, 13 May 1946, ibid., p. 424.

59. Paget to War Office, 23 April 1946, FO371/53517/J1828, PRO; Colonel Drew, War Office, to Lord Hood, 17 November 1945, FO371/50796/U9148, PRO; Utter report, 5 June 1946, Box 5, Records of the Office of African Affairs, RG 59, DSNA; Villard memorandum, 9 April 1946, Box 4, ibid. See also Schwartz to Villard, 23 May 1946, Box 5, ibid.

60. US Delegation Record, CFM, 2d sess., 10th informal meeting, 20 June 1946, *FRUS 1946*, 2: pp. 559, 562.

61. US Delegation Record, CFM, 2d sess., 13th informal meeting, 26 June 1946, ibid., pp. 676–7.

62. Taubman, *Stalin's American Policy*, p. 159; Ward, *Threat of Peace*, pp. 125, 177.

63. Charles de Gaulle, *The Complete War Memoirs of Charles de Gaulle, 1940–1946*, 3 vols in one (1967; reprint, New York: Da Capo Press, 1984), p. 338.

64. James Edward Miller, *The United States and Italy, 1940–1950: The Politics and Diplomacy of Stabilization* (Chapel Hill: University of North Carolina Press, 1986), p. 162; James Reston, 'U.S. Chiefs Divided on Italy's Colonies', *New York Times*, 2 September 1945, p. 15.

Chapter 5

1. Byrnes speech, *Foreign Relations of the United States, 1946: Paris Peace Conference Proceedings* (Washington: GPO, 1970), 3: pp. 33–4, 38 (hereafter cited as *FRUS* followed by the appropriate year).

2. The phrase is from Hamilton Fish, former chairman of the House Committee to Investigate Communist Activities and Propaganda, Senate Committee on Foreign Relations, *Hearings on the North Atlantic Treaty*, 81st Cong., 1st sess., 1949, pt. 3: p. 950.

3. Handy comment, House Committee on Appropriations, *Military Establishment Appropriation Bill for 1947, Hearings*, 79th Cong., 2d sess., 1946, pp. 26–7; Patterson to Stimson, 17 December 1945, General Correspondence Files, Robert P. Patterson Papers, Library of Congress, Washington, DC; quoted phrase from War Council meeting minutes, 5 September 1946, ibid.

4. Slim to chief, Imperial General Staff, 6 October 1945, included as annex to COS (45)607(0), 9 October 1945, CAB 122/495, Public Record Office, London, England (hereafter PRO).

5. Memorandums enclosed in J.C. Sterndale Bennett to Chiefs of Staff Committee, COS (45)533(0), 14 August 1945, CAB 122/495, PRO.

6. See 'Basic Plan for Operation EMBANKMENT', folder no. 284, Box 25, Entry 110, RG 226, Military Reference Branch, National Archives and Records Administration, Washington, DC (hereafter cited as MRB). It was expected that French officials would balk at such intelligence gathering: 'Since U.S. policy towards Indo-China is suspected by the French of being contrary to the expressed policy of complete economic subjugation to France of F.I.C., or the status of *status quo ante bellum*, American observers will be regarded with suspicion, it is believed'. Ibid.

7. Counasse, 'Saigon Mission', folder no. 85, Box 25, Entry 110, RG 226, MRB; Krull, 'Diary of Saigon, Following the Allied Occupation in September 1945', pp. 4–5, enclosure in Moffat to Vincent and Paul T. Culbertson (chief, Division of Western European Affairs), 24 February 1947, Records, Philippine and Southeast Asia Division, State Department Lot Files, RG 59, National Archives (hereafter cited as DSNA); Sergeant Nardella, 'Informal Report on Operation EMBANKMENT', folder no. 284, Box 25, Entry 110, RG 226, MRB.

8. Krull, 'Diary of Saigon', p. 7, RG 59, DSNA.

9. Mountbatten, *Post Surrender Tasks, Section E of the Report to the Combined Chiefs of Staff* (London: Her Majesty's Stationery Office, 1969), p. 286; Dening to Foreign Office, no. 506, 19 September 1945, as repeated to Washington, CAB 122/512, PRO.

10. Sterndale Bennett to secretary, Chiefs of Staff Committee, 25 September 1945, COS (45)589(0), CAB 122/512, PRO.

11. Gracey to Mountbatten, 22 September 1945, as reproduced in SACSEA to Chiefs of Staff, 23 September 1945, SEACOS 488, CAB 122/512, PRO. Gracey's 21 September proclamation is also available in Great Britain, Her Majesty's Stationery Office, *Documents Relating to British Involvement in the Indo-China Conflict 1945–1965*, Misc. No. 25, 1965, pp. 52–3; and a newsprint copy of the proclamation in French and Vietnamese can be found in folder no. 2151, Box 124, Entry 148, RG 226, MRB.

12. SACSEA to Chiefs of Staff, 24 September 1945, SEACOS 490, CAB 122/512, PRO. In his final report to the Chiefs of Staff, Mountbatten suggested that Gracey did overstep his authority by addressing his proclamation to the whole of southern Indochina; *Post Surrender Tasks*, p. 287.

13. Krull, 'Diary of Saigon', p. 19, RG 59, DSNA; see also George Sheldon, 'The Status of Viet Nam', *Far Eastern Survey* 15 (18 December 1946): p. 373.

14. Dennis, *Troubled Days of Peace: Mountbatten and South East Asia Command, 1945–46* (New York: St Martin's Press, 1987), pp. 46, 51. While Dennis contended that Gracey 'was no died-in-the-wool imperialist', other authors have attributed Gracey's actions to a colonial mentality nurtured by years of foreign service; see Hugh Tinker, *Men Who Overturned Empires: Fighters, Dreamers, and Schemers* (Madison: University of Wisconsin Press, 1987), p. 167, and V.G. Kiernan, *From Conquest to Collapse: European Empires from 1815–1960* (New York: Pantheon Books, 1982), p. 214. Peter M. Dunn, *The First Vietnam War* (New York: St Martin's Press, 1985), p. 367, lauded the 23 September coup, writing: 'Had the Chinese in North Vietnam done similar favors for the French, it is not impossible that the Viet Minh would have been smothered before reaching full bloom'.

15. William J. Donovan, OSS director, to President Truman, 28 September 1945, summarizing OSS reports from Saigon, folder: Chronological File,

OSS, September 1945, Box 15, Rose Conway File, Harry S. Truman Papers, Harry S. Truman Library, Independence, Missouri.

16.   Krock letter to the editor, *New York Times*, 3 October 1945; the letter was dated 1 October. Krock wrote that Dewey 'was not meant to perish in the way he did – from the gunfire of insurgents in a strange land who mistook him for a French officer, and therefore a symbol of what they consider their oppressor'. For a summary of Dewey's background, see R. Harris Smith, *OSS: The Secret History of America's First Central Intelligence Agency* (Berkeley: University of California Press, 1972), pp. 337–9.

17.   Bluechel to commanding officer, OSS Detachment 404, HQ SEAC, 30 September 1945, in Senate Committee on Foreign Relations, *Causes, Origins, and Lessons of the Vietnam War, Hearings*, 92d Cong., 2d sess., 1973, p. 284 (hereafter cited as *COLVW*); see also Bluechel and White affidavits on Dewey's murder, ibid., pp. 286–95; Small to Strategic Services Officer, IBT, 25 October 1945, ibid., pp. 296–7.

18.   Small to Strategic Services Officer, IBT, 25 October 1945, ibid., p. 297; Krull, 'Diary of Saigon', p. 21, RG 59, DSNA.

19.   Dening to Foreign Office, no. 530, 25 September 1945, as repeated to Washington, CAB 122/512, PRO. For reference to an earlier Dening memo based on similar fears, see Christopher Thorne, *Allies of a Kind: The United States, Britain, and the War Against Japan, 1941–1945* (New York: Oxford University Press, 1978, paperback), p. 539.

20.   Joint Planning Staff, 'French Indo-China – Measures for Responsibility for Internal Security by SACSEA', 30 September 1945, JP (45)258(Final), CAB 122/512, PRO; on Operation PYTHON, see Dennis, *Troubled Days of Peace*, pp. 14–15, 19.

21.   SACSEA to Chiefs of Staff, 2 October 1945, SEACOS 500, CAB 122/512, PRO.

22.   Vincent to Dean Acheson, under secretary of state, 28 September 1945, State Department Decimal Files, 851G.00/9-2845, RG 59, DSNA; Vincent to Acheson, 2 October 1945, 851G.00/10-245, ibid.; Moffat memorandum, 1 October 1945, filed with ibid.; Matthews to Acheson and Vincent, n.d., emphasis in original, attached to Vincent to Acheson, 28 September 1945, 851G.00/9-2845, ibid.; Acheson to Vincent, n.d., ibid.; Bonbright to Matthews, 2 October 1945, 851G.00/10-245, ibid. John F. Cady, *Contacts With Burma, 1935–1949: A Personal Account*, Papers in International Studies, Southeast Asia Series No. 61 (Athens, OH: Ohio University, Center for International Studies), p. 63, asserts that Matthews typically assumed a superior attitude toward what he considered the amateurish work of the Division of Southeast Asian Affairs. George C. Herring, 'The Truman Administration and the Restoration of French Sovereignty in Indochina', *Diplomatic History* 1 (Spring 1977): p. 102, observed that Matthews viewed Indochina affairs 'from an unabashedly pro-French standpoint'.

23.   Cady, *Contacts With Burma*, p. 64; personal interview with Hickerson, 26 June 1979.

24.   See, for example, SACSEA to Cabinet Offices, 17 October 1945, SEAC(RL) 159, CAB 119/189, PRO; SACSEA to Cabinet Offices, 20 October 1945, SEAC(RL) 170, ibid.

25.   On the politics of the Chinese occupation regime, see Ronald H. Spector, *Advice and Support: The Early Years of the United States Army in Vietnam, 1941–1960* (1983; reprint, New York: The Free Press, 1985), pp. 52–3.

26.   'Report by Arthur Hale of the U.S.I.S. Based on a Thirteen Day Stay in Hanoi in October 1945', Appendix I, pp. 28–30, in *The United States and*

Vietnam: 1944–1947, staff study no. 2 prepared for the Senate Foreign Relations Committee, 92d Cong. 2d sess., 1972.

27. Archimedes Patti, *Why Vietnam? Prelude to America's Albatross* (Berkeley: University of California Press, 1980), pp. 225–6, 245–6; Frank White comments, *COLVW*, pp. 149–50; Spector, *Advice and Support*, pp. 60–1.

28. Ripley to N. F. Allman, 3 March 1945, folder no. 24, Box 2, Entry 141, RG 226, MRB. Ripley was uncertain whether psychological warfare operations for the Netherlands East Indies should be mounted from the Southwest Pacific Area Command base in Australia or from Colombo, Ceylon, in the China-Burma-India theater.

29. Ripley to Whitney H. Shepardson, Memorandum no. 15, (October [?] 1943), folder no. 21, Box 2, Entry 141, RG 226, MRB.

30. Foote to MacArthur, 29 January 1944, quoted in Robert J. McMahon, *Colonialism and Cold War: The United States and the Struggle for Indonesian Independence, 1945–1949* (Ithaca: Cornell University Press, 1981), p. 75. McMahon wrote of Foote: 'Comfortable with the colonial lifestyle and close to many Dutch leaders, he considered the statements floating around Washington about the future of the European colonies to have no relevance to the Indies' (p. 74). See also Akira Iriye, *Power and Culture: The Japanese-American War, 1941–1945* (Cambridge: Harvard University Press, 1981, paperback), p. 78.

31. 'Problems Arising from a Sudden Liberation of NEI', 13 August 1945, Research and Analysis (R&A) Branch report no. 3229, Office of Strategic Services, RG 59, DSNA.

32. Theodore Friend, *The Blue-Eyed Enemy: Japan Against the West in Java and Luzon, 1942–1945* (Princeton University Press, 1988), p. 57.

33. Joyce C. Lebra, *Japanese-Trained Armies in Southeast Asia: Independence and Volunteer Forces in World War II* (New York: Columbia University Press, 1977), pp. 13, 89–90.

34. Ibid., pp. 111–12, 169–71; Friend, *Blue-Eyed Enemy*, p. 98; see also Christopher Thorne, *The Issue of War: States, Societies, and the Far Eastern Conflict of 1941–1945* (New York: Oxford University Press, 1985), p. 161. Lebra put the peak strength of Peta forces at 33 000 in 1944 (p. 109); Friend counted 37 500 members by the end of the war (p. 98). Such paramilitary training focused upon Java because it was the major supply base for Japanese military forces in the region.

35. Charles Wolf, Jr., *The Indonesian Story: The Birth, Growth, and Structure of the Indonesian Republic* (New York: John Day, 1948), p. viii, emphasis in original (Wolf was vice-consul in Batavia from February 1946 to June 1947); Hornbeck, 'The United States and the Netherlands East Indies', *Annals of the American Academy of Political and Social Science* 225 (January 1948): pp. 125–6, emphasis in original. The article was based on a lecture given on 2 July 1947. Hornbeck had been director of the Office of Far Eastern Affairs before being appointed ambassador to the Netherlands in September 1944.

36. Dennis, *Troubled Days of Peace*, pp. 78–9.

37. McMahon, *Colonialism and Cold War*, pp. 39–40, 93; Friend, *Blue-Eyed Enemy*, p. 17.

38. 'Transitional Period in Indonesia's Internal Political Situation', 24 August 1945, R&A report no. 3232, OSS, RG 59, DSNA.

39. 'Indonesian Unrest Portends Most Critical Situation in Southeast Asia Command', 28 September 1945, p. 5, R&A report no. 3265, OSS, RG 59, DSNA; Foster memorandum, 20 September 1945, folder no. 8, Box 21, Entry 110, RG 226, MRB; Foster to Lloyd George, 25 September 1945,

folder no. 77, Box 25, Entry 110, RG 226, MRB. George was chief of the SI branch, IBT, at this point. For a discussion of the wartime role of the Kempeitai (or Kenpeitai), see Friend, *Blue-Eyed Enemy*, pp. 68, 186–209.

40. *New York Times*, 11 November 1945, p. 6.

41. 'British Policy Toward Nationalists in Indonesia Strengthens Soekarno's Position', 5 October 1945, R&A report no. 3265, p. 2, OSS, RG 59, DSNA; Mountbatten, *Post Surrender Tasks*, p. 290.

42. Mountbatten, *Post Surrender Tasks*, p. 290; memorandum by the chief of the division of Northern European Affairs (Hugh S. Cumming, Jr.), 8 October 1945, *FRUS 1945*, 6: pp. 1159–61; memorandum of conversation by Acheson, 10 October 1945, ibid., pp. 1163–4. Cumming continued to adhere to the pre-war picture of the Indonesian peasantry: 'The mass of the population consists of uneducated, illiterate and passive peasants who have so far shown little interest in anything outside their local village' (p. 1162).

43. Dening to J. C. Sterndale Bennett, 5 October 1945, FO371/46353/F9305, PRO; memorandum of conversation by Abbot Moffat, 18 October 1945, *FRUS 1945*, 6: p. 1167.

44. Press conference, 24 October 1945, *Press Conferences of the Secretaries of State, 1922–1973* (Wilmington, DE: Scholarly Resources, n.d., microfilm), reel 10. For complaints about French use of American military equipment in the Levant in the summer of 1945, see Karl Mundt's comments, Committee on International Relations, *Selected Executive Session Hearings of the Committee, 1943–50*, vol. 2: *Problems of World War II and Its Aftermath*, 1976, pt. 2: p. 455.

45. Secretary of state to the ambassador in the United Kingdom (John G. Winant), 13 October 1945, *FRUS 1945*, 6: p. 1164; Foster to Lloyd George, 11 October 1945, folder no. 8, Box 21, Entry 110, RG 226, MRB.

46. See Truman letter to General Donovan, 20 September 1945, in *Public Papers of the Presidents of the United States: Harry S. Truman*, 1945 (1961), p. 330; Foster to George, 25 September 1945, folder no. 77, Box 25, Entry 110, RG 226, MRB.

47. Grew to William J. Donovan, 14 July 1945, 851G.00/7-1445, RG 59, DSNA, and same decimal file number and date for Grew to James Forrestal, and Grew to Henry Stimson; Garden to George, 20 September 1945, folder no. 2300, Box 136, Entry 148, RG 226, MRB. See also memorandum of conversation, by Kenneth P. Landon, SEA, regarding his talk with Major Austin Glass of OSS about matters in Indochina, 4 June 1945, 851G.00/6-445, RG 59, DSNA; Capt. W. B. Kantack, to William J. Donovan, 20 November 1945, covering memo and report of OSS activities during September 1945, pp. iii–iv, viii, 48, 50, folder no. 131, Box 95, Entry 99, RG 226, MRB. Garden was still receiving some intelligence information in January 1946, as he wrote to Lt. Col. Amos D. Moscrip about the 'last days' of an American military presence in Southeast Asian colonies. 'The material received over the past few months has been of a high order and it has been recognized as of major importance to various government agencies here', he wrote. Garden added: 'We hope the flow will continue as long as possible'. See Garden, chief, Southeast Asia Section, FESI, SSU, to Moscrip, Detachment 404, SSU, 22 January 1946, folder no. 2300, Box 136, Entry 148, RG 226, MRB.

48. Memorandum of conversation (Bonbright), 17 September 1945, 851G.00/9-1745, RG 59, DSNA; Hornbeck, 'United States and Netherlands East Indies', p. 132; Wolf, *Indonesian Story*, p. 28; McMahon, *Colonialism and Cold War*, pp. 82–3. Harold M. Vinacke, a former Asian specialist with the

Office of War Information, used terms similar to Hornbeck – characterizing US policy in Southeast Asia as 'acquiescent non-involvement'; 'United States Far Eastern Policy', *Pacific Affairs* 19 (December 1946): p. 353.

49. 'U.S. Participation in Southeast Asia Command (SEAC), After Cessation of Japanese Resistance', 4 September 1945, JCS 1494/1, folder: ABC 384 Burma (8-25-42), Box 406, ABC Decimal Files 1942–1948, RG 319, MRB; JCS memorandum for the CCS, 15 October 1945, CCS 930, in CAB 122/1068, PRO.

50. Vincent to Acheson, 2 November 1945, folder: ABC 384 Burma (8-25-42), Box 406, ABC Decimal Files 1942–48, RG 319, MRB; Lincoln memorandum, 28 November 1945, ibid.; McFarland to Brig. A. T. Cornwall-Jones, 5 December 1945, in CAB 122/1068, PRO. The formal announcement of US withdrawal from SEAC came in a CCS statement of 6 January 1946; see acting secretary of state to the ambassador in the Netherlands (Hornbeck), 18 January 1946, *FRUS 1946*, 8: p. 800.

51. Wilkinson to Donovan, 5 November 1945, folder no. 225, Box 20, Entry 110, RG 226, MRB. Wilkinson was summarizing American intelligence activity in the region for the month of October.

52. Koke memorandum, in Beltz to Bluechel, 9 December 1945, ZB-11, Box 21, Entry 110, RG 226, MRB; see also Beltz to Bluechel, 25 November 1945, ZB-8, ibid.

53. Koke and Stuart to Taylor and Bluechel, 21 December 1945, ZB-17, ibid. In November 1945, the US government had ordered an end to weapons sales to the Netherlands, though non-military materials continued to be made available; McMahon, *Colonialism and Cold War*, pp. 103–4.

54. Laurens van der Post, *The Night of the New Moon* (London: Hogarth Press, 1971), p. 45, italics in original; Martha Gellhorn, *The Face of War* (1959; reprint, New York: Atlantic Monthly Press, 1988), p. 2. Van der Post was from South Africa.

55. Sukarno to Mountbatten, quoted in Friend, *Blue-Eyed Enemy*, p. 223; Sukarno statement, quoted in 'British Policy Toward Nationalists in Indonesia Strengthens Soekarno's Position', 5 October 1945, R&A report no. 3270, OSS, RG 59, DSNA. See also Sukarno's letter to General Christison, 9 October 1945, quoted in McMahon, *Colonialism and Cold War*, p. 95.

56. 'British Policy Toward Nationalists in Indonesia Strengthens Soekarno's Position', 5 October 1945, R&A report no. 3270, OSS, RG 59, DSNA. Though technically part of the State Department as of 1 October, R&A people in the field still co-operated closely with their former OSS colleagues; see, for example, Wilkinson to Donovan, 5 November 1945, folder no. 225, Box 20, Entry 110, RG 226, MRB.

57. Diary entry of 5 October 1945, quoted in Dennis, *Troubled Days of Peace*, p. 107.

58. Taylor, *Richer by Asia*, 2d edn. (Boston: Houghton Mifflin, 1964), p. 381; Evelyn Colbert, 'The Road Not Taken: Decolonization and Independence in Indonesia and Indochina', *Foreign Affairs* 51 (April 1973): pp. 613–14; Mountbatten, *Post Surrender Tasks*, pp. 292–3; McMahon, *Colonialism and Cold War,* pp. 97–8; Dennis, *Troubled Days of Peace*, pp. 123–5. Friend, *Blue-Eyed Enemy*, pp. 226–30, argued that Surabaya was 'more mature for revolution' than other cities like Jakarta, Bandung, or Semarang, concluding: 'The shadow of Surabaya made both British and Dutch cautious thereafter'.

59. SACSEA to Cabinet Offices, 12 December 1945, in CAB 119/189, PRO.

60. 'Report on a Visit by Colonel Chapman-Walker to Indo-China', n.d., in CAB 122/512, PRO.

61. Vincent, 'The Post-War Period in the Far East', *Department of State Bulletin* 13 (21 October 1945): pp. 644–8; Vincent memorandum, 22 October 1945, *FRUS 1945*, 6: pp. 1167–8. See also Gary R. Hess, 'United States Policy and the Origins of the French-Viet Minh War, 1945–46', *Peace and Change* 3 (Summer–Fall 1975): p. 25.

62. Moffat to Vincent, 12 October 1945, folder: SEA 1946–49, Box 4, Records, Philippine and Southeast Asia Division, RG 59, DSNA; Moffat to Vincent, 19 November 1945, Box 5, ibid.; Moffat to Acheson, 27 December 1945, FW 811B.01/12-2645, RG 59, DSNA. In his 27 December memo, Moffat was affirming the judgment of veteran Asian expert Frank P. Lockhart, chief of the Division of Philippine Affairs, 811B.01/12-2645, RG 59, DSNA. For a discussion of US-British disagreements over the post-war status of Thailand, see Gary R. Hess, *The United States' Emergence as a Southeast Asian Power, 1940–1950* (New York: Columbia University Press, 1987), pp. 111–19.

63. Hess, *United States' Emergence as a Southeast Asian Power*, p. 180; McMahon, *Colonialism and Cold War*, pp. 110–11.

64. White testimony, *COLVW*, p. 150; Harold Isaacs, *No Peace for Asia* (New York: Macmillan Company, 1947), p. 175. Isaacs recalled: 'Annamite nationalists spoke of the United States as men speak of a hope they know is forlorn but to which they desperately cling all the same' (p. 174). See also General Gallagher's comments, memorandum of conversation, by Richard L. Sharp, 30 January 1946, *FRUS 1946*, 8: p. 19.

65. Sjahrir to Truman, 25 December 1945, *FRUS 1945*, 6: p. 1187.

66. Hornbeck to the secretary of state, 1 December 1945, *FRUS 1945*, 6: pp. 1176–7. Hornbeck had been a lecturer on Far Eastern history at Harvard in the late 1920s and served subsequently as chief of the Division of Far Eastern Affairs, then (briefly) as director of the Office of Far Eastern Affairs immediately before his appointment as ambassador to The Hague.

67. Moffat memorandum of conversation, 6 December 1945, ibid., pp. 1178–80. Other participants were Holden Furber, Division of British Commonwealth Affairs; Rupert Emerson, Division of Research, Office of Far Eastern Affairs; and John F. Cady of SEA.

68. The press statement was reproduced in acting secretary of state to the consul general at Batavia (Walter Foote), 19 December 1945, *FRUS 1945*, 6: pp. 1182–3; see also, McMahon, *Colonialism and Cold War*, pp. 111–12, and Dennis, *Troubled Days of Peace*, pp. 212–13.

69. Foote to secretary of state, 30 December 1945, *FRUS 1945*, 6: p. 1190.

70. Mountbatten, *Post Surrender Tasks*, p. 298.

71. Christison was given the Northern Command in Britain and replaced in NEI by Lt. Gen. Montague Stopford. Dennis, *Troubled Days of Peace*, p. 183, wrote that despite Christison's controversial public statements and his efforts to circumvent Dutch authorities, the general's 'no-nonsense approach undoubtedly injected a very necessary note of realism into the situation in Java'.

72. Memorandum of conversation, by Richard L. Sharp, 30 January 1946, *FRUS 1946*, 8: p. 17. Gallagher further believed that the Vietnamese were not yet ready for self-government. While he felt that DRV propaganda and organizational techniques bespoke a Soviet influence, he asserted that the Viet Minh 'should not be labelled full-fledged doctrinaire communists' (pp. 17, 19). State Department officials who spoke with Gallagher included Charles S. Reed, soon to be the US consul in Saigon; Woodruff Wallner (WE); and Moffat and Sharp from SEA. For the text of the Sino-French agreement, see Allan W. Cameron (ed.), *Viet-Nam Crisis: A Documentary History*, vol. 1:

1940–1956 (Ithaca: Cornell University Press, 1971), pp. 76–7. The Chinese, wrote Ellen Hammer, *The Struggle for Indochina, 1940–1955* (1954–55; reprint, Stanford University Press, 1967), p. 152, 'decided to sacrifice Vietnamese independence for French economic and political concessions'.

73.   Caffery to secretary of state, 6 February 1946, *FRUS 1946*, 8: p. 24; Landon to secretary of state, 5 February 1946, ibid., p. 23; Jean Sainteny, *Ho Chi Minh and His Vietnam, A Personal Memoir*, trans. Herma Briffault (Chicago: Cowles, 1972), p. 52.

74.   For the text of the 6 March accord, see Cameron, *Viet-Nam Crisis*, 1: pp. 77–9; SACSEA to Cabinet Offices, 13 March 1946, in CAB 119/189, PRO.

75.   Sainteny, *Ho Chi Minh*, p. 71; Lauristan Sharp, 'French Plan for Indochina', *Far Eastern Survey* 15 (3 July 1946): p. 193; Peter Scholl-Latour, *Death in the Ricefields: An Eyewitness Account of Vietnam's Three Wars, 1945–1979*, trans. Faye Carney (New York: St Martin's Press, 1979), pp. 24–5. Scholl-Latour was very sympathetic toward the French position in Indochina and viewed the Viet Minh as a fanatical communist movement which must be defeated. Correspondent George Weller, 'Can France Hold Her Eastern Empire?', *Saturday Evening Post*, 30 November 1946, p. 18, found it ironic that Germans in the Foreign Legion might well find themselves fighting against Japanese advisers to the Viet Minh.

76.   Hammer, *Struggle for Indochina*, p. 158.

77.   Sharp, 'French Plan for Indochina', p. 197; Hammer, *Struggle for Indochina*, p. 163.

78.   Enclosure B to 'Estimate of British Post-War Capabilities and Intentions', report prepared by the Joint Intelligence Committee, 13 February 1946, JIC 340/1, folder: ABC 092 France (15 Apr 45), Box 95, ABC Decimal Files, RG 319, MRB.

79.   Enclosures D and E, ibid.

Chapter 6

1.   Harold Isaacs, *No Peace for Asia* (New York: Macmillan Company, 1947), p. 179; Elizabeth P. MacDonald, *Undercover Girl* (New York: Macmillan, 1947), p. 227.

2.   Martha Gellhorn, *The Face of War* (1959; reprint, New York: Atlantic Monthly Press, 1988), pp. 2–3, 191–9; Laurens van der Post, *The Night of the New Moon* (London: Hogarth Press, 1971), p. 149; Isaacs, *No Peace for Asia*, p. 186.

3.   Hornbeck, 'The United States and the Netherlands East Indies', *Annals of the American Academy of Political and Social Science* 255 (January 1948): p. 132. This comment was made while discussing the importance of the Netherlands to US policymaking *vis-à-vis* the European theater of the cold war. Hornbeck did not feel that Indonesians were yet ready for independence (pp. 130–1).

4.   De Gasperi's remarks were made at the 11th plenary meeting of the conference, 10 August 1946, *Foreign Relations of the United States, 1946: Paris Peace Conference Proceedings* (Washington: GPO, 1970), 3: p. 184 (hereafter cited as *FRUS* followed by the appropriate year).

5.   William Attwood, *The Twilight Struggle: Tales of the Cold War* (New York: Harper & Row, 1987), p. 12.

6.   See, for instance, Richard A. Best, Jr., *'Cooperation with Like-Minded Peoples': British Influences on American Security Policy, 1945–1949* (Westport, CT: Greenwood Press, 1986), pp. 54, 64.

7. Nimitz testimony, House Committee on Naval Affairs, *Sundry Legislation Affecting the Naval Establishment, 1946, Hearings*, 79th Cong., 2d sess., 1947, p. 2750.
8. Entry of 5 March 1947, Walter Millis (ed.), *The Forrestal Diaries* (New York: Viking Press, 1951), p. 250.
9. Lippmann, *US Foreign Policy: Shield of the Republic* (Boston: Little, Brown, 1943), pp. 147, 5, 7, 82–4, 125–30, 174. Henry Butterfield Ryan, *The Vision of Anglo-America: The US-UK Alliance and the Emerging Cold War, 1943–1946* (New York: Cambridge University Press, 1987), p. 30, notes that Lippmann's book was well received in the British Foreign Office.
10. 'Problems and Objectives of United States Policy', 2 April 1945, enclosure in Donovan to Truman, 5 May 1945, folder: OSS, Chronological File April–May 1945, Box 15, Rose Conway File, Harry S. Truman Papers, Harry S. Truman Library, Independence, Missouri; Welles, Introduction to Crane Brinton, *The United States and Britain* (Cambridge: Harvard University Press, 1945), p. viii; Eisenhower testimony, 15 November 1945, House Committee on Military Affairs, *Universal Military Training, Hearings*, 79th Cong., 1st sess., 1946, p. 77; 'Estimate of British Post-War Capabilities and Intentions', 13 February 1946, JIC 340/1, folder: ABC 092 France (15 Apr 45), Box 95, ABC Decimal Files, Record Group (RG) 319, Military Reference Branch, National Archives and Records Administration, Washington, DC (hereafter cited as MRB).
11. 'We have pinned our hopes to the banner of the United Nations', *Department of State Bulletin* 14 (10 March 1946): pp. 355–8.
12. Harbutt, *The Iron Curtain: Churchill, America, and the Origins of the Cold War* (New York: Oxford University Press, 1986), pp. 169, 173–5. Harbutt wrote that Byrnes' 28 February speech 'must have suggested to the Russians not only an attempt to convert the United Nations into the militant instrument of a new American diplomacy, and a call for the maintenance and revival of American military power, but also the embryo of an Anglo-American alliance to counter Soviet power' (p. 175).
13. 'The Sinews of Peace', 5 March 1946, in Robert Rhodes James (ed.), *Winston S. Churchill: His Complete Speeches, 1897–1963* (London: Chelsea House Publishers, 1974), 7: pp. 7285–93; Eisenhower statement, 5 June 1946, House Committee on Appropriations, *Military Establishment Appropriation Bill for 1947, Hearings*, 79th Cong., 2d sess., 1946, p. 1122.
14. See, for example, Harbutt, *Iron Curtain*, pp. 151, 153, 164–5, 168–9, 267, 280–1; Best, *Cooperation with Like-Minded Peoples*, pp. 10, 114; Bruce Robillet Kuniholm, *The Origins of the Cold War in the Near East: Great Power Conflict and Diplomacy in Iran, Turkey, and Greece* (Princeton University Press, 1980), pp. xx, 300, 311–12. Ryan, *Vision of Anglo-America*, focuses on the importance of the decline of British power for American policymaking (p. 10), but he concludes that the turning point in US-Soviet relations did not come until the Truman Doctrine speech of March 1947 (pp. 106, 112, 172).
15. MacVeagh to Roosevelt, 15 October 1944, quoted in Kuniholm, *Origins of the Cold War in the Near East*, p. 98. MacVeagh was ambassador to the Greek government-in-exile in Cairo during the war and then took up duties in Athens after the liberation.
16. Lippmann, *US Foreign Policy*, pp. 147–8.
17. Kennan to secretary of state, 22 February 1946, *FRUS 1946*, 6: pp. 696–709.

18. Merchant to Lawrence B. Haley (ITP) and William Clayton (A-C), 11 June 1945, State Department Decimal Files, 851R.61311/6–1145, RG 59, Department of State records, National Archives (hereafter cited as DSNA).
19. Lawton to secretary of state, 4 November 1945, 851R.00/11-445, RG 59, DSNA; Finley to secretary of state, 23 May 1946, 851R.00/5-2345, RG 59, DSNA.
20. Finley to secretary of state, 23 May 1946, ibid.; Clifton Daniel, 'Moroccans Remote from other Arabs', *New York Times*, 1 June 1946; Caffery to secretary of state, 5 June 1946, 851R.00/6-546, RG 59, DSNA.
21. Acting secretary of state to officer in charge of the American mission in Paris, 2 July 1946 [stamped 11 July 1946], 851R.00/7-1145, RG 59, DSNA; the phrase in single quotes was taken from an earlier memorandum by Jefferson Caffery.
22. Acting secretary of state to American consular officer in charge, Algiers, 1 July 1946 [stamped 11 July 1946], attachment to 851R.00/7-1146, RG 59, DSNA.
23. Caffery to secretary of state, 26 July 1946, 851R.00/7-2646, RG 59, DSNA, emphasis added; Caffery restated his thesis in a note of 27 August, 851R.00/8-2746, ibid. Steven P. Sapp, 'Jefferson Caffery, Cold War Diplomat: American-French Relations 1944–49', *Louisiana History* 23 (Spring 1982): pp. 190–2, characterized Caffery as 'a committed Europeanist and staunch anti-Soviet' who effectively lobbied the State Department in favor of strong support for a 'Centrist solution' in France without regard for French colonial policies.
24. Schwartz, 'Communist Program in North Africa', 21 August 1946, 851R.00B/8-2146, RG 59, DSNA; Caffery to secretary of state, 27 August 1946, 851R.00/8-2746, ibid. Foreign Minister Georges Bidault, said Caffery, had made clear the resolve of the French government to retain control of Algerian affairs. The consul general in Algiers reported similar sentiments expressed by Governor General Chataigneau several days later: 'He said there were to[o] many ties uniting Algeria with France to permit its alienation, its abandonment or its secession'. Finley to secretary of state, 4 September 1946, 851R.00/9-446, RG 59, DSNA.
25. Harold Callender, 'France's Goal: Neither Moscow Nor Detroit', *New York Times Magazine*, 2 June 1946, p. 11.
26. Grew, 'Some Aspects of our Relations with France', *Department of State Bulletin* 12 (4 February 1945): pp. 151–3 (hereafter cited as *DSB*); McVey, 'An American's View of France', *DSB* 13 (7 October 1946): pp. 523–7. McVey was an adviser in the War Areas Economic Division of the Office of International Trade Policy.
27. Paul H. Alling (US diplomatic agent, Tangier) to secretary of state, 30 January 1947, 851R.00B/1-3047, RG 59, DSNA.
28. R. D. J. Scott Fox minute, 1 November 1946, FO 371/53520/J4516, PRO; Utter to Henry S. Villard, deputy director, NEA, 14 October 1946, Records, Office of African Affairs, Box 4, Lot files, RG 59, DSNA. Utter was serving as a member of the US delegation to the Council of Foreign Ministers and was much valued by the State Department for his expertise regarding North African affairs. For further materials dealing with the British working party, see FO371/53521.
29. Rupert Emerson, 'Nationalist Movements in Southeast Asia', in John Carter Vincent *et al.* (eds), *America's Future in the Pacific* (New Brunswick: Rutgers University Press, 1947), pp. 119–20; Churchill comment to James Forrestal, 10 March 1946, *Forrestal Diaries* p. 145; Ellen J. Hammer,

'Blueprinting a New Indochina', *Pacific Affairs* 21 (September 1948): p. 253. Churchill's comment, as recorded by Forrestal, read: 'Referring to the Russians, he said they had no understanding of such words as "honesty", "honor", and "truth" – in fact, that they regarded these as negative virtues. They will, he said, try every door in the house, enter all rooms which are not locked, and when they come to one that is barred, if they are unsuccessful in breaking through it, they will withdraw and invite you to dine genially that same evening'.

30.   Emerson, 'Nationalist Movements in Southeast Asia', pp. 121–6, 131. In addition to a stint with the State Department's Division of Southeast Asian Affairs, Emerson had previously been director of the Division of Territories and Island Possessions in the Department of the Interior.

31.   Caffery to secretary of state, 6 February 1946, *FRUS 1946*, 8: p. 24.

32.   Landon to secretary of state, Hanoi, n.d. (received 27 February 1946), *FRUS 1946*, 8: p. 27; Ho Chi Minh letter, 18 February 1946, Department of Defense, *United States-Vietnam Relations, 1945–1967* (Washington: GPO, 1971), vol. 1, pt. C: pp. 98–100. Gary R. Hess, 'United States Policy and the Origins of the French-Viet Minh War, 1945–46', *Peace and Change* 3 (Summer–Fall 1975): p. 26, has stressed that while all American observers in Indochina, both civilian and military, did not feel the same way about the DRV, 'their reports underscored the seriousness of the French-Vietnamese relationship and suggested the potential influence of the United States in helping to resolve the worsening situation'.

33.   Jean Sainteny, *Ho Chi Minh and His Vietnam: A Personal Memoir*, trans. Herma Briffault (Chicago: Cowles Book Company, 1972), pp. 70, 72–5.

34.   Reed to secretary of state, 1 April 1946, *FRUS 1946*, 8: p. 34; Secretary of State to the French Ambassador (Henri Bonnet), 10 April 1946, ibid., p. 35.

35.   Reed to secretary of state, 1 June 1946, *FRUS 1946*, 8: p. 45. The US consulate in Saigon had been raised to the status of consulate general effective 20 May 1946.

36.   George Sheldon, 'Status of Viet Nam', *Far Eastern Survey* 15 (18 December 1946): pp. 373, 377.

37.   Caffery to secretary of state, 2 August 1946, *FRUS 1946*, 8: p. 50.

38.   Moffat to John Carter Vincent, director of the Office of Far Eastern Affairs, 9 August 1946, *FRUS 1946*, 8: pp. 52–4.

39.   Sainteny, *Ho Chi Minh*, p. 88; *New York Times*, 16 September 1946. For a summary of the *modus vivendi*, see Caffery to secretary of state, 17 September 1946, *FRUS 1946*, 8: pp. 59–60.

40.   Sainteny, *Ho Chi Minh*, p. 89; memorandum of conversation, by Richard L. Sharp (SEA), 30 January 1946, *FRUS 1946*, 8: p. 18. The participants included Gallagher, Charles Reed, Woodruff Wallner (WE) and Moffat and Sharp from SEA.

41.   Acheson to Reed, 9 October 1946, *FRUS 1946*, 8: p. 61; Reed to secretary of state, 17 September 1946, ibid., p. 59; O'Sullivan to secretary of state, 1 November 1946, ibid., pp. 62–3. Caffery to secretary of state, 29 November 1946, ibid., p. 63, noted: 'The French are very concerned over developments in Indochina. A high Foreign Ministry official said they are particularly worried because they have "positive proof that Ho Chi Minh is in direct contact with Moscow and is receiving advice and instructions from the Soviets"'.

42.   Acheson to Reed, 5 December 1946, ibid., p. 68; Byrnes to Certain Missions Abroad, 17 December 1946, ibid., pp. 72–3.

43. Moffat letters, printed as Appendix II, in *The United States and Vietnam: 1944–1947*, staff study no. 2, prepared for the Senate Foreign Relations Committee, 92d Cong., 2d sess., 1972, pp. 36–8.

44. Acting secretary of state (Acheson) to the consul at Saigon (Reed), for Moffat, 5 December 1946, *FRUS 1946*, 8: pp. 67–9.

45. Moffat letters, *United States and Vietnam: 1944–1947*, p. 40.

46. Ibid., pp. 40–1.

47. Sainteny, *Ho Chi Minh*, p. 98.

48. Hailey to Merz, 31 December 1946, attachment to Landon to Vincent and Culbertson, 20 January 1947, Box 9, Records, Philippine and Southeast Asia Division, RG 59, DSNA.

49. Robert Trumbull, 'The West Loses "Face" in the East', *New York Times Magazine*, 1 December 1946, pp. 12, 58.

50. Memorandum prepared in the State Department, 26 December 1945, *FRUS 1946*, 8: pp. 787–9.

51. Memorandum of conversation, by Hugh S. Cumming, chief of the Division of Northern European Affairs, 10 January 1946, ibid., pp. 792–5. The other State Department official listening to Loudon's comments was John D. Hickerson, deputy director of EUR. A summary of the local situation from Walter Foote, the US consul general in Batavia, tended to sustain Loudon's complaints; see acting secretary to Hornbeck, 24 January 1946, ibid., p. 801.

52. See the text of Clark Kerr's instructions in Lord Halifax to the secretary of state, 26 January 1946, ibid., pp. 801–3; Foote to secretary of state, 26 January 1946, ibid., p. 804; Foote to secretary of state, 8 February 1946, ibid., p. 807. Peter Dennis, *Troubled Days of Peace: Mountbatten and South East Asia Command, 1945–46* (New York: St Martin's Press, 1987), pp. 162, 182–3, wrote that Christison had become an obstacle to the resolution of East Indies affairs and thus had to be replaced, despite the fact that 'his no-nonsense approach undoubtedly injected a very necessary note of realism into the situation in Java' (p. 183). Christison was given the Northern Command in Britain and replaced in NEI by Lt. Gen. Montague Stopford. Dutch officials removed from NEI included Adm. C. E. H. Helfrich and Lt. Gen. L. H. van Oyen.

53. Robert J. McMahon, *Colonialism and Cold War: The United States and the Struggle for Indonesian Independence, 1945–49* (Ithaca: Cornell University Press, 1981), p. 123; see also Leslie Palmier, *Indonesia and the Dutch* (New York: Oxford University Press, 1962), p. 51; Charles Wolf, Jr., *The Indonesian Story: The Birth, Growth and Structure of the Indonesian Republic* (New York: John Day, 1948), pp. 29–30.

54. Foote to the secretary of state, 8 March 1946, *FRUS 1946*, 8: p. 813; see also Foote to secretary of state, 21 October 1946, ibid., pp. 849–50, and Byrnes to Bloom, chairman of the House Committee on Foreign Affairs, 24 May 1946, ibid., pp. 822–5.

55. Foote to secretary of state, 31 March 1946, ibid., p. 818; McMahon, *Colonialism and Cold War*, p. 126; Palmier, *Indonesia and the Dutch*, pp. 52, 145–6.

56. Foote to secretary of state, 10 July 1946, *FRUS 1946*, 8: pp. 832–3.

57. Foote to secretary of state, 17 September 1946, ibid., p. 844. In London, meanwhile, the Foreign Office assured American diplomats that British representatives in NEI were scrupulously neutral and that in fact they would have offered less substantive concessions to Indonesian nationalists than did The Hague; see chargé in the United Kingdom (Waldemar J.

Gallman) to the secretary of state, 25 September 1946, ibid., p. 845. McMahon, *Colonialism and Cold War*, p. 135, has concluded: 'London succeeded admirably in maintaining an even-handed approach toward the Indonesian crisis'.

58.	Memorandum prepared for the acting secretary of state (Acheson), 27 November 1946, ibid., pp. 853–5.

59.	McMahon, *Colonialism and Cold War*, p. 135; 'Java Strife Minimized', *New York Times*, 1 December 1946; Foote to secretary of state, 2 December 1946, *FRUS 1946*, 8: pp. 856–68.

60.	Palmier, *Indonesia and the Dutch*, p. 55; 'Basic Dutch-Indonesian Issues and the Linggadjati Agreement', Central Intelligence Group, ORE 20, 9 June 1947, p. 1, Box 254, President's Secretary's Files, Truman Papers, Truman Library. See also Wolf, *The Indonesian Story*, pp. 45–6.

61.	Acheson to US embassy in the Netherlands, 12 March 1947, *FRUS 1947*, 6: p. 905; Gary R. Hess, *The United States' Emergence as a Southeast Asian Power, 1940–1950* (New York: Columbia University Press, 1987), p. 209. In mid-April, Acheson wrote to American officials in Holland, 'At your discretion you may reiterate [to the Netherlands] FonOff [the] US view ... [concerning the] importance [of an] agreement [the] soonest possible to permit world trade on [a] non-discriminatory basis with [the] entire area, stressing our view that such trade will prove [to be an] important factor in restoring economic stability [in] NEI'. Acheson to US embassy in the Netherlands, 18 April 1947, *FRUS 1947*, 6: p. 918.

62.	Acting secretary of state (Acheson) to US embassy in the Netherlands, 9 April 1947, *FRUS 1947*, 6: p. 916; Evelyn Colbert, 'The Road Not Taken: Decolonization and Independence in Indonesia and Indochina', *Foreign Affairs* 51 (April 1973): p. 617.

63.	Secretary of State (Marshall) to US embassy in the Netherlands, 16 May 1947, *FRUS 1947*, 6: pp. 924–6. Likewise, the British government stressed the importance of restored production and trade in the East Indies: 'Under settled conditions the Island of Java is a valuable source of oils and fats of which the British people and indeed most of the peoples of Europe stand in urgent need'. British embassy to the Department of State, aide-mémoire, 4 June 1947, ibid., pp. 939–41.

64.	Cumming/Moffat memorandum, to Hickerson and Vincent, 17 April 1947, *FRUS 1947*, 6: pp. 917–18; Moffat memorandum, 8 July 1947, 856E.00/7-847, RG 59, DSNA, quoted in McMahon, *Colonialism and Cold War*, pp. 164–5.

65.	Wolf, *The Indonesian Story*, pp. 132–3; the author was vice-consul at Batavia from February 1946 to June 1947. See Foote to secretary of state, 28 May 1947, *FRUS 1947*, 6: p. 930; Foote to secretary of state, 19 June 1947, ibid., pp. 952–3. Addressing the department's Far Eastern Luncheon Group on 20 October 1949, Foote (no longer in the Foreign Service) characterized the Javanese nationalists as Kremlin-dominated communists, whom the United States had acted to put in power. 'In answer to a question, Dr Foote said that if the United States only stops meddling in Indonesia the Dutch could settle all Indonesian problems by police action in three weeks.' John F. Melby to William S. Lacy, 21 October 1949, folder: Southeast Asia File, General–1948–49, Box 8, John F. Melby Papers, Truman Library.

66.	Memorandum of conversation, by the associate chief of the Division of Northern European Affairs (John H. Morgan), 24 July 1947, *FRUS 1947*, 6: pp. 986–7.

67. Patterson statement, 8 November 1945, House Committee on Military Affairs, *Universal Military Training, Hearings*, 79th Cong., 1st sess., 1946, pp. 3–13; Eisenhower and Martin remarks, ibid., pp. 68, 77, 82.
68. House Committee on Appropriations, *Military Establishment Appropriation Bill for 1948, Hearings*, 80th Cong., 1st sess., 1947, pp. 77–8 (Eisenhower, 19 February), p. 601 (Spaatz, 6 March), p. 1404 (Patterson, 1 April); House Committee on Appropriations, *Navy Department Appropriation Bill for 1948, Hearings*, 80th Cong., 1st sess., 1947, p. 21 (Forrestal, 21 January). Eisenhower also debunked what he called 'the Buck Rogers school of thought', *Military Establishment Appropriation Bill for 1948, Hearings*, p. 77.
69. Vandenberg statement, 4 March 1947, Senate Committee on Foreign Relations, *Treaties of Peace with Italy, Rumania, Bulgaria, and Hungary, Hearings*, 80th Cong., 1st sess., 1947, p. 2.
70. Deimel oral history interview, 5 June 1975, p. 67, Truman Library. For further discussion of the Europe-first priority, for both the United States and the USSR, see the following: Harold M. Vinacke, *The United States and the Far East, 1945–1951* (Stanford University Press, 1952), pp. 3–5; Russell H. Fifield, *Americans in Southeast Asia: The Roots of Commitment* (New York: Thomas Y. Cromwell, 1973), pp. 70–1; Roger E. Kanet, 'The Soviet Union and the Colonial Question, 1917–1953', in Roger E. Kanet (ed.), *The Soviet Union and the Developing Nations* (Baltimore: Johns Hopkins University Press, 1974), pp. 1–26; George McT. Kahin, 'The United States and the Anticolonial Revolutions in Southeast Asia, 1945–1950', in Yonosuke Nagai and Akira Iriye (eds), *The Origins of the Cold War in Asia* (New York: Columbia University Press, 1977), pp. 343, 347–8; Steven P. Sapp, 'The United States, France and the Cold War: Jefferson Caffery and American-French Relations, 1944–1949' (Ph.D. diss., Kent State University, 1978), pp. 151, 153; Scott L. Bills, 'The United States, NATO, and the Colonial World', in Lawrence S. Kaplan and Robert W. Clawson (eds), *NATO After Thirty Years* (Wilmington, DE: Scholarly Resources, 1981), pp. 149–64; and Geir Lundestad, *East, West, North, South: Major Developments in International Politics, 1945–1986*, trans. Gail Adams Kvam (Oslo: Norwegian University Press, 1986), pp. 67–8.
71. *New York Times*, 1 December 1946.
72. Foreign Office to Washington embassy, no. 846, 28 January 1947, enclosed in FO371/60998/AN252, PRO.
73. Alex J. Robertson, *The Bleak Midwinter 1947* (Manchester University Press, 1987), p. 10; see chap. 1, *passim*, for a brief overview of both weather and economic conditions in early 1947. See also Robert A. Pollard, 'Economic Security and the Origins of the Cold War: Bretton Woods, the Marshall Plan, and American Rearmament, 1944–1950', *Diplomatic History* 9 (Summer 1985): p. 277, and Charles W. Yost, *History and Memory* (New York: W. W. Norton, 1980), p. 224. Robert M. Hathaway, *Ambiguous Partnership: Britain and America, 1944–1947* (New York: Columbia University Press, 1981), chaps 10 and 12, contains a good summary of the central themes of the US–UK economic relationship during the immediate post-war years, including the negotiations for the British loan signed by President Truman on 15 July 1946. Robin Edmonds, *Setting the Mould: The United States and Britain, 1945–1950* (New York: W. W. Norton, 1986), p. 103, observed that Britain's economic distress in 1947 at last dispelled fears among Truman administration policymakers and members of Congress that England constituted a major rival to American commerce.

74.   British embassy to the Department of State, aide-mémoire, 21 February 1947, *FRUS 1947*, 5: pp. 32–5; for the accompanying aide-mémoire concerning Turkey, see ibid., pp. 35–7.
75.   Bevin to Orme Sargent, 2 September 1946, quoted in G. M. Alexander, *The Prelude to the Truman Doctrine: British Policy in Greece 1944–1947* (New York: Oxford University Press, 1982), p. 213.
76.   Dean Acheson, *Present at the Creation: My Years in the State Department* (New York: W. W. Norton, 1969), p. 219. Also see Vandenberg's speech to the Senate on 8 April 1947, in which he argued 'that the fall of Greece, followed by the collapse of Turkey, could precipitate a chain reaction which would threaten peace and security around the globe'; *On Assistance to Greece and Turkey* (Stamford, CT: Overbrook Press, 1947), p. 3.
77.   Henderson oral history interview, 14 June 1973, Truman Library.
78.   'Special Message to the Congress on Greece and Turkey: The Truman Doctrine', 12 March 1947, *Public Papers of the Presidents of the United States: Harry S. Truman,* 1947 (1963), pp. 176–80.
79.   Thus, Richard Best, *Cooperation with Like-Minded Peoples*, p. 132, saw US policy as 'formally redefined' by the Truman Doctrine speech, and much the same point was made by James L. Gormly, *The Collapse of the Grand Alliance, 1945–1948* (Baton Rouge: Louisiana State University Press, 1987), pp. 158–9. Ryan, *Vision of Anglo-America*, p. 172, asserted that the 12 March speech and the subsequent authorization bill 'provide a realistic point at which to mark America's full-fledged entry into the international politics of confrontation'. See also John Lewis Gaddis, 'Korea in America Politics, Strategy, and Diplomacy, 1945–1950', in *Origins of the Cold War in Asia*, p. 281, and, more importantly, Gaddis, 'Was the Truman Doctrine a Real Turning Point?', *Foreign Affairs* 52 (January 1974): pp. 386–402, for a strong assertion that the Truman Doctrine, despite its apparent globalism, did not signal a major reorientation of US foreign policy away from Europe. Pollard, 'Economic Security and the Origins of the Cold War', p. 279, asserts that the Truman Doctrine 'was primarily an instrument of economic containment in Western Europe'.
      On a related point, there has emerged no evidence to support the notion that the Soviets were directly involved in the Greek civil war: see Lawrence S. Wittner, *American Intervention in Greece, 1943–1949* (New York: Columbia University Press, 1982), pp. 255, 262; Alexander, *Prelude to the Truman Doctrine*, pp. 93, 99, 101, 114, 250. Wittner suggested that Stalin perceived a communist victory in Greece as 'likely to bolster Tito's hegemony in the Balkans, while at the same time angering the Western powers and thereby endangering Soviet holdings elsewhere in Eastern Europe' (p. 262). Alexander characterized Stalin's reluctance to become entangled in Greece as a product of his search for precedents which would give him a free hand in Eastern Europe (p. 251). Kuniholm, *Origins of the Cold War in the Near East*, p. 405, argued that even if there was no evidence of a direct Soviet role in Greek affairs, the USSR was indirectly supporting Yugoslavia, Albania and Bulgaria – who were aiding the Greek rebels – and that Moscow would certainly have taken advantage of any communist victory in Greece regardless of Stalin's previous thinking on the matter.
80.   McMahon, *Colonialism and Cold War*, p. 156; George F. Kennan, *Memoirs 1925–1950* (Boston: Little, Brown, 1967), pp. 53–4, 319–20, 322–4; Kuniholm, *Origins of the Cold War in the Near East*, pp. 415–16; Theodore Draper, 'Falling Dominoes', *New York Review of Books*, 27 October 1983, p. 18; Theodore Draper, 'American Hubris: From Truman

to the Persian Gulf', *New York Review of Books*, 16 July 1987, p. 41. See also Edmund Taylor, *Awakening From History* (London: Chatto & Windus, 1971), p. 281, for his discussion of 'officialized delusion'. James Gormly, *Collapse of the Grand Alliance*, pp. 134–5, suggests that the universalistic language of the Truman Doctrine was in part designed to 'play down the extent to which the United States was consciously moving to fill ailing Britannia's shoes'.

81. Wittner, *American Intervention in Greece*, pp. 307–8; see also Kuniholm, *Origins of the Cold War in the Near East*, pp. 419–20, and Richard J. Barnet, *Intervention and Revolution: The United States in the Third World* (New York: World Publishing, 1968), pp. 97, 100–01.

82. MacVeagh testimony, Senate Foreign Relations Committee, *Legislative Origins of the Truman Doctrine, Hearings held in Executive Session*, 80th cong., 1st sess., 1973, pp. 32–3, 39, 46.

83. Kennan, 'Reflections on Containment', in Terry L. Deibel and John Lewis Gaddis (eds), *Containing the Soviet Union: A Critique of US Policy* (New York: Pergamon-Brassey's International Defense Publishers, 1987), p. 17; see also Kennan, *Memoirs 1925–1950*, pp. 294–5, 315, 358–59, 367.

84. George comment, *Legislative Origins of the Truman Doctrine, Hearings*, p. 15; Kennan remark, *Memoirs 1925–1950*, p. 351; James Reston, 'The Case for Vandenberg', *Life*, 24 May 1948, p. 101.

85. Lincoln statement, 2 April 1947, *Legislative Origins of the Truman Doctrine, Hearings*, p. 160.

86. Jennings statement, 26 February 1947, House Committee on Appropriations, *Navy Department Appropriation Bill for 1948, Hearings*, 80th Cong., 1st sess., 1947, p. 1649. Congressman Errett P. Scrivener (Kansas) asked about the islands' people: 'They are scattered but what are we going to do, what is our policy to be, are we going to try to remake their entire lives or try to get the islands back somewhere to the place they were before the Japanese invasion and then let the people alone?' Jennings responded that yes, that would be appropriate for the former Japanese mandates, but that others, like Guam and American Samoa had been undergoing Americanization for a number of years before the Second World War (p. 1656).

87. Finley to secretary of state, 5 February 1947, 851R.00B/2-547, RG 59 DSNA. Finley saw little enthusiasm among the Algerian French for war in Vietnam – they were tired of war, he wrote, and did not want their sons dying in faraway jungles. See also Finley to secretary of state, 2 April 1947, 851R.00B/4–247, RG 59, DSNA; R. K. Beyer (Algiers) to secretary of state, 14 June 1947, 851R.00B/6-1447, RG 59, DSNA.

88. Secretary of state to US embassy in France, 10 June 1947, *FRUS 1947*, 5: pp. 686–9.

89. Caffery to secretary of state, 20 June 1947, ibid., 5: pp. 691–7.

90. Villard, acting director of NEA, to undersecretary of state, 31 July 1947, attachment to Henderson to Acting Secretary Lovett, 6 October 1947, 851R.00/10-647, RG 59, DSNA. Thus, wrote Villard, Ambassador Caffery had been instructed to make a high-level approach to French officials and urge adoption of a policy of 'gradual but sure evolution' of North African colonies toward something akin to dominion status. If this step were taken, US economic assistance for North Africa might be routed through planned Marshall Plan aid for the continent. Then, in terms reminiscent of Roosevelt's Vichy strategy, Villard proposed that if civil war erupted in mainland France, the United States might want to consider severing ties between the North African colonies and Paris – though French officials would naturally

expect the US government to operate along the lines of the 1942 Murphy-Weygand agreement. See also 'Policy Problems Summary French North Africa', memorandum by Harry Schwartz, Division of African Affairs, 29 August 1947, attachment to 851R.00/10-647, RG 59, DSNA. A 'Special Ad Hoc Committee: Country Report on Indochina', 15 July 1947, folder: ABC 400.336 (20 Mar 47) Sec 1–B, Box 531, ABC Decimal File 1942–48, RG 165, MRB, likewise noted that a civil war in France would foster a US policy toward French colonies that 'would be analogous to that which pertained during the Vichy regime'.

91. PPA paper quoted in Finley to secretary of state, 8 September 1947, 851R.00/9-847, RG 59, DSNA. *La Nation Algérienne* aggressively set forth the PPA platform of independence for Algeria, Tunisia, Morocco and the international zone of Tangier; independence for Libya; the withdrawal of foreign troops from Egypt and Sudan; an end to Jewish migration to Palestine; and the withdrawal of British troops from Iraq and Transjordan.

92. Henderson to Acting Secretary Lovett, 6 October 1947, 851R.00/10-647, RG 59, DSNA; 'Communists in North Africa', Joseph Palmer, 2d, to Raymond E. Murphy (EUR) and Francis B. Stevens (EE), 29 October 1947, 851R.00B/10-2947, RG 59, DSNA. In a response to Palmer's memo, Raymond Murphy agreed that sudden independence in North Africa would not necessarily mean that communists would come to power. With some relish, he observed: 'Fundamentally Moslems are anti-communists who are especially opposed to the anti-religious sentiments of communists. Lacking the fine appreciation of so-called liberal elements Moslems would probably act on primitive impulses and eliminate definitely and finally communist missionaries'. Murphy to Palmer, 3 November 1947, 851R.00B/10-2947, RG 59, DSNA.

93. See Touchette to secretary of state, 12 March 1947, 848T.00/3-1247, RG 59, DSNA; Touchette to secretary of state, 8 May 1947, 848T.00/5-847, RG 59, DSNA. Touchette relayed the latest population figures: overall, Kenya was 98.4 per cent black African, 1.3 per cent Asian (primarily Indian), and 0.3 per cent European; Touchette to secretary of state, 10 May 1947, 848T.00/5-1047, RG 59, DSNA.

94. Touchette to secretary of state, 28 July 1947, 848T.00/7-2847, RG 59, DSNA.

95. The phrase is from James Chace, 'Inescapable Entanglements', *Foreign Affairs* 67 (Winter 1988/89): p. 26; Acheson memorandum, 9 October 1945, *FRUS 1945*, 8: p. 45. See also remarks by John A. Loftus, chief of the Petroleum Division of the Office of International Trade Policy, 'Oil in United States Policy', *DSB* 15 (11 August 1946): pp. 276–81. Noting that supplies of oil often occurred in the 'industrially undeveloped areas' of the world, Loftus was concerned about the maintenance of 'peace and stability' in such regions. For the United States to have dependable sources of strategic materials, Loftus suggested a twofold approach: (1) to liberalize the contractual policies of petroleum companies in order to eliminate obvious inequities in resource arrangements with smaller nations, and (2) to institute the open door 'so that the distinction between have and have-not nations with respect to oil will become largely meaningless and the acquisitive greed of nations for control over external oil reserves will be correspondingly reduced'. Improved contractual relations would also reduce the likelihood that 'some other power' would 'play upon the uneasiness and suspicion latent in the minds of the granting government'.

96. JCS memorandum, 3 July 1947, 'The Military Implications Involved in the Disposal of the Italian Colonies', folder: ABC 092 Italy (27 Apr 44), Box 95, ABC Decimal Files 1942–48, RG 319, MRB; 'Significant Considerations Regarding the Disposition of the Italian African Colonies', Central Intelligence Group, ORE 39, 25 July 1947, p. 2, Box 254, President's Secretary's Files, Truman Papers, Truman Library.

97. British chargé (John Balfour) to secretary of state, 30 July 1947, *FRUS 1947*, 5: p. 268; Marshall to acting secretary of state (Lovett), 25 August 1947, ibid., p. 313.

98. Memorandum Prepared in the Department of State, 'The British and American Positions', n.d., ibid., pp. 511–21.

99. Comment by Maj. Allison K. Thomas, Deer Report no. 1, 17 July 1945, in Senate Committee on Foreign Relations, *Causes, Origins, and Lessons of the Vietnam War, Hearings*, 92d Cong., 2d sess., 1973, p. 246; see chap. 3 of this book.

100. See Caffery to secretary of state, 20 June 1947, 840.50 Recovery/6-2047, RG 59, DSNA.

101. Davies to George Kennan, 15 December 1947, Subject Files: Communism 1947–51, PPS Lot Files, RG 59, DSNA. Davies' purpose was to urge the department to 'now begin systematically to train one or more officers for each country in the Far East to specialize in communist activities'. Kennan wrote that Davies was 'basically right' in his analysis; see Kennan to Butterworth, 26 December 1947, ibid.

102. Acheson statement, 20 May 1947, *Executive Sessions of the Senate Foreign Relations Committee* (Historical Series), 80th Cong., 1st and 2d sess., 1947–48 (1976), pp. 53–4; Hodge remarks, 26 March 1947, House Committee on Appropriations, *Military Establishment Appropriation Bill for 1948, Hearings*, 80th Cong., 1st sess., 1947, p. 1476; Buhite, *Soviet-American Relations in Asia, 1945–1954* (Norman, OK: University of Oklahoma Press, 1981), pp. 155, 158, 160–1. For other accounts of the growing symbolic importance of the US commitment to southern Korea, see Charles M. Dobbs, *The Unwanted Symbol: American Foreign Policy, the Cold War, and Korea, 1945–1950* (Kent, OH: Kent State University Press, 1981), and William Whitney Stueck, Jr., *The Road to Confrontation: American Policy Toward China and Korea, 1947–1950* (Chapel Hill: University of North Carolina Press, 1981).

103. See Michael Schaller, 'Securing the Great Crescent: Occupied Japan and the Origins of Containment in Southeast Asia', *Journal of American History* 69 (1982): pp. 392–414; Kennan, *Memoirs 1925–1950*, p. 374.

104. Russell H. Fifield, *Americans in Southeast Asia: The Roots of Commitment* (New York: Thomas Y. Cromwell, 1973), p. 68; see also Hess, *United States' Emergence as a Southeast Asian Power*, pp. 218, 245, 248; McMahon, *Colonialism and Cold War*, pp. 139–40; and Vinacke, *United States and the Far East*, p. 9.

105. 'Proposed public position of the United States with respect to nationalist movements in colonial dependencies', Landon (SEA) to John P. Davies (S/P), 6 August 1947, Box 5, Records, Philippine and Southeast Asia Division, RG 59, DSNA.

106. Landon to John Carter Vincent, 18 July 1947, Box 12, Records, Philippine and Southeast Asia Division, Lot Files, RG 59, DSNA; 'Special Ad Hoc Committee: Country Report on Indochina', 15 July 1947, folder: ABC 400.336 (20 Mar 47) Sec 1–B, Box 531, ABC Decimal File 1942–48, RG 165, MRB. See also Edwin Stanton (US minister, Siam) to secretary of state, 7

January 1947, *FRUS 1947*, 6: p. 57; and Moffat to secretary of state, 7 January 1947, ibid., pp. 54–5.

107. Memorandum of conversation, by Cohen, 13 June 1947, 840.50 Recovery/ 6-1847, RG 59, DSNA. The criticism had come from James Shotwell of the Carnegie Foundation.

108. Marshall statement, House Committee on Foreign Affairs, *United States Foreign Policy for a Post-War Recovery Program, Hearings*, 80th Cong., 1st and 2d sess., 1948, pt. 1: p. 29; Vandenberg comment, *Legislative Origins of the Truman Doctrine, Hearings*, p. 14; 'Review of the World Situation as It Relates to the Security of the United States', 12 May 1948, CIA 5–48, *Declassified Documents Reference System*, Carrollton Press (microfilm), no. 179–D; Johnson statement, Senate Committee on Foreign Relations, *Reviews of the World Situation: 1949–50, Hearings Held in Executive Session*, 81st Cong., 1st and 2d sess., 1974, p. 233.

Chapter 7

1. Clayton remarks, 23 January 1950, House Committee on Foreign Affairs, *Atlantic Union, Hearings*, 81st Cong., 2d sess., 1950, pp. 3–4, 21–2, 20; Clayton was appearing before the committee in order to win support for the principle of 'Atlantic union' as the best defense against aggressive Soviet communism. For similar remarks, see also speech texts titled, 'Atlantic Union – The Road to Peace in an Atomic World', 17 January 1950, folder: Speeches & Statements – 1949–50, Box 80, William L. Clayton Papers, Harry S. Truman Library, Independence, Missouri, and 'What Atlantic Union Means to You and to Me', 27 September 1949, ibid. Historian Emily S. Rosenberg has recalled: 'One distinguishing feature of my generation, raised during the Cold War's most frigid years, is its collective childhood memory of red-bleeding maps. I have not traced the precise origins of these pedagogical devices, but they did effectively dramatize the concept of an expanding Communist Empire: it was *Them*, not *Us*'. See ' "The Empire" Strikes Back', *Reviews in American History* 16 (December 1988): p. 585.

2. 'Communists in North Africa', Joseph Palmer, 2d, to R. E. Murphy (EUR) and F. B. Stevens (EE), 29 October 1947, State Department Decimal Files, 851R.00B/10-2947, RG 59, National Archives and Records Administration, Washington, DC.

3. Douglas remark, 11 November 1947, Senate Committee on Foreign Relations, *Interim Aid for Europe, Hearings*, 80th Cong., 1st sess., 1947, p. 101; Romney statement, 14 November 1947, ibid., p. 252; Vandenberg to Truman, 30 September 1947, in House Committee on Foreign Affairs, *Emergency Foreign Aid, Hearings*, 80th Cong., 1st sess., 1947, p. 2.

4. Marshall comment, 6 May 1947, Senate Committee on Foreign Relations, *Treaties of Peace with Italy, Rumania, Bulgaria, and Hungary, Hearings*, 80th Cong., 1st sess., 1947, p. 180.

5. For a very spirited denunciation of American anticolonialism, see D. C. Watt, 'American Anti-Colonial Policies and the End of the European Colonial Empire, 1941–1962', in A. N. J. Hollander (ed.), *Contagious Conflict: The Impact of American Dissent on European Life* (Leiden: E. J. Brill, 1973), pp. 93–125. In particular, Watt criticized what he termed a naive, simplistic American perception of political consciousness among native peoples, particularly in India, Indochina and Indonesia; and he attacked the 'moral imperialism' of US policymakers.

6. Robert C. Good, 'The United States and the Colonial Debate', in Arnold

Wolfers (ed.), *Alliance Policy in the Cold War* (Baltimore: Johns Hopkins Press, 1959), p. 237.

7. John W. Dower, *War Without Mercy: Race and Power in the Pacific War* (New York: Pantheon Books, 1986), pp. 29, 309; see also V. G. Kiernan, *From Conquest to Collapse: European Empires from 1815–1960* (New York: Pantheon Books, 1982), p. 215.

8. I. A. Kirkpatrick, 'Visit to the B.I.S. in America', 10 January 1947, FO371/60998/AN187, Public Record Office, London, England. Kirkpatrick arrived on 27 November 1946 and left on 4 January 1947; in 38 days, he visited Washington, New York City, Chicago, Los Angeles, San Francisco, Dallas, Houston and New Orleans. He also spent a day at the State Department. Another British observer, Frederick Puckle believed that American public opinion had become much less critical of Britain's policy in India: 'We are generally considered to be making an honest attempt to give India independence – in fact to force it on them. The blame for present difficulties is generally laid on [the] Indians themselves. As usual, when we seem to be behaving ourselves, the matter gets little attention. But the dogs of criticism, asleep for the moment, could be wakened'. Puckle commentary, 6 December 1946, enclosure with Paul Patrick to Nevile Butler, 8 January 1947, FO371/60998/AN113, PRO.

9. Truman, *Memoirs*, vol. 1: *Year of Decisions* (Garden City, NY: Doubleday, 1955), pp. 275, 237–8, emphasis mine; see Good, 'The United States and the Colonial Debate', p. 237: 'We were firm in our principled espousal of self-determination, but regularly qualified it with adjectives like "eventual", and reservations concerning "timing and procedure"'.

10. 'Special Message to the Congress on Greece and Turkey: The Truman Doctrine', 12 March 1947, *Public Papers of the Presidents of the United States: Harry S. Truman*, 1947 (1963), pp. 176–80, italics in original.

11. Marshall statement, 10 November 1947, *Emergency Foreign Aid, Hearings*, pp. 3, 6.

12. James F. Byrnes, *Speaking Frankly* (New York: Harper, 1947), p. 229.

13. Harold Isaacs, *No Peace for Asia* (New York: Macmillan, 1947), pp. 235, 242; see also Eric Sevareid, *Not So Wild a Dream* (New York: Alfred A. Knopf, 1946), p. 243, on the puncturing of myths about the American presence in Asia.

14. Patricia Dawson Ward, *The Threat of Peace: James F. Byrnes and the Council of Foreign Ministers, 1945–1946* (Kent, OH: Kent State University Press, 1979), pp. 177–8.

15. Isaacs, *No Peace for Asia*, pp. 266, 276.

16. Hurley to Roosevelt, 21 December 1943, in Warren F. Kimball (ed.), *Churchill & Roosevelt: The Complete Correspondence*, 3 vols (Princeton University Press, 1984), 3: p. 6. While Hurley believed that most empires had collapsed or would soon crumble as a result of the war, he believed that the British empire had acquired an illusory 'new life' due to 'the infusion . . . of the blood of productivity and liberty from a free nation through lend-lease'. Ibid. General Hurley's remarks were enclosed in FDR to Churchill, 29 February 1944, in ibid., 3: p. 3. Churchill responded: 'The General seems to have some ideas about British imperialism which I confess make me rub my eyes'; Churchill to FDR, 21 May 1944, in ibid., 3: p. 140.

17. Philip C. Jessup, *The Birth of Nations* (New York: Columbia University Press, 1974), p. 20; Charles Wolf, Jr., *The Indonesian Story: The Birth, Growth and Structure of the Indonesian Republic* (New York: John Day, 1948), p. 162.

18.   'Draft Notes for Remarks by the United Kingdom at the Opening of the United States-United Kingdom Talks on the Middle East', 16 October 1947, *Foreign Relations of the United States, 1947* (Washington: GPO, 1971), 5: p. 566; Michael Schaller, 'Securing the Great Crescent: Occupied Japan and the Origins of Containment in Southeast Asia', *Journal of American History* 69 (1982): p. 392; McGhee, *Envoy to the Middle World: Adventures in Diplomacy* (New York: Harper & Row, 1983).

19.   H. Stuart Hughes, 'The Second Year of the Cold War: A Memoir & an Anticipation', *Commentary*, August 1969, pp. 27–9; Sally Marks, 'The World According to Washington', *Diplomatic History* 11 (Summer 1987): p. 266.

20.   Hugh Tinker, *Men Who Overturned Empires: Fighters, Dreamers and Schemers* (Madison: University of Wisconsin Press, 1987), p. 21. Tinker served with British forces in India and Burma during the Second World War.

21.   Walter Reich, 'Endless Fear and Endless Hate?', *New York Times Book Review*, 6 March 1988, p. 26; Reich was reviewing the book *Yellow Wind* (1988), by David Frossman. See also Adeed Dawisha, 'Anti-Americanism in the Arab World: Memories of the Past in the Attitudes of the Present', in Alvin Z. Rubinstein and Donald E. Smith (eds), *Anti-Americanism in the Third World: Implications for U.S. Foreign Policy* (New York: Praeger, 1985), p. 67.

22.   Edmund Taylor, *Awakening From History* (London: Chatto & Windus, 1971), p. 282; the latter phrase is from Walter A. McDougall, 'Technocracy and Statecraft in the Space Age – Toward the History of a Saltation', *American Historical Review* 87 (1982): p. 1028.

23.   Christopher Thorne, *Allies of a Kind: The United States, Britain, and the War Against Japan, 1941–1945* (New York: Oxford University Press, 1978, paperback), p. 729; see also William A. Williams' statement, House Committee on Foreign Affairs, *The Cold War: Origins and Developments, Hearings*, 92d Cong., 1st sess., 1971, p. 17.

24.   Ernest R. May, *'Lessons' of the Past: The Use and Misuse of History in American Foreign Policy* (New York: Oxford University Press, 1973), p. xi. British author D. C. Watt has complained about 'the substitution of crude historical myth for real historical advice in the US governmental process'; 'Every War Must End: War-Time Planning for Post-War Security, in Britain and America in the Wars of 1914–18 and 1939–45. The Roles of Historical Example and of Professional Historians', *Transactions of the Royal Historical Society*, 5th Ser., 1978, p. 172.

Select Bibliography

ARCHIVAL SOURCES

Great Britain

Public Record Office, London.
  FO 371, Foreign Office Files.
  CAB 65-66, War Cabinet Minutes and Memoranda.
  CAB 79, Chiefs of Staff Committee Minutes.
  CAB 119, Joint Planning Staff: Files.
  CAB 122, British Joint Staff Mission: Washington Office Files.

United States

National Archives and Records Administration, Washington, DC.
  RG 59, State Department Records.
  RG 165, War Department General and Special Staffs: Plans and Operations Division.
  RG 226, Office of Strategic Services.
  RG 319, Army Staff: Plans and Operations Division.
Library of Congress, Washington, DC.
  Philip C. Jessup Papers.
  Tom Connally Papers.
  Robert P. Patterson Papers.
Harry S. Truman Library, Independence, MO.
  Harry S. Truman Papers, White House Files.
    Confidential File.
    Rose Conway File.
    Naval Aide Files.
    Offical File.
    President's Secretary's File.
  William L. Clayton Papers.
  John F. Melby Papers.

ORAL HISTORY INTERVIEWS

Henry L. Deimel, 5 June 1975, Truman Library.
Loy W. Henderson, 14 June 1973, Truman Library.
John D. Hickerson, 26 June 1979, personal interview, Washington, DC.
Roger Makins, 10 August 1970, Truman Library.

PUBLISHED DOCUMENTS

Great Britain

Her Majesty's Stationery Office, *Documents Relating to British Involvement in the Indo-China Conflict 1945–1965*, misc. no. 25, 1965.

United States

Congress, House of Representatives
US Congress, House Committee on Appropriations, *Navy Department Appropria-tion Bill for 1946, Hearings before the Subcommittee of the Committee on Appropriations*, 79th Cong., 1st sess., 1945, Part I.

US Congress, House Committee on Appropriations, *Military Establishment Appropriation Bill for 1947, Hearings before the Subcommittee of the Committee on Appropriations*, 79th Cong., 2d sess., 1946.

US Congress, House Committee on Appropriations, *Military Establishment Appropriation Bill for 1948, Hearings before the Subcommittee of the Committee on Appropriations*, 80th Cong., 1st sess., 1947.

US Congress, House Committee on Appropriations, *Navy Department Appropria-tion Bill for 1948, Hearings before the Subcommittee of the Committee on Appropriations*, 80th Cong., 1st sess., 1947.

US Congress, House Committee on Appropriations, *Department of the Navy Appropriation Bill for 1949, Hearings before the Subcommittee of the Committee on Appropriations*, 80th Cong., 2d sess., 1948.

US Congress, House Committee on Appropriations, *Foreign Aid Appropriation Bill for 1949, Hearings before the Subcommittee of the Committee on Appropria-tions*, 80th Cong., 2d sess., 1948.

US Congress, House Committee on Appropriations, *Foreign Aid Appropriation Bill for 1950, Hearings before the Subcommittee of the Committee on Appropria-tions*, 81st Cong., 1st sess., 1949.

US Congress, House Committee on Appropriations, *National Military Establish-ment Appropriation Bill for 1950, Hearings before the Subcommittee of the Committee on Appropriations*, 81st Cong., 1st sess., 1949.

US Congress, House Committee on Appropriations, *Foreign Aid Appropriations for 1951, Hearings before the Subcommittee of the Committee on Appropriations*, 81st Cong., 2d sess., 1950.

US Congress, House Committee on Banking and Currency, *Defense Production Act of 1950, Hearings before the Committee on Banking and Finance*, 81st Cong., 2d sess., 1950.

US Congress, House Committee on Foreign Affairs, *To Create a Department of Peace, Hearings before the Committee on Foreign Affairs*, 79th Cong., 1st sess., 1945.

US Congress, House Committee on Foreign Affairs, *Emergency Foreign Aid, Hearings before the Committee on Foreign Affairs*, 80th Cong., 1st sess., 1947.

US Congress, House Committee on Foreign Affairs, *United States Foreign Policy for a Post-War Recovery Program, Hearings before the Committee on Foreign Affairs*, 80th Cong., 1st and 2d sess., 1948.

US Congress, House Committee on Foreign Affairs, *Extension of European Recovery, Hearings before the Committee on Foreign Affairs*, 81st Cong., 1st sess., 1949.

US Congress, House Committee on Foreign Affairs, *Atlantic Union, Hearings before the Committee on Foreign Affairs*, 81st Cong., 2d sess., 1950.

US Congress, House Committee on Foreign Affairs, *The Cold War: Origins and Developments, Hearings before the Subcommittee on Europe of the Committee on Foreign Affairs*, 92d Cong., 1st sess., 1971.

US Congress, House Committee on International Affairs, *Selected Executive Session Hearings of the Committee, 1943–50*, vol. 2: *Problems of World War II and Its Aftermath*, pt. 2; vol. 5: *Military Assistance Program*, pts. 1 and 2; vol. 7: *United States Policy in the Far East*, pt. 1 (Washington, DC: GPO, 1976).

US Congress, House Committee on Military Affairs, *Universal Military Training, Hearings before the Committee on Military Affairs*, 79th Cong., 1st sess., 1946.

US Congress, House Committee on Naval Affairs, *Sundry Legislation Affecting the Naval Establishment, 1945, Hearings before the Committee on Naval Affairs*, 79th Cong., 1st sess., 1946.

US Congress, House Committee on Naval Affairs, *Sundry Legislation Affecting the Naval Establishment, 1946, Hearings before the Committee on Naval Affairs*, 79th Cong., 2d sess., 1947.

Congress, Senate

US Congress, Senate Committee on Appropriations, *Military Establishment Appropriation Bill for 1947, Hearings before the Subcommittee of the Committee on Appropriations*, 79th Cong., 2d sess., 1946.

US Congress, Senate Committee on Appropriations, *Supplemental National Defense Appropriation Bill, 1948, Hearings before the Subcommittee of the Committee on Appropriations*, 80th Cong., 2d sess., 1948.

US Congress, Senate Committee on Armed Services, *Universal Military Training, Hearings before the Committee on Armed Services*, 80th Cong., 2d sess., 1948.

US Congress, Senate Committee on Foreign Relations, *The Charter of the United Nations, Hearings before the Committee on Foreign Relations*, 79th Cong., 1st sess., 1945.

US Congress, Senate Committee on Foreign Relations, *Interim Aid for Europe, Hearings before the Committee on Foreign Relations*, 80th Cong., 1st sess., 1947.

US Congress, Senate Committee on Foreign Relations, *Treaties of Peace with Italy, Rumania, Bulgaria, and Hungary, Hearings before the Committee on Foreign Relations*, 80th Cong., 1st sess., 1947.

US Congress, Senate Committee on Foreign Relations, *European Recovery Program, Hearings before the Committee on Foreign Relations*, 80th Cong., 2d sess., 1948.

US Congress, Senate Committee on Foreign Relations, *North Atlantic Treaty, Hearings before the Committee on Foreign Relations*, 81st Cong., 1st sess., 1949.

US Congress, Senate Committee on Foreign Relations, *Legislative Origins of the Truman Doctrine, Hearings Held in Executive Session before the Committee on Foreign Relations*, 80th Cong., 1st sess., 1973.

US Congress, Senate Committee on Foreign Relations, *The Vandenberg Resolution and the North Atlantic Treaty, Hearings Held in Executive Session before the Committee on Foreign Relations*, 80th Cong., 1st sess., 1973.

US Congress, Senate Committee on Foreign Relations, *Causes, Origins, and Lessons of the Vietnam War, Hearings before the Committee on Foreign Relations*, 92d Cong., 2d sess., 1973.

US Congress, Senate Committee on Foreign Relations, *The United States and Vietnam: 1944–1947*. Staff study, 92d Cong., 2d sess., 1973.

US Congress, Senate Committee on Foreign Relations, *Reviews of the World Situation: 1949–1950, Hearings Held in Executive Session before the Committee on Foreign Relations*, 81st Cong., 1st and 2d sess., 1974.

US Congress, Senate Committee on Foreign Relations, *Executive Sessions of the Senate Foreign Relations Committee* (Historical Series), vols 1–2, 80th Cong., 1st and 2d sess.; 81st Cong., 1st and 2d sess., 1976.

Department of Defense

US Department of Defense, *United States-Vietnam Relations, 1945–1967*, 12 vols (Washington, DC: GPO, 1971).

Department of State
US Department of State, *Foreign Relations of the United States: The Conferences at Washington, 1941–1942, and Casablanca, 1943* (Washington, DC: GPO, 1968).
US Department of State, *Foreign Relations of the United States: The Conference at Quebec 1944* (Washington, DC: GPO, 1972).
US Department of State, *Foreign Relations of the United States: The Conferences at Malta and Yalta, 1945* (Washington, DC: GPO, 1955; Reprint, Westport, CT: Greenwood Press, 1976).
US Department of State, *Foreign Relations of the United States: Conference of Berlin (Potsdam), 1945*, 2 vols (Washington, DC: GPO, 1960).
US Department of State, *Foreign Relations of the United States, 1944–47*, 35 vols (Washington, DC: GPO, 1965–75).

OTHER DOCUMENTS

Press Conferences of the Secretaries of State, 1922–1973 (Wilmington, DE: Scholarly Resources, n.d.), microfilm.
Public Papers of the Presidents of the United States, Harry S. Truman, 1945–47 (Washington, DC: Office of the *Federal Register*, National Archives and Records Administration, 1961–63).

MEMOIRS, DIARIES, PAPERS

Acheson, Dean, *Present at the Creation: My Years at the State Department* (New York: W. W. Norton, 1969).
Alvarez, Luis W., *Alvarez: Adventures of a Physicist* (New York: Basic Books, 1987).
Attlee, Clement R., *As It Happened* (New York: Viking Press, 1954).
Bohlen, Charles E., *Witness to History, 1929–1969* (New York: W. W. Norton, 1973).
Byrnes, James F., *Speaking Frankly* (New York: Harper, 1947).
Campbell, Thomas M. and George C. Herring (eds), *The Diaries of Edward R. Stettinius, Jr., 1943–1946* (New York: New Viewpoints, 1975).
Childs, J. Rives, *Diplomatic and Literary Quests* (Richmond, VA: Whittet & Shepperson, 1963).
Colville, John, *The Fringes of Power: 10 Downing Street Diaries, 1939–1955* (New York: W. W. Norton, 1985).
Davies, John Paton, Jr., *Dragon by the Tail: American, British, Japanese, and Russian Encounters with China and One Another* (New York: W. W. Norton, 1972).
De Gaulle, Charles, *The Complete War Memoirs of Charles de Gaulle, 1940–1946*, 3 vols, 1955–60, translated by Jonathan Griffin (vol. 1), and Richard Howard (vols 2 and 3) (New York: Simon & Schuster, 1967; reprint (3 vols in one), New York: Da Capo Press, 1984).
Dilks, David (ed.), *The Diaries of Sir Alexander Cadogan, 1938–1945* (New York: G. P. Putnam's Sons, 1972).
Eden, Anthony, *The Memoirs of Anthony Eden*, vol. 2, *The Reckoning* (Boston: Houghton Mifflin, 1965).
Ferrell, Robert H. (ed.), *Dear Bess: The Letters from Harry to Bess Truman, 1910–1959* (New York: W. W. Norton, 1983).

Hull, Cordell, *The Memoirs of Cordell Hull*, 2 vols (New York: Macmillan, 1948).
James, Robert Rhodes (ed.), *Winston S. Churchill: His Complete Speeches, 1897–1963* (London: Chelsea House, 1974).
Jessup, Philip C., *The Birth of Nations* (New York: Columbia University Press, 1974).
Kennan, George F., *Memoirs, 1925–1950* (Boston: Little, Brown, 1967).
Leahy, William D., *I Was There* (New York: McGraw-Hill, 1950).
Macmillan, Harold, *War Diaries: Politics and War in the Mediterranean, January 1943–May 1945* (New York: St Martin's Press, 1984).
Millis, Walter (ed.), *The Forrestal Diaries* (New York: Viking, 1951).
Lord Mountbatten, *Post Surrender Tasks, Section E of the Report to the Combined Chiefs of Staff* (London: Her Majesty's Stationery Office, 1969).
Murphy, Robert, *Diplomat Among Warriors* (Garden City, NY: Doubleday, 1964).
Reid, Escott, *On Duty: A Canadian and the Making of the United Nations, 1945–1946* (Kent, OH: Kent State University Press, 1983).
Roosevelt, Elliott, *As He Saw It* (New York: Duell, Sloan and Pearce, 1946).
Rosenman, Samuel I. (comp.), *The Public Papers and Addresses of Franklin D. Roosevelt*, 14 vols (New York: Harper, 1950).
Sainteny, Jean, *Ho Chi Minh and His Vietnam: A Personal Memoir*, translated by Herma Briffault (Chicago: Cowles, 1972).
Stettinius, Edward R., Jr., *Roosevelt and the Russians: The Yalta Conference*, edited by Walter Johnson (New York: Doubleday, 1949).
Stimson, Henry L., *Henry Lewis Stimson Diaries* (New Haven: Yale University Library Microfilm Edition, n.d.).
Truman, Harry S., *Memoirs*, 2 vols (Garden City, NY: Doubleday, 1955–56).
Vandenberg, Arthur H., Jr. (ed.), *The Private Papers of Senator Vandenberg* (Boston: Houghton Mifflin, 1952).

ARTICLES

Ash, Timothy Garton, 'From World War to Cold War', *New York Review of Books*, 11 June 1987, pp. 44–50.
Bell, Philip W., 'Colonialism as a Problem in American Foreign Policy', *World Politics* 5 (October 1952): pp. 86–109.
Bernstein, Barton J., 'Roosevelt, Truman, and the Atomic Bomb, 1941–1945: A Reinterpretation', *Political Science Quarterly* 90 (Spring 1975): pp. 23–69.
Bills, Scott L., 'The United States, NATO, and the Colonial World', in Lawrence S. Kaplan and Robert W. Clawson (eds), *NATO After Thirty Years* (Wilmington, DE: Scholarly Resources, 1981), pp. 149–64.
Blair, Leon Borden, 'Amateurs in Diplomacy: The American Vice Consuls in North Africa 1941–1943', *Historian* 35 (August 1973): pp. 607–20.
Bunche, Ralph, 'Trusteeship and Non-Self-Governing Territories in the Charter of the United Nations', *Department of State Bulletin* 13 (30 December 1945): pp. 1037–44.
Byrnes, James F., 'Report on First Session of the Council of Foreign Ministers', 5 October 1945, *Department of State Bulletin* 13 (7 October 1945): pp. 507–12.
——, 'Report by the Secretary of State on the Meeting of Foreign Ministers', *Department of State Bulletin* 13 (30 December 1945): pp. 1033–6.
——, 'We have pinned our hopes to the banner of the United Nations', *Department of State Bulletin* 14 (10 March 1946): pp. 355–8.

Callender, Harold, 'France's Goal: Neither Moscow Nor Detroit', *New York Times Magazine*, 2 June 1946.

Clayton, William L., 'The Foreign Economic Policy of the State Department', *Department of State Bulletin* 12 (27 May 1945): pp. 979–82.

Clymer, Kenton J., 'The Education of William Phillips: Self-Determination and American Policy Toward India, 1942–45', *Diplomatic History* 8 (Winter 1984): pp. 13–35.

Colbert, Evelyn, 'The Road Not Taken: Decolonization and Independence in Indonesia and Indochina', *Foreign Affairs* 51 (April 1973): pp. 608–28.

Dawisha, Adeed, 'Anti-Americanism in the Arab World: Memories of the Past in the Attitudes of the Present', in Alvin Z. Rubinstein and Donald E. Smith (eds), *Anti-Americanism in the Third World: Implications for U.S. Foreign Policy* (New York: Praeger, 1985), pp. 67–83.

Defourneaux, René J., as told to James Flowers, 'A Secret Encounter with Ho Chi Minh', *Look*, 9 August 1966, pp. 32–3.

Draper, Theodore, 'American Hubris: From Truman to the Persian Gulf', *New York Review of Books*, 16 July 1987, pp. 40–8.

———, 'Falling Dominoes', *New York Review of Books*, 27 October 1983, pp. 6 ff.

Dulles, Foster Rhea, and Gerald Ridinger, 'The Anti-Colonial Policies of Franklin D. Roosevelt', *Political Science Quarterly* 70 (March 1955): pp. 1–18.

Fosdick, Raymond B., 'The Challenge: One World or *None*', *New York Times Magazine*, 2 September 1945.

Gaddis, John Lewis, 'Korea in American Politics, Strategy, and Diplomacy, 1945–50', in Yonosuke Nagai and Akira Iriye (eds), *The Origins of the Cold War in Asia* (New York: Columbia University Press, 1977), pp. 277–98.

———, 'Was the Truman Doctrine a Real Turning Point?' *Foreign Affairs* 52 (January 1974): pp. 386–402.

Grieg, Benjamin, 'Significance of the Trusteeship System', *The Annals of the American Academy of Political and Social Science* 255 (January 1948): pp. 39–47.

Girard, Raymond P., 'City Man Helped to Train Guerrillas of Ho Chi Minh', *Evening Gazette* (Worcester, MA), 14 May 1968.

———, 'Ho Is Described as Clever, Yet Naive', *Evening Gazette* (Worcester, MA), 15 May 1968.

Good, Robert C., 'The United States and the Colonial Debate', in Arnold Wolfers (ed.), *Alliance Policy in the Cold War* (Baltimore: Johns Hopkins Press, 1959), pp. 224–70.

Grew, Joseph C., 'Some Aspects of Our Relations with France', *Department of State Bulletin* 12 (4 February 1945): pp. 151–3.

Lord Hailey, 'The Colonies and the Atlantic Charter', *Journal of the Royal Central Asian Society* 30 (1943): pp. 233–46.

Hammer, Ellen J., 'Blueprinting a New Indochina', *Pacific Affairs* 21 (September 1948): pp. 252–63.

Herring, George C., 'The Truman Administration and the Restoration of French Sovereignty in Indochina', *Diplomatic History* 1 (Spring 1977): pp. 97–117.

Hess, Gary R., 'Franklin Roosevelt and Indochina', *Journal of American History* 59 (September 1972): pp. 353–68.

———, 'United States Policy and the Origins of the French-Viet Minh War, 1945–46', *Peace and Change* 3 (Summer–Fall 1975): pp. 21–33.

———, 'The First American Commitment in Indochina: The Acceptance of the "Bao Dai Solution", 1950', *Diplomatic History* 2 (Fall 1978): pp. 331–50.

Hornbeck, Stanley K., 'The United States and the Netherlands East Indies', *The Annals of the American Academy of Political and Social Science* 255 (January 1948): pp. 124–35.

Hughes, H. Stuart, 'The Second Year of the Cold War: A Memoir & an Anticipation', *Commentary*, August 1969, pp. 27–32.

Just, Matthew J., 'The Great Dilemma of American Foreign Policy', *Virginia Quarterly Review* 34 (Spring 1958): pp. 224–39.

Kahin, George McTurnan, 'The United States and the Anticolonial Revolutions in Southeast Asia, 1945–50', in Yonosuke Nagai and Akira Iriye (eds), *The Origins of the Cold War in Asia* (New York: Columbia University Press, 1977), pp. 338–61.

Kanet, Roger E., 'The Soviet Union and the Colonial Question, 1917–1953', in Roger E. Kanet (ed.), *The Soviet Union and the Developing Nations* (Baltimore: Johns Hopkins University Press, 1974), pp. 1–20.

Kennan, George F., 'The Sources of Soviet Conduct', 1947. Reprinted in *Foreign Affairs* 65 (Spring 1987): pp. 854–68.

———, 'Reflections on Containment', in Terry L. Deibel and John Lewis Gaddis (eds), *Containing the Soviet Union: A Critique of US Policy* (New York: Pergamon-Brassey's International Defense Publishers, 1987), pp. 15–19.

Khenouf, Mohamed, and Michael Brett, 'Algerian Nationalism and the Allied Military Strategy and Propaganda during the Second World War: The Background to Sétif', in David Killingray and Richard Rathbone (eds), *Africa and the Second World War* (New York: St Martin's Press, 1986), pp. 258–74.

Kimball, Warren F., 'Naked Reverse Right: Roosevelt, Churchill, and Eastern Europe from TOLSTOY to Yalta – and a Little Beyond', *Diplomatic History* 9 (Winter 1985): pp. 1–24.

LaFeber, Walter, 'Roosevelt, Churchill, and Indochina: 1942–45', *American Historical Review* 80 (December 1975): pp. 1277–95.

Loftus, John A., 'Oil in United States Policy', *Department of State Bulletin* 15 (11 August 1946): pp. 276–81.

McDougall, Walter A., 'Technocracy and Statecraft in the Space Age', *American Historical Review* 87 (October 1982): pp. 1010–40.

McKay, Vernon, 'The Future of Italy's Colonies', *Foreign Policy Reports* 21 (1 January 1946): pp. 270–9.

McVey, Camden, 'An American's View of France', *Department of State Bulletin* 13 (7 October 1945): pp. 523–7.

Marks, Sally, 'The World According to Washington', *Diplomatic History* 11 (Summer 1987): pp. 265–82.

Pollard, Robert A., 'Economic Security and the Origins of the Cold War: Bretton Woods, the Marshall Plan, and American Rearmament, 1944–50', *Diplomatic History* 9 (Summer 1985): pp. 271–89.

Pratt, Julius W., 'Anticolonialism in United States Policy', in Robert Strausz Hupé and Harry W. Hazard (eds), *The Idea of Colonialism* (New York: Praeger, 1958), pp. 114–51.

Reston, James, 'U.S. Chiefs Divided on Italy's Colonies', *New York Times*, 2 September 1945.

———, 'The Case for Vandenberg', *Life*, 24 May 1948, pp. 101–6, 111–14.

Sapp, Steven P., 'Jefferson Caffery, Cold War Diplomat: American-French Relations 1944–49', *Louisiana History* 23 (Spring 1982): pp. 179–92.

Sbrega, John J., ' "First catch your hare": Anglo-American Perspectives on Indochina During the Second World War', *Journal of Southeast Asian Studies* 14 (March 1983): pp. 63–78.

———, 'The Anticolonial Policies of Franklin D. Roosevelt: A Reappraisal', *Political Science Quarterly* 101 (1986): pp. 65–84.

———, 'The Anticolonial Views of Franklin D. Roosevelt, 1941–1945', in Herbert D. Rosenbaum and Elizabeth Bertelme (eds), *Franklin D. Roosevelt: The Man, the Myth, the Era, 1882–1945* (Westport, CT: Greenwood Press, 1987), pp. 191–201.

Schaller, Michael, 'Securing the Great Crescent: Occupied Japan and the Origins of Containment in Southeast Asia', *Journal of American History* 69 (1982): pp. 392–414.

Sharp, Lauriston, 'French Plan for Indochina', *Far Eastern Survey* 15 (3 July 1946): pp. 193–7.

Sheldon, George, 'The Status of Viet Nam', *Far Eastern Survey* 15 (18 December 1946): pp. 373–7.

Singh, Anita Inder, 'Decolonization in India: The Statement of 20 February 1947', *International History Review* 6 (May 1984): pp. 191–209.

Siracusa, Joseph M., 'FDR, Truman, and Indochina, 1941–1952: The Forgotten Years', in Joseph M. Siracusa and Glen St John Barclay (eds), *The Impact of the Cold War: Reconsiderations* (Port Washington, NY: Kennikat Press, 1977), pp. 163–83.

Stettinius, Edward R., 'The Economic Basis for Lasting Peace', *Department of State Bulletin* 12 (8 April 1945): pp. 593–9.

Trumbull, Robert, 'The West Loses "Face" in the East', *New York Times Magazine*, 1 December 1946.

Vinacke, Harold M., 'United States Far Eastern Policy', *Pacific Affairs* 19 (December 1946): pp. 351–63.

Vincent, John Carter, 'The Post-War Period in the Far East', *Department of State Bulletin* 13 (21 October 1945): pp. 644–8.

Watt, D. C., 'American Anti-Colonialist Policies and the End of the European Colonial Empires 1941–1962', in A. N. J. Den Hollander (ed.), *Contagious Conflict: The Impact of American Dissent on European Life* (Leiden: E. J. Brill, 1973), pp. 93–125.

——, 'Every War Must End: War-Time Planning for Post-War Security, in Britain and America in the Wars of 1914–18 and 1939–45. The Roles of Historical Examples and of Professional Historians', *Transactions of the Royal Historical Society*, 5th Ser., 1978.

Weller, George, 'Can France Hold Her Eastern Empire?' *Saturday Evening Post*, 30 November 1946, pp. 18–19, 142–4.

Welles, Sumner, 'Problems of Dependent Peoples', *Washington Post*, 28 March 1945.

——, 'Britain's Empire', *Washington Post*, 8 August 1945.

Zingg, Paul J., 'The Cold War in North Africa: American Foreign Policy and Postwar Muslim Nationalism, 1945–1952', *The Historian* 39 (November 1976): pp. 40–61.

BOOKS

Aglion, Raoul, *Roosevelt and de Gaulle, Allies in Conflict: A Personal Memoir* (New York: Free Press, 1988).

Alexander, G. M., *The Prelude to the Truman Doctrine: British Policy in Greece 1944–1947* (New York: Oxford University Press, 1982).

Anderson, Terry H., *The United States, Great Britain, and the Cold War, 1944–1947* (Columbia: University of Missouri Press, 1981).

Attwood, William, *The Twilight Struggle: Tales of the Cold War* (New York: Harper & Row, 1987).

Barker, Elisabeth, *The British Between the Superpowers, 1945–50* (University of Toronto Press, 1983).

Barnet, Richard J., *Intervention and Revolution: The United States in the Third World* (New York: World, 1968).

Behr, Edward, *The Algerian Problem* (New York: W. W. Norton, 1961).

Best, Richard A., Jr., *'Cooperation with Like-Minded Peoples': British Influences on American Security Policy, 1945–1949* (Westport, CT: Greenwood Press, 1986).

Blum, Robert M., *Drawing the Line: The Origin of the American Containment Policy in East Asia* (New York: W. W. Norton, 1982).

Brinton, Crane, *The United States and Britain* (Cambridge: Harvard University Press, 1945).

Buhite, Russell D., *Decisions at Yalta: An Appraisal of Summit Diplomacy* (Wilmington, DE: Scholarly Resources, 1986).

——, *Soviet-American Relations in Asia, 1945–1954* (Norman, OK: University of Oklahoma Press, 1981).

Bullard, Reader, *Britain and the Middle East: From the Earliest Times to 1950* (London: Hutchinson's University Library, 1951).

Cady, John F., *Contacts with Burma, 1935–1949: A Personal Account*, Center for International Studies, Papers in International Studies, Southeast Asia Series, no. 61 (Athens, OH: Ohio University, 1983).

Cameron, Allan W. (ed.), *Viet-Nam Crisis: A Documentary History*, vol. 1: *1940–1956* (Ithaca: Cornell University Press, 1971).

Camus, Albert, *American Journals*, translated by Hugh Levick (New York: Paragon, 1987).

Carpenter, Humphrey (ed.), *The Letters of J. R. R. Tolkien* (Boston: Houghton Mifflin, 1981).

Charlton, Michael, and Anthony Moncrieff, *Many Reasons Why: The American Involvement in Vietnam* (1978; reprint, New York: Hill and Wang, 1989).

Clubb, Oliver E., Jr., *The United States and the Sino-Soviet Bloc in Southeast Asia* (Washington: Brookings Institution, 1962).

Colbert, Evelyn, *Southeast Asia in International Politics, 1941–1956* (Ithaca: Cornell University Press, 1977).

Cousins, Norman, *The Pathology of Power* (New York, W. W. Norton, 1987).

Cruickshank, Charles, *SOE in the Far East* (New York: Oxford University Press, 1983).

Dallek, Robert, *Franklin D. Roosevelt and American Foreign Policy, 1932–1945* (New York: Oxford University Press, 1979).

Dennis, Peter, *Troubled Days of Peace: Mountbatten and South East Asia Command, 1945–46* (New York: St Martin's Press, 1987).

Devillers, Philippe, *Histoire du Viêt-Nam de 1940 à 1952* (Paris: Editions de Seuil, 1952).

Dobbs, Charles M., *The Unwanted Symbol: American Foreign Policy, the Cold War, and Korea, 1945–1950* (Kent, OH: Kent State University Press, 1981).

Dougherty, James J., *The Politics of Wartime Aid: American Economic Assistance to France and French Northwest Africa, 1940–1946* (Westport, CT: Greenwood Press, 1978).

Dower, John W., *War Without Mercy: Race and Power in the Pacific War* (New York: Pantheon, 1986).

Dunn, Peter M., *The First Vietnam War* (New York: St Martin's Press, 1985).

Easton, Stewart C., *The Rise and Fall of Western Colonialism* (New York: Praeger, 1964).

Edmonds, Robin, *Setting the Mould: The United States and Britain, 1945–1950* (New York: W. W. Norton, 1986).

Evans-Pritchard, E. E., *The Sanusi of Cyrenaica* (London: Oxford University Press, 1949).

Fanon, Franz, *The Wretched of the Earth*, translated by Constance Farrington (New York: Grove Press, 1968).

Feis, Herbert, *Between War and Peace: The Potsdam Conference* (Princeton University Press, 1960).

Fifield, Russell H., *Americans in Southeast Asia: The Roots of Commitment* (New York: Thomas Y. Cromwell, 1973).

Friend, Theodore, *The Blue-Eyed Enemy: Japan Against the West in Java and Luzon, 1942–1945* (Princeton University Press, 1988).

Funk, Arthur Layton, *The Politics of TORCH: The Allied Landings and the Algiers Putsch 1942* (Lawrence: University Press of Kansas, 1974).

Gallicchio, Marc S., *The Cold War Begins in Asia: American East Asian Policy and the Fall of the Japanese Empire* (New York: Columbia University Press, 1988).

Gardner, Brian, *The Year that Changed the World: 1945* (New York: Coward-McCann, 1963).

Gardner, Lloyd C., *Approaching Vietnam: From World War II through Dienbienphu, 1941–1954* (New York: W. W. Norton, 1988).

Gaunson, A. B., *The Anglo-French Clash in Lebanon and Syria, 1940–45* (New York: St Martin's Press, 1987).

Gellhorn, Martha, *The Face of War* (1959; reprint, New York: Atlantic Monthly Press, 1988).

Gormly, James L., *The Collapse of the Grand Alliance, 1945–1948* (Baton Rouge: Louisiana State University Press, 1987).

Lord Hailey, *The Future of Colonial Peoples* (Princeton University Press, 1944).

Hammer, Ellen J., *The Struggle for Indochina, 1940–1955* (1954–55; reprint, Stanford University Press, 1967).

Harbutt, Fraser J., *The Iron Curtain: Churchill, America, and the Origins of the Cold War* (New York: Oxford University Press, 1986).

Hathaway, Robert M., *Ambiguous Partnership: Britain and America, 1944–1947* (New York: Columbia University Press, 1981).

Hess, Gary R., *America Encounters India, 1941–1947* (Baltimore: Johns Hopkins Press, 1971).

——, *The United States' Emergence as a Southeast Asian Power, 1940–1950* (New York: Columbia University Press, 1987).

Hoisington, William A., Jr., *The Casablanca Connection: French Colonial Policy, 1936–1943* (Chapel Hill: University of North Carolina Press, 1984).

Hurstfield, Julian G., *America and the French Nation, 1939–1945* (Chapel Hill: University of North Carolina Press, 1986).

Iriye, Akira, *Power and Culture: The Japanese-American War, 1941–1945* (Cambridge: Harvard University Press, 1981).

Isaacs, Harold R., *No Peace for Asia* (New York: Macmillan, 1947).

Isnard, Hildebert, *Géographié de la décolonisation* (Paris: Presses Universitaires de France, 1971).

Kahin, George McTurnan, *Nationalism and Revolution in Indonesia* (New York: Cornell University Press, 1952).

Kiernan, V. G., *From Conquest to Collapse: European Empires from 1815–1960* (New York: Pantheon, 1982).

Kimball, Warren F. (ed.), *Churchill & Roosevelt: The Complete Correspondence*, 3 vols (Princeton University Press, 1984).

Kolko, Gabriel *The Roots of American Foreign Policy* (Boston: Beacon Press, 1969).

——, *Anatomy of a War: Vietnam, the United States, and the Modern Historical Experience* (New York: Pantheon, 1985).

Kolko, Joyce, and Gabriel Kolko, *The Limits of Power: The World and United States Foreign Policy, 1945–1954* (New York: Harper & Row, 1972).

Kuniholm, Bruce Robillet, *The Origins of the Cold War in the Near East: Great Power Conflict and Diplomacy in Iran, Turkey, and Greece* (Princeton University Press, 1980).

Langer, William L., *Our Vichy Gamble* (1947; reprint, Hamden, CT: Archon Books, 1965).

Lebra, Joyce C., *Japanese-Trained Armies in Southeast Asia: Independence and Volunteer Forces in World War II* (New York: Columbia University Press, 1977).

Lippmann, Walter, *US Foreign Policy: Shield of the Republic* (Boston: Little, Brown, 1943).

Louis, William Roger, *Imperialism at Bay: The United States and the Decolonization of the British Empire, 1941–1945* (New York: Oxford University Press, 1978).

——, *The British Empire in the Middle East, 1945–1951: Arab Nationalism, the United States, and Postwar Imperialism* (New York: Oxford University Press, 1984).

Lukacs, John, *1945: Year Zero* (Garden City, NY: Doubleday, 1978).

Lundestad, Geir, *East, West, North, South: Major Developments in International Politics, 1945–1986*, translated by Gail Adams Kvam (Oslo: Norwegian University Press, 1986).

MacDonald, Elizabeth P., *Undercover Girl* (New York: Macmillan, 1947).

MacFarlane, S. Neil, *Superpower Rivalry and Third World Radicalism: The Idea of National Liberation* (Baltimore: Johns Hopkins University Press, 1985).

McGhee, George, *Envoy to the Middle World: Adventures in Diplomacy* (New York: Harper & Row, 1983).

McMahon, Robert J., *Colonialism and Cold War: The United States and the Struggle for Indonesian Independence, 1945–49* (Ithaca: Cornell University Press, 1981).

Mastny, Vojtech, *Russia's Road to the Cold War: Diplomacy, Warfare, and the Politics of Communism, 1941–1945* (New York: Columbia University Press, 1979).

May, Ernest R., *'Lessons' of the Past: The Use and Misuse of History in American Foreign Policy* (New York: Oxford University Press, 1973).

Memmi, Albert, *The Colonizer and the Colonized*, translated by Howard Greenfeld (New York: Orion Press, 1965).

Messer, Robert L., *The End of an Alliance: James F. Byrnes, Roosevelt, Truman, and the Origins of the Cold War* (Chapel Hill: University of North Carolina Press, 1982).

Miller, James Edward, *The United States and Italy, 1940–1950: The Politics and Diplomacy of Stabilization* (Chapel Hill: University of North Carolina Press, 1986).

Osada, Arata (comp.), *Children of Hiroshima*, edited by Yoichi Fukushima for the English-language edition (New York: Harper Colophon, 1980).

Palmier, Leslie, *Indonesia and the Dutch* (New York: Oxford University Press, 1962).

Patti, Archimedes L. A., *Why Viet Nam? Prelude to America's Albatross* (Berkeley: University of California Press, 1980).

Pendar, Kenneth, *Adventure in Diplomacy: Our French Dilemma* (New York: Dodd, Mead, 1945).

Pelt, Adrian, *Libyan Independence and the United Nations: A Case of Planned Decolonization* (New Haven: Yale University Press, 1970).

Rennell, Lord, *British Military Administration of Occupied Territories in Africa During the Years 1941–1947* (London: His Majesty's Stationery Office, 1948; reprint, Westport, CT: Greenwood Press, 1970).

Rivlin, Benjamin, *The United Nations and the Italian Colonies* (New York: Carnegie Endowment for International Peace, 1950).

Robertson, Alex J., *The Bleak Midwinter 1947* (Manchester University Press, 1987).

Romanus, Charles F., and Riley Sunderland, *Stilwell's Mission to China* (Washington: Department of the Army, 1953).

——, *Time Runs Out in CBI* (Washington: Department of the Army, 1959).

Ryan, Henry Butterfield, *The Vision of Anglo-America: The US-UK Alliance and the Emerging Cold War, 1943–1946* (New York: Cambridge University Press, 1987).

Scholl-Latour, Peter, *Death in the Ricefields: An Eyewitness Account of Vietnam's Three Wars, 1945–1979*, translated by Faye Carney (New York: St Martin's Press, 1979).

Sevareid, Eric, *Not So Wild a Dream* (New York: Alfred A. Knopf, 1946).

Smith, Bradley F., *The War's Long Shadow: The Second World War and Its Aftermath: China, Russia, Britain, and America* (New York: Simon and Schuster, 1986).

Smith, R. Harris, *OSS: The Secret History of America's First Central Intelligence Agency* (Berkeley: University of California Press, 1972).

Spector, Ronald H., *Advice and Support: The Early Years of the United States Army in Vietnam, 1941–1960* (Washington: Center of Military History, 1983; reprint, New York: Free Press, 1985).

Spykman, Nicholas John, *America's Strategy in World Politics: The United States and the Balance of Power* (1942; reprint, Hamden, CT: Archon Books, 1970).

Stueck, William Whitney, Jr., *The Road to Confrontation: American Policy Toward China and Korea, 1947–1950* (Chapel Hill: University of North Carolina Press, 1981).

Sulzberger, C. L., *Unfinished Revolution: America and the Third World* (New York: Atheneum, 1965).

Taubman, William, *Stalin's American Policy: From Entente to Détente to Cold War* (New York: W. W. Norton, 1982).

Taylor, Edmund, *Awakening From History* (London: Chatto & Windus, 1971).

——, *Richer by Asia*, 2d edn (Boston: Houghton Mifflin, 1964).

Taylor, George E., *America in the New Pacific* (New York: Macmillan, 1942).

Thomas, R. T., *Britain and Vichy: The Dilemma of Anglo-French Relations 1940–42* (New York: St Martin's Press, 1979).

Thorne, Christopher, *Allies of a Kind: The United States, Britain, and the War Against Japan, 1941–1945* (New York: Oxford University Press, 1978).

——, *The Issue of War: States, Societies, and the Far Eastern Conflict of 1941–1945* (New York: Oxford University Press, 1985).

Tinker, Hugh, *Men Who Overturned Empires: Fighters, Dreamers and Schemers* (Madison: University of Wisconsin Press, 1987).

Ulam, Adam B., *Expansion and Coexistence: The History of Soviet Foreign Policy, 1917–67* (New York: Praeger, 1968).

Van der Post, Laurens, *The Night of the New Moon* (London: Hogarth Press, 1971).

Vinacke, Harold M., *The United States and the Far East, 1945–1951* (Stanford University Press, 1952).

Vincent, John Carter, *et al.* (eds), *America's Future in the Pacific* (New Brunswick: Rutgers University Press, 1947).

Ward, Patricia Dawson, *The Threat of Peace: James F. Byrnes and the Council of Foreign Ministers, 1945–1946* (Kent, OH: Kent State University Press, 1979).

Welles, Sumner, *The Time for Decision* (New York: Harper, 1944).

————, *The World of the Four Freedoms* (New York: Columbia University Press, 1943).

————, *We Need Not Fail* (Boston: Houghton Mifflin, 1948).

————, *Where Are We Heading?* (New York: Harper, 1946).

Wieschhoff, H. A., *Colonial Policies in Africa* (Philadelphia: University of Pennsylvania Press, The University Museum, 1944).

Willkie, Wendell L., *One World* (New York: Simon and Schuster, 1943).

Wittner, Lawrence S., *American Intervention in Greece, 1943–1949* (New York: Columbia University Press, 1982).

Wolf, Charles, Jr., *The Indonesian Story: The Birth, Growth and Structure of the Indonesian Republic* (New York: John Day Company, 1948).

Woodward, Llewellyn, *British Foreign Policy in the Second World War* (London: Her Majesty's Stationery Office, 1970).

Woolf, Leonard, *Imperialism and Civilization* (New York: Harcourt, Brace, 1928).

Yost, Charles W., *History and Memory* (New York: W. W. Norton, 1980).

Ziegler, Philip, *Mountbatten* (New York: Alfred A. Knopf, 1985).

Index